M000251801

Collaborative Cyber Threat Intelligence

Collaborative Cyber Threat Intelligence

Detecting and Responding to Advanced
Cyber Attacks at the National Level

Edited by
Florian Skopik

CRC Press
Taylor & Francis Group

CRC Press is an imprint of the
Taylor & Francis Group, an **informa** business

AN AUERBACH BOOK

CRC Press
Taylor & Francis Group
6000 Broken Sound Parkway NW, Suite 300
Boca Raton, FL 33487-2742

MIX
Paper from
responsible sources
FSC
www.fsc.org
FSC® C014174

Library of Congress Cataloging-in-Publication Data

Names: Skopik, Florian, editor.
Title: Collaborative cyber threat intelligence : detecting and responding to advanced cyber attacks at the national level / [edited by] Florian Skopik.
Description: Boca Raton, FL : CRC Press, 2017.
Identifiers: LCCN 2017025820 | ISBN 9781138031821 (hb : alk. paper)
Subjects: LCSH: Cyber intelligence (Computer security) | Cyberspace operations (Military science) | Cyberterrorism--Prevention. | National security.
Classification: LCC QA76.9.A25 C6146 2017 | DDC 005.8--dc23
LC record available at https://lccn.loc.gov/2017025820

Visit the Taylor & Francis Web site at
http://www.taylorandfrancis.com

and the CRC Press Web site at
http://www.crcpress.com

Printed and bound in the United States of America by Sheridan

Contents

Foreword

This book provides a valuable foundation for the future development of cybersecurity information sharing both within and between nation-states. This work is essential—unless we can identify common threats and share common mitigation then there is a danger that we will become future victims of previous attack vectors. Without shared situation awareness, it is likely that different organizations facing the same threat will respond in inconsistent ways—and the lessons learned in combatting earlier incidents will be repeated and repeated until we develop more coordinated responses. There are further motivations for reading this work. Existing standards across many industries and continents agree on the need for risk-based approaches to cybersecurity. Too often these are based on subject introspection; they can be little more than the best guesses of chief information security officers. If we can encourage information sharing, then our assessments of probability, consequence, and our identification of potential vulnerabilities can be based on previous experience.

All of these benefits will only be realized if we can address a number of barriers to information sharing. First, it is clear that there may be limited benefits from sharing information about every potential attack. The sheer scale of automated phishing and DDoS (Distributed Denial-of-Service Attacks) means that without considerable support we may lose cyber situation awareness as we are overwhelmed by a mass of well-understood incidents. Second, the focus must never be on recording the incidents—the utility of these systems is derived from the decisions that they inform. We must allocate resources to identifying mitigations and preventing future incidents. Third, a host of questions must be addressed about the disclosure of compromising information and the violation of intellectual property through incident reporting. Simply revealing that an organization has been the target of an attack may encourage others to focus on them. Fourth, there are questions about what should be shared. The information needs are different both horizontally— between companies in different industries—and vertically between companies addressing different needs within the same supply chain. Finally, we must be sensitive to the limitations of incident reporting—it can be retrospective, focusing on gathering information about the previous generation of attacks rather than the next—which may be very different especially when state actors are involved.

The chapters of this book provide, arguably for the first time, a coherent and sustained view of these many different opportunities and potential pitfalls. It investigates the potential benefits of peer-to-peer systems as well as the legal obstacles that must be overcome. It looks at the key determinants of situation awareness at a national level and beyond. It does all of this in an accessible manner—focusing on generic issues rather than particular technologies.

I recommend it to you.

Chris Johnson
Head of Computing Science at Glasgow University
Glasgow, UK

Preface

The Internet threat landscape is fundamentally changing. A major shift away from hobby hacking toward well-organized cybercrime, even cyberwar, can be observed. These attacks are typically carried out for commercial or political reasons in a sophisticated and targeted manner and specifically in a way to circumvent common security measures. Additionally, networks have grown to a scale and complexity and have reached a degree of interconnectedness, that their protection can often only be guaranteed and financed as a shared effort. Consequently, new paradigms are required for detecting contemporary attacks and mitigating their effects.

Information sharing is a crucial step to acquiring a thorough understanding of large-scale cyber attack situations and is therefore seen as one of the key concepts to protect future networks. To this end, nation-states together with standardization bodies, large industry stakeholders, academics, and regulatory entities have created a plethora of literature on how cybersecurity information sharing across organizations and with national stakeholders can be achieved. Shared information, commonly referred to as threat intelligence, should comprise timely early warnings, details on threat actors, recently exploited vulnerabilities, new forms of attack techniques, and courses of action on how to deal with certain situations—just to name a few. Sharing this information, however, is highly nontrivial. A wide variety of implications, regarding data privacy, economics, regulatory frameworks, organizational aspects, and trust issues need to be accounted for.

This book is an attempt to survey and present existing works and proposes and discusses new approaches and methodologies at the forefront of research and development. It provides a unique angle on the topics of cross-organizational cyber threat intelligence and security information sharing. It focuses neither on vendor-specific solutions nor on technical tools only. Instead, it provides a clear view on the current state of the art in all relevant dimensions of information sharing, in order to appropriately address current—and future—security threats at a national level.

Regarding the intended readership, I foresee the book being useful to forward-looking practitioners, such as CISOs, as well as industry experts, including those with deep knowledge of network management, cybersecurity, policy, and compliance issues and are interested in learning about the vast state of the art, both in practice and applied research. Similarly, I suggest the book has value for academics and post-graduate students beginning their studies in this important area and seeking to get an overview of the research field. As an editor, I have encouraged the chapter authors to follow a "bath-tub" approach to the depth of knowledge required to read each chapter (i.e., the start and end of each chapter should be approachable and give high-level insights into the topic covered, whereas the core content of the chapter may require more attention from the reader, as it focuses on details).

Finally, a word on the authors of the single chapters: These are a mixed group of renowned experts and young talents from research institutions and universities across Europe, including the Austrian Institute of Technology, the Netherlands Organization for Applied Scientific Research (TNO), Queen's University Belfast, University of Vienna, and Catholic University of Leuven. Their contributions reflect existing efforts and argue the case for areas where they see future research and standardization is of paramount importance. Additionally, the authors comment on a number of open contentious issues, including building on the existing effort on network security, what is the next highest priority that should be addressed and why, and whether, despite the efforts of the community, the full realization of nationwide cybersecurity information sharing systems is possible in a privacy-preserving, legally sound, efficient, and, most importantly, secure manner. Without the authors' willingness and enthusiasm for this project, and their subject knowledge, this book would not have been possible. As an editor, I am grateful for their significant contributions.

I am happy to receive feedback, comments on the book, questions, and opinions of any kind. Please feel free to contact me—refer to www.flosko.at for details.

Florian Skopik
Vienna, Austria

Acknowledgment

Work presented in this book was partly funded by the Austrian FFG research program KIRAS in course of the project "Cyber Incident Situational Awareness" (CISA; grant no. 850199) and by the European Union FP7 project "European Control System Security Incident Analysis Network" (ECOSSIAN; grant no. 607577).

About the Editor

Florian Skopik currently works in the ICT Security Research Team at the Austrian Institute of Technology (AIT) as Senior Scientist, where he is responsible for national and international research projects (in course of the EU FP7). The main topics of these projects are centered on smart grid security, security of critical infrastructures, and national cybersecurity and cyber defense. Due to this research focus, the ICT Security Research Team works in close collaboration with national authorities, such as the Ministry of the Interior and the Ministry of Defense. Before joining AIT, Florian was with the Distributed Systems Group at the Vienna University of Technology as a research assistant and postdoctoral research scientist from 2007 to 2011, where he was involved in a number of international research projects dealing with cross-organizational collaboration over the Web. In the context of these projects, he also finished his PhD studies. Florian further spent a sabbatical at IBM Research India in Bangalore for several months. He published more than 100 scientific conference papers and journal articles, and is member of various conference program committees and editorial boards, as well as standardization groups, such as ETSI TC Cyber and OASIS CTI. He further holds 20 industry relevant security certifications, including Trusted Security Auditor, ISA/IEC 62443 Security Specialist, CCNA Security, and ISO27001 Information Security Manager. In 2017 he finished a professional degree in Advanced Computer Security at the Stanford University, USA. In parallel to his studies, he was working at numerous SMEs as firmware developer for microcontroller systems for about 15 years. Florian is an IEEE senior member and a member of the Association for Computing Machinery (ACM).

Contributors

Abdullah Al Balushi
CSIT Centre for Secure Information
  Technology
Queen's University Belfast
Belfast, United Kingdom

Damian Clifford
Centre for IT & IP Law – imec
Katholieke Universiteit Leuven
Leuven, Belgium

Roman Fiedler
Center for Digital Safety & Security
Vienna, Austria

Frank Fransen
Cyber Security & Robustness
Netherlands Organisation for Applied
  Scientific Research (TNO)
Hague, the Netherlands

Ivo Friedberg
Center for Digital Safety & Security
Vienna, Austria
and
CSIT Centre for Secure Information
  Technology
Queen's University Belfast
Belfast, United Kingdom

Vinzenz Heussler
Centre for Computers and Law
University of Vienna
Vienna, Austria

Walter Hötzendorfer
Digital Human Rights Center
Research Institute
Vienna, Austria

Boojoong Kang
CSIT Centre for Secure Information
  Technology
Queen's University Belfast
Belfast, United Kingdom

Richard Kerkdijk
Cyber Security & Robustness
Netherlands Organisation for Applied
  Scientific Research (TNO)
Hague, the Netherlands

Maria Leitner
Center for Digital Safety & Security
Vienna, Austria

Timea Pahi
Center for Digital Safety & Security
Vienna, Austria

Jessica Schroers
Centre for IT & IP Law – imec
Katholieke Universiteit Leuven
Leuven, Belgium

Erich Schweighofer
Centre for Computers and Law
University of Vienna
Vienna, Austria

Giuseppe Settanni
Center for Digital Safety & Security
Vienna, Austria

Florian Skopik
Center for Digital Safety & Security
Vienna, Austria

Markus Wurzenberger
Center for Digital Safety & Security
Vienna, Austria

Chapter 1

Introduction

Florian Skopik
Austrian Institute of Technology

Contents

1.1 Motivation for This Book

The smooth operation of critical infrastructures, such as those in telecommunication, energy supply, transportation, and banking, is essential for our society. In recent years, however, operators of critical infrastructures have increasingly struggled with cybersecurity problems. Through the use of ICT standard products and the increasing network interdependencies, the attack surfaces and channels have multiplied. Nowadays, private operators mainly provide the mentioned critical services, which often need to act under cost pressure. Those services are essential to maintaining public order and safety, and thus, it is in the interest and the responsibility of a state to guarantee the security of these infrastructures. Therefore, a formal arrangement of the public and private sector, some form of private–public partnership, has to be established. One of the visions of recent initiatives is that the state directly supports infrastructure providers to secure their service operations by distributing important security information, aka cyber threat intelligence, to target users, while they provide security-relevant information of their respective organization, such as their services' status, or spotted indicators of attacks in their networks, to the state. This data from every single organization is essential to create a clear picture of cyber threats and establish cyber situational awareness of the operational environment, and thus create the basis for justified and effective decision making by competent authorities at the national level.

This vision has recently made a huge leap forward toward its realization. With the political agreement on the US Cybersecurity Information Sharing Act (CISA) (The Senate of the United States, 2015) and the ratification of the European Network and Information Security (NIS) Directive (European Commission, 2016), both the United States of America and the European Union have put legal/regulatory frameworks in place that require operators of essential services and digital service providers to report high-impact cybersecurity incidents to competent authorities or national Computer Security Incident Response Teams (CSIRTs). It is further foreseen that mentioned authorities take and process information about security incidents to increase the network security level of all organizations by issuing early warnings, assisting with mitigation actions, or distributing recommendations and best practices.

However, while many of the essential building blocks to implement information sharing systems already exist today, there is a major lack of understanding on how they need to work together to satisfy the requirements of a state-driven cybersecurity approach—as foreseen by the US CISA and EU's NIS directive. Furthermore, in recent years, technical solutions for capturing network data and processing them within organizations have been developed, and high-level security strategies have been formulated in the national scope. The question of how security information from the organizations' information and communication systems can be shared, processed, and utilized at the national level turned out to be a challenging problem for which there are still no sufficient solutions. It is of paramount importance for all stakeholders, being infrastructure providers, heavy users, or state actors, to understand the major implications with respect to the technical, legal, economic, regulatory, and organizational dimensions when it comes to establishing effective national cyber threat intelligence sharing with the private sector.

This book is an attempt to survey and present existing works and proposes and discusses new approaches and methodologies at the forefront of research and development.

1.2 On the Ever-Changing Cyber Threat Landscape

The threat posed by cyber attacks on businesses, local governments, and critical infrastructures remains a key challenge in an increasingly connected world. As targets become more valuable to attackers, and techniques to protect them become more sophisticated, the tools used to exploit vulnerabilities in security systems have matured. The number of high profile attacks on such organizations as Anthem, Target, AOL, and eBay illustrates the scale and ambition of many attackers. In 2016, the number of records lost to cyber attacks is estimated to be over half a billion (Symantec, 2017). The threat is just as relevant however for smaller organizations where the resources are not available for advanced security systems and dedicated security personnel. As larger organizations put in place stronger defenses, these smaller businesses become attractive targets.

According to the ENISA report on the threat landscape for 2016 (ENISA, 2016), an evolution in cyber threats has taken place. A significant development of concern to smaller organizations is the rise of "Cyber-Crime-as-a-Service" where tools are made readily available to attackers without the technical need to develop their own. A recent Verizon report (Verizon, 2016) noted that the threat of cyber attacks has spread to all industries, including agriculture, retail, finance, public authorities, utilities, and healthcare, with a total of 64,199 security incidents in 2015, 2260 of which resulted in data loss.

The top five threats reported by ENISA in 2016 were malware, Web-based attacks, Web application attacks, Botnets, and denial-of-service (DoS). Malware remains the top threat. McAfee's recent threat report (McAfee Labs, 2016) identified an increase of 426% in the number of incidents of Adwind, a Java-based remote administration tool (RAT). Adwind, like many malware campaigns, is typically propagated through e-mail spamming approaches, malicious web pages and downloads. E-mail spamming campaigns are not a new approach but still remain successful through clever naming of subjects and deliberately articulated content designed to compromise soft targets.

Growth in mobile malware has remained stable in recent years, though a sharp rise was reported in Q4 2015 (McAfee Labs, 2016). This is representative of the increasing value of targeting mobile devices allowing attackers to gain access to personal and financial data. With almost 90% of phones shipped in 2016 running

Android (Strategy Analytics Wireless Smartphone Strategies Service, 2016), Android users are the main target, though other operating systems are not unaffected. A number of attacks in 2016 required the victim to open a malicious multimedia message, triggering an exploit in the operating system allowing the attacker to gain control of the device. A particular concern with mobile devices is the latency between the discovery of a vulnerability and the release of a patch from the various carriers and/or vendors. For older devices there is a significant risk that no patch will be pushed to them at all, leaving these devices vulnerable to a compromise.

Another development is that attacks increasingly target the hardware layer of systems, enabling attackers to subvert security applications operating at the operating system and application layers. Equation Group, a sophisticated cyber attack group, developed a module that allows them to install malicious data in the firmware of hard disks, making it more difficult to detected and repair. Targets of Equation Group include the following sectors: telecoms, government, energy, media, and finance.

Security vulnerabilities in popular websites remain a persistent threat, with over one million Web attacks recorded every day in 2016 (Symantec, 2017). Cyber criminals are able to exploit vulnerabilities in website security allowing them to run malicious code without any user interaction (i.e., the victim receives no notification or prompt in his or her browser). Over 75% of websites contain unpatched vulnerabilities, 15% of which were deemed critical. The rise of Wordpress, now powering a quarter of the world's websites, has increased the attack surface through plugin vulnerabilities that require regular updating for the latest patches. Another avenue of attack via websites is through the use of malvertising campaigns in which attackers host malicious ads on popular sites. Relaxed controls on hosting ads make it easy for cyber criminals to masquerade as legitimate businesses.

Social media has also come into prominence in 2016 as an integral part of social engineering campaigns. For example, so-called mocking bird, parrot, and egg accounts on Twitter create a network of legitimate looking accounts with the intention of attracting real accounts to which they can spam with advertisements redirecting to malicious websites (Narang, 2015). Another example of an attack on Gmail accounts involves the attacker requesting a password reset on the victim's account (using the victim's e-mail and mobile number). Google automatically texts a verification code to the victim's mobile. The attacker also texts the victim to respond to the message with the code he just sent. The unsuspecting replies with the code, and the attacker can now either reset the password (recovering whatever data is of interest to the attacker) or set up e-mail forwarding to perform a man-in-the-middle attack on the account.

According to an annual security report compiled by Arbor Networks (2016), Distributed Denial of Service attacks continued to hit records in 2016, with the largest ever recorded at 800 Gbps due to the weaponization of Internet-of-Things (IoT) devices. Additionally, in 2016 53% of service provider respondents reported more than 21 attacks per month, and 67% of service providers and 40% of enterprise, government, and education reported seeing multivector attacks on their networks.

While the most common motivation behind distributed denial-of-service (DDoS) attacks is typically to demonstrate attack capabilities or criminal extortion, DDoS attacks are increasingly being used as a diversionary tactic for primary malware infiltration or data exfiltration attacks.

High-profile attacks, such as the attack on the Ukrainian energy sector (SANS, 2016), were identified as the latest trend in cyber threats. In the report on this particular attack, several techniques were identified that enabled the attackers to gain a foothold ineside the target. These included spear phishing e-mails, malware, and the manipulation of Microsoft Office documents containing malware. Another high-profile ransomware in 2016 was the Trojan Locky, which is used by cyber criminals sending out mass e-mails with the malware attached to a .doc file. Once executed, the Trojan dials back home, receives a 2048-bit RSA public key, and proceeds to encrypt files on the disk. The victim is then prompted to pay a fee for the corresponding decryption key and regain access to files.

The continued rise of malware, in particular targeting mobile devices, is expected through 2017 and beyond. Targeted attacks such as those seen in 2016 are also expected to continue and increase in sophistication. Social engineering tactics remain an integral part of such attacks, enabling attackers to recover credentials from victims or to infect their devices with malware. While the impact of DDoS can be mitigated through the effective use of Cloud computing and building in countermeasures, such an attack is increasingly an indicator of a larger attack campaign.

Some of the threats described here are analyzed in detail and exemplarily demonstrated in the form of illustrative attack scenarios, based on real incidents, in Chapter 2.

1.3 An Introduction to Threat Intelligence and Cross-Organizational Information Sharing

In order to counter and adapt to advanced and quickly changing threats, all affected parties of the digital society need to collaborate. While this is already commonplace in some specific domains for certain purposes (Shackleford, 2015), e.g., the banking sector exchanges information about phishing campaigns or ransomware waves, strategic alliances and threat information sharing in general is still not fully developed.

1.3.1 Benefit of Threat Information Sharing

The expected advantages of information sharing, with respect to improving the fierce cybersecurity situation in many countries, are manifold. First and foremost, threat information sharing provides access to potentially vital threat information that might otherwise be unavailable to an organization. Using shared resources, organizations can enhance their individual security levels by leveraging the knowledge, experience, and capabilities of their partners in a cost-efficient manner. In particular, each organization is able to augment its internal view with external data and can thus extend, validate, and correct its cybersecurity situational awareness through collaborating with others in similar situations.

For instance, if a new vulnerability of a widely used software product is exploited and applied in multiple attacks on a broad scale, without sharing, every affected organization would need to investigate the root cause separately. Instead, with threat intelligence sharing, only one organization is required to do the detailed analysis and can then provide findings to partners who consume this intelligence and use it within their own organizational contexts. Eventually, this means that a piece of information might be relevant for many but trigger different actions, depending on the degree to which an organization is affected by said exploit.

Besides a more timely and cost-efficient mitigation of threats and response to actual incidents, this kind of collective defense also leads to significant knowledge enrichment in those organizations that actively share threat intelligence. In centralized hubs, often represented by national CERTs or ISACs, shared information is sanitized, verified, enriched and aggregated and eventually contributes to an enhanced situational awareness within a specific sector or a whole nation-state (or even beyond that). Knowing which organizations are currently facing what types of issues is a key prerequisite for defending against large-scale attacks, especially those targeting critical infrastructures. Advanced cyber situational awareness is a further key element to facilitating informed decision making—from an operational as well as a strategic perspective.

1.3.2 Challenges of Threat Information Sharing

Although sharing threat information undeniably makes sense, numerous challenges need to be addressed before this can be carried out. One of the most significant issues is trust between the organizations planning to exchange information. Since security-sensitive data can be harmful when leaked (e.g., information about internal infrastructure details can easily increase the risk level, and the announcement of security issues can harm a company's reputation) organizations are understandably reluctant to discuss their security incidents with external parties. Thus, trust is of paramount importance as are additional measures to protect sensitive data that are to be leaked outside a trusted community. One concrete measure that can help in this regard is to limit the attribution as much as technically feasible. For instance, if an organization can safely share information about a new vulnerability without being publicly linked to the incident that led to the discovery of this vulnerability, it will more likely do so.

Another major challenge is the integration of threat intelligence tasks into organizational processes. Especially when information is supposed to leave the organizational boundaries, it must be clearly specified which information can be released, how it needs to be anonymized, and who is responsible for that. But also, if some intelligence from partner organizations is received, it must be clear how new insights are being rated and used and which internal processes are triggered. Specific guidelines and well-documented procedures are key prerequisites for success. Furthermore, the creation of threat intelligence inside the organization requires extensive monitoring, logging, and analytics—setting these capabilities up and keeping them efficiently running are not just technical, but also organizational challenges.

Regarding the technical dimension, one of the biggest challenges is establishing interoperability between internal and external systems. In other words, incoming threat intelligence needs to be interpreted, rated, and seamlessly integrated into internal systems in order to be effective. Every additional manual step, required to translate and apply external information (e.g., to manually formulate a firewall rule based on incoming insights) requires extra effort and additional time. Therefore, automation is a key feature—however, one must keep in mind that a fully automated threat information import and export is for the most part not feasible. There should be human supervision to avoid any undesired side effects, such as unintentional system adaption or information leakage due to incorrectly applied automation. Eventually, smart tools that are able to deal with threat information and make suggestions for specific organizational contexts are required. This is a key feature of automated tools, because suspicious behavior can be malicious in one setting and completely normal in another setting—depending on the normal system behavior, risk, and utilization.

Finally, legal and regulatory requirements comprise one of the biggest hurdles. Every time two parties exchange information, they must be very careful to not harm any legal constraints. Data protection, competition regulations, and nowadays even notification obligations need to be precisely followed in order to avoid any serious consequences. Since this is such an important topic, we cover it in two separate chapters. Chapter 7 outlines different types of laws that need to be followed (with a major focus on the complex situation in Europe with its different Member States' legislations), and Chapter 8 highlights some concrete scenarios of threat intelligence sharing and analysis and argue which of the outlined laws are applicable under these circumstances.

1.3.3 Creating Cyber Threat Information

Threat information may originate from a wide variety of internal and external sources.

Internal sources include security sensors (e.g., intrusion detection systems, antivirus scanners, malware scanners), logging data (from hosts, servers, and network equipment such as firewalls), tools (e.g., network diagnostics, forensics toolkits, vulnerability scanners), security management solutions [security information and event management (SIEM) systems, incident management ticketing systems (e.g., Request Tracker[1])], and personnel who report suspicious behavior, social engineering attempts, and the like.

Typical external sources (meaning "external to an organization"), may include sharing communities (open public or closed ones; see Chapter 5), governmental sources (such as national CERTs or national cybersecurity centers), sector peers and business partners (for instance, via sector-specific ISACs), vendor alerts, and advisories and commercial threat intelligence services.

Stemming from these sources, it is already obvious that cyber threat intelligence can be (preferably automatically) extracted from numerous technical artifacts that are produced during regular IT operations in organizations:

1. Operating system, service, and application logs provide insights into deviations from normal operations within the organizational boundaries
2. Router, WiFi, and remote services logs provide insights into failed login attempts and potentially malicious scanning actions
3. System and application configuration settings and states, often at least partly reflected by configuration management databases help to identify weak spots due to unrequired but running services, weak account credentials, or wrong patch levels
4. Firewall, IDS, and antivirus logs and alerts point to probable causes but often with high false positive rates that need to be verified
5. Web browser histories, cookies, and caches are viable means for forensic actions after something happens, to discover the root cause of a problem (e.g., the initial drive-by download and the like)
6. SIEM systems already provide correlated insights across machines and systems
7. E-mail histories are a vital means to learn about and eventually counter (spear) phishing attempts and follow links to malicious sites
8. Help desk ticketing systems, incident management/tracking systems, and people provide insights into any suspicious events and actions reported by humans rather than software sensors
9. Forensic toolkits and sandboxing are vital means to safely analyze the behavior of untrusted programs without exposing a real corporate environment to any threats

Most of the more important sources of this list are studied in more detail in Chapter 3.

1.3.4 Types of Cyber Threat Information

The types of potentially useful information extracted from the sources mentioned above and utilized for security defense purposes are manifold. However, note that every type has its own characteristics regarding the purpose (e.g., to

---

[1] https://bestpractical.com/request-tracker/, last accessed in February 2017.

facilitate detection, to support prosecution, etc.), applicability, criticality, and "shareability" (i.e., the effort required to make an artifact shareable because of steps required to extract, validate, formulate, and anonymize some piece of information).

The remainder of this section investigates in more detail which information is considered cyber threat intelligence. In particular, we take a closer look at the following [list from NIST (2016) and details added from OASIS (2017)]:

- Indicators
- Tactics, techniques, and procedures (TTPs)
- Threat actors
- Vulnerabilities
- Cybersecurity best practices
- Courses of action (CoA)
- Tools and analysis techniques

Independent from the type of threat information, there are common desired characteristics of applicable cyber threat intelligence, which are as follows:

- Timely—allow sufficient time for the recipient to act
- Relevant—applicable to the recipient's operational environment
- Accurate—correct, complete, and unambiguous
- Specific—provide sufficient level of detail and context
- Actionable—provide or suggest an effective CoA

Indicators: An indicator is "a technical artifact or observable that suggests an attack is imminent or is currently underway, or that a compromise may have already occurred" (NIST, 2016). Examples are IP addresses, domain names, file names and sizes, process names, hashes of file contents and process memory dumps, service names, and altered configuration parameters. The idea behind indicators is to use them either for preventive measures (e.g., add the command and control server's IP address to a block list) or to scan systems (and artifacts) for the presence of an indicator in the past (e.g., the occurrence of a command and control server's IP address in archived log files may indicate a successful attack).

TTPs: TTPs characterize the *behavior of an actor. A tactic is the highest-level description of this behavior, while techniques give a more detailed description of behavior in the context of a tactic, and procedures an even lower-level, highly detailed description in the context of a technique.* (NIST, 2016). Some typical examples include the usage of spear phishing e-mails, social engineering techniques, websites for drive-by attacks, exploitation of operating systems and/or application vulnerabilities, the intentional distribution of manipulated USB sticks, and various obfuscation techniques—just to name a few. From these TTPs, organizations are able to learn how malicious attackers work and derive higher level and generally valid detection and remediation techniques, compared to quite specific measures based on indicators only.

Threat actor: This type of threat intelligence contains information regarding the individual or a group posing a threat. For example, information may include the affiliation (such as a hacker collective or a nation-state's secret service), identity, motivation, and relationships to other threat actors and even their capabilities (via links to TTPs). This information is used to better understand why a system might be attacked and work out more targeted and effective countermeasures. Furthermore, this type of information can be applied to collect evidences of an attack that will be used at court.

Vulnerability: A vulnerability is a software flaw that can be used by a threat actor to gain access to a system or network. Vulnerability information may include its potential impact, technical details, exploitability and the availability of an exploit, affected systems, platforms, and version and mitigation strategies. A common schema to rate the seriousness of a vulnerability is the common vulnerability scoring schema (CVSS) (Scarfone and Mell, 2009), which considers the enumerated details to derive a comparable metric. There are numerous Web platforms that maintain lists of vulnerabilities, such as the common vulnerability and exposures (CVE) database from MITRE[2] and the national vulnerability database (NVD)[3]. Notice that the impact of vulnerabilities usually needs to be interpreted for each organization (and even each system) individually, depending on the criticality of the affected systems for the main business processes.

Cybersecurity best practices: These include commonly used cybersecurity methods that have demonstrated effectiveness in addressing classes of cyber threats. Some examples are response actions (e.g., patch, configuration change), recovery operations, detection strategies, and protective measures. National authorities, CERTs, and large industries frequently publish best practices to help organizations build an effective cyber defense and rely on proven plans and measures.

CoA: CoAs are recommended actions that help to reduce the impact of a threat. In contrast to best practices, CoAs are very specific and shaped to a particular cyber issue. Usually, CoAs span the whole incident response cycle starting with detection (e.g., add or modify an IDS signature), response (e.g., block network traffic to command and control server), recovery (e.g., restore base system image), and protection against similar events in the future (e.g., implement multifactor authentication).

Tools and analysis techniques: This category is closely related to best practices but focuses more on tools instead of procedures. Within a community, it is desirable to align tools with each other to increase compatibility, which makes it easier to import/export certain types of data (e.g., IDS rules). Usually there are sets of recommended tools (e.g., log extraction/parsing/analysis, editor), useful tool configurations (e.g., capture filter for network protocol analyzer), signatures

---

[2] https://cve.mitre.org/.
[3] https://nvd.nist.gov/.

(e.g., custom or "tuned" signatures), extensions (e.g., connectors or modules), codes (e.g., algorithms, analysis libraries), and visualization techniques.

1.3.5 Cornerstones of Threat Information Sharing Activities

Having identified which information is useful to share and why, this section roughly outlines the required steps to establish sharing capabilities and keep sharing activities running. These steps are based on the NIST SP 800-150 guide (NIST, 2016).

1.3.5.1 Establish Cyber Threat Intelligence Sharing Capabilities

In order to establish a sharing capability, an organization needs to commit to the following basic steps:

- Define information sharing goals and objectives.
- Identify internal sources of cyber threat information.
- Define the scope of information sharing activities.
- Establish information sharing rules.
- Join a sharing community.
- Plan to provide ongoing support for information sharing activities.

These steps are defined as follows:

Define information sharing goals and objectives: Sharing itself is not the objective; rather, goals and objectives need to be aligned with mission, business, and security needs. All organizational stakeholders need to be involved in order for a plan to be beneficial to and accepted within an organization. The early involvement and commitment of upper management, the legal department, and the privacy officers is key to success. Typical objectives are to reduce specific risks or to enhance the cybersecurity level. It must be noted that, since threats and risks change rapidly over time, goals need to be reviewed and revised periodically.

Identify internal sources of cyber threat information: Some example sources have been identified in Section 1.3.3.

Define the scope of information sharing activities: The scope needs to be carefully selected based on current capabilities, information availability, information needs, available resources, and the degree of automation. A scope that is too broad might consume resources that an organization cannot afford to spend; on the other hand, a scope that is too narrow might make an organization miss or not properly exploit vital threat information. Again, this scope needs to be verified and adapted over time as the infrastructure's and people's maturity levels change and adapt to new needs.

Establish information sharing rules: Rules are usually modeled as sharing agreements (expressed in a memorandum of understanding, service level agreement, nondisclosure agreement, and so forth) and might consist of the following elements: the types of information that can be shared and the conditions and circumstances that allow sharing to be permitted, distribution to approved recipients, identification and treatment of personally identifiable information, decision whether information exchange should be attributed or anonymized, etc.

Join a sharing community: Potential partners and resources depend on the goals set initially. Potential sharing partners comprise governmental stakeholders, industry-sector peers, threat intelligence vendors, supply chain partners, vendor consortia, and so on. Several constraints might hinder an organization from joining a sharing community, such as eligibility criteria and membership fees; types of information being exchanged; delivery mechanisms, formats and protocols, and compatibility with its own technologies; frequency, volume, and timeliness of shared information; security and privacy controls and terms of use.

Plan to provide ongoing support for information sharing activities: Once the decision to join a community has been made and the required adaptations of organizational processes and technologies have been applied, it is important to create and periodically review a support plan that addresses involved personnel, funding, infrastructure, training, and processes for keeping the sharing activities alive.

1.3.5.2 Participating in Threat Information Sharing Relationships

Joining a sharing community is just half of the story. Continuous effort is required to keep up a sharing relation. Many communities even require their participants to actively contribute and oblige them to share a minimum amount of indicators, threat sightings or malware samples (refer to Chapter 5 for more details). This is a measure against free riders and to ensure a critical mass of active contributors, which ultimately facilitates trust among the partners.

Numerous standards and guidelines (NIST, 2016; ENISA, 2013) suggest at least the following fundamental activities in some form:

- Informal exchange of information in course of ongoing communications to build up trust
- Formal exchange of carefully selected and modeled information
  - Organizations consume cyber threat intelligence from peers to respond to alerts and incidents within their boundaries
  - Organizations report new threat intelligence and validate/improve existing information in a trusted community

In order to build up trust, regular meetings, virtual or physical, and the support of frequent communications is absolutely necessary. Effective sharing is not just about the formal exchange of indicators, but also about the informal discussion of current threats, the joint development of response and mitigation strategies, the mentoring of new community members to advance them to a similar maturity level as the rest of the community, the development of key practices, and the sharing of technical insights. Many of these activities are supported by national CERTs through mailing lists of different confidentiality levels and even sector-specific physical meetings (refer to Chapter 4 for more details). Informal communication and formal exchange of alerts, vulnerabilities, and indicators complement each other.

In addition to this informal communication, the formal exchange of information can be roughly categorized as incoming or outgoing. If security alerts or bulletins are consumed by an organization, there need to be procedures in place for

1. Establishing that the alert is from a trusted, reliable source.
2. Seeking confirmation from an independent source (if necessary).
3. Determining whether the alert affects systems, applications, or hardware that the organization owns or operates.
4. Characterizing the potential impact of the alert.
5. Prioritizing the alert.
6. Determining a suitable CoA.
7. Taking action (e.g., changing configurations, installing patches, notifying staff of threats).

On the other hand, if new cyber threat intelligence is reported to a trusted community, or existing information is verified or improved upon, the following basic steps (often modeled as sharing rules) need to be followed:

1. Validate finding internally and try to rule out misconfiguration or misinterpretation to a certain extent.
2. Validate that the finding is of general interest and its estimate potential impact.
3. Verify internal approval for sharing (either explicit approval or following pre-approved guideline); involve the legal department if necessary.
4. Run anonymization or pseudonymization measures (if useful and desired).
5. Check information representation and completeness of the modeled intelligence.
6. Assign dissemination level, e.g., via traffic light protocol labels.
7. Report finding to trusted peers.

Running through this reporting process allows an organization to contribute to the community by correcting errors in existing threat intelligence, making clarifications, validating findings, providing supplemental information, suggesting alternate interpretations, and exchanging analysis techniques or results.

1.3.6 The Role of Nation-States as Enablers of Information Sharing

Information sharing communities can implement different structures, ranging from a pure peer-to-peer model to an entirely centrally managed community. Even hybrid models are possible, with a central entity that controls the member subscription and management processes, however sharing is performed directly between peers.

Having a central entity seems to be an intriguing design, since some trusted entity is helpful in performing the required vetting before a member joins the community and coordinating and supervising the information sharing activities, e.g., stimulating sharing activities. Furthermore, a central entity that publishes carefully negotiated agreements and policies on how to involve new members, what level of sharing is obliged and how to provide feedback on requests of peers (e.g., to trigger the validation of new threat intelligence) is beneficial to establishing a stable community.

The main question, however, is who should run this central hub, and although examples of industry consortia exist, national authorities increasingly take over that role in the course of their individual cybersecurity strategies (ENISA, 2014). This role further enables a nation-state to keep informed about actual threats and incidents and their root causes, which is a strict requirement for establishing national cyber situational awareness (Franke and Brynielsson, 2014). On the other side, national authorities are responsible for ensuring the safety and security of the citizens, and thus it is part of their duties by law to protect critical infrastructure providers from adversaries (Lewis, 2014). Therefore, nation-states increasingly run national cybersecurity centers as public entities. Besides running national cybersecurity centers, a nation-state shapes information sharing activities through adaptations of the law [see NIS directive (European Commission, 2016), US CISA (The Senate of the United States, 2015), etc.].

Be aware that cybersecurity centers operated directly by a nation-state are controversial. Some argue that this ensures that a neutral stakeholder (i.e., one not interested in profits or in competition with any peer organization) runs the center. Others, however, think that the potentially close relationship with police or military personnel might hinder establishing trusting relations. On the other side, involving law enforcement early might be beneficial in the case of desired prosecution (Hewlett-Packard, 2016).

1.4 About the Structure of the Book

In light of the recent political developments towards establishing strategic security information sharing structures at state level, and the overwhelming daily amount of technical security information produced by critical infrastructure operators, it is obvious that new approaches are required to keep pace with the developments and maintain a high level of security in the future. Therefore, this book sheds light on the required building blocks for *a cross-organizational collaborative cybersecurity approach supported by the state* and especially emphasizes their connection, important interfaces, and multidimensional implications regarding legal, organizational, technical, economic, and societal issues. The book has the following structure:

Chapter 1: This book has already started with an extended introduction into the topic by describing the foundational basis of cyber threat intelligence and the potential role of nation-states. It further outlines the main challenges, points to a wide variety of open issues, and establishes the storyline for the rest of the book.

Chapter 2: This chapter outlines and compares five recent large-scale high-profile attacks and formulates common threat scenarios, including the large-scale distributed denial-of-service attacks, stealthy espionage, and industrial control systems manipulation. These scenarios motivate the need for coordinated cyber defense through threat information sharing and outline some actual challenges of collaborative cyber defense and establishing situational awareness at the national level.

Chapter 3: Next, we elaborate on methods that aid the isolation and extraction of cyber threat intelligence data from log data and network flows. For that purpose, we shortly introduce the numerous technical means of network monitoring, log data management, intrusion detection, anomaly detection, and SIEM solutions. Special emphasis will be put on novel methods that go beyond the state of the art (since the current state of the art does not seem to be sufficient in the long run).

Chapter 4: Once attacks and cyber threat indicators have been captured, we proceed to survey the wide variety of information sharing models and identify connected challenges and constraints. The state of the art will be rated (e.g., CERT associations, ISACs) especially with respect to compatibility with the mentioned CISA and NIS directive.

Chapter 5: We elaborate on (peer-to-peer and trust-circle based) cyber threat intelligence sharing communities that exist today, including their structures, modes of operation and used tools, such as the malware information sharing platform (MISP) and the tools used by national CERTs and CSIRTs as well as ISACs.

Chapter 6: Once information has been collected from various sources and/or shared among organizations and the state, it needs to be processed, i.e., normalized, filtered, and interpreted within a context, in order to establish situational awareness. Various models have been proposed to create common operating pictures at the state level to facilitate effective decision making. This chapter outlines them and gives recommendations for their application.

Chapter 7: We devote a chapter to legal implications of cyber incidents and information sharing across organizations and with a nation-state in light of the European NIS directive and the US CISA—as two exemplary frameworks. Please notice that we focus on the European case in greater detail, because the situation is much more complex than in the USA due to the legal status of the Member States.

Chapter 8: After highlighting the legal baseline and common frameworks, numerous case studies will discuss concrete and important legal questions, dealing with liabilities in case of data leakage, unintentional publication of privacy-relevant data, harm to reputation, or (physical) harm due to inappropriate mitigation measures.

Chapter 9: An extensive illustrative implementation of a Europe-wide incident analysis and sharing system based on results of the EU FP7 project ECOSSIAN[4], stakeholder-driven and with major industry participation, demonstrates how the discussed building blocks may interoperate in a real-world example. Additionally, lessons learned during an in-depth piloting phase in 2017 of this strategic project are discussed.

List of Abbreviations

CERT	Computer emergency readiness/response team
CISA	Cybersecurity information sharing act
CoA	Course of action
CVE	Common vulnerability and exposure
CVSS	Common vulnerability scoring schema
ECOSSIAN	European Control System Security Incident Analysis Network
ENISA	European Network and Information Security Agency
ICT	Information and communication technology
IDS	Intrusion detection system
ISAC	Information sharing and analysis center
MISP	Malware information sharing platform
NIS	Network and Information Security Directive
NIST	(US) National Institute of Standards and Technology
NVD	National vulnerability database
RAT	Remote administration tool
SIEM	Security information and event management
TTP	Tactics, techniques, and procedures

---

[4] http://ecossian.eu/.

References

Arbor Networks. 12th Annual Worldwide Infrastructure Security Report, https://www.arbornetworks.com/arbor-networks-12th-annual-worldwide-infrastructure-security-report-finds-attacker-innovation-and-iot-exploitation-fuel-ddos-attack-landscape; 2016; accessed April 2017.

European Commission. Directive (EU) 2016/1148 of the European Parliament and of the Council of 6 July 2016 concerning measures for a high common level of security of network and information systems across the Union. http://eur-lex.europa.eu/legal-content/EN/TXT/?uri=uriserv:OJ.L_.2016.194.01.0001.01. ENG&toc=OJ:L:2016:194:TOC; 2016; accessed March 2017.

ENISA. Detect, share, protect—Solutions for improving threat data exchange among CERTs. https://www.enisa.europa.eu/ activities/cert/support/data-sharing/detect-share-protect-solutions-for-improving-threat-data-exchange-among-certs/at_download/fullReport; 2013; accessed March 2017.

ENISA. An evaluation framework for national cyber security strategies. https://www.enisa.europa.eu/publications/an-evaluation-framework-for-cyber-security-strategies/at_download/fullReport; 2014; accessed March 2017.

ENISA. ENISA threat landscape 2016. https://www.enisa.europa.eu/publications/enisa-threat-landscape-report-2016; 2017; accessed April 2017.

Franke, Ulrik, and Joel Brynielsson. Cyber situational awareness: A systematic review of the literature. *Computers & Security* 46, 2014: 18–31.

Hewlett-Packard. Countering nation-state cyber attacks. http://h20195.www2.hpe.com/v2/getpdf.aspx/4AA6-6901ENW.pdf?ver=1.0; 2016; accessed March 2017.

Lewis, Ted G. *Critical Infrastructure Protection in Homeland Security: Defending a Networked Nation*. John Wiley & Sons, Hoboken, NJ, 2014.

McAfee Labs. Threats Report., https://www.mcafee.com/au/resources/reports/rp-quarterly-threats-mar-2016.pdf; 2016; accessed March 2017.

Narang, Satnam. Uncovering a persistent diet spam operation on Twitter, Symantec Whitepaper, Version 1.0.http://www.symantec.com/content/en/us/enterprise/media/security_response/whitepapers/uncovering-a-persistent-diet-spam-operation-on-twitter.pdf; 2015; accessed June 2017.

NIST. Guide to cyber threat information sharing. NIST special publication 800-150. http://nvlpubs.nist.gov/nistpubs/SpecialPublications/NIST.SP.800-150.pdf; 2016; accessed June 2017.

OASIS. Structured threat information expression v2.0. https://oasis-open.github.io/cti-documentation/; 2017; accessed June 2017.

Scarfone, Karen, and Peter Mell. An analysis of CVSS version 2 vulnerability scoring. *Proceedings of the 2009 3rd International Symposium on Empirical Software Engineering and Measurement*. IEEE Computer Society, Lake Buena Vista, FL, October 15–16, 2009.

Shackleford, Dave. Who's using cyberthreat intelligence and how? SANS Institute. https://www.sans.org/reading-room/whitepapers/analyst/cyberthreat-intelligence-how-35767; 2015; accessed June 2017.

Strategy Analytics Wireless Smartphone Strategies Service. Global smartphone OS market share by region: Q3. https://www.strategyanalytics.com/access-services/devices/mobile-phones/smartphone/smartphones/market-data/report-detail/global-smartphone-os-market-share-by-region-q3-2016#.WBi0jS2LSUk; 2016; accessed March 2017.

Symantec. Internet security threat report, Volume 22. https://www.symantec.com/en/ca/security-center/threat-report; 2017; accessed April 2017.

SANS, E-ISAC. Analysis of the cyber attack on the Ukrainian power grid: Defense use case. http://ics.sans.org/media/E-ISAC_SANS_Ukraine_DUC_5.pdf; 2016; accessed March 2017.

The Senate of the United States. Cybersecurity Information Sharing Act. https://www.congress.gov/114/bills/s754/BILLS-114s754es.pdf; 2015.

Verizon. Data breach investigations report. http://www.verizonenterprise.com/verizon-insights-lab/dbir/2016/; 2016; accessed April 2017.

Chapter 2

A Systematic Study and Comparison of Attack Scenarios and Involved Threat Actors

Timea Pahi and Florian Skopik
Austrian Institute of Technology

Contents

2.1 Introduction

Organizations and companies face a new worldwide level of sophistication in cyber attacks due to the continuous evolution of technology. Technological changes, such as the rise of cloud technology, widely available low-priced bandwidth, and cryptocurrency, bring new security threats. The resulting threat landscape calls for a paradigm shift and for fundamentally new approaches in cyber defense. Security breaches and cyber attacks of all kinds are becoming more professional, stealthy, automated, and complex. These advanced forms of cyber attacks and threat actors beat traditional defense methods and techniques.

This chapter gives a broad overview of the current threat landscape in the cyber domain. After discussing the commonly used terms related to cybersecurity in Section 2.2, a short description of the latest trends follows within the cyber landscape. Section 2.3 describes the characteristics of advanced persistent threats and the common steps of cyber attacks in the form of the cyber kill chain. Section 2.4 analyzes the five past cyber attacks and illustrates the scenarios in detail in order to give an overview of the relevant attack vectors and common tactics, tools, and procedures. Section 2.5 discusses the main categories of threat actors. Finally, Section 2.6 concludes the attack scenarios and common threat actors and their various characteristics and illustrates the most relevant cyber threats today.

2.2 The Definitions of Cybersecurity in a Nutshell

Security in general covers the protection of critical assets from numerous threats posed by various vulnerabilities (Von Solms and Van Niekerk, 2013). Therefore, the determination of assets deserving protection from threats helps to distinguish among the commonly used terms: information security, ICT security, and cybersecurity (see Table 2.1).

The aim of *information security* (IS) is to preserve business continuity and to minimize business damage by limiting the impact of security incidents. According to the international standards, such as the ISO 27002, information security deals with the protection of confidentiality, integrity, and availability of information stored electronically or on paper. The definition of electronically stored information is touching already another area, namely, information and communication technology (ICT). ICT and information technology (IT) are often used synonymously. IT covers a broad range of technologies based on computers, networks, and data storage, whereas ICT describes a broader concept (Von Solms, 2016), including telecommunications infrastructures. This chapter uses the term ICT for the underlying technical infrastructure. Therefore, it can be noted that *ICT security* deals with the protection of technology-based systems, including systems on which information is stored or transmitted, as the common area of these two terms.

The term *cybersecurity* is usually understood as an all-inclusive term covering information security, ICT security, and their combination. The prefix cyber is used to describe terms relating to ICT security and information security, but with a strong "cyber component." Thus, cybersecurity describes the protection of persons, societies, and nations, including their information- and non-information-based assets via tools, security concepts, guidelines, risk management approaches, best practices, and technologies in order to protect the interest of a person, society, or nation. In contrast to information security or ICT security, cybersecurity describes a rather

Table 2.1   Notions of Security

Notions of Security	Protection Of	Concerned Assets
Information security	Information	CIA of nonvirtual or virtual information
ICT security	Technology-based infrastructure	Technology related to computing data and communications
Cybersecurity	Person, society, or nation including their information and non-information-based assets	Identity, intellectual property, systems, networks (whether physical or virtual), critical infrastructures, etc.

broad scope. It aims to protect all information-based and non-information-based assets, including persons and knowledge, that are threatened via exploited ICT.

In general, cybersecurity is used as an umbrella term (Von Solms and Van Niekerk, 2013), whereas information security sets its focus on the preservation of the CIA triad—confidentiality, integrity, and availability—of information, and ICT security focuses on the underlying technical infrastructure. The notion of information security includes the underlying information resources, such as networked computing with various hardware devices and software solutions or virtualization equipment, which are partly provided by ICT. Cybersecurity takes a broader view and includes the human dimension in its operating and protection range.

2.3 On Cyber Attacks, Cybercrime, and Cyberwar: Emerging Trends and Threats

Cybersecurity aims to prevent, detect, and respond to cyber incidents and attacks, and mitigate cyber threats. Unlike physical threats, they are mainly stealthy, and the threat actors usually manage to remain anonymous. The spectrum of risks is limitless. Most definitions of cyber attacks focus only on information security or ICT security (NATO CCDCOE, 2017), but hardly ever address the holistic nature of these kinds of attacks. Strictly speaking, a *cyber attack* refers to an attack that is carried out through ICT and compromises the cybersecurity of persons, societies, or nation-states, targeting their information- and noninformation-based assets. Cyber attacks may include various consequences, such as breach of access, data exfiltration, identity theft, fraud, intellectual property theft, denial of service, and malware infection. Not every single cyber attack has the potential to escalate into serious conflicts.

A *cyber campaign* refers to a series of planned cyber attacks and other supporting operations. The chain of highly organized and complex cyber attacks, such as advanced persistent threats (APTs), could have serious consequences, even nationwide. Cyber attacks are becoming more sophisticated, and their tactics, techniques, and procedures (TTPs) are continuously developing. Sophisticated one-step and multistep cyber attacks augment their technical TTPs with nontechnical TTPs, such as social engineering or physical penetration. Therefore, the attack surface exploited by cyber attacks has expanded enormously.

Due to the variety of exploitable technologies and applied techniques, it has become quite hard to maintain a consistent categorization of cyber attacks. The documentations of cyber attacks use confusing categories that are partly overlapping with each other, such as cybercrime, data breaches, cyberwarfare, and government and corporate espionage. There are numerous ways to categorize cyber attacks, for instance, by TTPs, attacker's motivation, targets, and so on. The categorization of cyber attacks by their TTPs is a difficult task because of the diversity of widely applied TTPs. The categorization by motivation and threat actors is only possible after deeper investigations, because threat actors usually remain anonymous, and they attack a wide palette of targets driven by different, sometimes hidden motivations. Only hacktivist groups (Quaglia, 2016), such as Anonymous, Lizard Squad, Syrian Electronic Army, Inj3ct0r Team, and RedHack, periodically issue statements on their current hacking campaigns, often related to human rights or other political agendas. One preferable option is the categorization of cyber attacks by their targets, for example, government facilities, corporate facilities, or military facilities. However, the borderlines between these target categories are also blurred.

From a legal and law enforcement aspect, cyber attacks can be divided into two large categories: cybercrime and cyberwar. In this categorization, cyber espionage and cyberterrorism belong to cybercrime. The main difference is the attacker's motivation. In case of cyberterrorism, the threat actors have political, religious, or ideological motivation, whereas the motivation behind *cyberwar* is related to the protection of homeland and national assets (Interpol, 2016). State and non-state actors conduct cyber operations to achieve a variety of political, economic, or military objectives. The world has witnessed the development of cyber capabilities by nation-states quite extensively in recent years. The countries believed to have the most developed cyberwarfare capabilities are the United States, China, Russia, Israel, and the United Kingdom. Two other notable players are Iran and North Korea (Farwell and Rohozinski, 2011).

In the United States, the Department of Defense (DoD), together with other agencies, is responsible for defending the U.S. homeland and its interests from attacks, including those from cyberspace (U.S. DoD, 2015).

The DoD has developed capabilities for cyber operations and is still integrating capabilities into their portfolio of tools and thus the U.S. government. Additionally, the U.S. Cyber Command was created at the National Security Agency (NSA) for cyber operations in 2009. Installation owners and operators must partner with the Military Departments' Computer Emergency Response Teams (CERTs).

Among DoD's cyber personnel and forces, the Cyber Mission Force (CMF) has a unique role within the Department. In 2012, DoD began to build a CMF to carry out DoD's cyber missions (U.S. DoD, 2015). In 2016, all CMF teams achieved initial operating capability. The CMF currently comprises about 5000 individuals across the 133 CMF teams. By the end of the fiscal year 2018, the goal is for the force to grow to nearly 6200 and for all 133 teams to be fully operational (U.S. DoD, 2016).

After the cyber attack on the nuclear facility in Natanz, Iran made cyberwarfare a part of its military strategy and began to establish its capabilities. The cyber attack triggered the emergence of national hacker groups, such as the Iranian Cyber Army and the Islamic Revolutionary Guard Corps (Kraus, 2014). In 2011 and 2012, Iran launched a series of denial-of-service attacks on U.S. banks. Though Izz ad-Din al-Qassam Cyber Fighters took responsibility, U.S. officials claimed that Iran was retaliating for Stuxnet and UN sanctions (Zetter, 2015). Iran is rapidly developing its cyber capabilities; it is suspected to be the organizer of several major attacks in the region. For instance, in 2012, Iranian hackers struck Saudi Arabia's national oil company, Saudi Aramco, nearly obliterating its corporate IT infrastructure and bringing the company close to collapse (Bronk and Tikk-Ringas, 2013).

Currently, the term cyberwar has no official or generally accepted definition. After analyzing a great number of definitions of cyberwar, the following definition presents a trade-off among the diverse approaches (Uma and Padmavathi, 2013): *cyberwar* is an escalated state of conflict between or among nation-states in which cyber attacks are carried out against ICT systems of critical infrastructures as part of a military campaign (NATO CCDCOE, 2016).

EXAMPLE: CYBERWAR CASES

There is much skepticism about the degree of cyberwar, but the following cyber attacks appear to have all necessary ingredients of cyberwar:

- In 2007, the highly networked Estonian government was the target of cyber attacks. The DDoS attacks began on the foreign minister's web-site but spread to all government institutions and key businesses, such as banks. The large-scale attack had a significant effect on public life in the small country (Lesk, 2007).
- The Russian-Georgian cyberwar in August 2008 represented a long history of geostrategic conflicts between the two nations; it was based on many complex factors, such as geopolitical, legal, cultural, and economic (Hollis, 2015). Synchronized with the physical attack, Russia started attacking Georgia's military and government networks and assaulting websites related to communications, finance, and government to block communication with the citizens (Oltsik, 2009).
- There were also conflicts between Bangladesh and Myanmar (Burma) that escalated in continuous cyber attack, such as defacing governmental websites, by national hacktivists from both sides (Gandhi et al., 2011).

As the past incidents and attacks show, it is not unusual for political conflicts to escalate in cyberspace.

Although there is no universal definition of *cybercrime*, it is becoming increasingly accepted that the term is used to describe crime and other illicit activities (Hunton, 2009) that involve the use of ICT. Some organizations distinguish between advanced cybercrime and cyber-enabled crime (Interpol, 2016). Advanced cybercrime covers sophisticated attacks executed within cyberspace, whereas cyber-enabled crime includes "traditional" crimes enabled by technological (or ICT) achievements, such as financial crimes, online fraud, and even terrorism. There is a wide palette of cybercrimes putting every citizen at risk, from phishing e-mails through online blackmailing to data exfiltration.

Cybercrime is so fast growing that international law enforcement agencies opened an additional category for the most wanted cyber criminals. The nature of cybercrime has evolved remarkably in its quite short history. In the past, cybercrime was committed mainly by individuals (Interpol, 2016). Today, it is committed by highly organized and professional groups from all over the world. The crimes are not necessarily new, but the TTPs are continuously evolving with the opportunities presented by the evolving ICT. Cybercrime as a concept is much broader than just crime alone as it also covers the wider issues of unacceptable or undesirable behavior (Yar, 2013). Cybercrime often falls still into a regulatory gray area, and the ability to categorize the true scale and criminal nature of cybercrime remains difficult (Hunton, 2009). Past incidents revealed that even governments might recruit and sponsor hacker groups to support espionage (Geers et al., 2016). Some of these campaigns became public, such as GhostNet, Moonlight Maze, and Titan Rain, just to mention a few (Geers, 2015).

2.3.1 Emerging Technologies and Threat Trends in Cyberspace

There is still no common definition of *cyberspace*, but militaries especially usually treat it as an own domain, namely, as the fifth one (Lynn, 2010) after land, sea, air, and space. The fundamental difference between cyberspace and the other domains is that the hierarchy of the other domains is geophysical by nature. Cyberspace is embedded in all domains and it is transforming continuously (Welch, 2011). The NATO definition states that cyberspace is the name given to the global and dynamic domain composed of ICT. It has blurred borders, involving users in an unprecedented globalization that provides new opportunities but also entails new challenges, risks, and threats (NATO CCDCOE, 2017). One commonly described property is that cyberspace is in a continuous state of change. Cyberspace is still in expansion, as well as the resulting attack surface. In order to understand the challenges and risks posed by increasing cyberspace, we need to take a closer look at the emerging trends that are enormously broadening both cyberspace itself and its attack surface. Note that there are hundreds of technological, societal, economic, and regulatory/legal trends that constantly shape the appearance of cyberspace. Dealing with all of them goes far beyond the scope of the book—thus this chapter focuses on those that stick out of the masses and are relevant with respect to how cyber attacks are carried out today and will be carried out in the near future.

One of the most significant technology trends with impact on security is the *Internet of Things* (IoT). It multiplies exploitation opportunities, as it is expected to grow to an estimated 20 to 50 billion connected devices by 2020. Internet-connected devices (excluding traditional desktops, laptops, and mobile phones) are being rapidly adopted by both consumers and businesses, particularly in sectors such as manufacturing, healthcare, and entertainment. Considering how most organizations are still struggling with the phenomenon of bring your own device (BYOD), the emergence of the IoT might intensify the serious situation even more, particularly when considering that the IoT includes consumer devices that may support business purposes (Websense, 2015). IoT has begun to change the virtual but also the real world. On the one hand, the growing use of smart equipment in private and public life leads to the *continuous tracking* of its users. One the other hand, the IoT generates a huge amount of data, sometimes referred to as *Big Data*: the huge amount of data arriving especially from IoT devices. The concepts of Big Data and IoT are converging (Dull, 2015). Big Data is compiled from an increasing amount of data from sensors, smart systems, entertainment products, and social media applications—just to mention a few. The data volume will continue to grow and the analysis techniques must (and certainly will) improve. Processing Big Data, especially the merging of different large databases, faces already huge challenges— on the one side with privacy regulation and on the other side with security. A good example is the first wave of smart vehicles. Leading manufacturers have to deal with numerous privacy problems because of continuous tracking of the physical car and its geolocation. The first published cyber incidents targeting smart cars took place in summer 2015 (Ring, 2015). Hackers succeeded in intruding into some cars' systems via mobile telephone networks and were able to take over vital functions such as the brake system and engine (Schellekens, 2016). Another trend is the increased use of *wireless technology*, such as smart home platforms and fitness trackers. Generally speaking, the use of wireless devices increases the risk of potential cybersecurity threats. The increasing use of wireless office devices, such as the wireless keyboard and mouse, opens new opportunities for gaining access to potential target systems.

Another emerging trend is set by cryptocurrencies. Cryptocurrencies such as Bitcoin, Ether, or Solar Coin have the potential to significantly change the finance sector and the cyber domain by reviving the business of cyber attacks, especially ransomware. The news in 2015 and 2016 was full of stories about cyber attacks using ransomware focusing on public and private facilities (Pathak and Nanded, 2016). The main advantages of ransomware business for criminals are the

EXAMPLE: RECENT RANSOMWARE CASES

In the United States, numerous medical facilities, such as the Hollywood Presbyterian Medical Center, MedStar Georgetown University Hospital, Chino Valley Medical Center, and Desert Valley Hospital of Victorville, suffered damage from cyber attacks (Everett, 2016). In August 2016, FireEye

> ### EXAMPLE: RECENT RANSOMWARE CASES (*Continued*)
>
> reported a massive wave of attacks using Locky ransomware dropped via macro-enabled Word (.docm) documents in phishing e-mails, mostly targeting healthcare organizations, located as far away as Japan, Korea, and Thailand. Besides medical facilities, local governments attracted special attention of the attackers. In September 2016, researchers at Proofpoint identified a new strain of ransomware, called MarsJoke, which was pushed toward state and local government agencies and educational institutions in the United States. Universities have also been picked as targets for ransomware campaigns. The security firm SentinelOne found out that 56% of UK universities had been hit. In fact, one institution suffered no fewer than 21 attacks (Mansfield-Devine, 2016a,b).

low-maintenance and operation costs and the short path to anonymous monetization thanks to Bitcoin.

The anonymity provided by cryptocurrency, especially by Bitcoin, led to a rising number of ransomware attacks on soft target organizations. Modern ransomware attacks increasingly target small businesses, local government, and medical institutions due to their historically often poor information security maturity levels. Because of the lack of regular backups and suitable protective measures in these organizations, different ransomware tactics have evolved. The Hollywood Presbyterian Medical Center for example decided to pay the ransom in order to restore access to its files according to their official release (Hollywood Presbyterian Medical Center, 2016). There is a wide range of ransomwares in use, such as Locky, CryptoWall, TeslaCrypt, CoinVault, and CTB-Locker. The increasing cases of ransomware infections can be partly explained by the Ransomware-as-a-service (RaaS) business model for instance with Raas Shark, Stampado, or Encryptor. This particular strategy has been proven to be highly lucrative for cyber criminals, allowing malware creators to earn from their ransomware by enlisting a network of distributors. The scheme works because one type of ransomware can be sold and spread by multiple distributors, with the creator getting a cut from their profit (Trend Micro, 2016).

Distributed denial-of-service (DDoS) attacks represent a valid concern. DDoS attacks continue to increase in frequency, complexity, and size and focus mainly on cloud services, financial services, and the public sector (Verisign, 2016). DDoS-as-a-Service (DDoSaaS) is a flourishing business today thanks to the anonymity provided by cryptocurrency and the Deep Web (the part of the Internet that cannot be discovered by using traditional search engines. It contains web pages, databases, networks, and online communities that are hidden from average users). The terms Deep and Dark Web need further explanation: Dark Web is a part of the

Deep Web. The Dark Web is based on secured networks where connections are made between trusted peers (Ciancaglini et al., 2016), using TOR[1], Freenet[2], or I2P[3]. Nowadays information located on the Deep Web is estimated to be 400–550 times larger than the information on the Surface Web. Hence, the Deep Web is the largest growing part of the Internet (Bergman, 2001) and massively increases the number of threats. A series of new off-the-shelf tools are commoditizing the art of hacking. This makes it possible for everybody, even with little know-how, to launch attacks by renting services from the Dark Web. Available services allow, for instance, the renting of botnets for a small fee from botnet owners for the purpose of launching DDoS attacks. These Booters (botnet owners) are popular on the black market because they make tracking harder.

Another legitimate concern is the growing number of large-scale attacks against critical infrastructures and *industrial control systems* (ICS). There is an increasing interest in industrial products as targets. A significant incident was the successful attack on the Ukrainian power grid, which resulted in a large-scale power outage (U.S. DHS ICS-CERT, 2016). Countless organizations have fallen prey to cyber attacks, even large companies with advanced defense methods. In recent years, a new category of cyber threats hit the mainstream, namely, the *advance persistent threats (APTs)*. APTs are carried out by sophisticated and well-resourced adversaries targeting specific information in high-profile companies and governments, usually in a long-term campaign involving different methods and tools, such as the latest zero-day vulnerabilities, sophisticated toolkits, and social engineering techniques.

2.3.2 APT Characteristics

The history of APTs (focusing on cyber-nuclear espionage) goes back to the mid-1980s when computers and networks expanded throughout the defense and military establishment (RUSI, 2016). After the first "cyber espionage" case in 1968, the volume and scope of APTs have grown exponentially.

The U.S. National Institute of Technology (NIST) provides an appropriate definition of an APT, which also distinguishes between cyber attacks and the resulting APTs. According to the official definition, an APT is carried out by "an adversary that possesses sophisticated levels of expertise and significant resources which allow it to create opportunities to achieve its objectives by using multiple attack vectors (e.g., cyber, physical, and deception). These objectives typically include establishing and extending footholds within the information technology infrastructure of the targeted organizations for purposes of exfiltrating information, undermining or impeding critical aspects of a mission, program, or organization; or positioning itself to carry out these objectives in the future. The advanced persistent threat:

---

[1] Tor Project: Anonymity Online, https://www.torproject.org/, last accessed on 02-02-2017.
[2] Freenet Project, https://freenetproject.org/, last accessed on 12-12-2016.
[3] I2P, https://geti2p.net/en/, last accessed on 21-12-2016.

(i) pursues its objectives repeatedly over an extended period of time; (ii) adapts to defenders' efforts to resist it; and (iii) is determined to maintain the level of inter-action needed to execute its objectives" (NIST, 2011). Traditional cyber attacks focus on harvesting personal information of unaware users for financial gain. Unlike common cyber threats, which usually simply exploit a present vulnerability, independently from the user or owner, APTs focus on specific high-value targets and their intellectual property or classified information in order to gain strategic benefits. Another fundamental difference is the attack approach. While common cyber attacks try to gain personal information from a number of victims in a single attack with a few steps, in APTs an attacker carries out multiple steps over a lon-ger time span. Usually attackers try to directly lure victims to fake websites with the help of phishing e-mails, trying to make them enter their credentials or even their credit card information. APTs are much more sophisticated. Unlike the short-term attacks, they launch attacks in numerous stages while staying stealthy on the victim's systems. APTs start repeated attempts to access the target system within long-term campaigns. As APTs target advanced victims, mainly governmental organizations, finance, high-tech, and consulting companies (FireEye, 2016), they may need more time and advanced tools to penetrate the company's defense line while remaining undetected. Therefore, the threat actors of APTs are usually well-resourced and organized groups with deep technical know-how.

Generally, common cyber attacks can be considered battles, and an APT can be regarded as a military campaign combining methods of common cyber attacks. Like great military campaigns, APTs need precise planning, including multiple phases and steps. The experience of recent years shows that every large-scale cyber campaign applies its unique techniques. But the tactics of APT attacks are often similar; therefore, the phases are predictable. They differ mainly in the techniques used in the different phases (Chen et al., 2014). Table 2.2 provides an overview of the characteristics of common cyber threats and APTs.

Table 2.2 Attack Characteristics

	Aim	TTPs	Attack Scope	Time Scope	Attack
Common Cyber Attacks	Mainly financial profit	Common TTPs, even COST	Wide-range, targets with no or low security awareness	Hit-and-run approach (hours to days)	Roughly prepared, Finite resources
APTs	Espionage and/or sabotage	Newest TTPs, even self-developed	Specific targets, targets with even high security awareness	Long-lasting with solid preparation (months to years)	Carefully prepared, Programs with well-planned modular architecture, significant resources

2.3.3 Cyber Kill Chain

In order to describe the anatomy of advanced cyber threats, a concept called "cyber kill chain" is used. "A kill chain is a systematic process to target and engage an adversary to create desired effects" (Ryan, 2011). Basically, it is a simplified approach of the cyber kill chain model proposed by Lockheed (2014). APTs generally follow the following common phases in the cyber kill chain (cf. Figure 2.1): (1) reconnaissance, (2) weaponization, (3) delivery, (4) exploitation and initial intrusion, (5) command and control (C2 or C&C) and lateral movements, and (6) actions of intent. The following Sections 2.3.3.1–2.3.3.6 provides a deeper description of the phases of the cyber kill chain and analyzes the current attack methods that are used by today's threat actors.

2.3.3.1 Step 1: Reconnaissance

The first phase after choosing the potential target is reconnaissance. The reconnaissance process covers a wide range of information-gathering activities. In this phase, the threat actor tries to collect all relevant information about the target organization in order to discover the target's technical environment, organizational processes, and key personnel that could be exploited to achieve the threat actors' objective. The activities of the first phase are similar to black box penetration testing activities. As in black box testing, hackers do not have adequate knowledge about the victim organization and its target system in the early phase. The aim of the reconnaissance is to discover the attack surface of the target system and

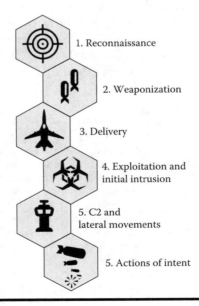

1. Reconnaissance

2. Weaponization

3. Delivery

4. Exploitation and initial intrusion

5. C2 and lateral movements

5. Actions of intent

Figure 2.1   APT kill chain.

to find the most efficient ways to penetrate it. A major difference to penetration testers, however, is that threat actors do not need to discover all vulnerabilities—a single exploitable weakness is enough to allow an initial compromise. The threat actors can gain valuable information from open source intelligence (OSINT) or gain internal information through *social engineering*.

The following OSINT sources might be relevant for information gathering or for further social engineering fraud: corporate websites, social networks, press releases, public documents, white papers, job offers, and search engines. There are two different methods of information gathering: passive and active reconnaissance (Pernet, 2014a,b). The main difference is the interaction between the attacker and the target. In passive reconnaissance, there is no direct interaction, and it usually leaves no traces. The threat actors use open information sources. Active reconnaissance could be the next step after passive reconnaissance. This step needs more preparation and leaves traces, e.g., as a result from active scanning activities.

> Input: Selected target
> Activity: Data gathering on the target
> Output: Solid knowledge of the target system, discovered vulnerabilities for further attacks
> Tools and techniques: Traditional or special search engines, social engineering (Tankard, 2011)

2.3.3.2 Step 2: Weaponization

Weaponization covers the preparation of malicious payloads for further attacks. In this phase, the threat actor has solid knowledge of the target's attack surface, and it has identified potential victim employees. Based on this information the threat actors prepare the next steps for the initial compromise. Weaponization refers to compiling tailored malware for the discovered vulnerabilities in order to gain remote access to the target system. The tailored malware with the suitable exploit is built into a deliverable payload, such as in Microsoft Office documents or Adobe PDF, in order to compromise at least one device in the target organization. The most effective method is to create a malicious payload, which uses certain zero day vulnerabilities, i.e., vulnerabilities not yet publically known).

> Input: Solid knowledge of target system, collection of potential entry points to the system
> Activity: Designing the initial compromise
> Output: Malicious payload
> Tools and techniques: Zero-day vulnerabilities, tailored malware

2.3.3.3 Step 3: Delivery

Delivery covers the transmission of the malicious payload to a target using different methods, for instance via e-mail attachments, websites, or USB sticks. The delivery of the exploits could be performed in a direct or indirect way (Chen et al., 2014). The direct delivery mechanisms utilize various social engineering techniques, such as spear phishing. As mentioned above, APT attackers combine traditional cyber attacks or enhance them in order to gain the required access to the system. Phishing attacks are usually one of two types: the common broad spreading of e-mail messages and advanced targeted spear phishing using customized e-mail bodies. Phishing e-mails usually contain a clickable link which forwards the user to a fake website. For instance, a copy of a legitimate website can lure to victims to enter their credentials or other personal information and then forwards this harvested information to the hacker in the background. There are numerous different variations of phishing e-mails using different social engineering schemes. Some are very sophisticated and succeed in luring the victim to even open malicious attachments, which are often executable files embedded in PDF or in Microsoft Office documents. These attachments contain a malware binary which exploits a software vulnerability and installs stealthy for example a Trojan horse that will steal information from the infected computer (Pernet, 2014a,b).

Another way for delivering the payload is provided by social networks. Professional business networks or social networks—such as LinkedIn, Data.com Connect, Xing, Beyond, and Facebook—provide a huge amount of useful information for the APT attackers. APT hackers just need to create a fake profile and send connection request to the members of the target company. Since high-profile companies have often hundreds of employees, a small number of the targets will likely accept the request. As a next step, the attacker sends a link, for instance, in the traditional phishing e-mail or a malicious attachment. The attacker hopes that people will fall in a trap while using the internal network of the target company. In that case, the attacker can compromise the victim's device within the company and move on to infect more hosts or even install a backdoor on the target system.

An example for direct delivery is to attack the companies' Internet servers, such as e-mail or DNS. After finding vulnerabilities (such as configuration weaknesses) on a publicly reachable server, the attacker can compromise further hosts and install a backdoor. Direct delivery can be reached also by physical access to the target company or by leaving USB sticks on crowded open places in the company in order to lure employees to plug the sticks into their office devices.

Indirect delivery happens through a trusted third party of the target company, causing APT attackers to be hard to trace. A trusted third party can be a supplier or a legitimate website that is frequently visited or contacted by the target company (Chen et al., 2014). In indirect delivery a watering hole (Kim and Vouk, 2015) attack can be used. The goal of these attacks is to compromise a host in the target company by infecting websites the employees frequently visit. The term watering hole attack originates from the tactic of predators in a natural world lurking near watering holes for their victims. According to this concept, the attacker is waiting for the target to visit the infected website. The consequence of a watering hole infection is not only that the member of the target organization but potentially every user visiting the infected website will be infected. APT attackers could sort the victims by IP addresses, since they mostly know the IP range of the target system from the first phase (reconnaissance) of the APT attack.

> Input: Tailored payload, solid knowledge of target system
> Activity: Delivery of the malicious payload
> Output: Malicious payload delivered, compromised hosts
> Tools and techniques: Phishing, spear-phishing, watering hole, physical access

2.3.3.4 Step 4: Exploitation and Initial Intrusion

After delivering the payload, vulnerability needs to be exploited in order to be able to execute the malicious code on the victim's system. The attackers do not necessarily need technical exploits if they obtain access credentials through social engineering and simply use them to gain access to the victim's systems. The execution of the exploit is relevant only when APT attackers take advantage of detected software or hardware vulnerabilities, in sophisticated cases zero-day exploits. Zero-day vulnerabilities are undisclosed computer-software vulnerabilities that hackers can exploit to adversely affect computer programs, data, additional computers, or a network. The term zero day relates to the fact that it is not publicly reported or announced before becoming active, leaving the software's author with zero days in which to create patches or advise workarounds to mitigate its actions (Kumar, 2014).

Installation refers to installing malware on the infected computer. The installation is relevant only if the APT attacker used malware as a part of the attack or malware is involved (Engel, 2014). The exploitation and installation make the initial intrusion to the target system possible. After accessing the target system, APT attackers establish a foothold in the network, typically by installing backdoor malware. Backdoors play a significant role in the next phase. They present a persistent point of entry to the target system for APT attackers.

> Input: Payload is delivered to the target
> Activity: Exploit the target's vulnerabilities, installation of further malware
> Output: Initial intrusion to the target system
> Tools and techniques: Backdoor malware, zero-day exploits, unpatched vulnerabilities

2.3.3.5 Step 5: C2 and Lateral Movements

The aim is to establish remote access to the target system for further attacks and investigation. This stage usually takes longer, hence the activities run slowly in order to evade detection. Backdoors allow attackers to establish connections to their command and control (C&C or C2) channel. The C2 mechanism takes control of the compromised hosts. The backdoor installation applies a number of strategies to enable successful intrusion, such as port binding, connect-back, connect availability use, or legitimate platform abuse (Chiu et al., 2014). In order to remain undetected, attackers increasingly use more advanced services and tools. Some APT attackers host their C2 servers in Tor to remain anonymous and avoid being blocked and blacklisted. APTs take advantage also of legitimate remote access tools (RATs, which are usually used by system administrators to remotely access and control computers). When they are used by a malicious user to control the system without the knowledge of the victim, they are known as Remote Access Trojans (Kienzle and Elder, 2013). In APT attacks, the commonly used RATs (Adachi and Omote, 2016) are Poison Ivy RAT, DakComet, Black Shades, njRAT, ZxShell, and Gh0st RAT (Fagerland, 2012).

The next step after infecting one endpoint or system within the target organization is spreading the malicious activity in order to establish a foothold. This can be carried out in various ways. On the one hand, the APT attacker might have managed to gain the credentials of a privileged user or managed to cause privilege escalation. The Active Directory service (AD) is a preferred target related to privilege escalation. Once successfully attacked, AD could enable control of the whole network to the threat actors. This step contains, for example, the hidden installation of many forms of malware, for instance viruses, worms, Trojan horses, and spyware. These software types have the ability to scan local files and browsing histories, install other programs, monitor keystrokes and screen, or sniff the network traffic, cookies, and other applications. These tools help to execute the further activities, called *lateral movement*, such as internal reconnaissance, compromising additional systems, privilege escalation, and identifying valuable assets and information location, such as password hashes in the Security Account Manager (Chen et al., 2014). Lateral movement is an essential part of the whole cyber kill chain. In this book, the kill chain does not foresee a step for lateral movement, because it is rather a

Input: Successful initial intrusion
Activity: Use of the tools to establish remote access, establishing foothold, lateral movements
Output: Control of the target system, establishing (persistent) access to the target
Tools and techniques: C&C server, RATs, backdoors

continuous activity. Others, however, treat it as a single step, and some treat it as part of the internal reconnaissance or exploitation step. Regardless of where lateral movement is conceptually located in the kill chain, it covers all secondary activities in moving deeper into the victim organization.

2.3.3.6 Step 6: Actions of Intent

After preparing the victim system, the threat actors execute the final attack phase in order to achieve their primary goal. This might include the destruction of essential control systems, DDoS attacks against critical services, or data exfiltration. Data exfiltration refers to copying or transferring the desired information to the C&C server or to an internal server where it is encrypted and prepared for transmission to the threat actor. The unauthorized exfiltration is executed in several steps so that the network traffic does not differ too much from the daily traffic. The attacker can use FTP or HTTP to send the files in order to obfuscate the exfiltration as legitimate communication within the target network. The sensitive data now can be delivered to the customer or be sold on anonymous marketplaces on the Deep Web.

> Input: APT attackers have established foothold and prepared the last attack
> Activity: Actions on target, such as data exfiltration, DDoS, paralyzing essential control systems, etc.
> Output: Primary goal achieved
> Tools and techniques: FTP, HTTP—both for illegitimate transfers.

2.3.3.7 Summary

Some of these steps overlap and are repeated by the threat actors if necessary. They represent the common course of actions of APT threat actors. There are different views on what makes a threat an APT. Some argue that APT is just a marketing term and that there is virtually no difference between an APT and a traditional threat; yet others say that an APT is a nation-state sponsored activity that is geared toward political espionage. APTs are often seen in nation-state sponsored attacks (which are hard to prove), and they do often use the same attack vectors that traditional threats leverage, but they also leverage different attack methodologies and have different characteristics than traditional threats (ISACA, 2014).

The following domains were targeted by APTs: governmental facilities, services and consulting; technology; financial services; telecommunication services; education; aerospace; and the defense and energy sector. In general, zero-day attacks are an important weapon in every APT arsenal, but in some cases attackers do not even need them to exploit the target system but rather use known vulnerabilities or social engineering (FireEye, 2013). APT attacks require complex resources and a high degree of stealth over a prolonged duration of operation in order to be successful. The drivers of those attacks may additionally be motivated by political and ideological reasons. All in all, traditional approaches to cybersecurity do not seem to provide a sufficient level of protection against current cyber threats, as the scenarios discussed in the next section will demonstrate.

2.4 Illustration of Recent Attack Scenarios

In order to gain a full picture of the current cyber threat landscape, this chapter provides a short description of the large cyber incidents and attacks of the past. A major part of these attacks was executed with the help of novel, quite recently discovered vulnerabilities—such as Heartbleed, Shellshock, Rootpipe, Stagefright, DROWN, Badlock or Dirty COW—or using the latest variations of malware, including Dexter, ZeuS, and ConFicker. The number of cyber attacks is growing continuously worldwide. Major incidents in recent years were the RSA SecureID compromise in 2011; 2011 PlayStation Network outage; LinkedIn Hack in 2012; Yahoo! data breaches between 2013 and 2014; Operation Tovar in 2014; the Sony Pictures Hack; Commission on Elections data breach in 2016 and many more. The following Section 2.4 presents detailed illustrations of five scenarios in order to provide insights into the applied TTPs and course of actions by different threat actors.

The following scenarios describe real recent attacks. The descriptions draw from publicly available sources, such as white papers, research reports, and official documentation. Due to the fact that (especially victim) organizations are usually not keen to share classified information—for instance the detailed environment and system information (see the second attack scenario)—and that threat actors attempt to work undercover without leaving (many) traces behind, the descriptions of the attack scenarios were enriched with justified assumptions on the infrastructure and attacker actions to draw a complete picture. These concern in particular are the common course of actions of the threat actors and their main tactics, techniques, and procedures (TTPs) applied within the selected attack scenarios. The selected scenarios cover attacks with a special focus on advanced cyber campaigns that need to be dealt with on a national level.

2.4.1 Scenario 1: Stuxnet (2010)

2.4.1.1 Introduction

Stuxnet was totally different from other cyber threats by the time it was recognized. It was the most sophisticated computer worm in June 2010. The sophistication of the malware and the specific systems it targeted led to the conclusion that such an attack could not be developed by a group of (private) persons but was likely rather enabled by a nation-state (Kriaa et al., 2015). The worm targeted industrial control systems, which was not usual at that time. Additionally, for the first time in history, a 500-kilobyte code caused major damage in the physical world. Today Stuxnet is considered to be an American-Israeli cyber weapon for attacking the development of Iran's nuclear research program (Broad et al., 2011). Stuxnet targeted a specific industrial control system in Natanz with the ultimate goal of sabotaging that facility by reprogramming programmable logic controllers (PLCs from Siemens) in order to operate outside their specified boundaries (Falliere et al., 2011).

2.4.1.2 Attack Scenario

Stuxnet was detected in July 2010 but was confirmed to have existed at least 1 year before. Multiple targets may exist, but one of the ultimate goals of the Stuxnet was presumably to stop the uranium-enrichment activities in the Natanz Nuclear Facility by targeting its industrial control systems. Industrial control systems (ICSs) are operated by a specialized assembly-like code on programmable logic controllers (PLCs). The PLCs are often programmed from Windows computers not connected to the Internet or even the internal network. In addition, the ICSs themselves are also unlikely to be connected to the Internet (Falliere et al., 2011). As each PLC has a unique configuration, the threat actors began with a deep reconnaissance of the victim system. Reconnaissance presents the most important activities of the cyber attack, including the mentioned reconnaissance as a common preparation activity. The Natanz fuel enrichment plant is Iran's largest gas centrifuge uranium enrichment facility. It began operating in February 2007, in contravention of UN Security Council resolutions (UN SC, 2006) demanding Iran to stop uranium enrichment.

After gaining the necessary information, the worm was designed to target the supervisory control and data acquisition (SCADA) systems running on Microsoft Windows that serves specific Siemens ICSs—namely, WinCC, PCS7, and Step 7 platforms—and connected to specific types of PLCs (see Step 2 in Figure 2.2). The complete Stuxnet code was presumably tested numerously in imitated target environments. In order to avoid suspicion, the contained driver files for the attack should have been signed with official digital signatures (Step 3). While the target was unlikely to have outbound Internet access, all functions were embedded directly in the Stuxnet executable (i.e., no payload was fetched in later stages from an external source) in order to sabotage the uranium enrichment activities. The preparation of a complex attack, such as performed by Stuxnet may have taken 6 months or more with 5–10 core developers (Kriaa et al., 2012). Due to the stringent security measures of the facility, the SCADA system was not directly connected to the Internet. The delivery of the malicious code happened by infecting an external device of the corporate network with the help of a USB drive (Step 4).

In order to reach the industrial network, Stuxnet used various propagation methods. Since the Windows computers used to program the PLCs were nonnetworked, Stuxnet tried to spread (see methods in Step 5.A and 5.B in Figure 2.2) to other computers on the LAN using numerous zero-day vulnerabilities. The number

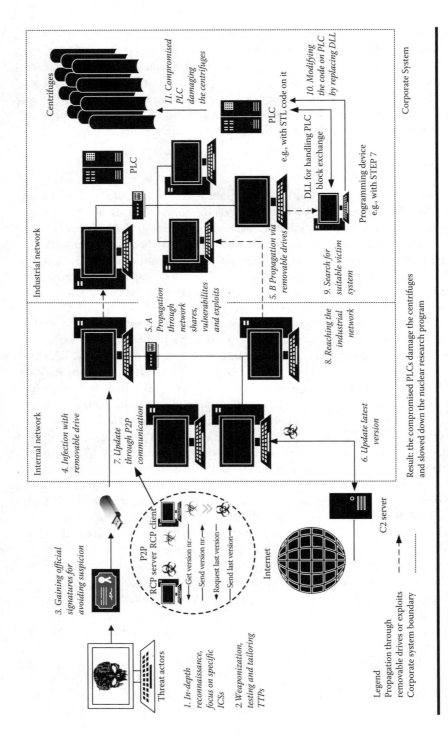

Figure 2.2 Simplified presentation of the Stuxnet attack.

of used zero-day exploits is unusual, as they are highly valued, and malware creators do not typically make use of four zero-day exploits in the same worm (Fildes, 2010). The Stuxnet worm used the following methods to spread: peer-to-peer (P2P) communication, infection of WinCC machines using hardcoded database server passwords (zero-day exploit), propagating through network shares (or using Windows Management Instrumentation operations), and propagation through MS10-061 Print Spooler Zero-Day (Microsoft, 2010) vulnerability and MS08–067 Windows Server Service vulnerability (Microsoft, 2008).

To update the latest version of the malware (Steps 6 and 7), Stuxnet could either establish a P2P communication by installing a remote procedure call (RPC) server on the infected machine and wait for connections from RPC clients or it could directly download the latest updates from a preconfigured C2 server if the host had a connection to the Internet. In P2P communication, the client and the server shared their version number. If the remote version were newer, then the local computer would request the new version and update itself (see Step 7). Through these methods, the worm propagated itself autonomously in order to reach the industrial network (Step 8) and continued the self-replication while searching for the ultimate target systems (Step 9).

When Stuxnet finally hit a suitable computer—on which the target ICS platform ran—it reprogrammed PLCs in a way that modified the system operation leading to damage to the physical equipment under control. Stuxnet targeted PLCs on sites using Siemens SIMATIC WinCC or Step 7 SCADA systems (Matrosov et al., 2011). When Stuxnet detected a system running the WinCC database software, it connected to the database using a further vulnerability with hardcoded passwords (CVE, 2010). It allowed a local user to access a back-end database and to gain privileged access to the system (Falliere et al., 2011). This means not only that the threat actors acquired the password through reverse engineering, but that the system would not continue to work if the password was changed (Matrosov et al., 2011). Once the connection was successful, Stuxnet performed two actions. First, it sent a malicious SQL code to the database that allowed a version of Stuxnet to be transferred to the computer and thus started to propagate itself. Second, it modified an existing view, such as the safety value related to pumps, and the worm deleted the traces of the modifications made. Because of the manipulated data displayed, the operators of the power plant were not aware of the corruption of their system.

Stuxnet took advantage of the MS10-061 Print Spooler vulnerability, which exists only where a printer is shared. The vulnerability allows remote code execution if an attacker sends a specially crafted print request to a vulnerable system that has a print spooler interface exposed over RPC. A further vulnerability, MS08-067, was used with similar effects. MS08-067 Windows Server Service vulnerability allows remote code execution if an affected system receives a specially crafted RPC request. Stuxnet used these vulnerabilities to propagate itself to unpatched remote computers besides the delivery via removable drives.

The ultimate attack was designed to modify PLCs through accessing the WinCC or Step 7 software (Step 10). PLCs run codes written in different languages, for instance STL or SCL. A specific dynamic link library (DLL) is responsible for handling PLC block exchange between the programming device and the PLC. Stuxnet was able to monitor PLC blocks, infect a PLC by inserting blocks, and mask the fact that a PLC is infected by replacing the required DLL file (Falliere, 2010). Eventually, the compromised PLCs caused heavy damage to the centrifuges used for uranium enrichment (Step 11) (Kriaa et al., 2011), and thus, Stuxnet resulted in slowing down Iran's whole nuclear research program (Matrosov et al., 2011).

2.4.2 Scenario 2: Power Outage in Ukraine (2015)

2.4.2.1 Introduction

After the Stuxnet incident, the number of similar cyber attacks against critical infrastructures increased (or was better recognized). Critical infrastructure (CI) sectors, from financial services and transportation to healthcare, all depend on massive information technology networks. Many traditional cyber defenses, sometimes used by critical infrastructure owners and operators to counter attacks, are outdated and ineffective. These systems remain highly vulnerable to hackers, who could gain control of nuclear plants, railways, and any number of other vital systems (Collier and Lakoff, 2008). These attacks against CIs are no longer just theories. In order to underline this, the second attack scenario presents a cyber attack against a CI, which resulted in a serious power outage, based on information collected during the Ukrainian cyber incident in December 2015 and the discovery of the Furtim malware (Mather, 2016).

The cyber attack in the Ukraine is the first publicly acknowledged incident to result in power outage (SANS-ICS, 2016). Distribution systems operators (DSOs) experienced unscheduled power outages impacting a large number of customers in the Ukraine. In addition, there were also reports of malware found in Ukrainian companies in a variety of critical infrastructure sectors. Based on the report of the U.S. Department of Homeland Security, three Ukrainian regional electricity distribution companies experienced coordinated cyber attacks that were executed within 30 minutes of each other (U.S. DHS ICS-CERT, 2016).

2.4.2.2 Attack Scenario

There is no conclusive evidence about the detailed reconnaissance steps executed by the threat actor. But due to the highly synchronized and multistage attack, deep reconnaissance of the targeted electricity distribution systems operators (DSOs) was required to find the potential victim e-mail addresses for the following phishing attempts (see Step 1 in Figure 2.3).

Referring to the model of the cyber kill chain, in the weaponization phase (Step 2) the threat actors tailored the applied malware and spear-phishing e-mails based on the information harvested in the reconnaissance step. This phase also

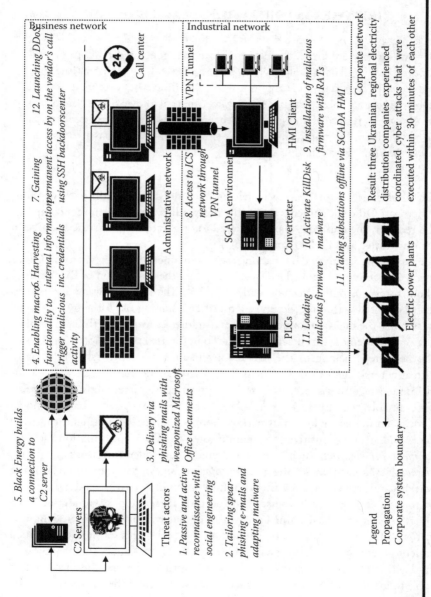

Figure 2.3   Attack illustration of the power outage in Ukraine.

covers the manipulation of Microsoft Excel and Word documents to embed the malware BlackEnergy 3.

FURTHER INFORMATION: BLACK ENERGY

BlackEnergy was first reported in 2007, named BlackEnergy 1, and was at this time a relatively simple form of malware that generated random bots to support distributed denial-of-service (DDoS) attacks. In 2010, BlackEnergy 2 emerged with some significantly improved capabilities that extended beyond DDoS—most notably a new plugin architecture that allowed BlackEnergy to subvert system resources and perform other activities such as data exfiltration and network traffic monitoring. At this time, BlackEnergy was first associated with crime ware (Shamir, 2016).

The BlackEnergy 3 malware was delivered via phishing e-mails with weaponized Microsoft Office documents to specific individuals within the target company. For the receiver, the crafted e-mails appeared to originate from a trusted source in the administrative and IT Network (Step 3).

The exploits were activated by enabling the macro functionality of Microsoft Office documents. Enabling the embedded macro triggered the installation of BlackEnergy 3 without using customized exploit codes (Step 4). The malware was only used to establish a foothold within the victim system. After installing BlackEnergy 3 on some victim systems, the malware connected to C2 IP addresses to activate the communication between the remote threat actors and the compromised systems (Step 5).

The next steps belong to the lateral movement step of the cyber kill chain. The threat actors began to deeply map (i.e., discover) the victim system, as a so-called internal reconnaissance. This activity prepared the later steps; therefore, it took presumably the largest amount of time in the whole attack. Lateral movement covers enumerating key information about the target environment, elevating privileges and stealing sensitive information (Step 6). Target information includes *environment information*, such as about domain controllers, network diagrams, user directories, and proxy settings; *system information*, for instance about running applications and services, active system configurations or antivirus vendors; and *user information*, such as logged-in users, admin account lists, and password hashes. The threat actors appear to have gained access to internal systems more than 6 months before the power outage. Within this period, they established a foothold and gained permanent access to the victim system by using SSH backdoors (Step 7). By harvesting legitimate credentials with the help of keystroke loggers, the threat actors were able to identify VPN connections without two-factor authentication from the business network into the ICS network. This made it possible for the attackers to enumerate the ICS network, as they did it within the enterprise network. The threat actors gained access with stolen credentials into network segments where SCADA dispatch workstations and servers existed (Step 8) (U.S. DHS ICS-CERT, 2016). They discovered and learned how to manipulate the distribution management systems and the uninterrupted power supplies of the three DSOs in order to execute later the coordinated attack. Additionally, the threat actors developed and tested a malicious firmware for some of the DSOs' devices in advance (Step 9). The delivery happened with the help of remote access Trojans, such as the updated version of BlackEnergy 3, and via VPN access into the IT environment.

Before executing the final attack, the threat actors added malware, called KillDisk, which destroyed essential parts of hard disks and made a last modification to take control of the operator workstations and lock the operators out of their systems (Step 10). In the final attack, they executed simultaneously three actions: take numerous substations offline using the HMI of the SCADA environment, load the malicious firmware onto the devices and execute denial-of-service attacks on the DSO's call centers (Steps 11 and 12). The combination of these measures was extremely effective for disturbing the incident response measures of the DSOs.

The threat actors succeed in disconnecting several substations for 4 hours and cut off 225,000 customers from electricity supply (U.S. DHS ICS-CERT, 2016).

Researchers from the Ukraine confirmed a second power outage on December 16, 2016, resulting from a cyber attack (Higgins, 2017). Ukrainian officials claimed to have identified Russian hackers as the perpetrators, and Ukraine President Petro Poroshenko revealed that his nation had suffered 6500 cyber attacks originating from Russia in a period of 2 months. The latest cyber attack targeted the Pivnichna remote terminal units (RTU). RTUs are microprocessor-controlled electronic devices used as interfaces between objects in the physical world and a SCADA system (Gordon et al., 2004). The attack hit the RTUs controlling circuit breakers and caused a power outage for about an hour.

2.4.3 Scenario 3: Sony Hack (2014)

2.4.3.1 Introduction

In November 2014, a group calling itself The Guardians of Peace (GOP) managed to break into some systems of Sony Pictures Entertainment (SANS, 2015). The supposed aim of the cyber attack was to prevent the release of the comedy movie *The Interview*, telling a story about the leader of North Korea. The threat actors threatened Sony to issue further actions after gaining administrative access to Sony's network. When Sony refused to cooperate, stolen data was posted on the Internet containing movies and personally identifiable information.

2.4.3.2 Attack Scenario

As all other complex cyber attack, this one began with a reconnaissance phase (Step 1 in Figure 2.4). It most likely started with a scan of the victim's network including active, random, or stealth scanning methods. In this phase the threat actors found out that like in many organizations, the relevant IT infrastructure of Sony is run on Microsoft Windows Server platforms. Their first aim was to become an authenticated user. By applying social engineering, the threat actors got an official account (e.g., as a temporary contractor) (Step 2). In this scenario, weaponization and therefore delivery and exploit steps were executed only after a first privilege escalation.

The initial intrusion was carried out after gaining legitimate user credentials. As an authenticated user, the threat actors got read access to internal information, such as to the list of all administrative accounts, which permit access to the Active Directory (Step 3) (Novetta, 2016). The next step was to escalate privileges of the utilized account to administrator level and then apply Active Directory (AD) Privilege Escalation (Step 4). Lateral movements enabled the attackers to gain the required knowledge about the machines on which the escalations could be performed. In Windows AD, there are two common methods to escalate privileges. The most used way is the Pass-the-Hash (PtH) attack. A typical hash-based login system, such as previously used by Sony, contains the following four basic steps: first, the user registers and assigns a password; second, the password is hashed and stored in the database; third, when later logging into the system, the hash of the entered password is checked against the hash saved in the database, and finally, if the hashes match, the user will be granted access. This procedure has weaknesses, such as exploitable password policies or weak hashes. PtH attacks exploit the design flaws in hash-based login systems by capturing and replaying hashes without the need for recovering the plain-text password. Another way of AD privilege escalation is performing password resets and applying tools to gain administrative access without logging into any specific machine (Shancang et al., 2016).

As part of the lateral movement, the attackers (GOP) installed the so-called wiper malware (named BKDR_WIPALL.A) used to establish a foothold within the victim system in Step 5. According to the experts at Trend Micro, once the BKDR_WIPALL.A successfully infects a machine, it drops the BKDR_WIPALL.B agent on the target, which is disguised as a file named "igfxtrayex.exe" and is the malware component ultimately responsible for causing the damage (Trend Micro, 2016). Once it has been installed, BKDR_WIPALL.B sleeps for 10 minutes, after which it starts deleting files and stops the Microsoft Exchange Information Store service. The malware then sleeps for 2 hours and forces a system reboot. The researchers explained that BKDR_WIPALL.B (Trend Micro, 2014a,b) is also able to execute copies of itself with various parameters, a feature that allows the malware to carry out several tasks, including deleting files and dropping additional payloads. The additional component "usbdrv32.sys" for example gives attackers read and write access to local files. Trend Micro discovered a different variation of the malware, named BKDR_WIPALL.D, which drops BKDR_WIPALL.C, this agent in turn drops an image file called "walls.bmp," which is the exact "Hacked by GOP" picture that was displayed on infected system at Sony Pictures (Pierluigi, 2016).

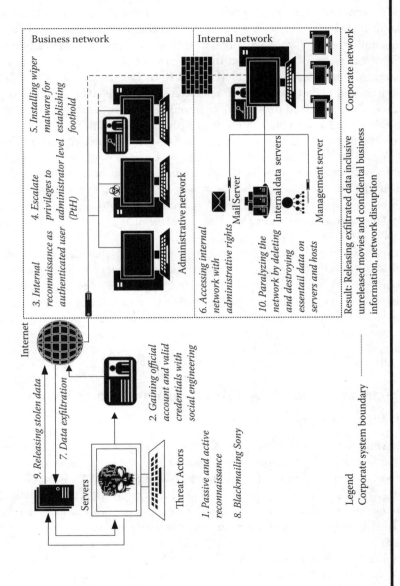

Figure 2.4   Attack illustration of the Sony hack.

After successful privilege escalation, the threat actors were able to perform internal reconnaissance in order to find all interesting documents, e-mails, and confidential data within the internal servers and began with data exfiltration (see Steps 6 and 7). The threat actors were able to copy, tamper, and delete all documents with administrator rights. These kinds of activities (or events) left traces in the audit logs, but organizations pay little attention to audit entries related to Domain Admin logons (Cyber Security, 2013). The GOP sent an e-mail addressed to the Sony Pictures CEO and forced the company not to release the movie and pay monetary compensation (Step 8) (Franceschi-Bicchierai and Warren, 2014). After Sony refused to do that, the GOP released the exfiltrated data into the public domain and caused the studio's network to be offline for a week due to the fact that the network needed to be rebuilt (Steps 9 and 10) (Abdollah, 2015).

According to official U.S. documents, North Korea conducted a cyber attack against Sony Pictures Entertainment, rendering thousands of Sony computers inoperable and breaching some of Sony's confidential business information. In addition to the destructive nature of the attacks, the attackers stole digital copies of a number of unreleased movies, as well as thousands of documents containing sensitive data regarding celebrities, Sony employees, and Sony's business operations (U.S. DoD, 2015).

In summary, the threat actors compromised one of the highly privileged accounts and gained access to all accounts and their passwords, all security policies, mobile devices, all servers, applications and data. Adversaries with sufficient resources (time, money, skills) and the motivation to invest these might be able to carry out similar attacks against a wide variety of organizations—some vague estimations state that up to 85% of all organizations worldwide are vulnerable to this sort of attack (Cyber Security, 2013).

2.4.4 Scenario 4: IoT DDoS Attack against Dyn (2016)

2.4.4.1 Introduction

The following section describes one of the latest distributed denial-of-service (DDoS) attacks by using a large-scale IoT botnet. The cyber attack involves multiple DDoS attacks targeting a large Domain Name System (DNS) provider on October 21, 2016, and the Dynamic Network Services Incorporation (Dyn). At the time of writing, the attack is still under investigation. The attack caused a serious Internet outage by making numerous platforms and services unavailable. Services and platforms affected by the attack include Airbnb, Amazon, BBC, The Boston Globe, GitHub, HBO, Netflix, The New York Times, PayPal, PlayStation Network, SoundCloud, Spotify, Twitter, and many other well-known services. Dyn disclosed that, according to the business risk intelligence firm FlashPoint and Akamai Technologies, the attack was a botnet coordinated through a large number of IoT-enabled devices, including cameras, residential gateways, and baby monitors, that had been infected with the Mirai malware (Hilton, 2016). With 60 of the most-used default usernames and passwords, such as "admin" and "1111," Mirai was able to break into 500,000 IoT devices (Cluley, 2016). The threat actors are still unknown due to the lack of convincing evidence. The hacker groups—Anonymous and NewWorldHackers—claimed responsibility for the attack (Pierluigi, 2014). With an estimated load of 1.2 terabits per second, the attack is, according to numerous experts, the largest DDoS on record (The Guardian, 2016).

2.4.4.2 Attack Scenario

The DDoS attack targeted the servers of Dyn with the help of infected computers as a part of the Mirai botnet. Recently, IoT devices were used to create large-scale botnets—networks of devices infected with self-propagating malware—that can execute crippling DDoS attacks (U.S. DHS US-CERT, 2016). An IoT botnet based on several variations of the Mirai malware created at least two waves of DDoS attacks. The Mirai malware continuously scans the Internet for vulnerable IoT devices, which are then infected and used in botnet attacks. Dyn estimated that the attack involved 100,000 malicious endpoints (Mansfield-Devine, 2016a,b).

There are different methods for distributing a particular bot. A common method is using web-based infections with malware, potentially through infected e-mail attachments. On the other hand, bots can automatically scan their environment for vulnerably hosts, exploit their vulnerabilities, and compromise them (see Figure 2.5). Botnets usually expand by remotely exploiting the vulnerability of new victims. In our attack scenario, the Mirai bot used a list of common default usernames and passwords to scan for vulnerable devices. Because many IoT devices are unsecured or weakly secured, this short dictionary allowed the bots to access hundreds of thousands of devices (Ducklin, 2016). Unlike other botnets, which are typically made up of computers, the Mirai botnet is largely made up of IoT devices such as routers, embedded Linux servers, digital video recorders (DVRs), residential gateways, and other IoT devices (see in Figure 2.5 as vulnerable IoT devices). Mirai—a piece of Linux malware—is used to transform IoT devices into DDoS botnets. The threat actors first gained shell access to the target devices by taking advantage of the fact that most have a default password set for the SSH or telnet account and then loaded the malware (Zorz, 2016). Another weakness of many IoT devices is that they, due to limited computing resources and intended low power consumption, store or send data with weak encryption or even in plaintext. When an infection was achieved, the victim executed a script and downloaded the actual bot binary. The bot binary installed itself to the victim IoT devices and started automatically. The new bot contacted a DNS server to get the IP address of the Internet Relay Chat (IRC) server (Step 4). This is, besides HTTP and P2P, the most common protocol for communication between the bots and the Botmaster. After getting the IP address of the IRC server, the bot established an IRC session with the server and joined the C2 channel. Then the bot automatically parsed and executed received commands.

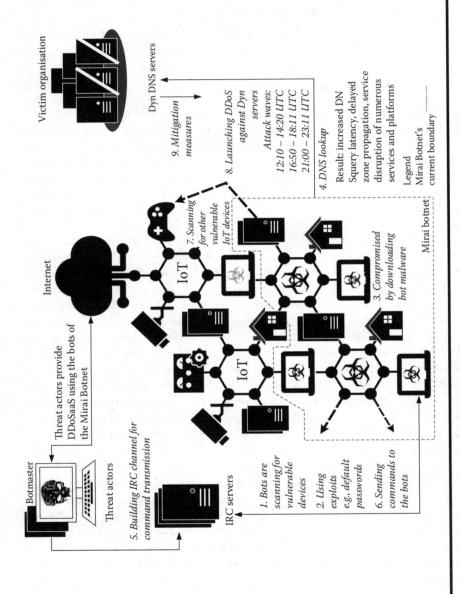

Figure 2.5   Attack illustration of the IoT DDoS attack.

Compromised hosts execute commands, which have been received from the Botmaster via IRC channels (Step 5). These commands include to compromise new hosts, steal sensitive data, send spam and phishing e-mails, or launch a DDoS attack such as in this case (Step 6) (Li et al., 2009). Additionally, the Mirai malware sets up several delayed processes and then deletes malicious files that might alert users of its existence (Zorz, 2016). Once an IoT device has been successfully compromised and integrated into the Mirai botnet, it immediately begins scanning for other vulnerable devices to expanding the botnet (Step 7). The original Mirai botnet had nodes observed in China, Hong Kong, Macau, Vietnam, South Korea, Thailand, Indonesia, Brazil, and Spain. The Mirai botnet served as the technical basis for DDoS-as-a-Service. DDoS-as-a-Service (DDoSaaS) allows attackers to launch their DDoS attacks against the target(s) of their choice in exchange for monetary compensation, generally in the form of Bitcoin payments. While the original Mirai botnet is still used today (February 2017), multiple threat actors have been observed to customize and improve the attack capabilities of the original botnet code, and additional Mirai-based DDoS botnets have been observed in the wild (Dobbins and Bjarnason, 2016).

The Botmasters gave the commands to attack the Dyn servers on September 21, 2016, in several waves (Step 8). According to the analysis of the attack made by the victim organization, the data centers were flooded with a packet volume 40–50 times higher than normal DDoS attacks. The attacks were launched in three waves against the Managed DNS platform mainly by using TCP and UDP packets (Hilton, 2016). In response to the attack, the victim organization activated some response techniques, such as traffic shaping, rebalancing by manipulation of anycast policies, application of internal filtering and deployment of scrubbing services (Step 9). Despite all mitigation measures, the DDoS attack resulted in increased DNS query latency, delayed zone propagation, and service disruption of several services and platforms hosted by the Dyn company, such as AirBnB, Box, Github, Reddit, Spotify, and Twitter.

2.4.5 Scenario 5: RUAG Cyber Espionage (2016)

2.4.5.1 Introduction

The last scenario presents a large-scale high-impact espionage case, the RUAG cyber espionage case based on the analysis by the Swiss GovCERT (2016). The RUAG case is a perfect example of how difficult the attribution of cyber attacks to threat actors is and how challenging the detection of APTs can be. The attackers showed great patience during the infiltration and lateral movement in course of the cyber attack. The threat actors seem to have not only infiltrated several governmental organizations in Europe, but also commercial companies in the private sector in the past decades. RUAG has been affected by this threat since at least September 2014.

FURTHER INFORMATION: THE COLD CYBERWAR

During the Cold War, governments raced against each other to create the strongest and most effective nuclear weapons in the world (Cowley and Parker, 1996). Today, governments race against each other to obtain sensitive information through cyber espionage (Windrem et al., 2013). Past cyber espionage attacks include for instance the Dragonfly cyber espionage attack against energy suppliers (Symantec, 2014), Chinese cyber spying against Tibetan institutions with the help of GhostNet network (F-Secure, 2009), and the espionage case dubbed Titan Rain against U.S. DoD facilities attributed to China (Lewis, 2005).

2.4.5.2 Attack Scenario

Similar to the previous scenarios, this started with an extensive reconnaissance phase. It covered passive and active information gathering about the victim organization. The gained information includes for instance target IP ranges, platforms, and actual user behavior derived from the collected data (see Steps 1 and 2 in Figure 2.6).

The weaponization phase draws from this information. For instance, the most visited site can be derived from the observed browsing behavior patterns and can be used for watering hole attacks (Greene, 2015). In order to ensure the successful intrusion into the victim's systems, the data collected in the reconnaissance phase should be matched to individual users. This approach is called fingerprinting. Every system has a digital fingerprint created by the personalized system configuration, such as fonts, screen-resolution, plug-ins, time zone, and system colors (Kurtz et al., 2016). Cookies were earlier used for browser fingerprinting, but in contrast to the digital fingerprints, cookies can be deleted from the system. In our scenario, active fingerprinting was applied by using mainly JavaScript in order to query the unique characteristics of the victim systems. The active fingerprinting enabled the selection of potential exploits depending on the target's configuration. In the case of a lack of suitable exploits, social engineering techniques were applied for the infection.

The delivery and intrusion were executed by activating watering holes and sending spear phishing e-mails. Based on the reconnaissance information, the threat actors were aware of the victims' most visited sites for water holing. The watering hole contains a redirection to malicious websites. According to the Swiss CERT report (Swiss GovCERT, 2016), the malicious site checked whether the IP address of the visitor was on the target list. If it was, a basic fingerprinting script was returned. The result of the fingerprinting process was delivered to the threat actors. The script collected fundamental information, such as current date and time of the device, and the external IP address. Based on the results, the threat actors decided whether a device was on the target list. In the following step, an advanced fingerprinting script was delivered in order to gain more information about the potential victim. The collected information helped the threat actor to decide whether the device should be infected by sending an exploit or by social engineering (see Step 3 in Figure 2.6). The social engineering activities were supported by various tools, for instance by the Browser Exploitation Framework (BeEF[4]). Whether compromised by a tailored spear phishing e-mail or browsing to an infected website (see Step 4), Trojans—either Trojan.Turla or Trojan.Wipbot—were installed onto the victim system (see Step 5.A and 5.B). The threat actors used Wipbot to download updated version of Turla after the initial infection (Symantec, 2016).

The delivery was followed by the exploitation phase, implemented in two stages. The exploitation enabled the internal reconnaissance within the victim system through various tools. Basic reconnaissance tools were applied in the first stage. The aim of the first stage was to figure out whether the infected device was actually interesting to the threat actors. In the second stage, the basic reconnaissance tools were replaced by advanced tools from the Turla malware family. These sophisticated reconnaissance tools injected themselves into already existing processes as additional threads in order to become invisible on the running systems. The victim company unfortunately preserved only the log files after September 2014, which makes a thorough analysis hard. However, these log files show communication between the infected machines and their C2 servers. Most of the C2 servers were actually deployed on legitimate machines, which had been hacked by the threat actors and misused for their own purposes. The infected devices built a kind of peer-to-peer network and communicated through windows named pipes (Step 6). The stage 2 malware tools set up a botnet hierarchy of the infected devices consisting of two groups. The group of the worker drones was responsible for executing the commands and gathering information, and the supervisory group of communication drones was responsible for communicating with the C2 servers and later for exfiltrating stolen data (drones are marked with letter W or C in Figure 2.6).

As usual, lateral movements included gaining credentials and escalating privileges. In the second stage of the infection, identified devices were compromised with Trojans with administrative privileges. Therefore, privilege escalation was required for gaining ultimate persistence. The lateral movements—for instance stealing credentials, privilege escalation, or remote code execution—were executed with the help of self-written scripts and publicly available tools and exploits (see Step 7). For instance, the Mimikatz tools were used for getting plaintext passwords, hashes, and Kerberos tickets out of the victim system; extracting certificates and private keys; and performing Pass-the-Hash and Pass-the-Ticket attacks (Swiss GovCERT, 2013). At the end of the patient lateral movement phase, the threat actors gained control of the Active Directory.

---

[4] The Browser Exploitation Framework Project, http://beefproject.com/, last accessed on 02-02-2017.

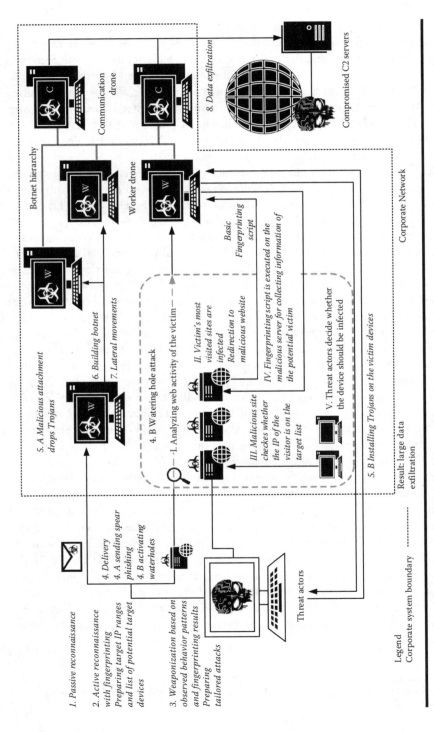

Figure 2.6   Attack illustration of the RUAG cyber espionage case.

In the last step, the threat actors began with the data exfiltration, performed slowly in order not to be discovered. As mentioned earlier, only the communication drones sent stolen data out of the victim system to the C2 servers (see Step 8). The available proxy logs of the victim system showed that data was exfiltrated in several stages. In total ~32 GB of data were sent to the C2 servers usually in a compressed form in an 8-month period.

According to investigations, the Swiss defense ministry and the government-owned defense firm (RUAG) were victim of industrial espionage. The threat actors caused no damage to the defense ministry or federal administration network, according to the statement of the Swiss defense ministry. Russia is suspected of being behind the computer attacks. This is not the first computer attack against government computer networks. The federal authorities have already been the target of hackers three times since 2011. In October 2009, hackers used malware to target the Swiss foreign ministry, entering its computer network and accessing various sensitive documents.

2.4.6 Comparison of Attack Scenarios

The presented attack scenarios show that the activities of threat actors cannot be mapped straight-forwardly to the various steps of the cyber kill chain. There are common parts, such as reconnaissance, initial intrusion, privilege escalation, and lateral movement, and occasionally some steps may be repeated or left out depending on the security level of the target system. For example, threat actors do not need individual weaponization if the target system is vulnerable by default. The main differences however stem from the applied TTPs utilized in the different cyber attacks.

The descriptions cover the following past cyber incidents: the Stuxnet incident (2010), the Ukrainian power outage (2015), the Sony Hack (2014), IoT DDoS attack against Dyn (2016), and RUAG cyber espionage (2013–2016) (see Table 2.3). The comparison of the attack scenarios is based primarily on three aspects, namely, the threat actors, attack complexity, and aim. Referring to threat actors, the attacks were executed by professionals with in-depth knowledge. However, the threat actors most likely received significant support—probably from nation-states—in the Stuxnet incident, the power outage, and the RUAG cyber espionage.

Numerous signs suggest that the perpetrators were not usual cyber criminals. The attacks targeted special devices and organizations (e.g., ICSs operated by specialized PLCs) and not a broad scale of potential victims. The attacks complexity required in-depth preparation, for instance, the number of used zero-day exploits was unusual within the Stuxnet case.

Malware creators or cyber criminals do not typically use several zero-day exploits in the same worm. They can make more profit by selling exploits separately at anonymous marketplaces. Since this did not happen in the previously presented cases, it seems financial support of the attackers was provided from another side.

FURTHER INFORMATION: ZERO-DAY EXPLOITS

Zero-day exploits are high-impact security vulnerabilities in software. The term "zero day" implies that the security flaw is publicly unknown, the larger security communities do not know of its existence (e.g., there is no corresponding entry in the larger CVE databases, which collect information about known vulnerabilities and their exploitability). Only APT groups, often state sponsored, have the resources to find and use zero day vulnerabilities to achieve their mission. In the case of Stuxnet, zero days were utilized to attack offline systems. Zero days are usually only discovered after a data breach takes place. It's not until after the damage has been done and information stolen that zero days are commonly discovered (Damballa, 2016).

These complex attacks require an intensive amount of resources—such as deep expertise, software, and hardware—and a high degree of stealth over a prolonged duration of operation in order to be successful. The preparation of these attacks can last over months, and some attacks can last even for years—e.g., RUAG cyber espionage. The Sony Hack and the IoT DDoS attack took advantage of inappropriately secured systems and devices; therefore, they belong to the cyber attacks with medium complexity. The threat actors of the Sony Hack used clever social engineering and privilege escalation for moving deeper into the victim's system, and the threat actors of the DDoS attack took advantage of vulnerable IoT devices—for instance by using default passwords—and expanded the Mirai botnet before

Table 2.3 Comparison of the Attack Scenarios

Attack Scenario	Threat Actors	Attack Complexity	Aim
Stuxnet	Nation-state-sponsored professionals	High	Sabotage
Power outage	Nation-state-sponsored professionals	High	Sabotage and espionage
Sony hack	Hacktivist	Medium	Sabotage and theft of IP
IOT DDoS attack	Unknown (hacktivist)	Medium	Sabotage
RUAG cyber espionage	Nation-state-sponsored professionals	High	Espionage and theft of IP

launching the waves of their DDoS attacks. The threat actors of these two incidents were likely hacktivists. The Guardians of Peace took the responsibility for the Sony Hack, and the hacker groups—Anonymous and NewWorldHackers—claimed responsibility for the Dyn DDoS attack. The common aspect of the advanced cyber attacks is their aim, mainly sabotage, espionage, and the theft of intellectual property—such as corporate or state secrets and strategy documents—for instance, for gaining economic or political advantage even at national and international levels.

Table 2.4 summarizes the steps of the cyber attacks mapped in the cyber kill chain. There are common steps required to carry out a successful cyber attack, such as the reconnaissance and lateral movement for establishing a foothold. Common TTPs to achieve the initial intrusion are stealing legitimate credentials by social engineering, use of backdoors, keyloggers, form-grabber or spyware, or brute forcing credentials. Another important issue is that even sophisticated attacks do not necessarily use technical exploits for initial intrusions, especially not zero-day exploits, but rather employ social engineering techniques with spear phishing or watering hole attacks. The common aim after delivery of the malware or after initial intrusion is a privilege escalation to facilitate movement within the compromised network. The lateral movements are very different since they depend on the ultimate goal of the cyber attack and the victim's infrastructure; however, this step usually prepares the actual attack inside the victim's system and aims at hiding the traces left behind.

All in all, the emerging TTPs continuously challenge current security solutions. Cyber attacks are becoming less linear in following the cyber kill chain. So they have become harder to detect, as steps are skipped, repeated, or only partially applied, thereby reducing the threat profile (Hanford, 2014).

2.5 Threat Actors

This section aims to define a number of different groups of threat actors. Threat actors cover a wide range of knowledge, abilities, motivation, applied tactics, techniques, and tools, and their actions have various effects and consequences from rather harmless local impact to national security impact. Threat actors are difficult to discover in cyberspace, because they invest quite some effort to not leave clear traces in order to preserve their anonymity. Threat actors use various hiding techniques, such as proxy servers, virtual private networks, or peer-to-peer software within cyberspace (Hanford, 2014). Attribution is also difficult and misleading based on time zone, location of the physical servers used in the attack, nation-specific tools and techniques, and language indicators (Summers, 2014).

The TTPs applied in cyber attacks are as diverse as the threat actors who are using them. A cyber threat actor or threat actor (often referred to as an adversary) is a person or group that targets another person or organization with a motivation. Threat actors can be external or internal to a target, and some can even be involved

Table 2.4   Steps of the Cyber Attack Scenarios

Cyber Kill Chain	Stuxnet	Power Outage in Ukraine	Sony Hack	IOT DDoS Attack	RUAG Cyber Espionage
◎ (reconnaissance)	☑ Passive and active reconnaissance about the specific ICS in Natanz	☑ Passive and active reconnaissance with social engineering	☑ Passive and active scanning ☑ Social engineering for gaining valid credentials	☑ Identify target ☑ Superficial reconnaissance	☑ In-depth passive and active reconnaissance ☑ Creating target IP list ☑ Fingerprinting
✕ (weaponization)	☑ Professional tailoring and testing the malware ☑ In-depth preparation	☑ Tailoring spear-phishing e-mails ☑ Adapting malware	☑ Preparing wiper malware (Weaponization only after first privilege escalation)	☑ Expanding the Mirai botnet ☑ Bots are scanning for further vulnerable IoT devices	☑ Tailoring spear-phishing e-mails ☑ Preparing watering hole attacks
✈ (delivery)	☑ Delivery by infecting an external device	☑ Delivery via phishing e-mails with weaponized Microsoft Office documents	☑ Delivery via authenticated user account	☑ Delivery of malware via web-based infection or malicious attachments	☑ Delivery via spear-phishing and social-engineering or activating watering holes

Table 2.4 (Continued) Steps of the Cyber Attack Scenarios

Cyber Kill Chain	Stuxnet	Power Outage in Ukraine	Sony Hack	IOT DDoS Attack	RUAG Cyber Espionage
	☑ Using various propagation methods partly via zero-day exploits and network shares	☑ Enabling macro functionality to trigger malicious activity	☑ Malicious activities taken as valid user ☑ Accessing the list of administrative accounts	☑ Remotely exploiting the vulnerabilities of new victims ☑ Exploit default or weak passwords	☑ Using previously prepared exploits ☑ Dropping Trojans
	☑ P2P communication between the infected devices ☑ Autonomous self-propagation	☑ BlackEnergy build connection to C2 server ☑ Gaining permanent access by using SSH backdoors	☑ Privilege escalation to admin. level ☑ AD Privilege escalation with PtH or resetting the password	☑ Transforming devices into DDoS bots ☑ Gaining shell access ☑ Deleting malicious files and traces	☑ Internal reconnaissance ☑ Creating botnet by sophisticated malware ☑ Gaining credentials and escalating privileges
	☑ Reprogramming the PLC on the ultimate targets ☑ Manipulating data displayed and deleting traces	☑ Installation of malicious firmware with RATs ☑ Activate KillDisk malware ☑ Taking substations offline ☑ Loading malicious firmware	☑ Exfiltrating data ☑ Blackmailing Sony ☑ Release stolen data ☑ Paralyzing network and releasing stolen data	☑ Launching DDoSaaS attack in several waves ☑ Causing service disruption	☑ Gaining ultimate persistence ☑ Performing PtH and PtT ☑ Gaining control over AD ☑ Stealthy data exfiltration

unknowingly (Chicone, 2015). Common threat actor classification distinguishes among hackers, criminals, or nation-states. Threat actors can also be defined by details. The following list is a combination of different categorization approaches (Surfwatch, 2017) and describes the following threat actors: state-sponsored threat actors, hacktivists, cyberterrorists, cyber criminals, insiders, script kiddies, crackers, and threat actors with unknown identity.

State-sponsored threat actors: State sponsored actors engage in cyber espionage to steal national secrets or sensitive intellectual property from a government or organization (Chicone, 2015). The actual actor or group is employed or often hired by the government of a nation-state for a specific purpose. The TTP is for instance the application of APTs that are using multiple attack vectors simultaneously. So, this kind of attack (actually campaign) lasts longer than many other forms of attack, on average up to 5 months (Recorded Future, 2016) or even years (such as the RUAG cyber espionage).

Examples: Chinese government hackers, NSA, United Kingdom Government Communications Headquarters

Hacktivists: These actors perform attacks in order to draw attention to a specific cause (such as free speech or human rights) or hinder the support of a cause. If the cause is political, and/or designed to inflict terror, they are instead considered cyberterrorists. Hacktivists typically engage organizations as a means of political protest. Their main motivation is to take a website offline for a period of time or deface webpages of their targets.

Example: Anonymous, Lulzsec_root, Syrian Electronic Army, RedHack, AnonGhost

Cyberterrorists: These actors carry out attacks designed to cause alarm or panic with ideological or political goals. There is a blurred line between hacktivism and cyberterrorism because of the similar nature of their motivation. The main difference is in the scope and the effect of the cyber attacks. When the attack endangers critical national assets, such as the safety and security of citizens, it is more than hacktivism, although they tend to apply the same TTPs. Therefore, depending on their activity all hacktivist groups could potentially evolve to more destructive threat actors.

Cyber criminals: These groups of criminals intend to engage in illegal activity, most commonly for monetary profit. Attacks are designed to extort money from the target, or the actors are funded to carry out an attack. The common TTPs are now mass phishing campaigns, ransomware, sophisticated off-the-shell tools, or using services on the Dark Web and even Clearnet, such as DDoSaaS (Radware, 2016).

Example: Producers of ransomware and malware, Black-market data thieves

Insiders: Some of the most common but heavily underestimated threat actors are employee, former (disgruntled) employees, or others with vast knowledge of an organization and its information. This type of threat actor is typically referred to as an insider threat and may aim to vandalize assets as a form of revenge, steal assets for resale on the Dark Web, or send sensitive data to third parties without authorization—such as corporate secrets, business information, personal information, sales and market strategies, etc. The tricky aspect with insiders is that they are extremely hard to detect, since they know the company-internal systems and processes usually quite well and thus mostly do not need apply an extensive lateral movement. Therefore, they do not leave traces caused by the application of malware and exploitation of actual vulnerabilities. Insider threats have led to some of the best-known and most harmful data breaches in history (Recorded Future, 2016).

Examples: Edward Snowden, who worked for NSA and disclosed classified information in 2013, or Jun Xie, a Chinese engineer who worked for a subsidiary of GE Healthcare, who stole about 2.4 million files of trade secrets and other confidential company information and sent it to China

Script kiddies: They are generally young persons with little or sufficient knowledge of routing, switching, Internet protocols, and so on. They often make mistakes and cause damage, even unintentionally, because of their inexperience (Barber, 2001). Script kiddies use mostly free or affordable tools on the Internet.

Crackers: Crackers are specific persons or groups acting on their own, not being members of any other threat actor category. Their motivations are manifold, but are often centered on impressing others with their capabilities or challenging themselves without political reason or looking for financial reward. Based on the poor quality of the applied tools and their limited knowledge, their activities are usually not stealthy enough to hide their actions.

Examples: Individuals, script kiddies, amateur hackers, etc.

Threat actors with unknown identity: In most cases, attacks cannot easily be attributed to particular threat actors. There are many methods and tools used by attackers to disguise their identity and thus maintain anonymity. The threat actors use for instance The Onion Router (TOR) to avoid traceability, insertion of misleading strings or website addresses into malicious binary files, dynamic DNS, and complex series of redirect chains (Websense, 2015).

Figure 2.7 summarizes the threat actor groups based on their motivations, tactics and procedures, tools, and common impact of their activities. Threat actors can certainly move between groups if they expand their skills (script kiddie to cyber criminal) or change their persuasion (state-sponsored threat actor to hacktivist).

Generally speaking, threat actors with little knowledge, such as script kiddies and crackers, have no concrete target. They usually target a wide range of systems with poor security levels. For these activities, they use simple, freely available, and affordable tools or take advantage of vulnerabilities, such as default passwords or nonhardened configurations. As they execute rather short opportunistic attacks, they usually have smaller effect (compared to other forms of attacks) on targets. Attacks by script kiddies usually have limited consequences (or can be quickly discovered), such as website defacement, increased communication latency, or short-term disruption of operations or functions of the targets. They usually have no political, ideological, or financial motivation; for this group the primary motivation is curiosity or their proud.

Threat Actor	Main Motivation	Tactics and Procedures	Tools	Possible Impact
State-sponsored threat actors / Nation states	Political, financial	Narrow target, long-term cyber campaign with strategic focus, targets with advanced security level, stealthy, professionals	In-house developed or tailored TTPs	National security impact, Disruption to CI, Loss of intellectual property, Monetary loss
Hacktivist / Cyber terrorists / Insiders	Ideological, political	Wide range of targets with advanced to poor security level, middle-term cyber attacks, more stealthy, professionals to skilled persons	COTS Products, special tools (expensive) and available tools	Disruption of business activities, Theft of intellectual property, Monetary loss, Trade secret disclosure, Operational disruption, Brand and reputation loss
Cyber criminals	Financial			
Script Kiddies / Crackers	Curiosity, challenging themselves, impressing others	Random targets, Opportunistic approach, targets with poor security level, short-term cyber attacks, less or not stealthy, beginners	Freely available or affordable tools	Annoying effects, such as website defacement or spamming, Disruption of operations, Increased latency

Figure 2.7 Threat actors.

The second group covers threat actors with advanced knowledge about security. According to their motivation they can be divided into two groups; threat actors with financial motivation belong to cyber criminals, and threat actors driven mainly by their ideology or political orientation belong to hacktivist, cyberterrorists, or individuals. As they have different but more concrete motivation than the first group, they have a narrower range of targets even with advanced security levels. Based on their solid knowledge, they have a better understanding of applicable malicious tools and have more resources for applying appropriate tools for achieving their aim while remaining undetected. They usually use advanced tools, even Commercial Off-the-Shelf (COTS) hacker tools or services, such as malware and malware toolkits, zero days, rented DDoS attacks, and so on. In contrast to the hit-and-run approach of the amateur hackers, they plan their steps in advance and work significantly more stealthily. Their activities can have a wide range of consequences, from short-term operational disruptions, through trade secret disclosure, to monetary loss or even disruption of business activities (see Figure 2.7).

At the top end are the highly capable and professional threat actors presumably with enhanced support. They can be motivated by their political orientation and through special monetary rewards. As these professionals work on behalf of special organizations or even nation-states, they carefully pick high-profile targets usually with advanced security levels. These attacks require in-depth reconnaissance and planning. The cyber attacks take a long time (months to years) because of the complexity and the unobtrusive way they are executed. Occasionally, threat actors need to create tools or exploits and tailor already existing tools for the unique tasks they receive from the contracting entity. As these activities are time consuming and cost-intensive, their impacts are more dangerous. The consequences can be monetary loss, loss of intellectual property, or operative disruption of critical infrastructures and can escalate to a considerable national security impact.

2.6 Conclusion

Today's cyber defense approaches and security solutions need to evolve as threat actors and attack scenarios change. Already existing cyber defense strategies usually have a defensive attitude, instead of a preventive and cooperative attitude. The presentation of the cyber kill chain and the comparison of past cyber attacks highlighted the current challenges in cyberspace. The attacks are becoming increasingly complex and sophisticated. On the one hand, this situation calls for new techniques and approaches in order to respond to the evolving threats and TTPs of the threat actors. And on the other hand, the situation requires a national and international cooperation for protecting a nation-state's essential infrastructures and its citizens. Research, industry, and international security communities are already working on a wide variety of possible solutions, which account for technical, organizational, and legal perspectives. The European Union, as well as the United States, demonstrates growing interest to enable information sharing (cf. Chapters 4 and 5), set up cybersecurity centers to establish effective cyber situational awareness and support fast decision-making (cf. Chapter 6), and elaborate on the legal background (cf. Chapters 7 and 8). These are the first steps on a long way to a secured cyberspace. The following chapters present the need for information sharing and new methods, techniques, and solutions in order to enhance cyber defense capabilities at both national and international levels and the protection of critical infrastructures within cyberspace.

List of Abbreviations

AD	Active Directory
APT	Advanced persistent threat
BYOD	Bring your own device
CERT	Computer Emergency Response Team
C&C or C2	Command and control
CMF	Cyber Mission Force
COTS	Commercial off-the-shelf
DDoS	Distributed denial of service
DDoSaaS	DDoS-as-a-Service
DLL	Dynamic link library
DNS	Domain Name System
DSOs	Distribution systems operators
Dyn	Dynamic Network Services
GOP	The Guardians of Peace
ICS	Industrial control system
ICT	Information and communication technology
IoT	Internet of Things

IS	Information security
LAN	Local area network
OSINT	Open source intelligence
PtH	Pass-the-Hash
PtT	Pass-the-Ticket
P2P	Peer-to-peer
PLC	Programmable logic controller
RPC	Remote procedure call
RTU	Remote terminal unit
SCADA	Supervisory control and data acquisition
TOR	The Onion Router
TTPs	Tactics, techniques, and procedures
USCYBERCOM	U.S. Cyber Command (USCYBERCOM)

References

Abdollah, T. 2015. Sony Pictures CEO had "no playbook" for mega-hack on studio, https://finance.yahoo.com/news/sony-pictures-ceo-had-no-063849901.html, last accessed on 12-12-2016.

Adachi, D. and Omote, K. 2016. A host-based detection method of remote access Trojan in the early stage. In International Conference on Information Security Practice and Experience (pp. 110–121). Springer International Publishing.

Barber, R. 2001. Hackers profiled: Who are they and what are their motivations? *Computer Fraud & Security*, 2001(2), 14–17.

Bergman, M. K. 2001. White paper: The deep web: Surfacing hidden value. *Journal of Electronic Publishing*, 7(1).

Broad, W., Markoff, J., and Sanger, D. 2011. Israeli test on worm called crucial in iran nuclear delay, *New York Times*. http://www.nytimes.com/2011/01/16/world/middleeast/16stuxnet.html, last accessed on 15-01-2011.

Bronk, C. and Tikk-Ringas, E. 2013. The cyber attack on Saudi Aramco. *Survival*, 55(2), 81–96.

Chen, P., Desmet, L., and Huygens, C. 2014. A study on advanced persistent threats. In *International Conference on Communications and Multimedia Security* (pp. 63–72). Springer, Heidelberg, Berlin.

Chicone, R. 2015. A layman's guide to cyber threats, threat actors, attacks, and intelligence, http://alliance.kaplan.edu/uploadedFiles/_Global_Content/Generic/Promotional contents/Laymans%20Guide%20to%20Cyber%20Threats%20Article.pdf, last accessed on 02-02-2017.

Chiu, D., Weng, S., and Chiu, J. 2014. Trend Micro research paper, backdoor use in targeted attacks, http://www.trendmicro.com/cloud-content/us/pdfs/security-intelligence/white-papers/wp-backdoor-use-in-targeted-attacks.pdf, last accessed on 23-07-2016.

Ciancaglini, V., Balduzzi, M., McArdle, R., and Rösler, M. 2016. Below the surface: Exploring the deep web. Trend Micro Incorporated.

Cluley, G. 2016. These 60 dumb passwords can hijack over 500,000 IoT devices into the Mirai botnet. N.p., 10 Oct. 2016. https://www.grahamcluley.com/mirai-botnet-password/, last accessed on 31-07-2017.

Collier, S. and Lakoff, A. 2008. The vulnerability of vital systems: how "critical infrastructure" became a security problem. *The Politics of Securing the Homeland: Critical Infrastructure, Risk and Securitisation*, 40–62. http://www.anthropos-lab.net/wp/publications/2008/01/collier-and-lakoff.pdf, last accessed on 31-07-2017.

Common Vulnerabilities and Exposures (CVE). 2010. CVE-2010-2772, http://cve.mitre.org/cgi-bin/cvename.cgi?name=cve-2010-2772, last accessed on 22-06-2016.

Cowley, R. and Parker, G. 1996. *The Reader's Companion to Military History*. Boston: Houghton Mifflin Harcourt (HMH).

Cyber Security Blog. 2013. Sony hack: Too easy and predicted by "The Paramount Brief" 5 years ago. http://www.cyber-security-blog.com/2014/12/sony-hack-act-of-cyber-vandalism-is-the-whole-world-sitting-on-a-ticking-bomb.html, last accessed on 23-08-2016.

Damballa. 2016. Advanced persistent threats: A brief description, https://www.damballa.com/paper/advanced-persistent-threats-a-brief-description/, last accessed on 22-07-2016.

Dobbins, R. and Bjarnason, S. 2016. Mirai IoT botnet description and DDoS attack mitigation, https://www.arbornetworks.com/blog/asert/mirai-iot-botnet-description-ddos-attack-mitigation/, last accessed on 02-02-2016.

Ducklin, P. 2016. Mirai "Internet of things" malware from Krebs DDoS attack goes open source, https://nakedsecurity.sophos.com/2016/10/05/mirai-internet-of-things-malware-from-krebs-ddos-attack-goes-open-source/, last accessed on 02-02-2017.

Dull, T. SAS. 2015. Big data and the Internet of things: Two sides of the same coin? http://www.sas.com/en_ph/insights/articles/big-data/big-data-and-iot-two-sides-of-the-same-coin.html, last accessed on 17-11-2016.

Engel, G. 2014. Deconstructing the cyber kill chain, DarkReading, http://www.darkreading.com/attacks-breaches/deconstructing-the-cyber-kill-chain/a/d-id/1317542, last accessed on 23-07-2016.

Everett, C.. 2016. Ransomware: to pay or not to pay? *Computer Fraud & Security*, 2016(4) 8–12.

Fagerland, S. and Norman, A. S. A. 2012. The many faces of Gh0st Rat, http://ver007.com/tools/APTnotes/2012/Faces_Ghost_RAT.pdf, last accessed on 11-12-2016.

Falliere, N. 2010. Symantec official blog, exploring Stuxnet's PLC infection process, https://www.symantec.com/connect/blogs/exploring-stuxnet-s-plc-infection-process,last accessed on 22-07-2016.

Falliere, N., Murchu, L. O., and Chien, E. 2011. W32. Stuxnet dossier. White paper, Symantec Corp., Security Response, 5, 6.

Farwell, J. P. and Rohozinski, R. 2011. Stuxnet and the future of cyber war. *Survival*, 53(1), 23–40.

Fildes, J. 2010. Stuxnet worm 'targeted high-value Iranian assets'. *BBC News*. http://www.bbc.com/news/technology-11388018, last accessed on 23-09-2010.

FireEye. 2013, FireEye advanced threat report 2013, http://www2.fireeye.com/rs/fireeye/images/fireeye-advanced-threat-report-2013.pdf, last accessed on 01-05-2016.

FireEye. 2016. M-Trends 2016, https://www.fireeye.com/current-threats/annual-threat-report.html, last accessed on 04-01-2017.

Franceschi-Bicchierai, L. and Warren, C. 2014. Hackers sent extortion email to Sony executives 3 days before attack. http://mashable.com/2014/12/08/hackers-emailed-sony-execs/#fRptVBHYMPqC, last accessed on 25-08-2016.

F-Secure. 2009. Tracking GhostNet: Investigating a cyber espionage network, https://www.f-secure.com/weblog/archives/ghostnet.pdf, last accessed on 29-01-2017.

Gandhi, R., Sharma, A., Mahoney, W., Sousan, W., Zhu, Q., and Laplante, P. 2011. Dimensions of cyber-attacks: Cultural, social, economic, and political. *IEEE Technology and Society Magazine*, 30(1), 28–38.

Geers, K., Kindlund, D., Moran, N., and Rachwald, R. 2016. FireEye report, world war C: Understanding nation-state motives behind today's advanced cyber attacks, https://www.fireeye.com/content/dam/fireeye-www/global/en/current-threats/pdfs/fireeye-wwc-report.pdf, last accessed on 23-06-2016.

Geers, K. 2015. Coder, hacker, soldier, spy. In *Cyber Security: Analytics, Technology and Automation*, Martti Lehto, Pekka Neittaanmäki (eds.) (pp. 73–87). Springer International Publishing. https://www.springerprofessional.de/cyber-security-analytics-technology-and-automation/2436834.

Gen. Larry D. Welch. 2011. Institute of Defense Analyses, Cyberspace: The fifth operational domain, https://www.ida.org/~/media/Corporate/Files/Publications/ResearchNotes/RN2011/2011%20Cyberspace%20-%20The%20Fifth%20Operational%20Domain.pdf, last accessed on 24-07-2016.

Gordon, R. Clarke, D. R., and Edwin, W. 2004. *Practical Modern SCADA Protocols: DNP3, 60870.5 and Related Systems*. Newnes, 19–21.

Greene, T. 2015. Biggest data breaches of 2015. *Network*, 10, 14.

Hanford, E. 2014. The cold war of cyber espionage. *Public Interest Law Reporter*, 20, 22.

Higgins, K. J. 2017. DarkReading, latest Ukraine blackout tied to 2015 cyberattackers, http://www.darkreading.com/threat-intelligence/latest-ukraine-blackout-tied-to-2015-cyberattackers/d/d-id/1327863? last accessed on 02-02-2017.

Hilton, S. 2016. Dyn analysis summary of Friday October 21 attack, http://dyn.com/blog/dyn-analysis-summary-of-friday-october-21-attack/, last accessed on 05-02-2017.

Hollis, D. 2015. Cyberwar case study: Georgia 2008. *Small Wars Journals*. http://smallwarsjournal.com/jrnl/art/cyberwar-case-study-georgia-2008, last accessed on 31-07-2017.

Hollywood Presbyterian Medical Center. 2016. Official release, http://hollywoodpresbyterian.com/default/assets/File/20160217%20Memo%20from%20the%20CEO%20v2.pdf, last accessed on 12-01-2017.

Hunton, P. 2009. The growing phenomenon of crime and the Internet: A cybercrime execution and analysis model. *Computer Law & Security Review*, 25(6), 528–535.

Interpol. 2016. Cybercrime, https://www.interpol.int/Crime-areas/Cybercrime/Cybercrime, last accessed on 12-12-2016.

ISACA. 2014. APT survey report, http://www.isaca.org/Knowledge-Center/Research/Documents/APT-Survey-Report-2014_whp_Eng_0614.pdf?regnum=277325, last accessed on 20-06-2016.

Kienzle, D. M. and Elder, M. C. 2013. Recent worms: A survey and trends. In Proceedings of the 2003 ACM Workshop on Rapid Malcode (pp. 1–10). Washington, DC, Oct. 27–30, 2003.

Kim, D., Vouk, M. A. 2015. Securing scientific workflows. In: Software Quality, Reliability and Security-Companion (QRS-C), 2015 IEEE International Conference on. IEEE, 2015. S. 95–104.

Kraus, J. 2014. Iranian Revolutionary Guard Corps and their influence on the Iranian government, military and economy. The International Annual Scientific Session Strategies XXI, 1, 171.

Kriaa, S., Bouissou, M., and Piètre-Cambacédès, L. 2012. Modeling the Stuxnet attack with BDMP: Towards more formal risk assessments. 2012 7th International Conference on Risks and Security of Internet and Systems (CRiSIS). IEEE.

Kriaa, S., Pietre-Cambacedes, L., Bouissou, M., & Halgand, Y. 2015. A survey of approaches combining safety and security for industrial control systems. *Reliability Engineering & System Safety*, 139, 156–178.

Kumar, A., Zero day exploit. 2014. https://papers.ssrn.com/sol3/papers.cfm?abstract_id=2378317, last accessed on 31-07-2017.

Kurtz, A., Gascon, H., Becker, T., Rieck, K., and Freiling, F. 2016. Fingerprinting mobile devices using personalized configurations. *Proceedings on Privacy Enhancing Technologies*, 2016(1), 4–19.

Lesk, M. 2007. The new front line: Estonia under cyberassault. *IEEE Security & Privacy*, 5(4), 76–79.

Lewis, J. A. 2005. Computer espionage, titan rain and China. Center for Strategic and International Studies-Technology and Public Policy Program, 1.

Li, C., Jiang, W., and Zou, X. 2009. Botnet: Survey and case study. *Innovative Computing, Information and Control (ICICIC), 2009 Fourth International Conference on* (pp. 1184–1187). IEEE.

Lockheed, M. 2014. Cyber kill chain, http://cyber. lockheedmar-tin.com/hubfs/Gaining_the_Advantage_Cyber_Kill_Chain.pdf, last accessed on 01-01-2017.

Lynn, W. J. 2010. Defending a new domain: The Pentagon's cyberstrategy. *Foreign Affairs* 89.5 (2010): 97–108.

Matrosov A., Rodionov E., Harley D., and Malcho J. 2011. Stuxnet under the microscope, ESET. Technical Report. Revision 1.31.

Mansfield-Devine, S. 2016a. DDoS goes mainstream: How headline-grabbing attacks could make this threat an organisation's biggest nightmare. *Network Security*, 2016(11), 7–13.

Mansfield-Devine, S. 2016b. Ransomware: Taking businesses hostage. *Network Security*, 2016(10), 8–17.

Mather, D., Security Zap. 2016. Researchers discovered a government-made malware on the deep web, http://securityzap.com/researchers-discovered-government-made-malware-deep-web/, last accessed on 24-07-2016.

Microsoft Corporation. Security Bulletin MS08-067. 2008. Microsoft Security Bulletin MS08-067. https://technet.microsoft.com/en-us/library/security/ms08-067.aspx, last accessed on 24-06-2016.

Microsoft Corporation. Security Bulletin MS10-061. 2010. Microsoft Security Bulletin MS10-061. 2010. https://technet.microsoft.com/library/security/ms10-061, last accessed on 23-06-2016.

NATO Cooperative Cyber Defence Centre of Excellence (NATO CCDCOE). 2017. Cyber definitions. https://ccdcoe.org/cyber-definitions.html, last accessed on 06-01-2017.

NIST, S. 800-39. 2011. Managing Information Security Risk–Organization, Mission, and Information System View. National Institute of Standards and Technology. Retrieved from http://csrc. nist. gov/publications/nistpubs/800-39/SP800-39-final. pdf., last accessed on 31-07-2017.

Novetta. 2016. Operation blockbuster: Unraveling the long thread of Sony attack, https://www.operationblockbuster.com/wp-content/uploads/2016/02/Operation-Blockbuster-Report.pdf, last accessed on 02-02-2017.

Oltisk, J. 2009. Russian cyber attack on Georgia: Lessons learned? http://www.csoonline. com/article/2236816/cisco-subnet/russian-cyber-attack-on-georgia---lessons-learned-. html, last accessed on 31-07-2017.

Pathak, P. B. and Nanded, Y. M. 2016. A dangerous trend of cybercrime: Ransomware growing challenge. *International Journal of Advanced Research in Computer Engineering & Technology (IJARCET)*, 5(2): 371–372.

Pernet, C. 2014a. Blog airbus cyber security, APT kill chain-Part 4: Initial compromise, http://blog.airbuscybersecurity.com/post/2014/06/APT-Kill-chain-Part-4-%3A-Initial-compromise, last accessed on 12-12-2016.

Pernet, C. 2014b. Blog airbus cyber security, APT kill chain-Part 3: Reconnaissance, http://blog.airbuscybersecurity.com/post/2014/05/APT-Kill-chain-Part-3-%3A-Reconnaissance, last accessed on 12-12-2016.

Pierluigi, P. 2016. NewWorldHackers & Anonymous behind massive DDoS attack on Dyn DNS service, http://securityaffairs.co/wordpress/52583/hacking/dyn-dns-service-ddos-3.html, last accessed on 03-02-2017.

Pierluigi, P. 2014. TrendMicro analyzed the wiper malware that infected Sony Pictures, http://securityaffairs.co/wordpress/30791/cyber-crime/trendmicro-analyzed-wiper-malware-infected-sony-pictures.html, last accessed on 22-06-2016.

Quaglia, F. 2016. Information and communication technology (ICT) and cyber threats: The main fields of analysis (Bachelor's thesis, Università Ca'Foscari Venezia), http://dspace.unive.it/bitstream/handle/10579/7945/831898-1192075.pdf?sequence=2, last accessed on 02-02-2017.

Radware. 2016. DDoS attacks via DDoS as a service tools, https://security.radware.com/ddos-threats-attacks/threat-advisories-attack-reports/ddos-as-a-service/, last accessed on 20-07-2016.

Recorded Future. 2016. Proactive defense: Understanding the 4 main threat actor types, https://www.recordedfuture.com/threat-actor-types/, last accessed on 12-01-2017.

Ring, T. 2015. Connected cars: The next target for hackers. *Network Security*, 2015(11), 11–16.

Royal United Services Institute for Defence and Security Studies (RUSI). 2016. Cyber threats and nuclear weapons, new questions for command and control, security and strategy, RUSI Occasional Paper. https://rusi.org/sites/default/files/cyber_threats_and_nuclear_combined.1.pdf, last accessed on 14-11-2016.

Ryan, J. 2011. *Leading Issues in Information Warfare and Security Research*, Volume 1, Reading, UK: Academic Publishing International.

SANS Institute. 2015. Case study: Critical controls that Sony should have implemented, https://www.sans.org/reading-room/whitepapers/casestudies/case-study-critical-controls-sony-implemented-36022, last accessed on 02-11-2016.

SANS-ICS. 2016. Analysis of the cyber attack on the Ukrainian power grid, https://ics.sans.org/media/E-ISAC_SANS_Ukraine_DUC_5.pdf, last accessed on 25-04-2016.

Schellekens, M. 2016. Car hacking: Navigating the regulatory landscape. *Computer Law & Security Review*, 32(2), 307–315.

Shamir, U. 2016. SentinelOne. Analyzing a new variant of BlackEnergy 3, https://www.sentinelone.com/wp-content/uploads/2016/01/BlackEnergy3_WP_012716_1c.pdf, last accessed on 03-01-2017.

Shancang, L. I., Romdhani, I., and Buchanan, W. 2016. Password pattern and vulnerability analysis for web and mobile applications. *ZTE Communications*, 32, 1.

Summers, D. J. (2014). Fighting in the cyber trenches. FORTUNE, http://fortune.com/2014/10/13/cold-war-on-business-cyber-warfare/, last accessed on 31-07-2017

Surfwatch. 2017. Cyber threat intelligence, section is mainly based on https://www.surfwatchlabs.com/threat-categories, last accessed on 12-12-2016.

Swiss GovCERT. 2013. Pass-the-hash-attacks, https://www.melani.admin.ch/melani/de/home/dokumentation/berichte/fachberichte/pass-the-hash-angriffe.html, last accessed on 02-02-2017.

Swiss GovCERT. 2016. Technical report about the malware used in the cyberespionage against RUAG. https://www.melani.admin.ch/melani/de/home/dokumentation/newsletter/technical_report_apt_case_ruag.html, last accessed on 28-01-2017.

Symantec. 2014. Dragonfly: Cyberespionage attacks against energy suppliers, https://www.symantec.com/content/en/us/enterprise/media/security_response/whitepapers/Dragonfly_Threat_Against_Western_Energy_Suppliers.pdf, last accessed on 30-01-2017.

Symantec. 2016. The Waterbug attack group. Security Response. Version 1.02 – January 14, 2016. https://www.symantec.com/content/en/us/enterprise/media/security_response/whitepapers/waterbug-attack-group.pdf, last accessed on 31-07-2017.

Tankard, C. 2011. Advanced persistent threats and how to monitor and deter them. *Network Security*, 2011(8), 16–19.

The Guardian. 2016. DDoS attack that disrupted internet was largest of its kind in history, experts say, https://www.theguardian.com/technology/2016/oct/26/ddos-attack-dyn-mirai-botnet, last accessed on 03-02-2017.

Trend Micro. 2014a. BKDR_WIPALL.A, https://www.trendmicro.com/vinfo/us/threat-encyclopedia/malware/bkdr_wipall.a, last accessed on 23-07-2016.

Trend Micro. 2014b. BKDR_WIPALL.B, https://www.trendmicro.com/vinfo/us/threat-encyclopedia/malware/BKDR_WIPALL.B, last accessed on 23-06-2016.

Trend Micro. 2016. Ransomware-as-a-service: Ransomware operators find ways to bring in business, http://www.trendmicro.com/vinfo/us/security/news/cybercrime-and-digital-threats/ransomware-as-a-service-ransomware-operators-find-ways-to-bring-in-business, last accessed on 24-11-2016.

U.S. Department of Defense. 2016. All cyber mission force teams achieve initial operating capability, https://www.defense.gov/News/Article/Article/984663/all-cyber-mission-force-teams-achieve-initial-operating-capability, last accessed on 12-12-2016.

U.S. Department of Defense. The Department of Defense cyber strategy. 2015. The DoD Cyber Strategy. https://www.defense.gov/Portals/1/features/2015/0415_cyber-straegy/Final_2015_DoD_CYBER_STRATEGY_for_web.pdf, last accessed on 12-12-2016.

U.S. Department of Homeland Security (DHS) US-CERT. 2016. Heightened DDoS threat posed by Mirai and other botnets, https://www.us-cert.gov/ncas/alerts/TA16-288A, last accessed on 02-02-2017.

U.S. Department of Homeland Security (DHS), ICS-CERT. 2016. Cyber-attack against Ukrainian critical infrastructure, https://ics-cert.us-cert.gov/alerts/IR-ALERT-H-16-056-01, last accessed on 15-12-2016.

Uma, M. and Padmavathi, G. 2013. A survey on various cyber attacks and their classification. *International Journal of Network Security*, 15(5), 390–396.

UN Security Council. Resolution 1696. 2006. Non-proliferation, http://www.refworld.org/docid/453786b00.html, last accessed on 15-01-2017.

Verisign. 2016. Verisign distributed denial of service trends report, https://www.verisign.com/assets/report-ddos-trends-Q12016.pdf, last accessed on 24-11-2016.

Von Solms, B. 2006. Information security: The fourth wave. *Computers & Security*, 25(3), 165–168.

Von Solms, R. and Van Niekerk, J. 2013. From information security to cyber security. *Computers & Security*, 38, 97–102.

Websense Security Labs. 2015. Threat report, http://www.dataconnectors.com/wp-content/uploads/2016/02/WebSense-Toronto-2015.pdf, last accessed on 22-06-2016.

Windrem, R., Producer, S. I., & Borg, S. (2013). Expert: US in cyberwar arms race with China, Russia. NBC News.

Yar, M.. 2013. *Cybercrime and Society*. Natalie Aguilera (ed.), SAGE Publications Ltd. ISBN 978-1-44620-193-0.

Zetter, K. Wired. 2015. We're at cyberwar: A global guide to nation-state digital attacks, https://www.wired.com/2015/09/cyberwar-global-guide-nation-state-digital-attacks/, last accessed on 10-11-2016.

Zorz, Z. 2016. Mirai Linux Trojan corrals IoT devices into DDoS botnets, https://www.helpnetsecurity.com/2016/09/07/mirai-linux-trojan-iot-ddos-botnets/, last accessed on 02-02-2017.

Chapter 3

From Monitoring, Logging, and Network Analysis to Threat Intelligence Extraction

Ivo Friedberg
Austrian Institute of Technology and Queen's University Belfast

Markus Wurzenberger
Austrian Institute of Technology

Abdullah Al Balushi and Boojoong Kang
Queen's University Belfast

Contents

3.1 Introduction

The importance and high connectivity of today's information and communication technologies motivate a more coordinated approach to cybersecurity than is common today. Sharing threat intelligence among companies (Section 3.5) and states (Section 3.4) is one approach that we argue is critical to achieving a coordinated push for cybersecurity.

To encourage participation and improve acceptance, it is critical that proposed solutions take existing security installations at the organization and the state level into account. Moreover, the existing solutions need to be integrated in information sharing solutions. This integration can happen in two ways. First, the feasibility of data monitored and generated at a local level already needs to be carefully considered to produce shareable threat intelligence, since it is unreasonable to expect that all existing monitoring solutions and processes will be changed to support cross-organizational information sharing. Second, the shared information needs to be supportive to existing organizational processes. This includes the automatic use of shared information in technical solutions like the automatic import of threat intelligence into intrusion detection systems and security incident and event management (SIEM) installations. It further means that operational security and incident response processes need to be extended.

In this chapter, we therefore focus on the following aspects:

■ Concepts of cybersecurity information sharing: We introduce a common nomenclature with respect to the types of information that are valuable candidates to be shared and introduce processes necessary to leveraging the benefits of information sharing.
■ Overview of common data sources: We provide an overview of the data sources that are usually monitored in ICT systems—from low-level network layers to the application layer. We highlight the monitoring infrastructures needed, the benefits, and limitations of each data type and its common use for incident detection.
■ Overview of high-level analysis techniques: We introduce and evaluate methods that are used to combine information from multiple data sources to identify more complex and sophisticated attacks. For each method, we highlight the respective possibilities to integrate with information sharing methodologies.

Figure 3.1 shows a general network diagram of an arbitrary organization that is loosely correlated to the scenarios in Chapter 2. It will be used throughout this chapter to highlight the implementation details of the concepts that are described. It is composed of four zones. The *public domain* hosts services that need to allow direct connections from the Internet. Examples are Web servers or mail servers that need to be accessible. The second zone is the *business network*. Nodes in the business network are able to connect to the public Internet. Direct connections from the Internet into the business network however are only possible through a virtual private network (VPN) tunnel. Connections between the business network and the public domain can be made to access more critical services or data needed to provide a service in the public domain but is located in the business network. The business network connects classical workstation machines and auxiliary services like servers for file storage and identity management. It is

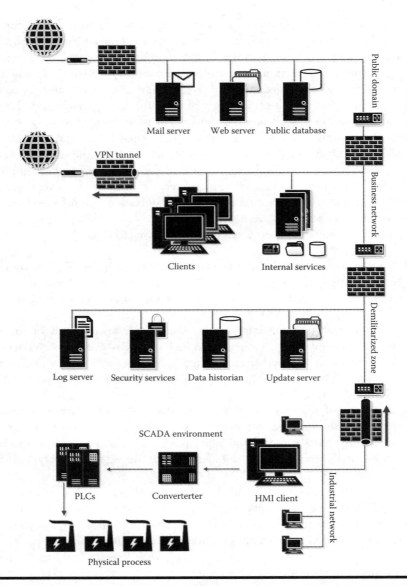

Public domain

Business network

Demilitarized zone

Industrial network

VPN tunnel

Mail server   Web server   Public database

Clients   Internal services

Log server   Security services   Data historian   Update server

SCADA environment

PLCs   Converterter   HMI client

Physical process

Figure 3.1   General network diagram of a corporate IT infrastructure with industrial control system components (loosely based on the examples in Chapter 2). The network has four zones (public domain, business network, demilitarized zone, and industrial network), which are segregated by different subnets and firewalls. When indicated by an arrow the firewall only allows connections being established in the direction of the arrow, unless a VPN tunnel is used. In the Industrial network, the wiring is not specified but does not necessarily have to be based in IP traffic.

further connected to the *demilitarized zone* (DMZ). The DMZ is a separate network segment that hosts services that manage critical data, host security services, or auxiliary services for the *industrial network* (e.g., Data Historian or Update Server). The industrial network is again isolated from the rest of the system. Human–machine interfaces (HMIs) are used to manage the industrial processes over supervisory control and data acquisition (SCADA) environments. They connect to programmable logic controllers (PLCs) that in turn control the physical processes. For management a VPN tunnel can be used to access the industrial network from the DMZ, but in general communication is only outgoing (e.g., to store sensor measurements in the Data Historian). The communication within the industrial network is not necessarily IP based; it can also make use of analog signals or bus systems.

The remainder of this chapter is structured as follows: Section 3.2 provides an introduction into the concepts of information sharing. It further highlights the need for corporate processes like asset management to leverage the benefits of information sharing effectively. Section 3.3 introduces different sources of information that are currently used to identify cybersecurity incidents on a system or corporate level. It highlights their benefits and shortcomings and describes the common setup of monitoring infrastructures. Section 3.4 provides details about analysis methods that combine information from multiple sources in different ways to derive higher-level alerts. These concepts include signature-based approaches, anomaly detection, stateful analysis, and ontologies. For each approach, the section discusses benefits and shortcomings and highlights the possible interfaces to information sharing. Section 3.5 concludes the chapter.

3.2 An Overview of Concepts in Cyber Threat Intelligence[1,2]

In order to understand the effective use of data generated and used on an organizational level for security analysis in the context of cyber threat intelligence, a shared terminology needs to be defined for different aspects of shareable information. Further, there is one particular important concept—namely, asset management—that is a basic requirement to make use of threat intelligence information. Terminology will be defined in Section 3.2.1, followed by an introduction to asset management in Section 3.2.2. Examples will be used to make the concepts more descriptive. These examples will be based on the cyber attack scenarios that were described in Chapter 2.

---

[1] http://stixproject.github.io/data-model/.
[2] http://www.openioc.org/.

3.2.1 Artifacts in Cyber Threat Intelligence

Observables: Observables are the lowest level of information used in threat intelligence. The term describes all *measurable events or stateful properties*[3] that can be detected in the cyber domain. An example of event-based observables is a change made to a file or a rule in an intrusion detection system (IDS) that is fired. On the contrary, stateful properties include the value of a registry key or system variable or the hash value of a file on the system. As such, the classification of an event or property as observable does not allow any conclusion about its nature (i.e., if the property is malicious or benign). The set of observables in a given system is merely the set system aspects that can be measured or detected. This is the main difference between observables and indicators.

Indicator: An indicator is an observable that suggests that

- A cyber attack is imminent.
- A cyber attack is currently present in the system.
- The system has been compromised at a previous point in time.

Thus, an indicator relates the states or events described by observables to malicious behavior. The examples for observables above can also be examples for indicators. The hash value of a file is an indicator if the file it belongs to is a known piece of malware. Similarly, a fired IDS rule is most likely an indicator for unwanted or malicious system behavior. Further, simple indicators might be logically combined to form more complex rules about a specific compromise[4] (Novetta, 2016).

EXAMPLE OF MALWARE INDICATORS

One piece of malware that was supposedly used in both the attack on the Ukraine power grid and the sony hack was a Server Message Block (SMB) worm that was classified by the US-CERT as Targeted Destructive Malware under Alert TA14-353A. With the alert, a list of indicators was published. These included file hashes of detected instances of different components of the malware, IP addresses commonly used for the command and control (C2) capabilities as well as rules for the Snort intrusion detection system that can detect network traffic that is characteristic for this worm. Some examples of this information can be found as follows:

---

[3] http://cybox.mitre.org/documents/Cyber%20Observable%20eXpression%20(CybOX)%20 Use%20Cases%20-%20(ITSAC%202011)%20-%20Sean%20Barnum.pdf.

[4] https://www.us-cert.gov/ncas/alerts/TA14-353A (accessed 16 February, 2017).

SMB WORM TOOL

Import hash: f6f48551d7723d87daeef2e840ae008f
Characterization: File Hash Watchlist
Notes: "SMB worm tool"
    Earliest PE compile Time: 20141001T072107Z
    Most Recent PE compile Time: 20141001T072107Z
An example of one common C2 IP addresses:

IP Address	Country	Port	Filename
203.131.222.102	Thailand	8080	Diskpartmg16.exe igfxtrayex.exe igfxtpers.exe

SNORT RULE

alert tcp any any -> any any (msg: "Wiper 1"; sid:42000001; rev:1; flow:established; content: "|be 64 ba f2 a8 64|"; depth:6; offset:16; classtype:bad-unknown;)

A whitepaper by the security company Crowdstrike[5] suggests two classes of indicators. While the classical Indicators of Compromise (IoC) are said to indicate attacks only after they occurr, Indicators of Attack (IoA) allow a more proactive approach, detecting attacks before they happen or while they are happening by looking at system behavior. This book will not differentiate between the two types, but examples of both will be given throughout this chapter under the term IoC. However, the discussion highlights that indicators, such as file hashes, destination IP addresses of Command and Control infrastructure communication, or URLs, that host malicious files can be easily changed by the attacker. It is therefore important to note that a database of indicators is never going to be sufficiently extensive to guarantee detection. The work necessary to keep indicator databases up to date is hard—if not impossible—to achieve by a single entity. Dividing this task among all participants of a community and sharing the relevant results is one of the goals behind threat intelligence sharing.

Threat actors and tactics, techniques, and procedures (TTPs): Sophisticated cyber attacks can usually not be described by a single IoC or a single vulnerability. Instead, only the successful execution of multiple steps results in a successful

---

[5] https://www.crowdstrike.com/blog/indicators-attack-vs-indicators-compromise.

attack. At each stage of the attack, different techniques can be used by the adversary to achieve a certain goal. For example, the initial infiltration of an IT system can be caused by a phishing e-mail, a drive-by download, an unchecked USB drive plugged into a machine in the network or through social engineering, just to name a view options. TTPs describe common behavioral patterns of adversaries. Threat actors tend to use similar attack patterns and pieces of malware in their attacks. They leverage resources including service providers (cloud infrastructure, registrars, etc.) and have certain targets and goals. TTPs structure this information to describe adversary behavior that can be used for attribution[6] (Wheeler and Larsen, 2003).

Incident: An incident describes the events that took place during a cybersecurity incident as well as the effects the incident had on the observed systems. On a technical level, it contains the vulnerabilities that were exploited, indicators that were found in the systems, and the TTPs used by the attacker. It further describes the impact of the attack on the systems and the organization as a whole: what was the impact on operations, was sensitive data exfiltrated, and what was the timeline of the attack? This information is necessary for internal reporting but can also be used to achieve awareness on a national level when shared with governmental organizations or as a guideline for other potential targets to identify the attack.

Course of action: When information about new types of malware, vulnerabilities, or attack campaigns is circulated, it usually also contains a set of recommendations or guidelines on how to detect and mitigate the described threat. These recommendations can contain actions that should be taken in advance to prevent a successful compromise or in response to an attack in order to mitigate the effects. This approach is usually used in published CVEs or in security advisories issued by national CERTs. Simple examples of preventive measures are software updates to remove vulnerable application versions or updated configurations. However, more complex actions can be shared, which should then also include information about efficacy, expected impact, and expected cost. Effective use of this information requires efficient asset management processes be in place to identify the potentially vulnerable components in the managed network (see Section 3.2.2).

Threat intelligence reports: In contrast to most of the previous items described, a report is not structured for automated processing but is instead a prose document aimed at decision makers in organizations. A report can be technical with details about a new piece of malware and how it is used by a threat actor or more abstract to provide situational awareness to an organization about a new attack campaign. It can contain specific IoCs useful for detecting future instances of the described attack. Therefore, it is a critical tool for information sharing.

---

[6] shttps://www.tenable.com/blog/attribution-is-hard-part-1 (accessed February 13, 2017).

OPERATION BLOCKBUSTER: THREAT INTELLIGENCE REPORT

One example of a very detailed Threat Intelligence Report is the Operation Blockbuster report from Novetta on the sony attack (see Chapter 2). It was generated in response to the sony attack incident to reconstruct the happenings, identify the *threat actor*, its *TTPs,* and relevant *IoCs.* While the general report provides a timeline of the threat actor's attacks, the general classes of malware used, and their procedures, the report is also extended with auxiliary material including specific IoCs in STIX format, using YARA signatures and a list of known hash values of the different malware families used.

3.2.2 Asset Management

As cyber threat intelligence is shared in the form of indicators or threat intelligence reports, asset management is vital for an organization to filter information streams. Not all shared information is relevant to every organization or party. The detection of a new vulnerability in a software product is only relevant if the product is deployed in the vulnerable version within an organization. If that is the case, it is necessary to quickly identify all exposed instances and the dependent components to identify the feasibility of provided courses of action. IT asset management is a corporate process to maintain software and hardware components in a way that guarantees visibility and controllability of the assets. This book can only give short descriptions of the aspects of asset management most relevant in the context of cyber threat information sharing. Standards and guides that provide a more complete picture about asset management were published by ISO in the 19770 suite (ISO/IEC, 2012, 2015a, 2016) and by NIST (Michael et al., 2015). Further, the Information Technology Infrastructure Library (ITIL),[7] which underpins the ISO/IEC 20000 (ISO/IEC, 2011) standard on IT service management, formalizes processes and checklists to design and operate IT services in alignment with the core business needs. These processes also include Software Asset Management and Asset and Configuration Management. The Control Objectives for Information and Related Technologies framework (Van Grembergen and De Haes, 2009) were designed by ISACA to provide best practices in IT governance and management. They have a similar scope to the ISO/IEC 38500 (ISO/IEC, 2015b) on Corporate Governance for Information Technologies, which focuses on six principles for governance of information technologies: Responsibility, Strategy, Acquisition, Performance, Conformance, and Human behavior.

Figure 3.2 gives an overview of the lifecycle of an asset and the tasks that need to be covered by asset management. Note that there is a wide variety of assets

---

[7] https://www.axelos.com/best-practice-solutions/itil.

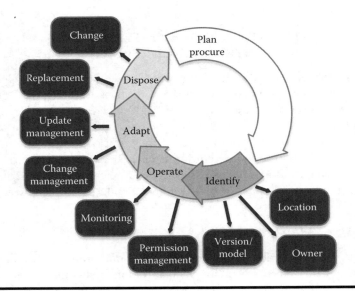

Figure 3.2 IT asset life cycle.

in IT systems. These can range from physical network equipment to services or software components. While each type of asset needs to be managed differently, the broad approach to asset management is generally applicable. This chapter will largely ignore the complexity of planning and procuring new assets. It should just be noted at this stage that the lifecycle of an asset starts long before it is actually deployed and does not end before the effects of its disposure are considered and mitigated in the remaining infrastructure of the organization. Instead, the chapter will focus on the four most critical parts of an asset's lifecycle with respect to cyber threat intelligence.

EXAMPLE: STUXNET

The Stuxnet attack (see Chapter 2) leveraged multiple zero-day exploits in the windows operating system to infect vulnerable machines during lateral movement. One of these exploits was the *Microsoft Windows Print Spooler Service Remote Code Execution Vulnerability* that allowed remote code execution during a vulnerable print spooler implementation in various versions of Windows including Windows XP SP3, Windows Vista SP2, and Windows Server 2008 SP2. Stuxnet was first spread in 2008, and the vulnerability was only published in 2010. It was a severe security risk, and proper asset management would have helped to minimize the attack surface for an organization.

3.2.2.1 Asset Identification

In the asset identification process, information about assets is collected and correlated. NIST issued report IR 7693 (John et al., 2011) that provides a formal specification of asset identification that the reader is referred to for more detailed information. Asset identification achieves the following goals:

1. Identification: Assets need to be correctly identified in different contexts of the organization. This is necessary to relate monitoring information with the correct asset. This is not to be confused with the asset identification step in the lifecycle, which describes the process of generating this data about each asset.
2. Responsibility: Each asset needs to have an owner responsible for the management and operation of the asset during its lifetime that can be held accountable for mismanagement.
3. Structured Access to Asset Information: Properties of each asset have to be stored and made accessible in a central database. This is necessary to quickly assess the vulnerability of the system to a newly received report or indicator.

To achieve these goals, the following information should be stored about each asset.

Identifiers: An asset appears in different organizational contexts with different identifiers. An office PC will have an inventory number to identify the physical PC, and it will be assigned a location (e.g., room number) to allow easy location. At the same time, it has an IP address in the company network. It will thus not be possible to correlate traffic that originates from the PC with the asset if the IP address of the PC is not stored as an additional identifier. In this way, sufficient identifiers need to be stored for each asset to allow efficient management.

Owner: Each asset needs to be owned by a real person in the organization. This is of high importance to ensure responsible operation and management of the asset. Further, only a real person can be held accountable in an incident that was caused by mismanagement of the asset in question.

Asset information: For each asset, a number of properties should be stored in a central asset database that can then be filtered. This is important to respond in a timely manner and appropriately to newly shared indicators. If a new exploit is found for a specific version of a software product, a list of machines running the product is not sufficient unless it also contains the currently installed version (and effective configuration) of each instance. Similarly, the vendor of a network router identified a problem with a number of components sold. A list of model numbers of all machines affected is publicly made available. A company, however, additionally requires an internal list of the model numbers of their deployed devices against which the affected model numbers in the public list can be compared. If such a company-specific list of model numbers does not exist, each hardware device has to be physically located and checked which again is not efficient.

EXAMPLE: STUXNET (*Continued*)

When the vulnerability was first published, a list of potentially vulnerable versions of Windows was also made available. In this case, there is no time to start and identify which workstation in an organization is running one of these vulnerable versions. Instead, a list should be ready, and the asset owners should be immediately contacted with information on the required steps to mitigate the vulnerability.

3.2.2.2 Asset Operation

Once the asset is properly identified, it has to be managed during operation. This includes two main aspects. One is the timely management of permissions. As project assignments or personnel changes, so should the permissions people have granted to assets. The owner of the asset is responsible for keeping the asset secure. The second aspect is monitoring. As indicators are shared, the behavior of each asset has to be continuously monitored for these indicators to guarantee timely detection of attack attempts and response to incidents. Information about monitoring and analyzing data will be provided in more detail in later sections of this chapter.

3.2.2.3 Asset Adaptation

During the lifetime of an asset, various changes to the environment force adaptations. The main causes for adaptations are as follows:

1. New information about the asset becomes available. For example, a CVE that describes a vulnerability in a software component should trigger mitigation strategies.
2. Updates are available for the asset. For each type of asset, there should be organization-wide update policies in place that regulate how updates must be handled. This also includes the management of new user accounts or changed configurations.
3. A related asset is changed. Each asset interacts with other assets. These interactions are usually well defined to ensure correct operation. Therefore, they need to be evaluated if one of the related assets is changed. For example, the installation of a software update in response to a newly found vulnerability might violate interoperability constraints.

To achieve secure asset operation, these adaptations need to be considered. At the same time, the changes need to be correctly documented in the asset database. Notice that the database is set up during the asset identification process in the beginning of the asset's operational phase. If it is not kept up to date, decisions on the risk level of the organization will be based upon outdated information.

> **EXAMPLE: STUXNET (*Continued*)**
>
> When the vulnerability exploited by Stuxnet was disclosed in July 2010, Microsoft had already issued a patch. In large organizations, security updates are often handled centrally so it is up to central update management to ensure that the updates are installed in a timely manner and on all vulnerable assets. It is however still necessary to keep track of additional assets that are not covered by the central update management (e.g., development machines). Since Stuxnet was targeting industrial control systems, this is of special interest because the necessary integration of general-purpose machines with legacy equipment often leads to policies that prevent updates from being installed without rigorous testing beforehand. In these cases, monitoring needs to get increased attention to detect a potential infection early and mitigate it manually.

3.2.2.4 Asset Disposal

Before the asset can be removed from the asset database (which concludes the life cycle) its disposal needs to be handled correctly. As mentioned earlier, assets depend on each other. Before an asset can be removed, it is therefore important to resolve all dependencies. Note that this will involve correct change management in the related assets. Due to the dependencies, assets are often not removed unconditionally but replaced. In this case, a new asset is introduced that in return needs to be properly identified. This process can be easier if relationships that were known for the old asset can be transferred and updated for the replacement rather than derived completely from scratch. At the same time, there is the risk of unmonitored assets that remain present, are removed from the asset management system only. This is often the case if it is not guaranteed that a replacement is able to support all dependencies. In this case, the old asset is operated parallel to the new replacement. At some point, the replacement takes over but the old asset is never properly disposed of. It is available but unmanaged, which leaves unmonitored vulnerabilities that can then be exploited by threat actors.

3.3 Raw Monitoring Data: Origin, Structure, and Insights

In order to detect indicators and attacks in systems, their state and behavior need to be monitored. During monitoring, different types of data elements are generated and then picked up by analysis tools to draw conclusions about the state of a monitored system. To understand how sharing of cyber threat intelligence can help to improve the overall security of information and communications technology (ICT) infrastructures, it is necessary to understand what data sources are available to the analysis techniques. This section introduces three sources of monitoring data: log data, network traffic, and information about files and processes. The information about each type of data is structured in the same way. After a short overview, the observables are described that can be described with the respective data. This is followed by a description of the necessary monitoring infrastructure. Finally, common evasion techniques (used by attackers to hide indicators from detection) are described. To understand the monitoring infrastructure, it is important to understand how it is installed in an operational network. Section 3.1 introduced a reference network (see Figure 3.1). Figure 3.3 highlights the locations of the different monitoring infrastructures within that network. For details about these infrastructures, please refer to the following sections.

3.3.1 Log Data

Log data contains automatically generated traces of all processes that run in ICT network environments and computer systems. Thus, it protocols all events occurring in such network infrastructures. Log data is usually represented in human-readable text format. This makes it easy to access the provided information. In opposed to other data sources, such as network packets, the information is available without any time, computational, or resource-intensive pre-processing. Therefore, log data is a valuable cybersecurity analysis tool (Babbin, 2006).

As visualized in Figure 3.3, logging takes place on various abstraction levels such as the data link layer (switch logs), the network and transport layer (firewall logs), to the application layer (web server logs, data base logs, mail server logs, etc.). One drawback of logging is that usually only lower log levels, i.e., warning and error logs, are used for security analysis. To carry out an extensive analysis, however, verbose logging-on information is required; in many cases, this is not performed. Reasons are that it is a resource-intensive task that produces large amounts of data (which might influence the performance of the target systems) that have to be stored somewhere. Furthermore, when log data is collected, organizations have to ensure protection of their employees' and customers' privacy. Log data contain sensitive information such as user names, names of machines, IP addresses, and machine fingerprints. Sometimes users' passwords are present in readable format, when users accidently enter them into the name field instead of the password field of a login dialogue.

3.3.1.1 Observables

A single log line usually consists of a time stamp and one protocolled event. The time stamp holds the information about when the logged event occurred. Depending on the configuration of the logging, it provides information about the day, the month, and the year, as well as the time the log line was produced. The event describes a

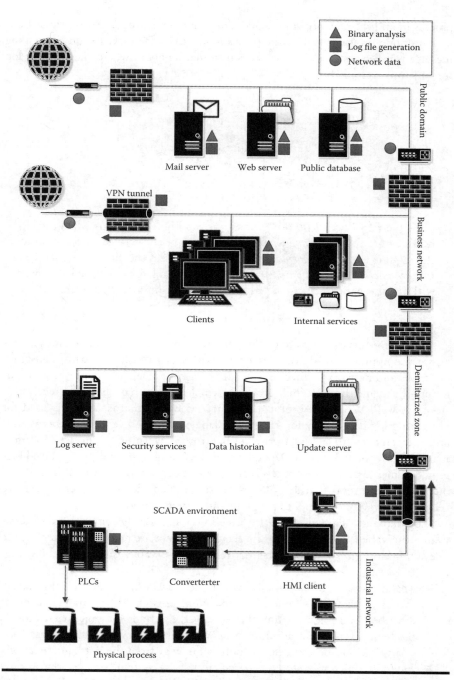

Figure 3.3 Reference network that highlights the locations of monitoring infrastructures for different observable types.

process in an ICT network, a network connection, or any other action carried out by a user or a program. While the time stamp carries the information when a log message was generated, the event stores information about where and why the log message was created.

EXAMPLE: LOG LINE

A typical log line looks as follows:

```
Jan 01 00:00:01 database.local mysql-normal Connect user@
database.host.local on
```

The timestamp *Jan 01 00:00:01* holds the month and the time when the log line was produced. *database.local* is the name of the service that produced the log line and *mysql-normal* specifies the type and the class of the service. *Connect user@database.host.local on* is the event that has been logged: The user with the username *user* connected to the database host *database.host.local*.

The protocoled events stored in log files include observables of malicious activities in a computer network. Besides user activities, observables of harmful program processes and network connections occur in log data. Depending on the configuration of the logging, information about which content has been sent/received is stored as well. When the protocol standard syslog (Gerhards, 2009) is used for generating log data, every log message is labeled with a severity level between 0 and 7: emergency (0), alert (1), critical (2), error (3), warning (4), notice (5), informational (6), and debug (7). Depending on the configuration of the deployed logging, log messages of different levels are stored. Log messages between level 0 and 3 contain only events that describe erratic system behavior and therefore security related observables that lead to program and system crashes.

Log messages of a higher severity level do not necessarily comprise security relevant observables. Therefore, tools for security analysis are required to filter out the relevant information describing security relevant observables, such as the following:

■ *Application-specific observables*, which holds security relevant information that is specific to a monitored application. This could be a malicious event described by a single log line of a ssh server, e.g., a log message that protocols the login of a system administrator with an unknown IP address assigned to a suspicious location, e.g., a country far away from the last login location.

■ *Environment-specific observables*, which describe system behavior that is only malicious for a specific ICT network environment. This could be a recorded communication flow between different hosts, such as access from a client machine to a Web server with a specific browser that is known to be used by malware.

■ *Collective observables*, which are described by a group of log lines. A collective observable can be obtained by a malicious sequence of log lines, an anomalous frequency of a log line, or an anomalous number of log lines in a specified time window. Such observables can be triggered for example by a database dump that produces an anomalous number of queries or a malicious access pattern.

Especially for legacy systems and products with small market shares, which are often not directly supported by security solution providers and vendors (e.g., SIEM vendors that provide parsers for well-known products), log data is an important source for observables.

3.3.1.2 Monitoring Infrastructure

Usually, by default, log files are stored as simple text files. This has the advantage of easy access in the case of a system crash. Using a database format raises the problem that the log data is reachable only if the database itself is available. Because of the growing digitalization in recent years, the amount of produced log data is increasing exponentially. Thus, suitable log management solutions are needed, and not only for large-scale network environments. These have to handle this large amount of data. Log management comprises collecting logs, storing log data, and analyzing log data, as well as searching and reporting log data (Chuvakin et al., 2013).

There are so-called logging frameworks for most programming platforms (see, e.g., the documentations of Java[8] and Python[9]), which aids the implementation of proper logging support in new software products. For logging, usually three components are required: a logger, a formatter, and a handler. The logger is responsible for collecting the information that should be logged. Usually for each class a separated logger is defined. The configuration of the logger defines at which level of detail information is finally logged. This so-called severity level can be defined for each logger. Based on the configuration of the severity level, the logging framework decides whether a log message is logged or not. After the logger forwards the log information to the logging framework, the formatter takes the object provided, which is usually represented as a binary object, and converts it for output into a string. Finally, the handler, which listens for log messages at or above the defined level of severity, displays the resulting log line in a console, writes it to a file, or forwards it to another application.

The common standard for transmitting log messages is syslog (Gerhards, 2009). The key advantage of the syslog protocol is that it is supported by a wide range of devices and network components. Its primary use is to send log messages to a

---

[8] https://docs.oracle.com/javase/8/docs/technotes/guides/logging/overview.html (03/03/17).
[9] https://docs.python.org/3.6/library/logging.html (03/03/17).

centralized location, a so-called syslog server. Hence, syslog assists in establishing centralized logging (Karen and Souppaya, 2006). Centralized logging makes log management much easier and simplifies the correlation of information collected at different locations of a network. Among its advantages, the syslog standard includes some drawbacks. First of all, syslog does not define a standard for formatting messages. This results in inconsistency, since every developer can define his/her own log message format. By default, syslog uses the User Datagram Protocol (UDP) to transmit the log messages over the network (Okmianski, 2009). Since UDP is connectionless, log messages can be lost because of network congestion and packet loss. A more reliable protocol for transmitting log data is the Transmission Control Protocol (TCP) (Gerhards and Lonvick, 2012).

3.3.1.3 Evasion Techniques

While the information log data carries is essential for detecting security incidents and invaders, it can also be used as a source of information about an ICT network infrastructure by the attacker. Especially the (stealthy) passive phase of advanced persistent threats can be used to learn about the logging mechanisms in place. This information can then be used during the active phase to hide the attack through the manipulation of logs. An attacker could for example disable the database log to hide a SQL-injection. Therefore, it is critically important to protect the logging from manipulation. A simple solution is offered by digital signatures that can be added to new log entries; however, resource constraints (space and computational power, such as in sensor networks) may practically prohibit such a solution. Thus, efficient and lightweight protection measures appear necessary. Centralized logging solutions have advantages regarding security compared to decentralized logging solutions: (1) Only one node has to be secured; (2) if an attacker, e.g., takes over a Web server, he/she can manipulate log lines locally, but not the centrally stored version, because in combination with a data diode, data only flows to the log server, and there are no write operations to old data.

3.3.1.4 Current Applications

Data logging has a widespread application area in the ICT sector. Log data is an important source for system monitoring that comprises acquisition of data and knowledge (Hansen and Atkins, 1993). Therefore, system analysis and diagnostics rely on system monitoring. Empirical and statistical properties of logs are analyzed to acquire knowledge about changes is the system behavior. In this course, e.g., log data can be used for error analysis (Lin and Siewiorek, 1990).

Furthermore, log data is investigated in course of digital forensics (Raghavan, 2013). The field of digital forensics is broad. It can be applied after an attack was detected to investigate its origin and find information about the attacker and the purpose of the attack. But digital forensic analysis is not limited to cybersecurity.

It can also be used to detect the reasons for other system failures: misconfiguration or crashed network components.

Besides forensic analysis, log data can be used for real-time intrusion detection (Liao et al., 2013). Therefore, signature-based detection methods that analyze single log lines to identify erratic and malicious system behavior, which might be caused by an attacker or malware, can be utilized. More intelligent anomaly detection methods (Chandola et al., 2009) that, e.g., correlate log lines over time can be applied to detect more sophisticated and tailored attacks, such as advanced persistent threats (APTs).

Database logs can be used to back up and restore database content in case of a system crash or destruction caused by an access violation (Frühwirt et al., 2012). Transactions and activities stored in a text format in log data are easier to restore than those in a corrupted binary file.

Firewall logs can be used to validate, if implemented firewall rules are working properly. Furthermore, they can provide information if the firewall is the reason for application errors. They can also be used to detect malicious activities such as multiple unsuccessful attempts to overcome the firewall, which is an indication of an intrusion attempt. Also suspicious outgoing connections might be an indication that malware is used to launch an attack (see, e.g., the attack scenarios described in Chapter 2).

3.3.2 Network Traffic

3.3.2.1 Observables

As IT systems become connected, networks are formed that enable communication between assets. This communication manifests in network traffic from which observables can be extracted and compared to indicators. In corporate IT networks, traffic is usually transmitted with the use of packet-switched network protocols. In these protocols, the bit stream of information is broken up into multiple packets that are sent over the network independently. The full information stream is then reassembled at the target. During incidents, the threat actors need to make use of network communications for various attack steps like reconnaissance, lateral movement, or exfiltration (see the Cyber Kill Chain in Chapter 2). The events during the incident will alter existing network traffic or introduce new traffic, and this can be monitored through various observables and detected with the use of indicators.

To handle the transmission of packets, the payload is put into an "envelope." It consists of a protocol header (added before the actual data) and a tail (added after the actual data) and contains information on how the packet should be handled during transmission and on reception. To handle the complexity of data transmission, this process is performed multiple times in a layered fashion to allow different levels of abstraction of network operations. The most commonly used model for this layered networking approach is the ISO OSI model as defined in ISO 7498

(Braden, 1989; Bush and Meyer, 2002). It defines seven layers used in the transmission of data between two applications. While the data make their way through the layers, each layer attaches a further envelope around the packet. Figure 3.4 shows the process.

This also means that each router in the network removes layer one and two protocol information to uncover the network layer header. It then decides on the correct port to forward the packet, makes any adaptions to protocol information necessary (such as replacing IP addresses), and rewraps it into layer two and one before the physical transmission is started.

An alternative to the ISO/OSI model is the TCP/IP model widely used on the Internet (Braden, 1989; Bush and Meyer, 2002). It defines only four layers (Application, Transport, Internet, and Data Link), which partly fulfills the tasks of multiple layers in the ISO/OSI model.

There are two approaches to monitoring network traffic. When traffic flow is monitored, only the data contained in the protocol envelopes is stored and analyzed. Packet captures on the other hand store the full packet, which contains the header information as well as the payload (see Section 3.3.2.2 for details). Observables are present in both parts of a packet: the envelope and the payload. This chapter categorizes them as follows in four categories: transport oriented observables, application oriented observables, payload, and general traffic observables. While transport-oriented and application-oriented observables are found in the protocol envelopes, payload observables require access to the actual data. General traffic observables are found in helper protocols that are used implicitly by network components or by analyzing traffic occurrence over time.

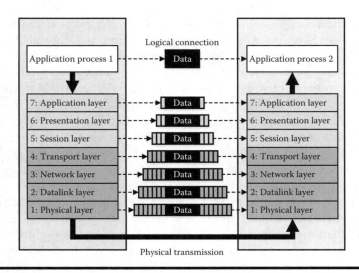

Figure 3.4 Overview of the packing and unpacking process in the OSI model.

3.3.2.1.1 Transport-Oriented Observables

> **EXAMPLE: SONY HACK**
>
> In the sony hack (see Chapter 2) the loader malware was programmed to connect to the C2 infrastructure over various IP addresses. The addressed machines were mainly unaffiliated with the threat actor. Instead, infected machines (e.g., mail servers, gaming servers, public VPNs, etc.) were used as proxies to disguise the real C2 infrastructure. The high number of accessible IP addresses that can be leveraged on the Internet by threat actors as proxies makes it hard for any one organization to detect novel malware reliably. However, with the use of cyber threat intelligence, this high number of IP addresses can easily be shared as indicators and automatically used in local monitoring infrastructures to detect infections quickly.

Transport-oriented observables are found in the packet envelopes that are introduced at the layers 1–4 of the ISO/OSI model. The information in the packet headers provides the most common observables used in network traffic monitoring. Due to its wide acceptance and use, this section focuses on the Internet protocol suite also known as TCP/IP (Braden, 1989; Bush and Meyer, 2002). It can be related to the OSI model where TCP is the transport layer protocol and IP is the network layer protocol. Layers 5–7 are combined into the application layer (more details on application layer protocols are given in Section 3.3.2.1.2).

Figure 3.5 shows the header structure of the IP and the TCP protocol. Transport-oriented observables are found in the various fields of these protocol headers. When the packet is received by a network device, it interprets the IP header to identify how the packet should be handled and routed to get to the intended destination. When the encapsulated protocol (in this case TCP) can be interpreted, the TCP header fields can also be recorded and used as observables. Examples for observables are the source and destination IP address of a given packet. One example of how these observables can be used as indicators is to detect the presence of a botnet client in the monitored network. Whenever the malware connects to the command and control server, the packets with the suspicious IP address in the source IP address field can be detected. Another example is to monitor network traffic to detect beaconing (Villeneuve and Bennett, 2012). Whenever the initial infection of a host happened, the malware pings the C2 infrastructure regularly to make it aware that it is ready to accept further commands. This traffic usually leverages ports of well-known protocols that are most likely not blocked by firewalls in operative networks (e.g., HTTP (80), HTTPS (443). However, the destination port of the traffic is often abnormal for regular traffic. The reason for this is that the traffic is often routed through multiple proxies that are unaffiliated with the attackers. These proxies have their regular ports used by benign services. So the

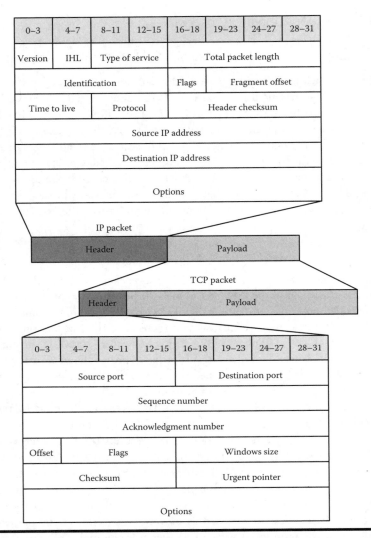

Figure 3.5   Packet and header structure of IPv4 and TCP packets. The header fields are ordered by their byte size and position where each line is a 32-byte block.

malicious traffic needs to be directed to unbound ports that are not used normally. Finally, tools such as nmap[10] make use of TCP among other protocols to perform port scans. Depending on the detailed settings in the response packets, the identified asset can be fingerprinted to identify its operating system, for example. This behavior can also be detected through network traffic monitoring through analysis of the number of connection attempts and the range of ports that are probed.

---

[10] https://nmap.org/.

The shortcoming of packet header information is that it is easy to manipulate during an incident. Depending on the protocol in use, various aspects of the header can be manipulated in an arbitrary fashion by the adversary to evade detection.

3.3.2.1.2 Application-Oriented Observables

The application layer protocols manage higher level functionality of services rather than the classical transmission. As such, they often contain valuable observables that can be used to detect the use of well-known application protocols for malicious activities. For threat actors, the use of well-known protocols is very beneficial. Malicious traffic can be hidden more easily between the large amounts of legitimate traffic sent with the same protocols. Table 3.1 gives an overview of the most common application-layer protocols, their standard TCP port mappings, and the application in which they are used.

Based on observables at the application layer, it is possible to monitor whether the respective underlying application is used as expected. The HTTP connection attempts to various well-known paths of the administration section of widely used content management systems (CMSs) can be an indicator for probing, which could be part of the reconnaissance phase. However, nowadays, these brute-force attempts are widely considered regular noise when a machine is reachable from the Internet.

EXAMPLE: POWER OUTAGE IN UKRAINE

In the case of the attack on a Ukrainian power distributor, the initial intrusion was achieved through spear fishing. After intensive reconnaissance with the use of social engineering, it is believed that a well-targeted mail (sent to a victim in the organization) contained a weaponized Microsoft Office document that installed the initial loader malware. While the most important step to limiting the effectiveness of this type of attack is user education, the header information of the delivered mail could have contained clues about the malicious intent of the attachment (i.e., the path of the mail would not have matched the path contained in the headers of previous mails).

Another example is the header information in e-mails that were sent using SMTP. They contain the route of the mail over various mail servers between sender and receiver. This information can be used to detect suspicious routes between two mail addresses, which can be an indication for a spoofed mail. This can be detected if mails appear to come from the same office network (e.g., from one employee to another in the same company), but the route either does not originate on the office mail server or seems to leave the domain before entering it again.

Table 3.1   List of the Most Well-Known Application Layer Protocols Used on the Internet and Their Standard TCP Port Mappings

Protocol	Full Name	Standard Port	Description
HTTP	Hypertext Transfer Protocol	80	Stateless application layer protocol for data transfer which is usually used to access Web sites
HTTPS	Hypertext Transfer Protocol Secure	443	HTTP with additional encryption using SSL/TSL
DNS	Domain Name System	53	Application layer protocol that is used to translate domain names to the IP address where the domain can be accessed
IMAP	Internet Message Access Protocol	143/993	Text-based application layer protocol used for the communication between e-mail servers and clients to access mails
SMTP	Simple Mail Transfer Protocol	25	Application layer protocol used to send and forward e-mails
SFTP	Secure File Transfer Protocol	990/989	Application layer protocol for file access, transfer and modification. It is implemented as an extension to SSH, to enable secure and reliable communication
SSH	Secure Shell	22	Cryptographic protocol to securely perform network operations over an otherwise insecure network

3.3.2.1.3 Payload

Another source for observables is the payload of the packets. The information that is encapsulated in the protocols can be reassembled by a monitoring system to discover malicious content. This capability is especially helpful in ICSs where clear-text measurements and control actions are sent between assets. With information about the underlying physical system, indicators can be designed to detect malicious (or erroneous) measurements or set points. It can however also be used in traditional Internet applications. Section 3.3.3 gives a detailed introduction about the observables contained in binaries that can be used to detect malware. The same tools can be used directly on the monitored network traffic. Attachments to e-mails are good examples of payloads that can be monitored at the mail server before the mail is transmitted to the end user to limit the risk for infection. Similarly, outgoing FTP or HTTP file transfers can be monitored to check for confidential documents that leave the controlled perimeter.

EXAMPLE: POWER OUTAGE IN UKRAINE (*Continued*)

In the example of the attack on the Ukraine power distributor, the spear fishing mail contained a weaponized attachment. With the use of threat intelligence, the malicious content could have been discovered from reconstructed packet captures or at the mail server before it was transmitted to the target machine. This could have prevented the initial infection, which in turn would have broken the kill chain.

The analysis of payloads is getting increasingly difficult with the use of encryption techniques, especially the wide adoption of SSL/TLS. While encryption has to be encouraged from a security standpoint, it is also heavily used by adversaries to circumvent the monitoring of payloads.

3.3.2.1.4 Traffic-Specific Observables

Packet-switched networks are configured dynamically. This is the main reason for the success of the Internet as we know it today. It was originally designed to withstand large-scale physical attacks. In order to dynamically handle the network setup, helper protocols are used by network equipment and hosts to connect the network nodes and ensure connectivity where possible. These protocols were designed without IT security in mind, and they still provide attack vectors in modern networks. They usually make no use of encryption techniques and are therefore easy to use for reconnaissance and as observables. In the following part, this chapter discusses three of the most widely used helper protocols.

The *Dynamic Host Configuration Protocol (DHCP)* (Droms, 1997, 2004) is used by clients that connect to DHCP-managed IP networks. A DHCP server listens for client requests and assigns them a free IP address through a DHCP lease, which is time limited. As DHCP does not include encryption, an infected or malicious node in the network can act as a rogue DHCP server. As a consequence, manipulated leases can be issued that can either cause a denial-of-service attack (invalid IP addresses will prohibit the client from connection) or a man-in-the-middle attack (e.g., when the lease specifies a wrong DNS server for DNS lookups, which redirects HTTP traffic to malicious servers).

At the same time, DHCP can be used to identify new hosts that connect to a network. The monitored packets can indicate rogue machines that send out invalid DHCP leases or clients that try to forge DHCP requests to take over IP addresses.

The *Address Resolution Protocol (ARP)* (Plummer, 1982) is used within the boundaries of a single network (it is not routed) to find out the MAC address for a machine when the IP address is known. This is important as the TCP/IP information is most often used to identify the intended receiver of a data stream rather than the link layer information (MAC). IP to MAC mappings that are known once are stored in a local buffer to minimize communication. If an intended receiver's mapping is not known, a broadcast request (ARP request) is sent to all machines in the local network. All machines receive this request, but only the machine with an active interface with the requested IP responds with its own MAC address.

Despite well-known vulnerabilities (e.g., ARP cache poisoning), the broadcast nature of this protocol makes it a prime candidate for monitoring the behavior of machines in a network.

The *Internet Control Message Protocol (ICMP)* is designed to manage IP traffic through control and error messages. It is usually used directly by networking hardware and not through user interaction. However, the ICMP ping command and traceroute are example cases for ICMP in the user domain. Pings use the ICMP echo command to determine if a host is available and reachable. Similarly, traceroute makes use of *time-to-live exceeded in transit* and *host unreachable* ICMP error messages. Due to their vulnerabilities, many switches filter ICMP messages. However, they are often used by network administrators for fault analysis and attackers for reconnaissance.

By monitoring a stream of network traffic, other patterns can also be identified and used as observables. This can include the traffic load on a certain node that is different from the expected traffic behavior. Similarly, traffic flows between specific assets can be identified. While a public Webserver is expected to have a large amount of traffic aimed for destinations outside the company's borders, the same does not hold for an internal database server. In the second case, a significant increase in data sent out of the company network can indicate data exfiltration.

EXAMPLE: SONY HACK (CONTINUED)

In the case of the sony hack (see Chapter 2), the attackers were hard to detect once they had acquired administrator privileges. However, the amount of confidential data released after the hack indicate that the exfiltration process could have been detected based on the outgoing traffic patterns. Specifically, it is usually not the case that large amounts of data are sent out of the corporate network from machines that store sensitive or confidential data.

3.3.2.2 Monitoring

The challenge of network traffic monitoring is getting a complete picture of the traffic in a network. Modern packet-switched networks use network switches to distribute packets to the intended receivers. The hosts only receive the packets that are relevant to that host. Monitoring at host level is useful for error analysis but not for network monitoring; a complete picture cannot be seen at one host. Instead, the common approach is to monitor network traffic at the network switches on the border between segregated subnetworks. This is shown in the reference network in Figure 3.3. Monitoring is installed on the network switches between the different domains; for example between the Corporate Network and the public Internet. Industrial network switches provide so-called mirroring ports. The switch can be configured to send a copy of every network packet seen on one switch port out through the mirroring port. Attached to this mirroring port is the monitoring infrastructure that collects and analyzes traffic. In Cisco systems, port mirroring is generally referred to as Switched Port Analyzer (SPAN).[11] One problem with port mirroring is that traffic within the network is usually not completely monitored. Only traffic that transcends the borders between segregated networks or broadcast traffic is captured and analyzed. The reason is that the switch does not have the bandwidth to redirect the traffic from all ports to a single mirroring port. Neither is there a mirroring port for each regular port. A decision needs to be made as to what traffic is most important to monitor, and this is usually the traffic that transcends network borders.

In case of additional critical communication links within the subnetwork, in-line monitoring can be applied. In-line monitoring is implemented by a network bridge that receives all traffic between two communication partners and can then read but also manipulate all traffic before forwarding it. This is also done to support intrusion prevention systems (IPSs) that need this type of installation to actively intercept malicious traffic. In-line monitoring systems pose a connectivity risk in the case that the in-line system powers down due to errors or power loss. Therefore, they are installed with the use of bypass switches. These special switches can detect the state of the in-line system and forward the traffic directly if the connection is lost due to a fault. Figure 3.3 does not show any in-line monitoring, but in-line monitoring could be helpful to monitor all traffic from and to a specific internal service in the corporate network. For example, it would be helpful to monitor all access to the server that stores the credit card information of customers.

Helper protocols often send some commands in a broadcast fashion. This means that the packet can be seen by every host in the subnet. It can therefore also be analyzed by monitoring systems at all three locations (host based, port mirroring, or in-line monitoring).

---

[11] http://www.cisco.com/c/en/us/tech/lan-switching/switched-port-analyzer-span/index.html.

Depending on the monitoring, there are two main formats in which network traffic is usually collected. The first type is network traffic flow information. It was first developed by Cisco as NetFlow (Introduction to Cisco IOS NetFlow—A Technical Overview, 2017) but later adapted by multiple companies. The router collects and aggregates the information about different flows of IP traffic. A NetFlow record contains: Version, Sequence Number, Input and Output Interface ID, timestamps for start and end time of the flow, number of bytes and packets observed, IP header information (most important here are source and destination IP address and port numbers), and a union of all TCP flags that were observed throughout the lifetime of the flow. The flow records observed at the router are then forwarded to a collector using UDP and deleted at the router. To limit the overhead from the newly introduced network traffic, the collector should be located in close proximity to the recording device. In Figure 3.3, the collector would be situated in the DMZ with the security services node. This leaves at most one network segment between the collector and the recording switches (with exception of the switch that connects the public domain to the Internet, which is acceptable). The generation of flow records is very resource demanding at the router. Further, the content of the packets is not stored and therefore cannot be analyzed when flow records are used for monitoring.

Packet captures are the second type of network monitoring. In this case, the complete packet (i.e., header information and payload) is collected, stored and parsed. This approach is usually necessary for deep-packet inspection and is performed by tools like tcpdump[12] and wireshark.[13] Since the complete packet information is stored, the same observables that are captured by flow records are also present in packet captures. However, the amount of data stored in packet captures is much greater, and thus, algorithms need to be applied to process the data and extract observables of interest.

3.3.2.3 Evasion Techniques

Adversaries can use various approaches to disguise attack indicators in network traffic in order to circumvent detection.

With the increased use of encryption in communication protocols (e.g., HTTPS) encrypted traffic is a normal occurrence in monitored traffic. While encryption is an important security and privacy feature, it is also widely used by adversaries to prevent payload analysis. A detection mechanism can only analyze the payload if it has a copy of the private key used during the encryption. Packet headers of transport protocols, however, usually cannot be encrypted by the attacker, as they need to be readable by the network equipment to ensure correct delivery. If the transport layer protocol uses encryption, however, then the header information of the application layer protocols cannot be monitored.

---

[12] http://www.tcpdump.org/.
[13] https://www.wireshark.org/.

Another possibility to evade payload inspection is fragmentation. The attacker can split the payload in multiple very small packets that need to be reassembled by the IDS to identify the malicious payload. The attacker can then send packets out of order or introduce random delays during transmission to make the reassembling process harder for the IDS in the hope that the IDS times out or fails to reassemble while the target machine does not. This is not an unreasonable assumption, as the IDS is often responsible for the traffic of multiple hosts. Therefore, simpler algorithms and shorter timeouts are necessary to handle the complexity in time.

Similar to encryption, encoding can be used to circumvent detection by signatures. For example, Web servers accept ASCII strings that are encoded in hexadecimal. If the IDS is not aware of the full range of encoding possibilities, signatures can be avoided, while the victim accepts the attack.

In the same category, multiple approaches exist that exploit differences between target host and IDS when it comes to the interpretation of encodings or packet structure. When fragments of the data are defined to be overlapping, the IDS and the host might use different portions of the overlapping data when the payload is reassembled (Bittau, 2005). Similarly, various operating systems handle specific protocol flags differently. These ambiguities between the protocol standard and the implementations can be exploited by the attacker.

Packet headers contain information about the intended receiver of a packet and also the sender. If the sender information is not validated, it is often possible to spoof the information about the sender with the address of another machine or with dummy data to disguise the attacker's location in the network or to make it look like the packet is sent from a valid machine. Similarly, helper protocols can be used to take over network configurations from other machines to disguise.

3.3.3 Files and Processes

Malware, short for malicious software, refers to software programs designed to damage a computer system[14] or perform other unwanted actions. Since malware tries to access computer systems, collect sensitive information, disrupt system operations, and cause damage to the system, malware detection is essential to secure a computer system. Not only are general ICT systems targeted by malware, but ICSs have also been victims of malware operations that were able to take control over physical processes and cause severe physical damage. Stuxnet (Karnouskos, 2011), Havex (ICS-CERT, 2014), and BlackEnergy (ICS-CERT, 2016) are well-known malware examples that targeted power infrastructures in recent years as highlighted in the examples about Stuxnet and the attack on a Ukraine grid operator in Chapter 2.

Malware detection was widely researched in computer science for decades, and detection methods include static analysis, dynamic analysis, and hybrid approaches. Static analysis is a process of the analysis of a file's data without execution of the

---

[14] http://techterms.com/definition/malware.

file itself. Dynamic analysis performs runtime analysis that runs the executable file, monitors its behavior, and investigates how the program affects the host machine. This is possible since malware includes at least one executable file that contains malicious contents. Some malware detection methods, as hybrid solutions, combine both analysis methods to overcome drawbacks of each.

Malware detection methods capture any malicious content or behavior by monitoring observables at the host machine including binary patterns, instructions, or system calls.

3.3.3.1 Observables

Depending on the method of analysis, different observables are used to identify malware. Some of the most widely used observables will be described in the following. However, as new techniques are developed, new observables are identified or the way observables are grouped to form indicators are adopted.

3.3.3.1.1 Binary Patterns

Malware consists of single or multiple files that contain malicious contents. These files are usually stored as binaries after they are compiled by the threat actor. Often, these binaries contain unique code patterns that can be extracted directly or from decoded data. Malware may further include additional information such as commands, the control server, or target locations. The additional information can be written as alphabet strings, and those strings can be used as unique patterns. Patterns are derived from executable code or additional configuration and meta-information of malware. Combined, sets of unique patterns form signatures to later detect the same malware file in different locations. The pattern analysis can then be triggered by any new file or any update on existing files in the monitored memory space. These signatures can also be shared as indicators (IoC) and used by various organizations in their detection processes.

Unfortunately, malware authors use obfuscation techniques (e.g., code compressions and encryption) (You and Yim, 2010) and write variants of the same malware to avoid binary pattern based malware detection. However, unique binary patterns can be identified and used to detect known malware, and sometimes obfuscation techniques fail to generate a significant number of variants. For example, if the same encryption key or small number of keys is used, the encrypted patterns remain the same or the number of the encrypted patterns is not big.

3.3.3.1.2 Operation Codes (opcodes)

As malware is a program, executable code can be extracted and analyzed for malware detection in addition to static binary analysis. Executable code reveals more information about the program than the binary does, e.g., instructions, functions, or system calls. In order to perform its task, the program executes various instructions sequentially where any instruction consists of exactly one opcode and optionally (depending on the opcode) one or more operands. Opcodes are primitive operations of programs such as register and memory operations, but they represent the behavioral information of the programs. Opcode-based malware detection methods include sequence, frequency analysis, or both.

Bilar (2007) used the difference of opcodes histograms between known malware and benign programs for malware prediction. Similarly, other methods employ frequency (Santos et al., 2010) of opcodes and sequences (Santos et al., 2013) of opcodes to model the malicious behavior. Runwal et al. (2012) proposed a graphical technique to find the similarity of the opcode sequence.

For opcode analysis, it is essential to translate a binary file into executable code and extract opcodes from the executable code. For the translation, disassemblers can be used and different types of opcode information extracted depending on the method. In order to overcome obfuscation methods, debuggers or instrumentation techniques can be used to extract opcode information, or operating system level tools can be used.

Dynamic approaches analyze the program behavior during execution. Principal dynamic techniques include virtual machine inspection (Garfinkel et al., 2003), function call monitoring (Forrest et al., 1996; Bayer et al., 2006; Canali et al., 2012; Chandramohan et al., 2013; Creech and Hu, 2014; Lanzi et al., 2010; Xue et al., 2015), dynamic binary instrumentation (Newsome and Song, 2005; Santos et al., 2013; Bilar, 2007), and information flow tracking (Christodorescu et al., 2008; Gascon et al., 2013). Although these approaches can potentially detect the obfuscated malware and the malware variants, they require a large amount of resources and cause substantial overhead. These difficulties often limit malware detection to a static approach (e.g., antivirus, scanners); however, they can be easily evaded due to the known limitations.

3.3.3.1.3 System Calls

System calls are responsible for primitive and essential functions in operating systems, such as memory access, network communication, etc. It is almost impossible to develop a program with no system call. System calls have been recognized as a promising feature that can be monitored and used for malware detection. System call patterns provide effective information about the runtime activities of a program, which can be used to characterize malicious behavior.

Clustering techniques, like the n-gram approach (Canali et al., 2012), can be used to group the system calls of a sample to identify malicious patterns. Another approach is to group the system calls based on common operating system resources to identify malicious intent (Chandramohan et al., 2013; Bayer et al., 2009). Another approach considers system call sequences that can indicate a sequence of malicious activities (e.g., read important file(s) and transfer the file(s) through a socket). Frequency distribution of system calls can also be used to characterize programs as benign and malicious in order to identify suspicious files. An abstract example of this concept is described in Table 3.2. Graph algorithms can be adopted to build program behavior information based on system calls.

What system calls are used in a program can be found from the executable code that is disassembled from the binary file through static analysis. Dynamic

Table 3.2   Example for Sequences of System Calls

Sequence 1	Sequence 2	Sequence 3	Malicious Sequence
S1	S1	S1	S1
S2	S2	S2	S2
S3	S3	S3	S3
S4	S4	S4	S4
S5	S5	S5	S5
S6	S6	S6	S6
S7	S4	S4	S4
S8	S5	S5	S5
S9	S6	S6	S6
S10	S7	S4	S7
S11	S8	S5	S8
S12	S9	S6	S9
S13	S10	S7	S10
	S11	S8	S15
	S12	S9	S16
	S13	S10	S11
		S11	S13
		S12	S15
		S13	S16

Note: The relative frequencies of system calls (S1–S13) performed by a process stay fairly constant. In this case, the difference among the three sequences is the number of iterations in a loop (S4–S6 are called in the loop). In the case of an attack, however, these calls would change which can be detected.

analysis, such as debugging and instrumentation, can also track the system calls during the runtime. In order to avoid more advanced obfuscation techniques like sandbox detection, researchers came up with ways to monitor the program behavior in hardware. NumChecker (Wang and Karri, 2013) detects malicious modifications to a kernel function (system call) by checking the hardware events including total instructions, branches, returns, and floating point operations. Ozsoy et al. (2015) proposed the design of a malware-aware processor using architectural events (e.g., frequency of memory read/writes, immediate branches taken, frequency of opcodes) as the features and machine learning for the classification of malware. All the above methods use low-level hardware features to model the malicious behavior. Rahmatian et al. (2012) proposed host-based intrusion detection using FPGA, which uses system call sequences to characterize the correct system behavior. The main limitations of this approach are as follows: Each program needs to be assisted by system calls-based FSM; it does not allow unknown programs to run; and FSM of system calls would be significantly large for complex programs, thus demanding large memory size. While these approaches are harder to circumvent by the attacker, they are also more cost intensive to implement and hard to deploy in an operational environment.

3.3.3.1.4 Information Flow

Opcode and system call information focus on what operations programs do, but what (or how) information (or data) a specific program handles is another perspective of program behavior analysis. In this case the analysis method is not interested in how data are handled but what data are handled.

Data can be located (or generated) inside programs or delivered from outside (e.g., input files, data transmission, and user actions). What data (or resource) are accessed by programs can be traced, and links between data accesses can be identified that might indicate suspicious activities. Hidden information can be identified by monitoring operations that programs perform on data rather than monitoring all operations. As one obfuscation technique, garbage instructions can be injected between real instructions. However, by filtering out instructions that are not related to specific data, the garbage instructions can be removed (Tang et al., 2014). Information flow can be traced in both static and dynamic analysis, but dynamic analysis is more robust to obfuscation techniques.

Similar approaches can again be done in hardware to circumvent specific obfuscation techniques. Demme et al. (2013) proposed the use of a hardware performance counter to monitor lower level micro-architectural parameters such as instruction per cycle and cache miss rate. Tang et al. (2014) built baseline models of benign program execution using unsupervised machine learning to detect the deviations that occur as a result of malware exploitation.

3.3.3.2 Obfuscation Methods

Typical static solutions, such as antivirus, scanners, and anti-malware tools, use signatures for malware detection. Unique sequence of bytes can be identified from malware and used to detect the same malware. Unfortunately, malware authors use obfuscation techniques (e.g., code compressions and encryption) and write variants of the same malware to avoid the signature detection (You and Yim, 2010). Besides that, signature generation requires a lot of manpower and time to extract the signatures of each malware.

As a first line of defense against signature detection, malware can be encrypted or "packed" (i.e., compressed). The advantage of encryption is that a signature that is present in the unencrypted code will not appear in the encrypted version. From the malware author's perspective, the disadvantage of encryption is that the code must be decrypted at some point, and the decryption code itself cannot be encrypted. Consequently, the decryption code can be the signature.

Polymorphic malware is the next logical step in the arms race between SD and malware authors. Polymorphic malware morphs the decryption code, and consequently there is no fixed decryption code that can be used as a signature. Ideally, new decryption code would be generated for each infection. Robust detection of polymorphic malware is difficult (Runwal et al., 2012).

Metamorphic malware is sometimes said to be "body polymorphic" (Konstantinou and Wolthusen, 2008; Péter and Ferrie, 2001) That is, instead of morphing the decryption code, metamorphic code morphs the entire malicious code. If the morphing is sufficiently thorough, no common signature will exist and therefore, no encryption is necessary. A wide variety of techniques can be employed to create metamorphic software. Such techniques include register swapping, general code obfuscation, equivalent instruction substitution, code shuffling, and subroutine permutation.

Malware authors use advanced techniques (e.g., anti-virtual machine inspection and anti-debuggers) to hide the malicious activity and finally avoid detection (Chen et al., 2008). For example, a malware uses anti-debugger techniques including anti-ptrace, anti-sigtrap and anti-breakpoint to detect the presence of malware detectors on the host machine and exits cleanly once it finds any malware detectors.

3.4 Evaluation and Analysis of Monitoring Data to Derive Cyber Incident Alerts

The previous section highlighted the different observables that can be monitored in traditional ICT systems. It further showed examples of IoCs that can be used to identify cyber attacks. However, observables and indicators are often not sufficient on their own to identify complex cyber attacks reliably. Various analysis techniques can be applied on top of observables for more effective detection. This section presents five categories of analysis techniques: (1) signature-based analysis, (2) stateful analysis, (3) cross-layer analysis, (4) anomaly detection, and (5) ontologies. Signature based analysis and stateful analysis are described under the umbrella of rule-based analysis, whereas cross-layer analysis is described with anomaly detection.

This section describes general concepts and the possibilities for integrating each approach with information sharing frameworks. One central question is how each approach can benefit from shared information and how it can be used to generate new information that should be shared. Figure 3.6 presents the approaches on a plane, where one axis describes their requirements on the analyzed information, while the other axis shows for each approach whether it is more suitable for detecting known attacks or novel or highly sophisticated attacks. It can be seen that rule-based approaches are more suitable for the detection of known attacks. In contrast, anomaly detection approaches can be used to get indications of novel or unknown

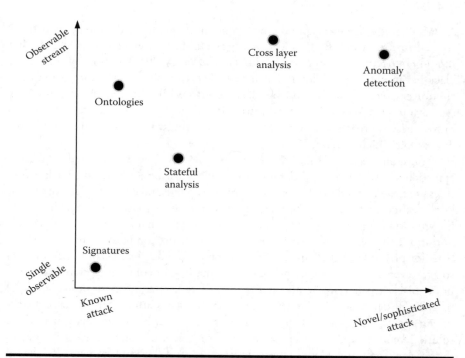

Figure 3.6 Classification of the five analysis categories. The position on the plane indicates if a specific approach operates on single observables or a stream of observables. It further shows if a method is more suitable to detect known attacks or novel and highly sophisticated attacks.

attacks. With the use of streams of observables, more data can be used and more complex situations can be classified. In contrast, simpler rule-based approaches often give more reliable results in known attacks.

3.4.1 Rule-Based Analysis

There are two concepts for establishing rule-based analysis:

1. Black-listing
2. White-listing

While black-listing is about detecting pre-defined malicious activities, the focus of white-listing is on allowing pre-defined normal activities.

Sections 3.4.1.1 - 3.4.1.4 discusses rule-based security analysis.

3.4.1.1 Black-Listing

A black-listing rule detects pre-defined values in the monitored data. Black-lists are applied to detect specific IP addresses, port numbers, user names, or clients that should not occur in an organization's network (Vacca, 2013). A major drawback of black-list approaches is that it is easy for attackers to avoid the prohibited values and circumvent security tools applying black-listing. While those approaches are very effective to prevent known attacks, it is difficult to keep them up to date, which makes these approaches vulnerable to unknown attacks that, e.g., make use of zero-day exploits (Liao et al., 2013).

Common security solutions such as firewalls, signature-based detection approaches, and antivirus programs utilize black-listing approaches. Black-listing rules are in general relatively easy to set-up and update and are very effective against known attacks, which are the majority of malicious activities. Hence, they form the important base of security analysis especially in smaller companies that cannot afford the resources and the personnel to set up complex security solutions. Also for private use, they are a preferred solution. Since black-listing rules forbid specific events, such as occurring malware signatures or communication on specific ports, black-lists have to be updated frequently to keep a sufficient protection level of an ICT network infrastructure. Since this is a resource-intensive task, black-listing approaches are usually based on centralized distribution mechanisms, where solution vendors update their customers with predefined signatures and rules to detect new malware. Hence, those approaches profit from automatically shared Indicators of Compromise (IoC). This process benefits from the fact that rules to detect malware signatures do not have to be configured for a specific network infrastructure—they rather look the same in each environment. However, a drawback of such widely distributed and general rules is that they are not able to detect infrastructure-specific undesired behavior, e.g., due to the exploitation of zero-day vulnerabilities (refer to Chapter 2).

3.4.1.2 White-Listing

In contrast to black-listing, white-listing does not prohibit specific actions or values visible in the monitored data per se. Those approaches allow a specific baseline of normal system behavior, which forms the so-called ground truth. Continuously collected data are then compared against the previously defined ground truth. It is more difficult for an attacker to not violate this ground truth, since the attacker's actions usually cause the generation of log and network events that differ from the normal system behavior. Simple white-listing rules (i.e., the model of the ground truth) can analyze single events, such as one log line, and allow using, e.g., only specific IP addresses, ports or Web browsers, and the correlation of multiple events. This means that in contrast to black-listing approaches, where specific system behavior is prohibited, a baseline of normal system behavior is allowed ("ground truth"). The model for this baseline of normal system behavior can be obtained from data sources such as log data and network traffic (see Section 3.3.2). Thus, white-listing approaches attempt to avoid the drawback of black-listing, that rules can be possibly avoided by an attacker, after s/he recognizes them. Furthermore, white-listing approaches enhance security against unknown attacks that make use of zero-day exploits or attack vectors nobody thought about when designing the rules, because they only allow normal user and system activities.

3.4.1.3 Black- vs. White-Listing

Security mechanisms applying black-listing form the base of organizations' cyber defenses. However, in order to avoid being detected by blacklist security approaches, they adapt their strategies and make their attacks more sophisticated and tailored to an organization (e.g., through using customized malware with unique signatures originating from toolkits (Symantec, 2016).

On the other side, intelligent anomaly detection systems that apply white-listing approaches are able to discover slight deviations of the system behavior and thus traces of unknown attacks. Many attackers exploit vulnerabilities at different network levels and abuse different network areas as entry points for launching a successful attack (see also Chapter 2). To counter sophisticated APTs, an appropriate synthesis of different approaches is required. Therefore, often applied and easy to deploy black-listing approaches that work sufficiently against known attacks, have to be extended with more complex and intelligent white-listing solutions that allow for detection of unknown attacks. ICT and enterprise networks are usually unique infrastructures that differ and are used differently. Therefore, they account for adaptive solutions that can be customized to those situations. This can

Table 3.3 Advantages and Disadvantages of Black-Listing and White-Listing

	Black-Listing	*White-Listing*
Advantages	• Simple and effective against known attacks • Detailed contextual analysis • Easy to share	• Effective to detect unknown attacks • More independent from OS • Easy to keep up to date
Disadvantages	• Ineffective against unknown attacks • Hard to keep up to date • Time consuming to maintain • Vulnerable to incompleteness of black-list	• High false positive rate (FPR) • Unavailable while behavior profiles are rebuilt

be achieved by the application of white-listing approaches, while black-listing is based on distributing pre-defined signatures that are not developed with focus on a specific network. Furthermore, especially for legacy systems and systems with small market shares, the application of black-listing is problematic because of the lack of periodic rule updates through major vendors. Table 3.3 provides a comprehensive comparison of the advantages and disadvantages of both approaches.

3.4.1.4 Sharing

Rule-based analysis is the vital backbone of a working security solution. While black-listing approaches are well established for many years, white-listing approaches are just about to gain more importance. From this development, black-listing approaches can also profit. White-listing does not rely on frequent updates of signatures and allows the detection of deviations from normal system behavior and therefore the observation of new, as yet unknown attacks. Based on this, observable IoCs can be defined. For enabling a useful processing of these IoCs, system information and event management (SIEM) systems can be used. SIEM systems can interpret alarms by combining the provided information from security solutions (e.g., firewalls, IDS, etc.) and organizational context as well as shared open/external threat intelligence from vulnerability databases, mailing lists, and online platforms. All this information then can be used to define signatures for black-listing approaches based on the IoC that have been obtained from white-listing approaches.

Furthermore, SIEM systems can be used to correlate alarms with information from risk management, configuration management, compliance management, etc. The particular challenge here is to apply the data fusion methods suitable to the context in which a network is used to limit the vast amount of information without losing important insights. Through applying the right mix of data fusion and contextualization approaches, detected alarms can be interpreted more accurately, thus contributing to increasing situational awareness (refer to Chapter 6 for more information on situational awareness).

3.4.2 Intrusion and Anomaly Detection

The following section focuses on anomaly detection approaches that are applied for intrusion detection in ICT network infrastructures. Anomaly detection deals with identifying patterns in an ICT network that contradict normal system behavior. Reasons for this anomalous system behavior that usually refers to malicious activities include the following:

- Invaders
- Cyber attacks
- Misconfiguration
- System failures

3.4.2.1 What Are Anomalies?

There are different types of anomalies (Chandola et al., 2009) that can indicate malicious system behavior:

- A *point anomaly* is the simplest form and is often also referred to as outlier, i.e., an anomalous single event. In a two-dimensional space, a point anomaly is an element at a large distance from all the other elements. In an ICT network, this could be an unexpected login-name or IP address.
- A *contextual anomaly* is an event that is anomalous in a specific context but might be normal in another one. In an ICT network, this can be an anomalous event parameter, such as an unexpected timestamp. A contextual anomaly could, e.g., be a system login of an employee outside the normal working hours, while this login would be normal during normal working time.
- A *collective anomaly* usually originates in an anomalous frequency of a usually normal single event. In an ICT network, this could be a database dump, which could be caused by a SQL-Injection. During a database dump, a large number of log lines that refer to normal SQL-Queries are generated. In this case, the single lines are normal, but their high frequency is anomalous.

Anomalies that refer to the described types might also be detected with simpler detection methods mentioned in previous sections. But these kinds of anomalies are usually not caused by APTs (see also Chapter 2), which aim to stay below the radar. An APT is a tailored and sophisticated attack that is difficult to detect, usually aims at a specific target, and results in significant damage, such as high

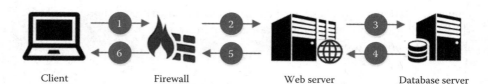

Client   Firewall   Web server   Database server

Figure 3.7   The normal log in process to an online shop: (1) the client tries to log into an online shop on a web server, (2) a connection through firewall occurs, (3) the Web server checks credentials through a database query, (4) the database query returns some result, (5) a response through firewall: access acceptance or denial, (6) client receives response.

financial loss, stolen intellectual property, or sabotaged systems. Furthermore, it is difficult to detect this sort of attacks in a timely manner—it usually takes months (Mandiant Consulting, 2016). Another type of anomaly that can be detected and also expose APTs is sequential anomalies.

A sequential anomaly represents an anomalous sequence of single events usually categorized as normal. In an ICT network, a sequential anomaly can be caused, e.g., by violating an access chain. For example, a normal database server access is usually only allowed via a firewall and a Web server (see Figure 3.7). Therefore, it would be malicious if someone accessed the database server directly without accessing the Web server.

3.4.2.2 Intrusion and Anomaly Detection Approaches

In Section 3.4.1 two basic concepts of detecting malicious system behavior were discussed. This section (Section 3.4.2.2) reviews methods of intrusion detection and focuses especially on anomaly detection. These approaches usually make use of statistical methods and machine learning (Tsai et al., 2009). Anomaly detection tools can use various types of input data, such as network traces and textual log data (see also Section 3.3.2).

There are three general methods that are used in intrusion detection systems (IDS): (1) signature-based detection (SD), (2) stateful protocol analysis (SPA), and (3) anomaly-based detection (AD) (Liao et al., 2013).

1. *SD* uses predefined signatures and patterns to detect attackers. This method is simple and effective for detecting known attacks. The drawbacks of this method are as follows: it is ineffective against unknown attacks or unknown variants of an attack, which allows attackers to evade IDS based on SD. Furthermore, since the attack landscape is rapidly changing, it is difficult to keep the signatures up-to-date, and thus maintenance is time consuming (Whitman and Mattord, 2012).

2. *SPA* uses predetermined profiles that define benign protocol activity. Occurring events are compared against these profiles to determine whether protocols are used in the correct way. IDSs based on SPA track the state of network, transport, and application protocols. They use vendor-developed universal profiles and therefore rely on their support (Karen and Mell, 2007).

3. *AD* approaches learn a baseline of normal system behavior, a so-called ground truth. Against this ground truth, all occurring events are compared to detect anomalous system behavior. In contrast to SD- and SPA-based IDS, AD-based approaches allow detection of previously unknown attacks. A drawback of AD-based IDS is the usually high false positive rate (García-Teodoro et al., 2009).

SD and SPA use signatures and rules that describe malicious events and thus can be categorized as black-listing approaches. AD approaches are more flexible and are also able to detect novel and previously unknown attacks. They permit only normal system behavior and therefore implement white-listing approaches. While SD and SPA are relatively easy to deploy, they usually require the support of vendors that share signatures. On the other hand, AD-based approaches are more flexible and can adapt to different situations (see next section about self-learning), but are usually harder to set up.

IDS approaches can be distinguished by the level on which the detection takes place and can be roughly categorized as host-based IDS (HIDS), network-based IDS (NIDS), and hybrid or cross-layer IDS (Sabahi and Movaghar, 2008; Vacca, 2014):

- *Host level:* HIDS is the initial form of IDS and was invented for the purpose of securing military mainframe computers (Intrusion Detection System/Intrusion Prevention System (IDS/IPS) Market (Host Based, Network Based, Wireless, On-Premise & Cloud Deployment, Appliances, Software, Professional Services)—Global Advancements Forecasts & Analysis (2014–2019), 2014). Similar to simple security solutions such as anti-viruses, this sort of IDS has to be installed on every system (host) in the network to be monitored. While HIDS delivers specific high-level information about an attack and allows comprehensive monitoring of a single host, it can be disabled by, e.g., a denial-of-service (DoS) attack, because once a system is compromised the HIDS is as well.

- *Network level:* NIDS monitors and analyzes the network traffic of a whole network. The optimal application of NIDS would be monitoring inbound as well as outbound traffic. However, this might create a bottleneck and slow down the network. For monitoring a whole network with a NIDS, a single sensor node is sufficient, and the functionality of the sensor is not effected if one system of the network is compromised. A major drawback of NIDS is that if the NIDS's band width is overloaded, complete monitoring cannot be guaranteed, because some network packets and therefore possibly essential information might be dropped.

Table 3.4 Describes Which Type of IDS Considers Which Data Source

Data Source	HIDS	NIDS	Cross-Layer
Network traffic	−	+	~
Log data	+	~	~
Files and binaries	+	−	~

- *Cross-layer:* Cross-layer anomaly detection approaches and so-called Hybrid IDS combine different methods. Hybrid IDS usually provide a management framework that combines HIDS and NIDS to reduce their drawbacks and make use of their advantages. Cross-layer anomaly detection approaches aim to maximize the available information and therefore optimize detection capability and minimize the false alarm rate at the same time. Therefore, various data sources, such as textual log data and network traffic data described in previous sections can be used for anomaly detection. Timely detection of attacks and invaders accounts for lightweight solutions that allow a high data throughput to enable real-time analysis and evaluation of the collected information.

Table 3.4 visualizes which data types are considered by which type of IDS to detect attacks and invaders.

3.4.2.3 Self-Learning and Adaptive Approaches

As previously mentioned, a drawback of black-listing is that they are only capable of detecting already known attack patterns. Therefore, these approaches account for developers who update the rule base. Especially small companies cannot afford the resources and the personnel required to maintain their security solutions in house. Hence, they rely on the support of vendors and their rule sets or costly Managed Security Service Providers (MSSPs) that manage the security solutions for them. Consequently, the rule sets are not tailored to a company's specific ICT network infrastructure and requirements.

Another problem, for large companies as well, are legacy systems or systems with small market shares that are part of their network infrastructures. These systems often lack proper documentation and are often no longer supported by vendors. Legacy systems are especially weakly secured, since in the past, software developers often did not give security the required attention. Legacy devices are, e.g., a problem in cyber physical systems (CPS), such as smart grids and supervisory control and data acquisition (SCADA) systems that are used to connect and control devices in the energy and manufacturing sector (Sridhar et al., 2012). Because of the lack of documentation and maintenance support, there are often no rules that can be applied for detecting attacks and invaders. But usually these systems produce some logs, and network packets can be collected for monitoring the system status and errors. Thus, flexible anomaly detection approaches are required so they can adapt to the available data and the quickly changing threat landscape and secure these systems.

One solution to solve problems, such as missing signatures, lacking vendor support, and challenges created by a quickly changing threat landscape are self-learning anomaly detection approaches. Generally, there are three methods for implementing self-learning features to build a baseline of normal system behavior that then serves as the "ground truth" (Goldstein and Uchida, 2016):

1. *Unsupervised:* This method does not require any labeled data; it is able to learn to distinguish normal from malicious system behavior during a training phase. Based on the findings, it classifies any other given data after the training is completed.
2. *Semi-supervised:* This method is applied when the training set only contains anomaly-free data and is therefore also called "one-class" classification.
3. *Supervised:* This technique requires a labeled training set containing both normal and malicious data.

These three methods do not require active human intervention during the learning process. While unsupervised self-learning is entirely independent from human influence, for the other two methods the user has to ensure that the training data is anomaly free or correctly labeled. Consequently, the previously described methods can be categorized as unsupported self-learning approaches. Using completely unsupported self-learning raises some challenges. While providing training data for unsupervised self-learning is rather easy and does not require any pre-processing of the data, these approaches might learn actual malicious system behavior as normal. Semi-supervised approaches try to avoid this problem by using anomaly-free training data. Applying these methods raises the problem of obtaining training data guaranteed to be anomaly free. Retrieving such a dataset from a running productive system is usually difficult. Also for self-learning based anomaly detection, it is true that the more information provided during the training phase the more accurately the system works later while an ICT network is monitored. Thus, supervised self-learning approaches provide the most detailed ground truth, but providing suitable training datasets for specific network environments is time and resource consuming. Consequently, the false positive rate is the lowest for AD-based IDS that apply supervised learning.

To avoid drawbacks such as learning malicious behavior as normal and vice versa, supported self-learning approaches can be applied, where also system administrators can influence the anomaly detection process. This means, e.g., that when an event occurs for the first time (therefore, not part of normal system behavior) and as a consequence is classified as anomalous, the administrator can decide whether the event comprises an anomaly or is a false alarm so the event should be considered normal system behavior in the future. Furthermore, self-learning can be used to adapt the baseline, which describes the normal behavior and keep it actual, when, e.g., new devices are added to or removed from a network or if the used software changes because of updates.

DETECTION CAPABILITIES OF IDS

The following table gives an overview of the most important statistics to evaluate the detection capabilities of any IDS. A high true positive rate (TPR) and a low false positive rate (FPR) characterize a well-performing, appropriately configured IDS according to its detection capabilities:

		Predicted Condition		
		Attack Detected	No Attack	
True condition	Attack happened	True positive (TP)	False negative (FN)	True positive rate (TPR) $$TPR=\frac{TP}{TP+FN}$$
	No attack happened	False positive (FP)	True negative (TN)	False positive rate (FPR) $$FPR=\frac{FP}{FP+FN}$$

Although anomaly detection systems that apply white-listing and self-learning are capable of detecting unknown attack patterns and adapting to changing situations, they tend to raise a high number of false alarms. A promising way to counter that problem is to establish cross-layer anomaly detection approaches. This means that information and alarms from various anomaly detection systems are combined and ranked to determine whether an anomaly occurred.

3.4.2.4 Sharing

In Section 3.4.2.2, the three methods of IDS were introduced. Since SD and SPA comprise black-listing approaches and AD implements white-listing, the points discussed in Section 3.4.1.4 are also valid for IDS. Furthermore, since AD-based IDS are especially suitable for reveal ng modern sophisticated attacks, such as APTs, a victim to such an attack can share detailed information on detected observables e.g., IoC) and the different steps the attacker carried out. A CERT can adopt this information and provide advise on which systems should be monitored in more detail or what kind of anomalies (e.g., frequency anomalies or detailed sequential anomalies, cf. Section 3.4.2.1) should be looked for, to detect the attacker in a timely manner. Based on these so-called threat intelligence (TI), organizations can configure their AD systems to monitor affected parts of their cyber infrastructure more sensitively. This could be, e.g., to specifically look for anomalies in DNS query logs, because there is a new botnet variant, and because the IP address and URL of the command and control server changes rapidly, there are no concrete signatures available that could be applied to detect this threat. Hence, organizations are advised to monitor their DNS logs more thoroughly than usual. Such a dynamic configuration of anomaly thresholds (i.e.., the sensitivity with which an AD system raises alarms) would only lead to a higher FPR for those specific parts of the organization's network, would not increase the administrative overhead for dealing with false alarms for the whole network, but would ensure a higher detection rate for actual threats. Finally, by sharing TI and tactics, techniques and procedures (TTPs), organizations can increase their cyber situational awareness and can decide where (i.e., on which systems, protocols, etc.,) they should spend their limited monitoring resources, because the more detailed they monitor and analyze log and network data, the more human resources they need to investigate whether found results are accurate alarms or false positives.

3.4.3 Ontologies

3.4.3.1 What Is an Ontology?

An ontology is a knowledge representation technique that concerns understanding and representing important concepts along with their relationship in a particular domain of interest. The term ontology was originally taken from a branch of philosophy called metaphysics, associated with studying the nature of existence. This term was adopted by researchers in the artificial intelligence (AI) field in the mid-1970s due to its recognized applicability in mathematical logics and building computational models that enable automated reasoning (Hayes, 1985). In the context of computer and information sciences, an ontology is defined as "an explicit specification of conceptualization" (Gruber et al., 1993), which formally represents the knowledge within a domain as a set of concepts and their relationships to model the domain and support reasoning of concepts. The main representational primitives used by an ontology to specify captured knowledge in the domain are:

Classes or concepts are collections or abstracted groups that can be unambiguously defined using a property shared by all its members. A concept can be anything in the domain such as description of a task, function, action, strategy, process, or classification of objects. For instance, people or system groups in the organization, departments, roles, or processes could be specified into classes or subclasses in the ontology. The subclasses can inherit the common attributes specified in their root class.

Instances or individuals are concrete objects in the domain such as people, systems, attacks, or resources. These objects represent an individual or specific system in the domain such as John, Employee01 or ERPserver03. An instance could be attached to the class to which it belongs. Instances on a technical level are also connected to assets discussed in Section 3.2.2.

Attributes or properties are mainly used to describe the relationship that may exist between classes or to attach data values. There are two types of properties: object properties and data properties. Object properties are used to represent the relations between classes such as binary relationships of subclass-and superclass. The data properties on the other hand are used to attach values and information to classes or their individual members. These values can be the raw packet features or any information extracted for the input data.

Rules and axioms are a set of statements and assertions that enable inferring implicit information based on existing facts on the knowledge. The axioms are used to model sentences that are always true.

An example of the described ontology primitives and their logical relationship is illustrated in Figure 3.8. Consider a cyber security domain where an attacker exploits an input validation vulnerability on a database server to perform SQL injection attack and steal sensitive information. In this case, main classes of [Attack, Attacker, Vulnerability, Asset, Impact] could be defined in the ontology,

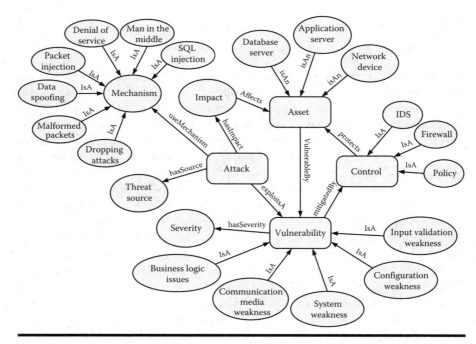

Figure 3.8 An example of ontology primitives around cyber attacks.

while subcategories such as type of attacks (e.g., database attacks, Web attacks, network-attacks) are added as subclasses of the attack class. Moreover, the SQL injection is represented an instance of the database attacks class. Therefore, the described connections between various classes are the logical relationships such as an attacker [*exploits*] a vulnerability.

3.4.3.2 Features of an Ontology (Why to Use an Ontology?)

An ontology possesses several features for knowledge engineering and modeling in the computer science field which include, but not limited to the following:

Formal representation of domain knowledge: An ontology formally represents the knowledge within a specific domain in a format that is easily understood and interpreted by machines. Therefore, machines can have better access and search capabilities on information and their semantic meaning.

Flexibility on the level of information abstraction: The represented knowledge can be flexibly expressed at various levels of granularity (abstraction) which allows better information analysis. Therefore, nonrelevant attributes can be eliminated from the information while other attributes are attached using the ontology data annotation capability. This makes it possible to construct high-level views of the overall network security and summarize anticipated activities in complex cyber attacks.

Interoperability on heterogeneous knowledge sources: An ontology enables the integration of heterogeneous information collected from different sources and in different formats. Therefore, it bridges the application gap between technical and operational knowledge. For instance, physical environment information and organizational policies may be linked to the raw data captured in the network (see Section 3.3.2). This feature may reduce the manual efforts required by analysts when investigating detected attacks and may allow eliminating false alarms that do not involve the required context.

Powerful semantic-level search and reasoning capabilities: An ontology formally represents knowledge in a machine-interpretable format and enables powerful semantic-level capabilities such as reasoning over the acquired knowledge to derive additional information or identify the logical relationships between concepts.

Extensibility and reusability: The nature of ontologies makes them eligible for reuse by different communities and possibly in different applications. An ontology usually aims at providing shared agreements of the conceptualization of a domain through a common vocabulary that can be shared and integrated by the community. This helps to reuse domain expertise and captured knowledge for automated analysis of information with less human intervention by nonexpert users.

The described features of an ontology makes it very applicable to many applications that require automated analysis of large volumes of data and attaching meaning to the terms and relations used to describe the domain. In comparison to traditional taxonomies used in the field, an ontology is a more complex but flexible solution that allows its designer to capture the knowledge of a domain and to express better relationship definitions among various pieces of information at different levels in the taxonomy. For example, taxonomies only allow limited relationship definitions of parent-child type while ontologies allow the definition of further relationships among classes on other levels. This makes it possible to link all related information even when it is located in different contexts such as mapping cyber attack scenarios, cyber physical and human knowledge, vulnerabilities, and asset information to network packet instances in the dataset.

A visualization of the ontological view on the real-life malware example (Stuxnet) is can be found in work by Kim and Lee (2015). It describes the connection between various elements used in Stuxnet attack scenario which include attacker goals, exploited vulnerabilities, assets information, and related resources.

3.4.3.3 What Are Ontologies Used For?

Ontology approaches are mainly utilized for knowledge engineering and reasoning on datasets which enable solving a particular problem in a specific domain. The powerful capabilities of ontology which include data modeling, description logics incorporation, reasoning over data, and representing information in a machine-readable format resulted in its adoption in multiple applications. In recent years, ontologies are gaining substantial popularity among researchers from different fields (Blanco et al., 2008; Dou et al., 2015; Jain and Singh, 2013; Souag et al., 2015, 2016). This includes the use of ontology for context management (Gu et al., 2004; Kabir et al., 2014; Joshi et al., 2014), incident handling (Shen et al., 2012; Mundie and Ruefle, 2012), system modeling and simulation (Walter et al., 2014) alert correlation (Sadighian et al., 2014; Liu et al., 2013), data mining (Keet et al., 2015; Ławrynowicz and Potoniec, 2016; Li et al., 2016; Yao et al., 2014), intrusion detection and security event management (Tsoumas and Gritzalis 2006), and cyber attack classification and prediction (Bhandari and Gujral, 2014; Salahi and Ansarinia, 2013; Heerden et al., 2013). A comprehensive list of 303 practical ontology examples in different domains along with their source codes and associated academic publications are available in an online Website repository (LOV4IoT)[15].

In general, the main objectives of ontologies as presented in the literature can be summarized as follows:

- To share a common understanding of concepts and information within the domain among the members of a community and software agents (machines)
- To facilitate integration and interoperability on heterogeneous knowledge sources
- To enable reuse of the domain knowledge
- To automate the analysis of knowledge in the domain

---

[15] http://www.sensormeasurement.appspot.com/index.html?p=ontologies#security_onto.

3.4.3.4 Ontology Design and Implementation

Ontology building may be considered as a crafting art rather than an understood engineering process. Different people's thoughts can result in different ontology structures. It is clear that produced ontology quality and its potential application could depend on several factors such as followed activities, available expertise in the domain, and its defined scope and role. There are five core design criteria for ontologies: clarity, coherence, extensibility, minimal encoding bias (encode the information as independent from the used symbols as possible), and minimal ontological commitment (minimize domain claims in ontology).

Furthermore, there are various methodologies for the development of ontologies that provide a set of guidelines to be used during the ontology lifecycle. Examples of the most common methodologies are TOVE[16], KBSI IDEF5[17], or Ontolingua[18]. Besides, a set of formal languages to encode the information required for the ontology model are available. Those include the Knowledge Interchange Format (KIF), the Frame Logic (Flogic), the Extensible Markup Language (XML), the Resource Description Framework (RDF), the RDF Schema (RDFS), the DARPA Agent Markup Language (DAML+OIL) or the Web Ontology Language (OWL and OWL2). Each of the referred methodologies and languages has its advantages and limitations, and it is the sole decision of the designer to choose what suits his desires.

3.4.3.5 Ontological Approaches for Cybersecurity Information Sharing

The large-scale volume of available information in the domain and its complexity make the exchange process a challenging task. Moreover, various pieces of information may be generated by different tools, systems, and sensors in different formats, which create interoperability issues when integration of these data is required.

A number of standards and initiatives have been proposed to facilitate the modeling of threat intelligence and enable cybersecurity information exchange. Common examples of these standards include the European Information Sharing and Alert System (EISAS), Common Vulnerabilities and Exposures (CVE), Common Platform Enumeration (CPE), Common Configuration Enumeration (CCE), Common Attack Pattern Enumeration and Classification (CAPEC), and the Open Vulnerability and Assessment Language (OVAL), Incident Object Description Exchange Format (IODEF), and Cybersecurity Information Exchange Framework (CYBEX). However, the adoption of different standards and formats of the represented cybersecurity information often led to isolated pieces of information and

---

[16] http://www.eil.utoronto.ca/theory/enterprise-modelling/tove/.
[17] http://www.idef.com/idef5-ontology-description-capture-method/.
[18] http://www.ksl.stanford.edu/software/ontolingua/.

caused interoperability issues. Furthermore, this issue may be more visible when attempts to integrate information from operational context or human knowledge or mapping it to technical features in the dataset is approached. For instance, the detection of some cyber attacks in many critical infrastructures may require evaluating information about the involved processes and system configurations and not to solely rely on network packet traces.

Current state-of-the-art solutions for cybersecurity event management and information exchange are mainly hampered by the large volumes of heterogeneous data to be integrated, modeled, and analyzed. Furthermore, the absence of automated approaches to deal with dynamic context information, missing data, and finding the logical connections between various pieces of information is limiting their ability in detecting modern sophisticated attacks such as Stuxnet malware. Therefore, recent research efforts toward addressing these issues and improving cybersecurity analysis and information exchange using ontology are being reported. The main advantages of ontology-based systems may include its ability in flexibly modeling big data while enable capturing and integrating contextual information, extracting the logical relationship among various information pieces, and reasoning capabilities to deal with data quality issues such as missing or bad data (Leenen and Meyer, 2015).

Takahashi and Kadobayashi (2015) proposed a reference ontology for cybersecurity operational information exchange on a global scale. The authors structured cyber information knowledge into four databases which are user resources, provider resources, incidents, and warning to be integrated and shared among different organizations. Similarly, Dandurand and Serrano (2013) proposed an approach for mapping common standards such as STIX and IODEF into ontologies to enable cybersecurity information integration and sharing. The authors concluded that the use semantic approaches can enable a more powerful sharing format and leads to improvements in decision making by security professionals. In addition, Asgarli and Burger (2016) provided an analysis on the cybersecurity data exchange requirements and proposed an ontology framework that addresses these requirements including correlating data from different domains or in different formats, automating data interpretation and sharing.

Ontology-based approaches have been also adopted in security information and event management (SIEM) platforms to enable automated analysis and sharing of information. Kotenko et al. (2013) presented the design and implementation of a hybrid ontological-relational data repository for SIEM systems which enables retrieving vulnerability information from external databases and ontologically integrate them with other information for attack modeling and security evaluation. Moreover, Kenaza and Aiash (2016) proposed the use of ontological representation for event correlation in SIEM. In this approach, an ontology is developed to represent and logically link events, vulnerabilities, attacks, contextual information and users that may be retrieved from in different formats from different sources such as IDMEF, TAXII, STIX, OVAL, and NVD.

3.4.3.6 Limitations and Research Challenges

Despite the claimed success of the ontology approach in representing and analyzing diverse cybersecurity information, some open research challenges are being reported which explain the limited use of it in practical implementations. These challenges are mainly centered (1) on the difficulty in reaching an agreed vocabulary to define different terms in the domain, (2) on how to address privacy issues when sharing sensitive information about security incidents (Denker et al., 2005), (3) on the assurance of domain experts' availability when developing the models, and (4) on the high computational requirements associated with ontology technique implementation (Wache et al., 2001). However, several researchers proposed numerous techniques to overcome these issues. First, an upper level ontology could be built to minimize the conflicts in terms definitions and to reach an acceptable agreement on a common vocabulary (Niles and Pease, 2001). Second, a unified effort from domain experts in the domain is suggested to ensure comprehensive expertise knowledge required to build a complete ontology. Considering the reusability of ontologies and possibility of multiple ontologies integration this objective seems easier to achieve. Third, the privacy concerns could be mitigated by having a top trusted authority that defines how information to be presented, processed, used, and protected (Kim et al., 2002). Finally, a distributed ontology-based architecture and distributed scalable storage (e.g., using Hadoop and Map-Reduce frameworks) is proposed to reduce the high computational requirements (Urbani et al., 2009; Jagvaral and Park, 2015). Some of these challenges, especially, privacy issues, are discussed in further details in the remaining chapters of this book.

3.5 Conclusion

Various different technical solutions are in use nowadays to detect and manage cyber incidents. While no silver bullet exists, the increasing amount and variety of low-level sensor data provides a promising source of information to detect cyber attacks reliably and timely. With the use of different analysis techniques like signature-based detection, anomaly detection, stateful analysis or ontologies, the industry tries to manage the data effectively. Still, success rates cannot live up to the expectations. While it is not sensible to aim at a replacement of all existing technologies, information sharing can be used to support the existing tools. Signatures of attacks can be shared and automatically applied to enable timelier detection of novel attack campaigns. Anomaly detection techniques still need a lot of manual analysis to understand the underlying attack but provide valuable insights when it comes to the detection of APTs or truly novel attack vectors. Finally, ontologies provide the means to identify causality between alerts rather than pure correlation. Not only is this critical to human investigators, but ontologies are also provided in a structured format that is sharable between organizations. It becomes clear that the current tools can benefit from a more collaborative approach to cybersecurity. The next chapters will therefore discuss remaining challenges and current approaches to information sharing.

List of Abbreviations

AD	Anomaly detection
AI	Artificial intelligence
APT	Advanced persistent threat
C2	Command and control
CAPEC	Common Attack Pattern Enumeration and Classification
CCE	Common Configuration Enumeration
CERT	Computer emergency response team
CPE	Common Platform Enumeration
CPS	Cyber-Physical System
CVE	Common Vulnerabilities and Exposures
CYBEX	Cybersecurity Information Exchange Framework
DMZ	Demilitarized zone
DoS	Denial of service
EISAS	European Information Sharing and Alert System
FPGA	Field programmable gateway array
FPR	False positive rate
FSM	Finite-state machine
HIDS	Host-based intrusion detection system
HMI	Human–machine interface
ICS	Industrial control system
ICT	Information and communication technology
IDMEF	Intrusion Detection Message Exchange Format
IDS	Intrusion detection system
IoA	Indicator of Attack
IoC	Indicator of Compromise
IODEF	Incident Object Description Language
MSSP	Managed Security Service Provider
NIDS	Network-based intrusion detection system
NVD	National Vulnerability Database
OS	Operating system
OVAL	Open Vulnerability and Assessment Language
PLC	Programmable logical controller
SCADA	Supervisory, control, and data acquisition
SD	Signature-based detection
SIEM	System information and event management
SPA	Stateful protocol analysis

SQL	Structured query language
STIX	Structured Threat Information Expression
TAXII	Trusted Automated eXchange of Indicator Information
TPR	True positive rate
TTPs	Tactics, techniques, and procedures
VPN	Virtual private network

References

Asgarli, E. and E. Burger. 2016. Semantic ontologies for cyber threat sharing standards. In *2016 IEEE Symposium on Technologies for Homeland Security (HST)*, 1–6, May 2016, Waltham, MA. doi:10.1109/THS.2016.7568896.

Babbin, J., ed. 2006. *Security Log Management: Identifying Patterns in the Chaos*. Rockland, MA: Syngress Publishing.

Bayer, U., P. Comparetti, C. Hlauschek, C. Kruegel, and E. Kirda. 2009. Scalable, behavior-based malware clustering. In *NDSS*, 9:8–11. San Diego, CA: Citeseer.

Bayer, U., A. Moser, C. Kruegel, and E. Kirda. 2006. Dynamic analysis of malicious code. *Journal in Computer Virology* 2(1): 67–77. doi:10.1007/s11416-006-0012-2.

Bhandari, P. and M. S. Gujral. 2014. Ontology based approach for perception of network security state. In *2014 Recent Advances in Engineering and Computational Sciences (RAECS)*, 1–6, 6–8 March 2014, Chandigarh, India. doi:10.1109/RAECS.2014.6799584.

Bilar, D. 2007. Opcodes as predictor for malware. *International Journal of Electronic Security and Digital Forensics* 1(2): 156–168. doi:10.1504/IJESDF.2007.016865.

Bittau, A. 2005. The fragmentation attack in practice. In *IEEE Symposium on Security and Privacy, IEEE Computer Society*, May 2005, Oakland, CA

Blanco, C., J. Lasheras, R. Valencia-García, E. Fernández-Medina, A. Toval, and M. Piattini. 2008. A systematic review and comparison of security ontologies. In *2008 Third International Conference on Availability, Reliability and Security*, 813–820, 4–7 march 2008, Barcelona, Spain. doi:10.1109/ARES.2008.33.

Braden, R. 1989. Requirements for internet hosts: Communication layers. STD 3. RFC Editor. http://www.rfc-editor.org/rfc/rfc1122.txt.

Bush, R. and D. Meyer. 2002. Some internet architectural guidelines and philosophy. RFC 3439. RFC Editor. http://www.rfc-editor.org/rfc/rfc3439.txt.

Canali, D., A. Lanzi, D. Balzarotti, C. Kruegel, M. Christodorescu, and E. Kirda. 2012. A quantitative study of accuracy in system call-based malware detection. In *Proceedings of the 2012 International Symposium on Software Testing and Analysis*, 122–132. ISSTA 2012. New York: ACM. doi:10.1145/2338965.2336768.

Chandola, V., A. Banerjee, and V. Kumar. 2009. Anomaly detection: A survey. *ACM Computing Surveys* 41(3): 15:1–15:58. doi:10.1145/1541880.1541882.

Chandramohan, M., H. B. K. Tan, L. C. Briand, L. K. Shar, and B. M. Padmanabhuni. 2013. A scalable approach for malware detection through bounded feature space behavior modeling. In *2013 28th IEEE/ACM International Conference on Automated Software Engineering (ASE)*, 312–322. doi:10.1109/ASE.2013.6693090.

Chen, X., J. Andersen, Z. M. Mao, M. Bailey, and J. Nazario. 2008. Towards an understanding of anti-virtualization and anti-debugging behavior in modern malware. In *2008 IEEE International Conference on Dependable Systems and Networks with FTCS and DCC (DSN)*, 177–186. doi:10.1109/DSN.2008.4630086.

Christodorescu, M., S. Jha, and C. Kruegel. 2008. Mining specifications of malicious behavior. In *Proceedings of the 1st India Software Engineering Conference*, 5–14. ISEC '08. New York: ACM. doi:10.1145/1342211.1342215.

Chuvakin, A. A., K. J. Schmidt, C. Phillips, and P. Moulder. 2013. *Logging and Log Management: The Authoritative Guide to Understanding the Concepts Surrounding Logging and Log Management.* Amsterdam, the Netherlands: Elsevier/Syngress.

Creech, G. and J. Hu. 2014. A semantic approach to host-based intrusion detection systems using contiguousand discontiguous system call patterns. *IEEE Transactions on Computers* 63(4): 807–819. doi:10.1109/TC.2013.13.

Dandurand, L. and O. S. Serrano. 2013. Towards improved cyber security information sharing. In *2013 5th International Conference on Cyber Conflict (CYCON 2013)*, 1–16, 4–7 june, Tallinn, Estonia.

Demme, J., M. Maycock, J. Schmitz, A. Tang, A. Waksman, S. Sethumadhavan, and S. Stolfo. 2013. On the feasibility of online malware detection with performance counters. In *Proceedings of the 40th Annual International Symposium on Computer Architecture*, 559–570. ISCA '13, 23–27 June, Tel-Aviv, Israel. New York: ACM. doi:10.1145/2485922.2485970.

Denker, G., L. Kagal, and T. Finin. 2005. Security in the semantic web using OWL. *Information Security Technical Report* 10(1): 51–58. doi:10.1016/j.istr.2004.11.002.

Dou, D., H. Wang, and H. Liu. 2015. Semantic data mining: A survey of ontology-based approaches. In *Proceedings of the 2015 IEEE 9th International Conference on Semantic Computing (IEEE ICSC 2015)*, 244–251, 7–9 February, Anaheim, CA. doi:10.1109/ICOSC.2015.7050814.

Droms, R. 1997. Dynamic host configuration protocol. RFC 2131. RFC Editor. http://www.rfc-editor.org/rfc/rfc2131.txt.

Droms, R. 2004. Stateless dynamic host configuration protocol (DHCP) service for IPv6. RFC 3736. RFC Editor. https://tools.ietf.org/html/rfc3736.

Forrest, S., S. A. Hofmeyr, A. Somayaji, and T. A. Longstaff. 1996. A sense of self for Unix processes. In *Proceedings 1996 IEEE Symposium on Security and Privacy*, 120–128, 6–8 May, Oakland, CA. doi:10.1109/SECPRI.1996.502675.

Frühwirt, P., P. Kieseberg, S. Schrittwieser, M. Huber, and E. Weippl. 2012. InnoDB database forensics: Reconstructing data manipulation queries from redo logs. In *Availability, Reliability and Security (ARES), 2012 Seventh International Conference on*, 625–633, 20–24 August, Prague, Czech Republic. IEEE.

García-Teodoro, P., J. Díaz-Verdejo, G. Maciá-Fernández, and E. Vázquez. 2009. Anomaly-based network intrusion detection: Techniques, systems and challenges. *Computers & Security* 28(1–2): 18–28. doi:10.1016/j.cose.2008.08.003.

Garfinkel, T., and M. Rosenblum. 2003. A virtual machine introspection based architecture for intrusion detection. In *NDSS*, 3:191–206, 6–7 February, San Diega, CA.

Gascon, H., F. Yamaguchi, D. Arp, and K. Rieck. 2013. Structural detection of Android malware using embedded call graphs. In *Proceedings of the 2013 ACM Workshop on Artificial Intelligence and Security*, 45–54. AISec '13. New York: ACM. doi:10.1145/2517312.2517315.

Gerhards, R. 2009. The syslog protocol. RFC 5424. RFC Editor. http://www.rfc-editor.org/rfc/rfc5424.txt.

Gerhards, R. and C. Lonvick. 2012. Transmission of syslog messages over TCP. RFC 6587. RFC Editor. https://tools.ietf.org/html/rfc6587.

Goldstein, M. and S. Uchida. 2016. A comparative evaluation of unsupervised anomaly detection algorithms for multivariate data. *PLoS One* 11(4): e0152173. doi:10.1371/journal.pone.0152173.

Gruber, T. R., et al. 1993. A translation approach to portable ontology specifications. *Knowledge Acquisition* 5(2): 199–220.

Gu, T., X. H. Wang, H. K. Pung, and D. Q. Zhang. 2004. An ontology-based context model in intelligent environments. In *Proceedings of Communication Networks and Distributed Systems Modeling and Simulation Conference*, 2004:270–275. San Diego, CA.

Hansen, S. E and E. T. Atkins. 1993. Automated system monitoring and notification with swatch. In *LISA*, 93:145–152, 01–05, November, Monterey, CA.

Hayes, P. J. 1985. The second naive physics manifesto. In *Computation & Intelligence*, ed. George F. Luger, 567–585. Menlo Park, CA: American Association for Artificial Intelligence. http://dl.acm.org/citation.cfm?id=216000.216035.

Heerden, R. van, L. Leenen, and B. Irwin. 2013. Automated classification of computer network attacks. In *2013 International Conference on Adaptive Science and Technology*, 1–7, 25–27 November, Pretoria, South Africa. doi:10.1109/ICASTech.2013.6707510.

ICS-CERT. 2014. ICS focused malware (update A). *ICS-ALERT-14-176-02A*. https://ics-cert.us-cert.gov/alerts/ICS-ALERT-14-176-02A.

ICS-CERT. 2016. Ongoing sophisticated malware campaign compromising ICS (update E). *ICS-ALERT-14-281-01E*. https://ics-cert.us-cert.gov/alerts/ICS-ALERT-14-281-01B.

Introduction to cisco IOS NetFlow: A technical overview. 2017. http://www.cisco.com/c/en/us/products/collateral/ios-nx-os-software/ios-netflow/prod_white_paper0900a-ecd80406232.html.

Intrusion detection system/intrusion prevention system (IDS/IPS) market (host based, network based, wireless, on-premise & cloud deployment, appliances, software, professional services): Global advancements forecasts & analysis (2014–2019). 2014. Markets and Markets. http://www.marketsandmarkets.com/Market-Reports/intrusion-detection-prevention-system-market-199381457.html.

ISO/IEC. 2011. ISO/IEC 20000-information technology: Service management. Standard 20000. International Organisation for Standardisation. https://www.iso.org/standard/51986.html.

ISO/IEC. 2012. ISO/IEC 19770-1:2012-information technology: Software asset management: Part 1: Processes and tiered assessment of conformance. https://www.iso.org/standard/56000.html.

ISO/IEC. 2015a. ISO/IEC 19770-2:2015-information technology: Software asset management: Part 2: Software identification tag. https://www.iso.org/standard/65666.html.

ISO/IEC. 2015b. ISO/IEC 38500:2015-information technology: Governance of IT for the organization. Standard 38500. International Organisation for Standardisation. https://www.iso.org/standard/62816.html.

ISO/IEC. 2016. ISO/IEC 19770-3:2016-information technology: IT asset management: Part 3: Entitlement schema. https://www.iso.org/standard/52293.html.

Jagvaral, B. and Y. T. Park. 2015. Distributed scalable RDFS reasoning. In *2015 International Conference on Big Data and Smart Computing (BIGCOMP)*, 31–34, 9–11 February, Jeju, South Korea. doi:10.1109/35021BIGCOMP.2015.7072845.

Jain, V. and M. Singh. 2013. Ontology based information retrieval in semantic web: A survey. *International Journal of Information Technology and Computer Science (IJITCS)* 5(10): 62.

John W., A. Halbardier, and D. Waltermire. 2011. NIST IR 7693-specification of asset identification 1.1. Interagency Report 7693. NIST National Institute of Standards and Technology. https://nccoe.nist.gov/publication/draft/1800-5c/#t=ITAMHowTo%2FCover%2FCover.htm.

Joshi, A., T. W. Finin, and M. L. Mathews. 2014. *System and Method for Semantic Integration of Heterogeneous Data Sources for Context Aware Intrusion Detection.* US Patent App. 14/253,569.

Kabir, M. A., J. Han, J. Yu, and A. Colman. 2014. User-centric social context information management: An ontology-based approach and platform. *Personal and Ubiquitous Computing* 18(5): 1061–1083. doi:10.1007/s00779-013-0720-9.

Karen K., and M. Souppaya. 2006. NIST SP 800-92: Guide to computer security log management. Special Publication. National Institute for Standards and Technology. http://nvlpubs.nist.gov/nistpubs/Legacy/SP/nistspecialpublication800-92.pdf.

Karen S. and P. Mell. 2007. NIST SP 800-94: Guide to intrusion detection and prevention systems (IDPS). Special Publication. National Institute for Standards and Technology. http://nvlpubs.nist.gov/nistpubs/Legacy/SP/nistspecialpublication800-94.pdf.

Karnouskos, S. 2011. Stuxnet worm impact on industrial cyber: Physical system security. In *IECON 2011-37th Annual Conference on IEEE Industrial Electronics Society*, 7–10 November, Melbourne, VIC. doi:10.1109/IECON.2011.6120048.

Keet, C. M., A. Ławrynowicz, C. d'Amato, A. Kalousis, P. Nguyen, R. Palma, R. Stevens, and M. Hilario. 2015. The data mining optimization ontology. *Web Semantics: Science, Services and Agents on the World Wide Web* 32(May): 43–53. doi:10.1016/j.websem.2015.01.001.

Kenaza, T., and M. Aiash. 2016. Toward an efficient ontology-based event correlation in SIEM. *Procedia Computer Science*, The 7th International Conference on Ambient Systems, Networks and Technologies (ANT 2016)/The 6th International Conference on Sustainable Energy Information Technology (SEIT-2016)/Affiliated Workshops, 83(January): 139–146. doi:10.1016/j.procs.2016.04.109.

Kim, A., L. J. Hoffman, and C. D. Martin. 2002. Building privacy into the semantic web: An ontology needed now. In *Proceedings of Semantic Web Workshop,* HI, USA.

Kim, B-.J. and S-.W. Lee. 2015. Conceptual framework for understanding security requirements: A preliminary study on Stuxnet. In *Requirements Engineering in the Big Data Era*, 135–146. Springer, Berlin, Heidelberg. doi:10.1007/978-3-662-48634-4_10.

Konstantinou, E. and S. Wolthusen. 2008. *Metamorphic Virus: Analysis and Detection.* Royal Holloway University of London, 15, 15 january.

Kotenko, I., O. Polubelova, A. Chechulin, and I. Saenko. 2013. Design and implementation of a hybrid ontological-relational data repository for SIEM systems. *Future Internet* 5(3): 355–375. doi:10.3390/fi5030355.

Lanzi, A., D. Balzarotti, C. Kruegel, M. Christodorescu, and E. Kirda. 2010. AccessMiner: Using system-centric models for malware protection. In *Proceedings of the 17th ACM Conference on Computer and Communications Security*, 399–412. CCS '10. New York: ACM. doi:10.1145/1866307.1866353.

Ławrynowicz, A., and J. Potoniec. 2016. Pattern based feature construction in semantic data mining. *http://Services.igi-Global.com/Resolvedoi/resolve.aspx?doi=10.4018/978-1-4666-8751-6.ch036*, 823–864. doi:10.4018/978-1-4666-8751-6.ch036.

Leenen, L. and T. Meyer. 2015. The use of semantic technologies in cyber defence. In *Proceedings of the 10th International Conference on Cyber Warfare and Security: ICCWS2015*, 170, 24–25, March, Kruger National Park, South Africa. Academic Conferences Limited.

Li, Y., M. A. Thomas, and K-. M. Osei-Bryson. 2016. Ontology-based data mining model management for self-service knowledge discovery. *Information Systems Frontiers* 19(4): 925–943, August 2017. doi:10.1007/s10796-016-9637-y.

Liao, H-. J., C-. H. Richard Lin, Y-. C. Lin, and K-. Y. Tung. 2013. Intrusion detection system: A comprehensive review. *Journal of Network and Computer Applications* 36(1): 16–24. doi:10.1016/j.jnca.2012.09.004.

Lin, T-. T. Y. and D. P. Siewiorek. 1990. Error log analysis: Statistical modeling and heuristic trend analysis. *Reliability, IEEE Transactions on* 39(4): 419–432.

Liu, Y., B-. C. Seet, and A. Al-Anbuky. 2013. An ontology-based context model for wireless sensor network (WSN) management in the internet of things. *Journal of Sensor and Actuator Networks* 2(4): 653–674. doi:10.3390/jsan2040653.

Mandiant Consulting. 2016. *M-Trends 2016*. Mandiant.

Michael, S., H. Perper, L. Kauffman, C. Irrechukwu, and D. Wynne. 2015. NIST SP 1800-5-IT asset management. Special Publication 1800-5. NIST National Institute of Standards and Technology. https://nccoe.nist.gov/publication/draft/1800-5c/#t=ITAMHowTo%2FCover%2FCover.htm.

Mundie, D. A. and R. Ruefle. 2012. Building an incident management body of knowledge. In *2012 Seventh International Conference on Availability, Reliability and Security*, 507–513, 20–24 August, Prague, Czech Republic. doi:10.1109/ARES.2012.83.

Newsome, J and D. Song. 2005. *Dynamic Taint Analysis for Automatic Detection, Analysis, and Signature Generation of Exploits on Commodity Software*. In 12th Annual Network and Distributed System Security Symposium (NDSS), 3–4 February, San Diego, CA.

Niles, I. and A. Pease. 2001. Origins of the IEEE standard upper ontology. In *Working Notes of the IJCAI-2001 Workshop on the IEEE Standard Upper Ontology*, 37–42, 4–10 August, Seattle, WA. Citeseer.

Novetta. 2016. Operation blockbuster. Unraveling the long thread of the Sony attack. https://www.operationblockbuster.com/.

Okmianski, A. 2009. Transmission of syslog messages over UDP. RFC 5426. RFC Editor. https://tools.ietf.org/html/rfc5426.

Ozsoy, M., C. Donovick, I. Gorelik, N. Abu-Ghazaleh, and D. Ponomarev. 2015. Malware-aware processors: A framework for efficient online malware detection. In *2015 IEEE 21st International Symposium on High Performance Computer Architecture (HPCA)*, 651–661, 7–11 February, Burlingame, CA. doi:10.1109/HPCA.2015.7056070.

Péter S., and P. Ferrie. 2001. Hunting for metamorphic. Symantec security response. Symantec. https://www.symantec.com/avcenter/reference/hunting.for.metamorphic.pdf.

Plummer, D. C. 1982. Ethernet address resolution protocol: Or converting network protocol addresses to 48.bit Ethernet address for transmission on Ethernet hardware. STD 37. RFC Editor. http://www.rfc-editor.org/rfc/rfc826.txt.

Raghavan, S. 2013. Digital forensic research: Current state of the art. *CSI Transactions on ICT* 1(1): 91–114.

Rahmatian, M., H. Kooti, I. G. Harris, and E. Bozorgzadeh. 2012. Hardware-assisted detection of malicious software in embedded systems. *IEEE Embedded Systems Letters* 4(4): 94–97. doi:10.1109/LES.2012.2218630.

Runwal, N., R. M. Low, and M. Stamp. 2012. Opcode graph similarity and metamorphic detection. *Journal in Computer Virology* 8(1–2): 37–52. doi:10.1007/s11416-012-0160-5.

Sabahi, F. and A. Movaghar. 2008. Intrusion detection: A survey. In *2008 Third International Conference on Systems and Networks Communications*, 23–26, 26–31 October, Sliema, Malta, Malta. doi:10.1109/ICSNC.2008.44.

Sadighian, A., J. M. Fernandez, A. Lemay, and S. T. Zargar. 2014. ONTIDS: A highly flexible context-aware and ontology-based alert correlation framework. In *Foundations and Practice of Security*, 161–177. Springer. doi:10.1007/978-3-319-05302-8_10.

Salahi, A. and M. Ansarinia. 2013. Predicting network attacks using ontology-driven inference. *arXiv:1304.0913 [Cs]*, April. http://arxiv.org/abs/1304.0913.

Santos, I., F. Brezo, J. Nieves, Y. K. Penya, B. Sanz, C. Laorden, and P. G. Bringas. 2010. Idea: Opcode-sequence-based malware detection. In *Engineering Secure Software and Systems*, 35–43. Springer, Berlin, Heidelberg. doi:10.1007/978-3-642-11747-3_3.

Santos, I., F. Brezo, X. Ugarte-Pedrero, and P. G. Bringas. 2013. Opcode sequences as representation of executables for data-mining-based unknown malware detection. *Information Sciences*, Data Mining for Information Security, 231 (May): 64–82. doi:10.1016/j.ins.2011.08.020.

Shen, H., J. Hu, J. Zhao, and J. Dong. 2012. Ontology-based modeling of emergency incidents and crisis management. In *Proceedings of the 9th International ISCREAM Conference*, Vancouver, Canada.

Souag, A., R. Mazo, C. Salinesi, and I. Comyn-Wattiau. 2016. Reusable knowledge in security requirements engineering: A systematic mapping study. *Requirements Engineering* 21(2): 251–283. doi:10.1007/s00766-015-0220-8.

Souag, A., C. Salinesi, R. Mazo, and I. Comyn-Wattiau. 2015. A security ontology for security requirements elicitation. In *Engineering Secure Software and Systems*, 157–177. Springer. doi:10.1007/978-3-319-15618-7_13.

Sridhar, S., A. Hahn, and M. Govindarasu. 2012. Cyber: Physical system security for the electric power grid. *Proceedings of the IEEE* 100(1): 210–224. doi:10.1109/JPROC.2011.2165269.

Symantec. 2016. Internet security threat report. https://www.symantec.com/content/dam/symantec/docs/reports/istr-21-2016-en.pdf.

Takahashi, T. and Y. Kadobayashi. 2015. Reference ontology for cybersecurity operational information. *The Computer Journal* 58(10): 2297–2312. doi:10.1093/comjnl/bxu101.

Tang, A., S. Sethumadhavan, and S. J. Stolfo. 2014. Unsupervised anomaly-based malware detection using hardware features. In *Research in Attacks, Intrusions and Defenses*, 109–129. Springer, Cham. doi:10.1007/978-3-319-11379-1_6.

Tankard, C.. 2011. Advanced persistent threats and how to monitor and deter them. *Network Security* 2011(8): 16–19. doi:10.1016/S1353-4858(11)70086-1.

Tsai, C-. F., Y-. F. Hsu, C-. Y. Lin, and W-.Y. Lin. 2009. Intrusion detection by machine learning: A review. *Expert Systems with Applications* 36(10): 11994–12000. doi:10.1016/j.eswa.2009.05.029.

Tsoumas, B. and D. Gritzalis. 2006. Towards an ontology-based security management. In *20th International Conference on Advanced Information Networking and Applications-Volume 1 (AINA'06)*, 1:985–992, 18–20 April, Vienna, Austria. doi:10.1109/AINA.2006.329.

Urbani, J., E. Oren, and F. Van Harmelen. 2009. RDFS/OWL reasoning using the MapReduce framework. *Science*, 1–87, University is Vrije Universiteit, Amsterdam; Faculty of Science.

Vacca, J. R., ed. 2013. *Computer and Information Security Handbook*. 2. ed. Amsterdam, the Netherlands: Elsevier/Morgan Kaufmann.

Vacca, J. R., ed. 2014. *Managing Information Security*. 2. ed. Amsterdam, the Netherlands: Elsevier/Syngress.

Van Grembergen, W. and S. De Haes. 2009. *Enterprise Governance of Information Technology: Achieving Strategic Alignment and Value*. New York: Springer.

Villeneuve, N. and J. Bennett. 2012. *Detecting APT Activity with Network Traffic Analysis*. Trend Micro Incorporated.

Wache, H., T. Voegele, U. Visser, H. Stuckenschmidt, G. Schuster, H. Neumann, and S. Hübner. 2001. Ontology-based integration of information: A survey of existing approaches. In *IJCAI-01 Workshop: Ontologies and Information Sharing*, 2001:108–117, 4–6, August, Seattle, WA. Citeseer.

Walter, T., F. S. Parreiras, and S. Staab. 2014. An ontology-based framework for domain-specific modeling. *Software & Systems Modeling* 13(1): 83–108. doi:10.1007/s10270-012-0249-9.

Wang, X. and R. Karri. 2013. NumChecker: Detecting kernel control-flow modifying rootkits by using hardware performance counters. In *Proceedings of the 50th Annual Design Automation Conference*, 79:1–79:7. DAC '13. New York: ACM. doi:10.1145/2463209.2488831.

Wheeler, D. A. and G. N. Larsen. 2003. *Techniques for Cyber Attack Attribution*. Defense Technical Information Center.

Whitman, M. E. and H. J. Mattord. 2012. *Principles of Information Security*. 4. ed., International ed. Stamford, CT: Course Technology, Cengage Learning.

Xue, Y., J. Wang, Y. Liu, H. Xiao, J. Sun, and M. Chandramohan. 2015. Detection and classification of malicious JavaScript via attack behavior modelling. In *Proceedings of the 2015 International Symposium on Software Testing and Analysis*, 48–59. ISSTA 2015. New York: ACM. doi:10.1145/2771783.2771814.

Yao, Y., X. Ma, H. Liu, J. Yi, X. Zhao, and L. Liu. 2014. A semantic knowledge base construction method for information security. In *2014 IEEE 13th International Conference on Trust, Security and Privacy in Computing and Communications*, 803–808, 24–26 September, Beijing, China. doi:10.1109/TrustCom.2014.106.

You, I. and K. Yim. 2010. Malware obfuscation techniques: A brief survey. In *2010 International Conference on Broadband, Wireless Computing, Communication and Applications*, 297–300. doi:10.1109/BWCCA.2010.85.

Chapter 4

The Importance of Information Sharing and Its Numerous Dimensions to Circumvent Incidents and Mitigate Cyber Threats[1]

Florian Skopik, Giuseppe Settanni,
and Roman Fiedler
Austrian Institute of Technology

Contents

---

[1] Parts of this chapter appeared first in "Florian Skopik, Giuseppe Settanni, Roman Fiedler: A problem shared is a problem halved: A survey on the dimensions of collective cyber defense through security information sharing. Computers & Security 60: 154-176 (2016)". Reuse with permission from Elsevier.

4.1 Introduction

The smooth operation of critical infrastructures such as telecommunications and electricity supply is essential for our society. In recent years, however, operators of critical infrastructures have increasingly struggled with cybersecurity problems (Langner, 2011). Through the use of standard information and communications technology (ICT) products and increasing network interdependencies (Rinaldi, 2004), the surfaces and channels of attacks have increased significantly. New approaches are required to tackle this serious security situation.

One promising approach is the exchange of network monitoring data and status information (Hernandez-Ardieta et al., 2013) of critical services across organizational boundaries with strategic partners and national authorities. The main goal is to create an extensive situational awareness picture (cf. Chapter 6) about potential threats and ongoing incidents, which is a prerequisite for effective preparation and assistance in large-scale incidents. Collaboration based on threat information sharing is believed to be effective in a multitude of cybersecurity scenarios (cf. Chapter 2) including financially driven cybercrimes, cyberwar, hacktivism, and terrorism (see Dacey, 2003; Denise and James, 2015). The attack morphology can be different depending on the scenario, e.g., cybercrime might use stealthy advanced persistent threats (APTs) to steal intellectual property, while cyberwar or cyberterrorism uses botnets to run distributed denial-of-service (DDoS) attacks. However, information sharing enables the victims to run coordinated and effective countermeasures and provides preventive support to potential future targets on how to effectively protect their ICT infrastructures (see NIST, 2016).

We argue that since attacks are becoming increasingly sophisticated, customized, and coordinated, we also need to employ targeted and coordinated countermeasures. Typical commercial-off-the-shelf (COTS) virus scanner and firewall systems appear incapable of sufficiently protecting against APTs (Tankard, 2011). The rapidly growing complexity of today's networks, emergence of zero-day exploit markets (Miller, 2007), and often underestimated vulnerabilities (e.g., outdated software or policies) lead to novel forms of attacks appearing daily. Thus, numerous information security platforms and knowledge bases have emerged on the Web. From there, people can retrieve valuable information about identified threats, new malware, and spreading viruses, along with information about how to protect their infrastructure (e.g., see national Computer Emergence Response Teams (CERTs)).[2] However, this information is usually quite generic, not shaped to particular industries, and often lacks in-depth knowledge.

In order to make such platforms more effective, sector-specific views along with rich information and experience reports are required to provide an added value to professional users. Many standardization bodies, including NIST (2014), ITU-T (2012), and ISO (2015), have proposed the establishment of centrally coordinated national cybersecurity centers, which are currently emerging all over the world.

However, effective cybersecurity centers are hard to establish, and often neither governmental bodies nor companies and customer organizations are well prepared to run and use them. The challenges are grounded in the fact that cybersecurity information sharing requires a great deal of multidisciplinary research. Although the setup of such systems is often reduced to addressing technical aspects, it is a similarly significant challenge for legal experts, standardization committees, and social as well as economic scientists. For example, questions dealing with the sharing-process design (i.e., who is allowed to share what and when in a corporate environment) legal dependencies and regulatory compliance, as well as what can we learn from existing implementations of CERTs, are of equal importance.

Moreover, while there are many works that deal with information sharing among CERTs, such as the European Network and Information Security Agency (ENISA, 2011a, 2013a), there is little experience so far with peer-to-peer (P2P) sharing of such information among companies (cf. Chapter 5). This is due to numerous reservations (ENISA, 2010), such as low quality information, reputational risks, and poor management. Raising awareness of these issues and providing an overview of potential solutions are two goals of this chapter.

It is therefore critical to take a closer look into all of these aspects in a structured form—from the economic motivation (and requirements) on information sharing, over legal and regulatory aspects, to structural and technological matters. Therefore, this chapter provides further insights into the following aspects:

- *A holistic picture of cybersecurity information sharing.* We shed light on the numerous economic, legal, and regulatory aspects that are often neglected.
- *Survey on existing methods, technologies, protocols and tools.* We survey existing approaches and solutions as a prerequisite to identifying open gaps.
- *Evaluation of the state-of-the-art and key findings for future systems.* We critically evaluate the current situation and emphasize likely future developments regarding standards, norms, and technologies.

The remainder of this chapter is structured as follows: Section 4.2 describes the various dimensions of cybersecurity information sharing that need to be considered. For

---

[2] http://www.cert.org; April 2016.

that purpose, we group all relevant aspects into five distinct categories. After that, relevant regulations, standards, concepts, supporting tools, and protocols that are essential for setting up effective information-sharing procedures are discussed. In particular, Section 4.3 outlines cooperation and coordination aspects and presents some sample sharing scenarios. Section 4.4 reviews existing regulatory directives and legal recommendations. Subsequently, Section 4.5 refers to well-recognized standards in this area, while Section 4.6 covers concrete implementations in terms of organizational structures. Section 4.7 deals with technologies, tools, and applicable protocols. In Section 4.8, we critically review the applicability of existing solutions in a large-scale national security information-sharing network (as set up in the context of a number of projects together with national stakeholders). Section 4.9 provides an overview of further readings; finally, Section 4.10 concludes the chapter.

4.2 The Dimensions of Information Sharing

A multitude of dimensions need to be considered in order to realize effective information sharing. In contrast to many others who primarily focus on the technical aspects, we argue that the biggest challenges are not entirely located in this area, but span the different dimensions of technical, legal, regulatory, and organizational means.[3]

In this work we made an extensive literature survey to identify a large base corpora of literature and references; we then clustered the identified references according to their main subjects. Following this strategy we took into account all the significant dimensions that holistically capture the relevant State-of-the-Art in the domain of cybersecurity information sharing only. However, other dimensions may emerge or become more important in the future.

Figure 4.1 shows the dimensions of security information sharing, which need to be considered when setting up a large-scale organizational or even national cybersecurity center:

1. *Efficient cooperation and coordination:* Real world experiences highlight the economic need for coordinated cyber defense (Gal-Or and Ghose, 2005; Gordon et al., 2003), e.g., due to increased system complexity and attack surfaces, as well as the sophistication of attacks. This coordinated cyber defense is mainly realized through information sharing. A wide variety of shared information classes is viable for a wide range of stakeholders: indicators of

---

[3] Notice that we intentionally left out social aspects, such as personal incentive and motivation to share, as well as reward and trust. These issues have been extensively studied in the literature (cf. Abrams et al., 2003; Fernandez Vazquez et al., 2012; Golle et al., 2001; Parameswaran et al., 2001; Skopik and Li, 2013) and are thus omitted here for the sake of brevity. Moreover, incentive and motivation of individuals are comparatively neglectable where sharing is either legally enforced or performed due to compliance issues.

Figure 4.1   The primary dimensions of information sharing and their concerns.

compromise (IoCs), technical vulnerabilities, zero-day exploits, social engineering attacks, or critical service outages.

2. *Legal and regulatory landscape:* However, in order to be adopted by a critical
   mass of stakeholders, information sharing requires a legal basis. Therefore,
   the European Union, some of its Member States, and the US have recently
   begun to create a set of directives and regulations.

3. *Standardization efforts:* As a further step toward enabling information sharing,
   standards and specifications must be compliant with legal requirements. NIST,
   ENISA, ETSI, and ISO—just to name a few—have already released documents
   to start this effort and will further develop existing guidelines in the near future.

4. *Regional and international implementations:* Taking these standards and specifications, organizational measures, and sharing structures need to be realized
   and integrated. Important work contributing to this step has been performed
   by CERTs and national cybersecurity centers so far.

5. *Technology integration in organizations:* Eventually, a set of sharing protocols
   and management tools on the technical layer need to be selected and set into
   operation. Here it is essential that selected technical means are compatible
   with organizational processes and can be handled appropriately.

After the full implementation of information-sharing procedures, a periodic reeval-
uation of their effectiveness (e.g., in terms of detecting and combating new and
emerging threats etc.) needs to be performed and—if necessary—certain measures
in the numerous dimensions reconsidered accordingly.

The next sections will deal with these dimensions and their concerns in detail.

4.3 Dimension I: Efficient Cooperation and Coordination

The increased presence of information technology in modern critical infrastructures has stimulated the proliferation of a significant number of new types of threats. These threats are global in nature and are shifting in focus and intensity, exploiting opportunities enabled by new technologies. Mitigation measures exist to respond to these evolving threats, but in most of the cases technological means need to be supported by cross-organizational (and even cross-border) collaboration to be effective.

4.3.1 Cyber Defense as a Joint Endeavor

International collaboration is of the utmost importance for effective response mechanisms. Indeed, digital boundaries are not clearly defined and do not correspond to national frontiers. Moreover, recent publications show that threats such as malware (and botnets, in particular) are no longer an issue that people should deal with individually but are increasingly a social and civic responsibility that affects all sectors of the digital society (Anonymous, 2012; ENISA, 2017).

According to Helmbrecht et al. (2013), response mechanisms, containing numerous established policy initiatives, have been in place from the early days of ICT development. However, the deployment of ICT solutions used by citizens in their day-to-day lives is threatened by cyber attacks, targeting areas such as online payment, e-government services, and in general every critical infrastructure relying on computer networks (refer to Chapter 2 for detailed examples). Finally, ICT is increasingly used in vandalism, terrorism, hacktivism, war, and fraud that reduce the level of confidence citizens have in trustfully adopting such technology and expose them to higher and higher danger.

Securing ICT systems within a confederation of countries needs to be coherent across geographical borders and consistently pursued over time. ENISA is the main European body aiming at improving the convergence of efforts from the different Member States by encouraging the exchange of information, methods, and results and avoiding duplication of work. To this end, one of ENISA's tasks is to support European institutions and Member States by facilitating a coordinated approach to responding to network and information security threats.

The NIST supports the coordination of existing Computer Security Incident Response Teams (CSIRTs), when responding to computer security incidents, by identifying technical standards, methodologies, procedures, and processes related to Computer Security Incident Coordination (CSIC). NIST provides guidance on how multiple CSIRTs should cooperate while handling computer security incidents and how CSIRTs should establish synergies with other organizations within a broader information-sharing community.

4.3.2 The Threat Landscape

The cyber threat landscape evolves rapidly. Innovative methods to achieve malicious objectives are constantly taking shape in cyberspace. Cyber criminals and certain nation-states are aggressively pursuing valuable data assets, such as financial transaction information, product design blueprints, user credentials to sensitive systems, and other intellectual property. Attackers are armed with the latest zero-day vulnerabilities, high-quality toolkits, and social engineering techniques to perpetrate advanced targeted attacks. These threats use several stages and vectors to duck traditional defenses and find vulnerable systems and sensitive data (FireEye, 2013).

Attacks have changed in form, function, and sophistication from just a few years ago. The new generation of threats utilizes both mass-market malware designed to infect multiple systems and sophisticated, zero-day malware to infect targeted systems. They leverage multiple attack vectors cutting across Web-, email-, and application-based attacks. Today's attacks are aimed at getting valuable data assets, sensitive financial information, intellectual property, authentication credentials, and insider information, and each attack is often a multistaged effort to infiltrate networks and spread and ultimately exfiltrate the valuable data (FireEye, 2013).

Modern cyber attackers are motivated by not only economic reasons; their actions are increasingly driven by impulses of social and political nature. International groups of associated activists and hacktivists, such as Anonymous, are nowadays well known for attacks on government, religious, and corporate websites (Olson, 2012).

EXAMPLE: LARGE-SCALE HIGH-IMPACT CYBER ATTACKS

In April 2007, Estonian government networks were harassed by a denial-of-service (DoS) attack by unknown foreign intruders, following the country's spat with Russia over the removal of a war memorial. Some government online services were temporarily disrupted, and online banking was halted. The attacks were more like cyber riots than crippling attacks and provoked outages lasting several hours or days (Herzog, 2011). In October 2010, Stuxnet, a complex piece of malware designed to interfere with Siemens Industrial Control Systems (ICS), was discovered in Iran, Indonesia, and elsewhere, leading to speculation that it was a government cyber weapon aimed at the Iranian nuclear program (Farwell and Rohozinski, 2011). On November 24, 2014, data belonging to Sony Pictures Entertainment, including personal information about Sony Pictures employees and their families, emails between employees, information about executive salaries at the company, copies of unreleased Sony films, and other information were released by hackers who called themselves the Guardians of Peace or GOP (State of California Department of Justice Office of the Attorney General, 2014). They demanded the cancelation of the planned release of the film *The Interview*, a comedy about a plot to assassinate the North Korean leader.

Refer to Chapter 2 of this book for more detailed information on how those attacks were carried out and Chapter 3 to learn which data are vital for future security analytics and information-sharing approaches to counter those attacks.

In order to develop effective defense strategies, it is necessary to understand the cyber threats and the methodologies put in place to deploy them. The components of the evolving cyber threat landscape are becoming increasingly complex. A comprehensive analysis of the reported cyber incidents is needed to characterize the multitude of aspects a cyber threat involves. Cyber threats, threat agents, attack methods, and threat trends all need to be taken into consideration. This information is useful for cybersecurity experts assessing risks to various systems and developing cybersecurity policies for defending valuable information. Nevertheless, care should always be taken when analyzing such data—the fact that an event has happened frequently in the past does not guarantee that it will continue to happen. Given that the cyber threat landscape develops very dynamically, the main challenge is to capture the trends as early as possible (cf. ENISA report, Helmbrecht et al., 2013).

Since 2014 for drive-by-exploits, there has been a shift from botnets to malicious URLs as the preferred means to distribute malware, because URLs are a more difficult target for law enforcement take-downs. Regarding code injection, a notable issue is attacks against popular content management systems (CMSs). Due to their wide use, popular CMSs make up a considerable attack surface that has drawn the attention of cyber criminals. An interesting aspect is the increased use of P2P botnets—more difficult to locate and take down. Also, the use of botnet infrastructures to mine the "virtual currency" bitcoins is an emerging trend.

After the 2013 Spamhaus attack (Arstechnica, 2013), domain name system (DNS) reflection attacks have gained popularity within the DoS attacks. Further, there is an increase in rogueware/scareware reported. One reason for this growth is the expansion of ransomware and fake antivirus distribution to mobile platforms such as Android. Cyber espionage attacks reached a dimension that went far beyond expectations (ENISA, 2013b). Several mass surveillance campaigns run by nation-states have been recently uncovered (see Clarke, 2011; Hudson, 2014), generating the indignation of the population. Identity theft led to some of the most successful attacks by abusing SMS-forwarders to commit significant financial fraud. These attacks were based on known financial Trojans (e.g., Zeus, SpyEye, Citadel) that have been implemented on mobile platforms and attack two-factor authentication. Search engine poisoning has also moved to mobile devices. These developments led to the conclusion that attackers remain one step ahead; quite often, exploiting simple and well known weaknesses can cause havoc.

Although information sharing might seem in contrast with the attitude of some nation-states performing espionage on other countries, this should not void information-sharing efforts among organizations (especially those with similar infrastructures, thus suffering from similar vulnerabilities or being potentially similarly attractive to attackers) from these countries on another layer. The key message of ENISA is to transfer knowledge from the cybersecurity community to the user groups for the purpose of strengthening cyber defense. To this end, effective information sharing, not only between security professionals, but also between all stakeholders dealing with critical ICT systems, needs to be enabled.

4.3.3 Incident Taxonomies

In order to uniquely identify and compare events, incidents, and revealed attacks, security communities have defined numerous taxonomies over the last years. Existing incident taxonomies are either specifically developed by individual CERTs (e.g., those defined by the Latvian[4] and Hungarian CERTs[5]), or universal and internationally recognized. In this section we briefly describe two of the most commonly adopted taxonomies.

One of the oldest schemas, developed at the Sandia National Laboratories, is the so called "Common Language" (Howard and Longstaff, 1998). This taxonomy defines three main terms: event, attack, and incident. An event comprises available information about a target of the attack and an action undertaken against it. When more information about it is available, such as a tool used to perform the attack, vulnerability exploited and a result of the attack, then the attack can be fully described. According to this taxonomy, an incident is described only if, along with the information about the attack, the source of the incident and the objective of the attack are known. This taxonomy is quite extensive and allows one to identify and classify incidents in detail according to several criteria. However, it can be time consuming and ambiguous; often security experts are not able to collect all the information required to fully describe an incident. This taxonomy is therefore mostly used for research purposes and theoretical considerations and as a starting point for creating custom taxonomies.

Another taxonomy worth considering is the IDEA (*Intrusion Detection Extensible Alert*) taxonomy developed within the European CSIRT Network project[6], and represented in Table 4.1. It is essentially based on the taxonomy by a Swedish CERT team (TS-CERT[7]) and is currently adopted by many European

---

[4] http://www.cert.lv/; April 2016.
[5] http://www.cert-hungary.hu/en; April 2016.
[6] http://www.ecsirt.net/; April 2016.
[7] http://www.teliasonera.com/; April 2016.

Table 4.1   IDEA Incident Classification

Category	Subcategory	Description
Abusive	Spam	Unsolicited bulk email, this means that the recipient has not granted verifiable permission for the message to be sent and that the message is sent as part of a larger collection of messages, all having a functionally comparable content
	Harassment	Discreditation or discrimination of somebody (e.g., cyberstalking, racism, and threats against one or more individuals)
	Child	Child pornography
	Sexual	
	Violence	Glorification of violence
Malware	Virus	Software that is intentionally included or inserted in a system for harmful purpose. A user interaction is normally necessary to activate the code
	Worm	
	Trojan	
	Spyware	
	Dialer	
	Rootkit	

(Continued)

Table 4.1 (Continued) IDEA Incident Classification

Category	Subcategory	Description
Recon	Scanning	Attacks that send requests to a system to discover weak points This includes also some kind of testing processes to gather information about hosts, services, and accounts. Examples: fingerd, DNS querying, ICMP, SMTP (EXPN, RCPT, …), port scanning and host sweeping
	Sniffing	Observing and recording of network traffic (wiretapping)
	SocialEngineering	Gathering information from a human being in a nontechnical way (e.g., lies, tricks, bribes, or threats)
	Searching	Google hacking or suspicious searches against site
Attempt	Exploit	An attempt to compromise a system or to disrupt any service by exploiting vulnerabilities with a standardized identifier such as CVE name (e.g., buffer overflow, backdoors, cross site scripting, etc.)
	Login	Multiple login attempts (guessing/cracking of passwords, brute force)
	NewSignature	An attempt using and unknown exploit
Intrusion	AdminCompromise	A successful compromise of a system or application (service). This can have been caused remotely by a known or new vulnerability but also by an unauthorized local access. Also includes being part of a botnet
	UserCompromise	
	AppCompromise	
	Botnet	

(Continued)

Table 4.1 (*Continued*) IDEA Incident Classification

Category	Subcategory	Description
Availability	DoS	System bombarded with so many requests (packets, connections) that the operations are delayed or the system crashes. DoS examples are ICMP and SYN floods, Teardrop attacks, and mail-bombing. DDoS often is based on DoS attacks originating from botnets, but also other scenarios exist like DNS amplification attacks
	DDoS	
	Sabotage	Outage, caused by local actions (destruction, disruption of power supply, etc.)—willfully or caused by deliberate gross neglect
	Outage	Outage, caused by Act of God, spontaneous failures, or human error, without malice or deliberate gross neglect being involved
Information	UnauthorizedAccess	Besides a local abuse of data and systems the information security can be endangered by a successful account or application compromise. Furthermore, attacks are possible that intercept and access information during transmission (wiretapping, spoofing, or hijacking). Human configuration/software error can also be the cause
	UnauthorizedModification	

(Continued)

Table 4.1 (*Continued*)   IDEA Incident Classification

Category	Subcategory	Description
Fraud	UnauthorizedUsage	Using resources for unauthorized purposes including profit-making ventures (e.g., the use of email to participate in illegal profit chain letters or pyramid schemes)
	Copyright	Offering or installing copies of unlicensed commercial software or other copyright protected materials (Warez)
	Masquerade	Type of attacks in which one entity illegitimately assumes the identity of another in order to benefit from it
	Phishing	Masquerading as another entity in order to persuade the user to reveal a private credential
	Scam	Fraud on a person by falsely gaining confidence. Prominent example is Nigerian 419 scam
Vulnerable	Open	Open for abuse, solvable preferably by patch, update, etc.–vulnerabilities apparent from Nessus and similar scans
	Config	Open for abuse, solvable preferably by configuration hardening/fixing-open resolvers, world readable printers, virus signatures not up-to-date, etc.

(Continued)

Table 4.1 (*Continued*)   IDEA Incident Classification

Category	Subcategory	Description
Anomaly	Traffic	Anomalies not yet identified as clear security problem
	Connection	
	Protocol	
	System	
	Application	
	Behaviour	
Other		Yet unknown/unidentified type of attack or attack unrecognized automatically by machine
Test		Meant for testing

CERTs. This taxonomy (see Kácha, 2014) groups incidents into eight main categories (incident classes) and 25 subcategories (incident types). Several features make this taxonomy convenient to use. The main categories are actual and universal, while the subcategories became a part of the description rather than a concrete schema for classification.

4.3.4 Sharing Scenarios

Facing the given threat landscape, there are a multitude of economic reasons for sharing (Gal-Or and Ghose, 2005; Gordon et al., 2003) in order to lower security expenses for all partners in an alliance (Phillips et al., 2002; Skopik and Li, 2013). Besides connecting organizations in a P2P manner, many national initiatives foresee (national) cybersecurity centers, which provide help and support on request, specifically to critical infrastructure providers. In this work, we identified four scenarios that in sum demonstrate the strong need for sharing and the high economic potential.

Notice that the applicability of the concepts proposed in this work is not limited to information sharing among (non-ICT) CI organizations; it rather spans a broader scope comprising ICT network service providers, cybersecurity providers, and other infrastructure providers.

4.3.4.1 Sharing Information about Recent or Ongoing Incidents

This scenario enables sharing of information on current incidents including the status of services, organizational impacts and consequences, and the attack vector (as far as known) or reasons for malfunction together with an estimation for the recovery time. This information is considered very sensitive and could possibly be used to harm the reputation of organizations; however, it is an important prerequisite for enabling mutual aid and help, issuing prewarnings, or enabling partner organizations to learn from recent incidents. In this scenario, we foresee three different use cases.

- Victim organizations report detailed information about the cyber incident to a national cyber center.
- A national cyber center informs critical-service organizations about incidents currently or recently affecting one or more of the federated organizations.
- Organizations within a confederation inform one another (especially business customers) about major service degradations due to current incidents.

Eventually, all these measures are suitable for increasing cyber situational awareness.

FURTHER INFORMATION

Compare the scenarios of Chapter 2 with the available information at different stages of an attack (cf. Chapter 3). Clearly, in different stages of an attack varying levels of information are available to different stakeholders. Connecting those parties and enabling them to exchange vital information, in an early stage to trigger timely prewarnings and in later stages to help investigations, is the key to success—and eventually a partial goal of the European NIS directive (see Chapter 7).

4.3.4.2 Sharing Information about Service Dependencies

This scenario deals with sharing static service dependencies to better predict the impact of a (potential) service degradation or outage. This is especially relevant for proper risk assessment if services from different companies depend on each other, e.g., the outage of a cloud provider has negative impact on services of other organizations that use the cloud for back-end storage. In this scenario, the consumer of the service reports about the service dependencies in the following three cases:

- Organizations report to a national cyber center about the services on which their activities depend.
- The national cyber center informs federated organizations about other organizations' services dependencies.
- Federated organizations inform one another on their services' dependencies.

4.3.4.3 Sharing Information about the Technical Service Status

In this scenario, dynamic information about the technical status of services, e.g., their availability, confidentiality, and integrity, is shared. In case of outages, predictions for the required restore time are included. This information can be used for modeling or informing dependent organizations about the service status. In this scenario the provider of the service reports about the service status in one of the following three cases:

- Organizations inform the national cyber center about the status of the services they provide.
- The national cyber center informs organizations about other organizations' service status.
- Organizations inform one another about their service status.

4.3.4.4 Request Assistance of Organizations

If an organization cannot handle a cyber incident on its own, it might request help from external experts of the national cyber center. Furthermore, a national cyber center can request help from external organizations or individuals (e.g., if certain expertise is required but not available). Eventually, a cyber center can act as a broker who connects the right people in time to tackle a cyber incident. We distinguish between two cases here:

- An organization asks for assistance from other organizations that might have dealt with similar issues in the past.
- The cyber center asks federated organizations for support for organizations facing a particular issue.

4.4 Dimension II: Legal and Regulatory Landscape

Internationally, CI cybersecurity has become a fundamental, delicate subject in the last years. The European Union and the United States are becoming increasingly sensitive to this topic, which has resulted in the release of indications and publishing strategies and the issuing of directives that regulate a secure digital environment for their Member States.

The European Commission, together with the High Representative of the Union for Foreign Affairs and Security Policy, has published a cybersecurity strategy alongside a commission directive concerning measures to ensure a high common level of network and information security (NIS) across the Union (European Commission, 2016).

In February 2013, the president of the United States signed Executive Order (EO) 13636, "Improving Critical Infrastructure Cybersecurity," and the Presidential Policy Directive (PPD)-21, "Critical Infrastructure Security and Resilience." The policies set forth in these directives will strengthen the security and resilience of critical infrastructure against evolving threats and hazards. These documents call for an updated and overarching national framework that reflects the increasing role of cybersecurity in securing physical assets. The provisions introduced by the EO, regarding the protection of CIs against cyber threats, are additionally supported by the Cybersecurity Information Sharing Act of 2015 (see The Senate of the United States, 2015), which makes it easy for companies to share personal information with the government, especially in cases of cybersecurity threats. Without requiring such information sharing, the bill creates a system for federal agencies to receive threat information from private companies. The main difference between the EO and the CISA is that:

- The EO specifically concerns the security of critical infrastructures and identifies the sharing of threat information as a necessary measures to achieve security.
- The CISA focuses only on security information sharing and should be applicable to any technology and manufacturing company.

Several smaller countries, outside the EU and the US, are currently discussing the essential aspects of Critical Information Infrastructure Protection (CIIP) to be regulated in their upcoming policies and directives. Due to resource limitations, the cybersecurity strategies being developed by Latin American countries such as Argentina, Colombia, Uruguay, and Trinidad and Tobago are mostly based on best practices and models adopted from more developed countries (see Micro and Organization of American States, 2015). According to BSA-The Software Alliance and Galexia (2015), a study providing a comprehensive overview on cybersecurity policy environment in ten Asia-Pacific markets, the markets included in the study have historically been slow to produce comprehensive national cybersecurity strategies and to implement the necessary legal frameworks for security and critical infrastructure protection. However, in order to strengthen the protection of critical infrastructure from cyber threats, in the Asia-Pacific region public and private stakeholders are now cooperating to the establishment of proper policy, legal, and operational frameworks; improve collaboration with various relevant stakeholders' communities; effectively share meaningful cybersecurity information; and prioritize the protection of critical infrastructures.

In the following we focus on the most prominent regulatory efforts and report excerpts, related to cybersecurity in critical infrastructure and information sharing, collected from the aforementioned European and American bills. Notice that these will be studied in more detail in Chapters 7 and 8 of this book.

4.4.1 EU Cybersecurity Strategy: "An Open, Safe and Secure Cyberspace"

This strategy (European Commission, 2013) clarifies the principles the European Union intends to follow with regard to cybersecurity policy within the Union and internationally. Through this document, the European Commission (EC) aims to tackle crucial challenges such as protecting fundamental rights, freedom of expression, personal data and privacy, and guaranteeing the Internet's integrity and security to allow safe access for all, supporting a multistakeholders governance approach, generating awareness on the shared responsibilities of public authorities, the private sector, and individual citizens to protect themselves, and ensure a coordinated response to strengthen cybersecurity. Several strategic priorities and actions that can enhance the EU's overall performance are identified within the strategy.

Particularly relevant for the scope of this work is the recent establishment of the NIS directive (European Commission, 2016) and the subsequently planned implementation in all European Member States. The NIS directive requires each Member State to set up a well-functioning CERT and adopt a national and international NIS cooperation plan. Sharing information and mutual assistance among the national NIS competent authorities is identified as a primary requirement for coordinating prevention, detection, mitigation, and response to cyber attacks. Private and public players in different areas (i.e., energy, transport, banking, public administration, etc.) are requested to perform appropriate risk management and share identified information with the national NIS competent authorities. Incidents with a significant impact on the continuity of core services must be reported to the same authorities that will in turn exchange this information, if necessary, with cooperating regulatory bodies and law enforcement authorities.

Another priority in this strategy is the fight against cybercrime. For this purpose, the EC is asked to support the European Cybercrime Centre (EC3) in providing analysis, intelligence, investigation of forensics, facilitation of cooperation, and creating of channels for information sharing among the competent authorities in the Member States, the private sector, and other stakeholders.

Moreover, the EC aims to develop a cyber defense policy framework to protect networks according to the Common Security and Defence Policy (CSDP) mission. Implementing dynamic risk management, threat analysis, and information sharing is a crucial objective of this mission.

In order to face the complexity of managing cyber incidents within the interconnected networks of the Union, the strategy instructs all the different involved actors (NIS competent authorities, CERTs, law enforcement, and industry) on roles and responsibilities they should take both on a national and an EU level. National governments are most suitable for carrying out prevention and response to cyber incidents and attacks and establishing contacts and networks with the private sector. At the same time, to be effective a national response requires EU-level involvement.

4.4.2 EU Network Information Security Directive

The Network Information Security Directive (European Commission, 2016) is a key component of the overall strategy and requires all Member States, key Internet enablers, and critical infrastructure operators, such as e-commerce platforms, social networks, and operators in energy, transport, banking, and healthcare services, to ensure a secure and trustworthy digital environment throughout the EU.

The directive appoints the ENISA to assist Member States and the Commission by providing expertise and advice. ENISA should ensure effective and timely information sharing between the Member States and the Commission through the establishment of a cooperation network. Within the cooperation network, a secure information-sharing infrastructure should be put in place, allowing the exchange of sensitive and confidential information. Only Member States proving that their technical, financial, and human resources and processes fulfill the high security requirements will be eligible to get access to the sharing infrastructure.

According to the Directive, early warnings should be made within the network only in the case of significantly severe incidents or risks that may affect more than one Member State and therefore require coordination of the response at the Union level. In the notification process, particular attention should be paid to preserving informal and trusted channels of information sharing between market operators and between the private and public sectors.

The Commission shall be empowered to adopt a Union NIS cooperation plan providing for:

1. A definition of the format and procedures for the collection and sharing of compatible and comparable information on risks and incidents by competent authorities
2. A definition of the procedures and the criteria for the assessment of the risk and incidents by the cooperation network

Incidents resulting in personal data breaches and the sharing of information on risk and incidents within the cooperation network should require the processing of personal data; the competent authorities shall work in close cooperation with personal data protection authorities in order to meet the objectives of public interest legitimate under Article 7 of Directive 95/46/EC.

4.4.3 U.S. White House Executive Order (EO 13636): Improving CI Cybersecurity

This Executive Order (EO) (White House, 2013a) published on February 12, 2013, strengthens the cybersecurity of CI by increasing information sharing and by jointly developing and implementing a framework of cybersecurity practices with U.S. industry partners. The EO strengthens the U.S. government's partnerships with critical infrastructure owners and operators to address cyber threats through:

1. New information-sharing programs to provide both classified and unclassified threat and attack information to U.S. companies[8]
2. The development of a cybersecurity framework. The EO directs the NIST to lead the development of a framework of cybersecurity practices to reduce cyber risks to critical infrastructure (see Section 4.5.3 for further details)

The EO requires federal agencies to produce high-informative unclassified reports of cyber threats and requires the reports to be shared with U.S. private sector entities

---

[8] The implementation of these programs has been further detailed in the Cybersecurity Information Sharing Act (CISA) of 2015, Section 103(a)(4).

in a timely manner to enable these entities to protect themselves against potential cyber attacks. Moreover, classified reports should also be generated and disseminated only to critical infrastructure entities authorized to receive them. A system for tracking the production, the dissemination, and the disposition of classified reports should be established. The EO also expands the Enhanced Cybersecurity Services program (Department of Homeland Security, 2013), enabling near real-time sharing of cyber threat information to assist participating critical infrastructure companies in their cyber-protection efforts.

The framework also assists the organizations in incorporating privacy and civil liberties as part of their cybersecurity program.

4.4.4 U.S. Presidential Policy Directive (PPD-21): Critical Infrastructure Security and Resilience

This Directive (White House, 2013b) updates the national approach on critical infrastructure security and resilience. According to this Directive, security and resilience of American critical infrastructures should be strengthened by embracing the following three strategic imperatives.

- *Imperative 1*: Refine and clarify functional relationships across the Federal Government to advance the national unity of effort to strengthen critical infrastructure security and resilience. Collaboration and information exchange between and among the federal government, critical infrastructure owners, and operators should be facilitated. As part of a redefined structure, two national critical infrastructure centers operated by the Department of Homeland Security shall be established: one for physical infrastructures and another for cyber infrastructures. They shall serve as focal points for critical infrastructure partners to obtain situational awareness and integrated, actionable information.
- *Imperative 2*: Enable effective information exchange by identifying baseline data and systems requirements for the federal government. Efficient exchange of information between governments and critical infrastructure owners and operators is essential for secure and resilient critical infrastructures. It should be enabled through timely exchange of threat and vulnerability information, as well as information allowing the development of a situational awareness capability during incidents. Requirements for data and information formats and accessibility, system interoperability, and redundant systems need to be therefore identified.
- *Imperative 3*: Implement an integration and analysis function to inform planning and operations decisions regarding critical infrastructures. Operational and strategic analysis on incidents, threats, and emerging risks should be performed at the intersection of the two national centers (as identified in

Table 4.2 Subjects Addressed in the Different EU and U.S. Regulatory Initiatives

Regulated Subject	EU CS Strategy	EU NIS Directive	US WH EO 13636	US PPD-21
Scope of the regulation	Cyberspace	CI NIS	CI cybersecurity	CI cybersecurity
Cooperation type	Public–private sector	Public–private sector	Public–private sector	Public–private sector
Coordination between entities	National and international NIS cooperation plan	ENISA coordinates and establishes cooperation network between Member States and the Commission	NIST leads the development of a framework of cybersecurity practices	DNS shall establish and operate national critical infrastructure centers
Information-sharing infrastructure	National CERT in each Member State. Stakeholders shall share info with NIS competent authorities	Info-sharing platform for exchange of sensitive information within the cooperation network	—	Two national CI centers: one for physical infrastructures and another for cyber infrastructures
Cyber defense policy	Implement risk management, threat analysis, info sharing	Union NIS cooperation plan defines risk assessment procedures	Federal agencies produce and share unclassified reports of cyber threats with CI operators in a timely manner	Operational and strategic analysis on incidents, threats, and emerging risks performed at the intersection of the two national centers

(Continued)

Table 4.2 (Continued) Subjects Addressed in the Different EU and U.S. Regulatory Initiatives

Regulated Subject	EU CS Strategy	EU NIS Directive	US WH EO 13636	US PPD-21
Format and procedure for collection and sharing information	—	Compatible and comparable information on risks and incidents shall be shared by Member States	Provide classified and unclassified threat and attack information to companies. Near real-time sharing of cyber threat information	Timely exchange of threat and vulnerability information. Identify data formats and accessibility, system interoperability, and redundant systems
Privacy	Considered but only partly addressed	Personal data protection authorities shall be involved when required	Considered but only partly addressed	—

Strategic Imperative 1). It shall include the capability to collate, assess, and integrate vulnerability and consequence information with threat streams and hazard information to aid in prioritizing assets and managing risks to critical infrastructure, anticipate interdependencies and cascading impacts, recommend security and resilience measures for critical infrastructure prior to, during, and after an event or incident, and support incident management and restoration efforts related to critical infrastructure.

The legal initiatives reviewed in the previous sections are summarized in Table 4.2. The table provides an overview on the main subjects the documents analyze. It also highlights the different approaches the initiatives suggest or demand in order to address the various issues.

4.5 Dimension III: Standardization Efforts

Official recommendations from standardization bodies such as NIST or ENISA are a valuable source of information when setting up information-sharing procedures.

4.5.1 ENISA: Proactive Detection of Network Security Incidents

ENISA carried out a study to investigate ways in which CERTs detect incidents, the tools and services they utilize for discovering malicious activities, identify good practices and recommend measures to other CERTs, and analyze the problems they face. The results of the study are presented in Proactive Detection of Network Security Incidents (ENISA, 2011b), which also offers recommendations to relevant stakeholders on what can be done to further push this process. The study has identified that CERTs are currently not fully utilizing all possible external sources at their disposal; some of them do not collect incident data about other constituencies or do not share these data with other CERTs. These and other shortcomings in the process of detection of incidents are examined in the report, both on a technical and a legal/organizational level, and for each identified shortcoming one or more recommendations are formulated. They are aimed at (1) data providers, (2) data consumers, and (3) organizations at the EU or national level.

For *data providers* key recommendations focus on suggestions on how to better reach out to CERTs, more suitable data formats, and distribution approaches as well as data quality improvement and enrichment. In order to fulfill the high-privacy constraints about shared information, *data providers* should screen potential data recipients for eligibility, establish contacts with security institutions and communities, and create an easy process of registration for clients.

To attract high-quality data sources and allow sharing of information in one of the commonly accepted ways and formats, *data providers* should adopt existing standards for sharing of incident information, use standard data transportation methods such as HTTPS, SCP, or SFTP, include in the delivered data information that would allow correlation between various sources (e.g., timestamps of events, Autonomous System Number (ASN), affected IP addresses or domain names, type of incident/exploit/malware, etc.), deliver the information to clients as soon as it becomes available, include detailed description of the methods that are used for acquiring information about incidents, and, finally, add context and classification.

For the purpose of increasing the quality of delivered data, ENISA (2011b) recommends *data providers* enrich incident information with additional meta-data and thus provide insights into observed events. In order to decrease the number of false positive classifications, strict filtering, consequent verification, and correlation of data are also suggested. According to the report, it would be moreover necessary to keep data stored for historical reference and research purposes and offline analysis while implementing data aging mechanisms to remove data from blacklists.

For *data consumers* a guide on how to acquire access to datasets is given in ENISA (2011b). The report puts forward suggestions on better integration of external feeds with internal monitoring systems, additional activities that can be performed by a CERT to verify the quality of data feeds, and specific deployments of new technologies.

According to this report, *organizations* that apply access to a data source should first select the most appropriate sources for their situation; they should then develop their own monitoring capabilities or install sensors in their networks to allow providers to gather data for the use of the service. Moreover, it is recommended that they establish relationships with security communities (e.g., with FIRST, TF-CSIRT, APCERT, etc.) to gain trust and speed up the process of verifying the eligibility to access restricted data feeds. Finally, data consumers are asked to be aware of potential legal issues concerning data sharing when applying for services that require setting up a sensor or sharing data.

With respect to best practices, *data consumers* should implement automation systems that allow the processing of incident data. These systems should therefore be able to handle data in many different formats, storing it in a database that allows offline analysis, correlation, and visualization, and integrate their own data with data from external sources. Incoming data feeds need constant verification. Therefore, *data consumers* should develop methods and criteria for assessing the quality of the data sources and verifying incident information before submitting it to database or incident handling software. Data correlation with external services is recommended in order to enrich it with additional data and filter duplicate events. If a feedback mechanism is in place, a *data consumer* should eventually use it to give data providers information to improve the quality of the service they offer.

Since a data-consuming CERT may become a data provider, data-consumer CERTs are encouraged to deploy their own monitoring mechanisms, such as sensor networks, client honeypot technologies, sandbox technologies, and passive DNS monitoring.

Finally, at the EU or national level, activities are pointed out that are aimed at achieving a balance between privacy protection and security provision needs, the encouragement of the adoption of common formats and underused technologies, and the integration of statistical incident data on a wider scale. Research is also suggested in the area of data-leakage reporting.

4.5.2 ISO/IEC27010: Information Technology—Security Techniques—Information-Security Management for Inter-Sector and Inter-Organizational Communications

This international standard (ISO, 2015) provides guidelines and general principles on how to share confidential information regarding IT security threats, vulnerabilities, and/or incidents between organizations or within a community of organizations, for example when private companies, governments, law enforcement, and CERT-type bodies are collaborating on the investigation, assessment, and resolution of serious pan-organizational and often international or pan-jurisdictional cyber attacks. The standard is designed to support the creation of trust when exchanging and sharing sensitive information, thereby encouraging the international growth of information-sharing communities.

Among the general recommendations, the standard demands the establishment of information-sharing communities. To be effective, these communities should have common interests that define the scope of the shared sensitive information. Moreover, organizational structures and management functions applying to community information security management should be clearly defined. Information exchanged within the community needs to be classified in terms of its value, legal requirements, sensitivity, credibility, and criticality to the organization. Adequate protection of shared information has to be guaranteed in a consistent manner. Where anonymity is requested, any information identifying the source of the information exchange should be removed.

To securely exchange sensitive information among the information-sharing community parties, designing, implementing, and monitoring processes to provide a secured flow of information on a timely basis is required. Information should, through this process, be disseminated to the appropriate persons, providing reasonable assurance that the information will not be used for malicious purposes or inappropriately redistributed. Secure and resilient communications between community members should also include risk knowledge and management, monitoring, and dissemination.

The greatest benefits in sharing information can be experienced by organizations operating within the same sector or with the same corporate objectives, sharing sector-specific categories of information security risk. Nevertheless, sharing information across sectors can be fruitful, either if communities are defined by geographical location or if a hierarchical structure of communities is in place.

Information-sharing communities should moreover define rules and conditions governing their operations, including objectives of the community, procedures for joining and leaving the community, obligations of community members, disciplinary and expulsion processes and criteria, rules for usage of shared information, and legal and financial obligations.

An information-exchange agreement should specify the types of information (e.g., announcements, alerts and warnings, incident handling, information requests, quality of service predictions, etc.) that may be exchanged between members of the community in order to allow the members to design and implement appropriate security measures for the sensitivity level of the shared information. Sharing too much information could be as bad as sharing too little, unless a suitable method of data filtering is utilized.

Refer to Chapter 5 to learn about concrete information-sharing communities and their individual setup and structure.

4.5.3 NIST: Framework for Improving CI Cybersecurity

As mentioned before, the EO calls for the development of a voluntary risk-based cybersecurity framework. The resulting framework (NIST, 2014),[9] created through collaboration between government and the private sector, was published on February 12, 2014, and addresses and manages cybersecurity risk in a cost-effective way based on business needs.

The framework focuses on using business drivers to guide cybersecurity activities and consider cybersecurity risks as part of the organization's risk-management processes. It consists of three parts:

1. The framework core
2. The framework profile
3. The framework implementation tiers

The *Framework Core* is a set of cybersecurity activities, outcomes, and informative references that are common across critical infrastructure sectors. It provides detailed guidance for developing individual organizational profiles. It presents industry standards, guidelines, and practices in a manner that allows for communication of cybersecurity activities and outcomes across the organization, from the executive level to the implementation/operations level. The framework core consists of five concurrent and continuous functions: identify, protect, detect, respond and recover. When considered together, these functions provide a high-level, strategic view of the life cycle of an organization's management of cybersecurity risk. The

---

[9] An updated version (Version 1.1) of this framework is being drafted and will be published by NIST in autumn 2017. Providing new details on managing cyber supply chain risks, clarifying key terms, and introducing measurement methods for cybersecurity, the updated framework aims to further develop NIST's voluntary guidance to organizations on reducing cybersecurity risks.

framework core then identifies underlying key categories and subcategories for each function and matches them with example informative references such as existing standards, guidelines, and practices for each subcategory.

Profiles are defined to help organizations align their cybersecurity activities with their business requirements, risk tolerances, and resources. A framework profile represents the outcomes based on business needs an organization has selected from the framework categories and subcategories. The profile can be characterized as the alignment of standards, guidelines, and practices to the framework core in a particular implementation scenario. Profiles can be used to identify opportunities for improving cybersecurity posture by comparing a "current" profile with a "target" profile. To develop a profile, an organization can review all of the categories and subcategories and, based on business drivers and a risk assessment, determine which are most important; they can add categories and subcategories as needed to address the organization's risks. The current profile can then be used to support prioritization and measurement of progress toward the target profile, while factoring in other business needs including cost effectiveness and innovation. Profiles can be used to conduct self-assessments and communicate within an organization or between organizations.

The *tiers* support organizations in understanding the characteristics of their approach to managing cybersecurity risk. Framework tiers provide context on how an organization views cybersecurity risk and the processes in place to manage that risk. Tiers describe the degree to which an organization's cybersecurity risk management practices exhibit the characteristics defined in the framework (e.g., risk and threat aware, repeatable, and adaptive). The tiers characterize an organization's practices over a range, from partial (tier 1) to adaptive (tier 4). These tiers reflect a progression from informal, reactive responses, to approaches that are agile and risk-informed. During the tier-selection process, an organization should consider its current risk management practices, threat environment, legal and regulatory requirements, business/mission objectives, and organizational constraints.

The framework also includes a methodology to protect individual privacy and civil liberties when critical infrastructure organizations conduct cybersecurity activities. While processes and existing needs will differ, the framework can assist organizations in incorporating privacy and civil liberties as part of a comprehensive cybersecurity program. Moreover, the framework enables organizations to apply the principles and best practices of risk management to improving the security and resilience of critical infrastructure. The framework finally provides organization and structure to today's multiple approaches to cybersecurity by assembling standards, guidelines, and practices that are working effectively in the industry today.

4.5.4 Recommendation ITU-T X.1500 Cybersecurity Information-Exchange Techniques

Recommendation ITU-T X.1500 (ITU-T, 2012) was approved in April 2011 and describes techniques to enhance cybersecurity through coherent, comprehensive, global, timely, and assured information exchange. It presents a cybersecurity information exchange (CYBEX) model and discusses techniques that can be used to facilitate the exchange of cybersecurity information. The techniques include the structured global discovery and interoperability of cybersecurity information in such a way as to allow for continual evolution to accommodate the significant activities and specification evolution occurring in numerous cybersecurity forums. The general cybersecurity information exchange model used in this recommendation consists of basic functions, listed in the following, that can be used separately or together as appropriate and extended as needed to facilitate assured cybersecurity information exchanges.

- Structuring cybersecurity information for exchange purposes
- Identifying and discovering cybersecurity information and entities
- Establishing trust and information exchange policy agreements between exchanging entities
- Requesting and responding to cybersecurity information
- Assuring the integrity of the cybersecurity information exchange

For the exchange of cybersecurity information to occur between any two entities, the exchange must be structured and described in some consistent manner that is understood by both of those entities. For the purposes of accomplishing these exchanges, cybersecurity information includes structured information or knowledge concerning the following characteristics: the state of equipment, software, or network-based systems as related to cybersecurity, especially vulnerabilities; forensics related to incidents or events; heuristics and signatures gained from experienced events; cybersecurity entities involved; specifications for the

Table 4.3 Cybersecurity-Information Exchange Groups and Corresponding Relevant Techniques, Standards, and Protocols

Group	Techniques/Standards/Protocols
Weakness, vulnerability and state	CVE, CVSS, CWE, CWSS, OVAL, XCCDF, CPE, CCE, ARF
Event, incident, and heuristics	CEE, IODEF, CAPEC, STIX
Information exchange policy	TLP
Identification, discovery, and query	OID arc, CYIQL
Identity assurance	TPM, TNC, entity authentication assurance, and extended validation certificate framework
Exchange protocol	RID, HTTPS, BEEP, SOAP, TAXII

exchange of cybersecurity information (including modules, schemas, terms, and conditions) and assigned numbers; the identities and assurance attributes of all cybersecurity information; and implementation requirements, guidelines, and practices.

As a means of describing at a general level the desired attributes of cybersecurity information exchange, the structured information capabilities are organized into six clusters of techniques for distinct cybersecurity information exchange groups. The clusters along with the corresponding relevant techniques, standards and protocols are reported in Table 4.3.

4.5.5 Overview on Information-Sharing Standardization Efforts

The standardization efforts described in the previous sections are summarized in Table 4.4. The table provides an overview on the principle matters the different documents aim to address with their recommendations.

While the ENISA report provides generic recommendations covering a wide set of matters regarding cybersecurity information sharing, the NIST framework

Table 4.4 Aspect Addressed by the Different Standardization Efforts

Recommended Matter	ENISA Report	ISO/IEC 27010	NIST Framework	ITU-T X.1500
Protection of shared information	✓	✓		✓
Cybersecurity risk management		✓	✓	
Privacy preservation in information sharing	✓	✓	✓	
Data format, protocols and standards	✓			✓
Data quality improvement	✓			
Incident handling process	✓	✓		✓

targets American (and non-American) organizations, focusing mostly on risk-management procedures and privacy-preservation aspects. The guidelines included in the ISO/IEC27010 standard and in the ITU-T X.1500 are oriented toward the protection of the data exchanged in the information-sharing process, as well as to the collection, analysis, and correlation of cyber incidents in order to obtain an effective mitigation strategy. Techniques standards and protocols for systems monitoring, threat detection, vulnerability inventory, and incident exchange are analyzed in detail in the ITU-T X.1500 document, but are also taken into account by the ENISA report and the NIST framework.

4.6 Dimension IV: Regional and International Implementations

CERTs are a vital part of every regional cybersecurity ecosystem. They collect information on new threats, maintain mailing lists to issue early warnings, and, in certain cases, provide help on request. CERT cooperation has proved to be the most effective within regions. This can be easily explained, as short travel times and overall relatively low costs stimulate more frequent personal meetings. Another important aspect is the similarity of the cultural backgrounds of the participating teams, which makes social networking easier and facilitates common projects.

However, the global nature of cyber threats calls for international collaborations. Therefore, CERTs are also internationally well connected with each other, and well-connected (national) cyber centers are emerging. These initiatives and their background are studied in this section.

4.6.1 CERTs

Asia: APCERT[10]: Formed during the first Asia-Pacific Security Incident Response Coordination (APSIRC) meeting in Japan in March 2002, with the aim of improving working relationships between CERT neighbors across national borders, APCERT is the vehicle for regional cross-border cooperation and information sharing. In February 2003, 15 CERT teams from the 12 Asia-Pacific economies accepted the APCERT agreement. APCERT aims at maintaining a trusted network of computer security experts in the Asia-Pacific region to improve the region's awareness and competency in relation to computer security incidents, enhance Asia-Pacific regional and international cooperation on information security, jointly develop measures to deal with large-scale or regional network security incidents, promote collaborative research and development on subjects of interest to its members, assist other CERTs in the region in conducting efficient and effective computer emergency response, and provide input and/or recommendations to help address legal issues related to information security and emergency response across regional boundaries.

---

[10] http://www.apcert.org; April 2016.

Europe: TERENAs TF-CSIRT[11]: Due to different interests and needs of various networks in Europe, CERT teams agreed that establishing a permanent operational European CERT coordination center would not be possible. Nevertheless, cooperation and development in certain areas are common interests for some teams. Sharing statistical data about incidents in order to observe common trends, developing a European accreditation scheme, establishing education and training, and assisting new teams are some of the main common objectives of this cooperation that led the Euro-CERT group, in May 2000, to form a task force of TERENA called TF-CSIRT.

Europe: NORDUnet CERT[12]: One of the regional CERT initiatives that aim to better coordinate incident handling and cooperation among Northern European countries is NORDUnet CERT. NORDUnet CERT performs security incident handling in cooperation with the Nordic national research networks. As NORDUnet is the Nordic Internet highway to research and education networks in Denmark, Finland, Iceland, Norway, and Sweden, NORDUnet CERT fulfills the coordination role for all the national CERTs in these countries. Each CERT operates in its own country, is independent in operation, and can be a member of international organizations (TERENA TF-CSIRT, FIRST). Nevertheless, those teams have established a network of peers that is also a "Web of Trust." NORDUnet CERT also plays a role in international contacts since it is a member of FIRST and TF-CSIRT.

South America: CLARA (Cooperation of Advanced Networks in Latin America) has established a working group, among CERTs in the region of South America and the Caribbean, to address two major security issues. The group focuses on the protection of the critical infrastructure of REDClara.[13] It also deals with the creation of security working groups in the NRENs called CLARA WG-CSIRT. With regard to this, the goals of CLARA WG-CSIRT are: (1) to establish a work framework, in terms of security, for each NREN; (2) to promote the development of new working groups dealing with security in Latin America and the region through training programs aimed at working group members; (3) to promote the exchange of data and information on related problems, incident management, etc.; (4) to promote coordinated and prompt reactions for security incidents occurring on REDClara's infrastructure and that of each NREN; (5) to build a data base of contact points responsible for security in each NREN; and (6) to cooperate with similar initiatives, such as TF-CSIRT and APCERT.

North America: USCERT (United States Computer Emergency Readiness Team)[14] in the United States, with the support of the CERT/CC team, has organized several CSIRT meetings, which brought together product vendors, security vendors, service providers, industry, academia, and government. The United States

---

[11] http://www.terena.org/activities/tf-csirt/; April 2016.

[12] http://www.nordu.net/; April 2016.

[13] REDClara is the network connecting Latin America National Research and Education Networks (NRENs) with each other and Europe. More at http://www.redclara.net; April 2016.

[14] https://www.us-cert.gov; April 2016.

government also cooperates with the sector Information Sharing and Analysis Centers (ISACs), hosting meetings limited to organizations dealing with the protection of critical national infrastructure. Specifically, the Information Technology Information Sharing and Analysis Center (IT-ISAC) is established as a trusted community of security specialists, from companies across the Information Technology industry, dedicated to protecting the Information Technology infrastructure by identifying threats and vulnerabilities to the infrastructure and sharing best practices on how to quickly and properly address them. The IT-ISAC also communicates with other sector-specific ISACs, enabling members to understand physical threats, in addition to cyber threats. Taken together, these services provide members a current and coherent picture of the security of the IT infrastructure.

4.6.2 International Cooperations

A crucial factor for successful incident handling is a well-established cooperation among countries (Herzog, 2011) and/or CERTs, respectively. These collaborations aim to better address the global character of Internet security-threat propagation. Moreover, many CERT services are strongly dependent on collaborations with other teams located in different parts of the world. Here, we briefly review the role of the Forum for Incident Response and Security Teams (FIRST) in building the international community of CERTs. Furthermore, we show some examples of sector cooperation initiatives; finally, we report two cross-regional cooperation cases: region to region cooperation and cooperation among Member States from two different regions in the same organization.

4.6.2.1 FIRST

FIRST is an organization formed in 1990 with the goal of establishing better communication and coordination between incident response teams. Today the FIRST membership consists of 286 teams across 61 countries from a variety of organizations including educational, commercial, vendor, government, and military. Membership in FIRST enables incident response teams to respond to security incidents by providing access to best practices, tools, and trusted communication with member teams. FIRST members develop and share technical information, tools, methodologies, processes, and best practices. FIRST encourages and promotes the development of quality security products, policies, and services, develops and publishes best practices, promotes the creation and expansion of incident response teams and memberships from organizations from around the world.

4.6.2.2 Sector Cooperation

A sector-specific CERT is mainly characterized by the type of constituency and the responsibilities it has. Common constituency and similar responsibilities represent incentives to cooperate; some teams, being in private or public sector, affiliate and start cooperation because of their common area of interest.

The European government CSIRTs group (EGC) is an informal group of governmental CERTs. Given the similarity in constituencies and problem sets between its members, this group aims at developing methods for incident response, taking advantage of the cooperation between its members. EGC members carry out different activities in order to reach this objective. They develop measures to deal with network security incidents, enable information-sharing and technology exchange relating to IT security incidents and malicious code threats and vulnerabilities, identify areas of specialist knowledge and expertise to share within the group, identify areas of collaborative research and development, and communicate common views with other initiatives and organizations. Moreover, EGC members cooperate with other international CERT initiatives dealing with vulnerabilities and incident management on a global scale (e.g., many EGC teams are members of FIRST and TF-CSIRT).

4.6.2.3 Cross-Regional Cooperation

Cross-regional cooperation between different teams and organizations is usually based on the exchange of knowledge and experience at physical meetings.

One example is the Central and Eastern European Networking Association (CEENet),[15] which comprises 23 national academic, research, and educational organizations from European and Asian regions. CEENet's mission is to coordinate the international aspects of the academic, research, and education networks in Central and Eastern Europe and in adjacent countries. Since there are substantial differences in ICT developments among members of this organization, sharing of information between those countries is a key element to achieving an acceptable average level of ICT security across the whole region.

Another example of cross-regional cooperation is the NATO Cooperative Cyber Defence Centre of Excellence (NATO CCD CoE). It is one of the NATO Centres of Excellence, located in Tallinn, Estonia. The Centre was established on May 14, 2008; it received full accreditation by NATO and attained the status of an International Military Organization. NATO CCD CoE, is an international military organization with a mission to enhance the capability, cooperation, and information sharing among NATO, its member nations and partners in cyber defense by virtue of education, research and development, lessons learned, and consultation. Among others, NATO CCD COE develops recommendations, manuals, and guidelines for national and international cybersecurity (see NATO Cooperative Cyber Defence Centre of Excellence, 2012; NATO Cooperative Cyber Defence Centre of Excellence, 2011; NATO Cooperative Cyber Defence Centre of Excellence, 2010).

---

[15] http://www.ceenet.org; April 2016.

4.6.3 IT Crisis Management

Some (mainly) Western countries have recently started to establish IT crisis-management centers with the purpose of addressing cybersecurity issues and generating cyber situational awareness (D'Amico et al., 2005; Jajodia et al., 2010) (refer to Chapter 6 for more information on how cyber situational awareness might be established). These centers are the main sources of information with regard to national cybersecurity for critical infrastructures. They offer expertise and advice through services available on a 24/7 basis. Besides providing information, a crisis management center must always have a reliable picture of the current IT security situation in the country. For this reason, monitoring procedures are put in place on the governmental and critical infrastructure networks. Tight cooperation with the national CERT is usually also established in order to keep close contact with national and international partners. Germany and the Netherlands have been among the first European countries deploying national IT crisis-management centers.

EXAMPLE: THE GERMAN AND DUTCH IT CRISIS-MANAGEMENT CENTERS

In the German case, a clear separation of tasks among 4 different entities is foreseen.[16] The CERT-Bund performs the computer emergency response operations; the BSI IT Situation Center carries out monitoring functions, reports alerts and early warnings, and reacts to IT security incidents; the BSI IR Crisis Reaction Center is in charge of national crisis management by resolving disruptions of the information infrastructure; finally, the Cyber Response Center cooperates with other federal agencies when necessary.

The Dutch IT crisis management operations are, instead, concentrated in a single entity called the National Cyber Security Center (NCSC).[17] The services delivered by this center are very similar to those provided by the German centers. Moreover, the NCSC plays a key role in operational coordination during an ICT crisis. It provides support in (large-scale) cyber exercises and scenarios, contributing to the development of high-level preparedness. Finally, it facilitates the ICT RE-SPONSE Board (IRB), allowing public–private partnerships to take place; meeting and cooperation processes are organized by the IRB, while an ICT crisis is occurring or is threatening the security of the country. An example of a non-European IT crisis management center is the Canadian Cyber Incident Response Centre (CCIRC).[18]

---

[16] https://www.bsi.bund.de/EN/Topics/IT-Crisis-Management/itcrisismanagement_node.html; April 2016

[17] https://www.ncsc.nl/english/; April 2016.

[18] http://www.publicsafety.gc.ca/cnt/ntnl-scrt/cbr-scrt/ccirc-ccric-eng.aspx; April 2016

4.7 Dimension V: Technology Integration into Organizations

As described in the previous section, much progress has been made recently in establishing national/governmental cybersecurity centers worldwide. All these entities are at different maturity levels and face the challenge of coordinating responses to global cyber attacks not only within national boundaries, but also at a cross-border level. Cooperation between many of these centers has led to visible results (TF-CSIRT, CEENET, North America CSIRT meeting, FIRST SIGs, and E-COAT are examples of development of best practices, code of conduct, recommendations for legislation, etc. obtained by effective collaboration of international teams; ENISA, 2006), but there are still obstacles to seamless security information exchange and sharing. Among the main problems hindering effective information sharing are technical barriers. This section highlights the state-of-the-art[19] technical platforms, tools, technology standards, and open protocols regarding security information exchange and management.

4.7.1 Open Web-Platforms and Open-Source Tools

As reported in ENISA (2013a), a number of initiatives aim to make data sharing effective among CERTs. These initiatives are developed by CERTs, NATO, or private companies and are driven by "cyber community" interests. Some initiatives have already attracted solid user communities, and they tend to be user-friendly and flexible, as they are mostly open source. On the other hand, as pointed out in ENISA (2011b), CERTs are still often focused on detecting and remedying a single incident rather than identifying and understanding larger events that encompass small individual attacks.

Even in the case of simple cyber incidents, correlation has been proven useful to gain better insight, eliminate false positives, or detect duplicates. Incident correlation is the process of comparing different events, coming from multiple sensors and data sources, in order to identify patterns and relationships, enabling the identification of events belonging to one attack or indicator of broader malicious activity. It allows for better understanding of the nature of an event, reducing the work-load needed to handle incidents, and automating the classification and forwarding of incidents that are only relevant to a particular constituency. Correlation is useful for both processing data from multiple tools on a monitored network and using multiple different external services that supply incident data.

---

[19] Notice that we left commercial products out intentionally, as it is not our goal to advertise certain products here, and thus rather survey tool/solution categories with open-source alternatives.

SIEM (Security Information and Event Management) tools are used to perform correlation on the enterprise level, by analyzing information derived from varying datasets, and are already available on the market. However, commercial solutions often come at high costs, while the open-source solutions are usually harder to manage. There is still no standard framework that defines how to get to the root cause of an incident by fully utilizing all data feeds available to a CERT/CSIRT team. Emerging solutions that enable correlation of external services that provide incident data, such as Megatron[20] or AbuseHelper,[21] are becoming available now, but are still not mature. The need for such tools is recognized by many CERTs, but they remain underemployed.

In the following section, we provide a short comparison of some of the open web-platform and open-source tools that are currently employed by CERTs and cybersecurity centers, for information sharing and data correlation.

4.7.1.1 Threat-Intelligence Sharing

It has become hard to reliably detect security breaches with only traditional signature-based methods, because today's highly sophisticated attacks aim to circumvent known signatures and exploit multiple vulnerabilities on different systems at the same time (FireEye, 2013). Therefore, organizations need to share higher-level threat-intelligence data to be able to quickly adapt their systems to new threats using machine-digestible formats that remove human delay from intelligence sharing. Some of the most popular intelligence sharing tools are here revisited and compared.

OpenIOC (Open Indicators of Compromise)[22] is an open framework for sharing threat intelligence and consists of an extensible XML schema describing the technical characteristics that define a known threat, an attack methodology or other artifacts left by an intrusion. Organizations that join the OpenIOC community get access to threat intelligence shared within a network of more than 1000 entities. In order to enable an organization to document and categorize forensics artifacts of an intrusion identified on a host or network, a simple XML schema needs to be filled in with the related information about the IoCs. Simplicity is indeed one of the biggest advantages of using OpenIOC. Further usage of OpenIOCs is straightforward, given that utilities to parse and convert XML into other formats are easy to implement. On the other hand, OpenIOC is not largely adopted outside of Mandiant products and has limited support for network-based IoCs, focusing more on file-based IoCs (refer to Chapter 3 to learn more about the various types of IoCs).

---

[20] https://www.cert.se/; April 2016
[21] http://www.abusehelper.be; April 2016.
[22] http://www.openioc.org; April 2016

The Malware Information Sharing Platform (MISP)[23] is another open-source software developed by the Belgian Defense CERT and the NATO Computer Incident Response Capability (NCIRC). MISP provides a central IoC database where technical and nontechnical information about malware and attacks are stored in a structured format. It automatically creates relations among malware, events, and attributes. It allows integration with other systems by generating IDS, OpenIOC, plain text, and XML outputs. Automatic sharing of information is enabled between trust groups, but also subcommunities can be created in order to selectively share certain data with certain parties. Finally, an automatic notification system, using PGP, is foreseen.

FURTHER INFORMATION

One of the main challenges of any type of information-sharing platform is to motivate participants to share valuable information. The MISP solves this issue in an elegant way: People can query the platform for any information about a suspicious process name, log entry, file, or hash value (and more types of information fragments)—in the background requests are transformed into hash values. However in order to do that, they also contribute. For instance, if multiple people query the platform for information on a specific process name, they mutually reinforce their suspicion, so that everyone knows others have seen a similar possibly unwanted information fragment.

4.7.1.2 Data Correlation Tools

As pointed out in ENISA (2013a), data providers are recommended to employ correlation methods to remove false positives and duplication of data. The data consumers, on the other hand, are strongly recommended to implement their own solutions for verifying datasets to help improve the quality of data before forwarding them to their constituencies. Some organizations try to implement event correlation mechanisms on both received datasets and the output generated from their own monitoring solutions, but extracting common behavior patterns and relations between incidents is no trivial task.

We reviewed the main open-source solutions for data correlation and categorized them in three different groups: generic correlation tools, SIEM tools, and tools for incident handling providing information correlation features. The main characteristics of each tool along with the input and output data type are reported in Table 4.5.

---

[23] https://github.com/MISP/MISP; April 2016

Table 4.5 Comparison between Main Open-Source Correlation Tools

Tool	Developer	Type	Input Format	Output Format	Description
SEC	Risto Vaarandi, Tallin University of Technology	Generic	Files, named pipes, standard input	Files, mails, TCP and UDP packets, etc.	Text lines are processed in order to detect certain event groups occurring in a predefined time window, according to rules defined in a configuration file
LogHound	Risto Vaarandi, Tallin University of Technology	Generic	Log files	Files	Finding frequent patterns from event log data sets with the help of a breadth-first frequent item set mining algorithm
iView	Cyberoam	SIEM	Logs and reports related to intrusions, attacks, spam and blocked attempts	Reports based on the user identity	Centralized reporting from multiple devices across geographical locations; it allows viewing information across hundreds of users, applications and protocols; it correlates the information, giving the user a comprehensive view of network activity
OSSIM	AlienVault	SIEM	Logs and information from security controls and detection systems	Summary and statistical reports related to the operation of the system threat reports provided by the community	Combines log management and asset management and discovery with information from dedicated information security controls and detection systems. This information is then correlated together to create contexts to the information not visible from one piece alone

(Continued)

Table 4.5 (Continued) Comparison between Main Open-Source Correlation Tools

Tool	Developer	Type	Input Format	Output Format	Description
Abuse Helper	CERT.FI (Finland) and CERT.EE (Estonia)	Incident handling	Incidents notifications and Internet abuse handling related information	Reports in different formats, via different transports	Aggregates Internet abuse-handling related information, retrieved via several sources, based on different keys, such as AS numbers or country codes
BGPrank	Computer Incident Response Centre Luxemburg (CIRCL)	Incident handling	Dshield, Shadowserver, Arbor ATLAS	BGP Ranking	Ranks autonomous system (AS) numbers based on malicious activities. A trust-ranking scheme is implemented based on existing dataset of compromised systems, malware C&C IP and existing datasets of the ISPs
CIF	Wes Young at REN-ISAC	Incident handling	IP addresses, domains and URLs that are observed to be related to malicious activity	Series of messages "over time" (e.g., reputation)	Combines known malicious threat information from many sources and uses that information for identification (incident response), detection (IDS) and mitigation (null route)

4.7.2 Technical Standards and Protocols

In order to achieve effective defensive actions while performing incident analysis, automated systems that assist operators need to be put in place. To cope with the growing complexity of the threat landscape, the increasing frequency at which cyber events occur, and the growing amount of data that need to be handled in cyber threat intelligence and threat-information sharing, human analysis alone is no longer sufficient. Automation is therefore becoming a fundamental asset for building defensive capabilities. Moreover, given the heterogeneous architectures, products, and systems being used as sources of data for information-sharing systems, standardized, structured threat information representations are required to allow a satisfying level of interoperability across organizations.

The exchange of information in both a human-readable and machine-parsable form has clear advantages: while basic data collection, categorization, and correlation are best performed by machines, the intelligence information generation itself is largely driven by human analysts, who perform types of analysis that are usually unsuitable for automation.

Performing a two-stage process where incident data are first automatically collected, parsed, filtered, and subsequently thoroughly analyzed by human experts to generate intelligence is essential in incident handling for critical infrastructure. This approach leverages the benefits of machine-learning methods to preliminarily process large amounts of raw data and dramatically reduces the chance of overlooking critical security information (lowering therefore the false positive rate) by employing human experts able to identify, highlight, and analyze the most relevant data.

In addition, because of the different quality of shared threat information, the intelligence analyst has to assess the fidelity based on the sources and methods adopted to generate the threat information. All these issues underline the need for structured representations of threat information that are expressive, flexible, extensible, automatable, and human readable.

An overview of the existing efforts is given in Figure 4.2 where concurrent standards are grouped into six different knowledge areas: asset definition (inventory); configuration guidance (analysis); vulnerability alerts (analysis); threat alerts (analysis); risk/attack indicators (intrusion detection); and incident report (management). The figure depicts how some standards cover different knowledge areas providing a more exhaustive service, while others are developed to be employed in a specific area. For further details on the standards analyzed in the figure, see Hernandez-Ardieta et al. (2013).

Some of the aforementioned standards define the way cyber threat information should be described; they are mostly based on the exchange of IoCs. After IoCs have been identified in a process of incident response and computer forensics, they can be shared for early detection of future attack attempts. In order to obtain a more efficient automated processing of these indicators, initiatives work to standardize

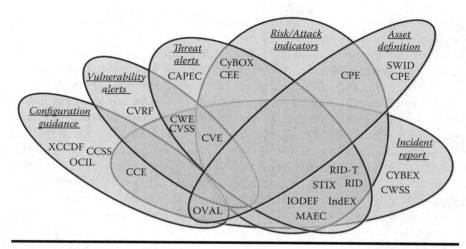

Figure 4.2   Knowledge areas covered by the different existing standards. (From Hernandez-Ardieta, J.L. et al., *2013 5th International Conference on Cyber Conflict (CyCon),* **IEEE, pp. 1–28, 2013. With permission.)**

formats for IoC descriptions. In the following, we briefly describe the two most prominent initiatives from OASIS (formerly developed by MITRE) and the IETF.

4.7.2.1 OASIS Standards: STIX, TAXII, and Others

OASIS Cyber Threat Intelligence (CTI)[24] is a technical committee of a U.S. standardization organization, which supports a number of (community-driven) efforts to design standards for security-information sharing, including noncommercial solutions for threat modeling and transport protocols. These efforts have been started by the MITRE Corporation but transitioned to OASIS in June 2015.

Structured Threat Information eXpression (STIX)[25] is a standardized language for structured cyber threat information representation. The STIX language aims at providing comprehensive cyber threat information as well as flexible mechanisms for addressing such information in a wide range of use cases. STIX's architecture comprises a large set of cyber threat information classes, including indicators, incidents, adversary tactics, techniques, and procedures, exploit targets, courses of action, cyber attack campaigns, and cyber threat actors. Existing structured languages, such as Cyber Observable Expression (CybOX), Malware Attribute Enumeration and Characterization (MAEC), and Common Attack Pattern Enumeration and Classification (CAPEC), can be leveraged to provide an aggregate solution for any single use case. Furthermore, numerous flexibility mechanisms are designed into

---

[24] https://www.oasis-open.org/committees/cti; March 2017
[25] https://oasis-open.github.io/cti-documentation/; March 2017

the language so that portions of the available features are independently usable, accounting for the relevance of a specific use case.

Trusted Automated eXchange of Indicator Information (TAXII)[26] defines a set of services and message-exchange mechanisms for the detection, prevention, mitigation, and sharing of cyber threat information across organization and service boundaries. It allows organizations to achieve improved situational awareness about emerging threats, enabling them to share subsets of information with a selected list of partners they choose. TAXII is the preferred method to securely and automatically exchange information represented in the STIX language. TAXII use cases include public alerts or warnings, private alerts and reports, push and pull content dissemination, and set-up and management of data sharing between parties. It uses a modular design that can accommodate a wide array of optional sharing models. Sharing models supported by TAXII include (but are not limited to):

- *Source-subscriber*: A single entity publishes information for a group of consumers.
- *P2P*: A group of data producers and data consumers establish direct relationships with each other. All sharing exchanges are between individuals.
- *Hub-and-spoke*: A group of data producers and consumers share information with each other. The information is sent to a central hub, which then handles dissemination to all the other spokes as appropriate.
- *Push or pull sharing*: Data consumers are automatically provided with new data (push), or the consumer can request updates at times of their choosing (pull).

FURTHER INFORMATION

STIX and TAXII are currently (January 2017) under heavy development. STIX 2 is going to be released soon with major improvements. The types of entities and their relations have been revised, as well as the underlying technology completely changed from XML to JSON. Furthermore, OASIS CTI plans to integrate STIX 2 with TAXII into one consistent standard. For most recent information, interested readers should refer to the OASIS CTI web page: https://oasis-open.github.io/cti-documentation/

---

[26] https://oasis-open.github.io/cti-documentation/; March 2017

4.7.2.2 IETF Standards: IODEF and RID

The Managed Incident Lightweight Exchange (MILE) IETF Working Group defined two main standards for describing (IODEF) and exchanging Real-time Internetwork Defense (RID) incident information. Although the current implementations of IODEF and RID are mostly limited to the technical description and local exchange of IoCs, the standards are designed to allow large-scale sharing of complex incidents.

The Incident Object Description Exchange Format (IODEF) specification described in RFC 5070 (Danyliw et al., 2007) provides an XML representation for conveying incident information across administrative domains. The data model comprises information about hosts, networks, services running on the systems, attack methodology and associated forensic evidence, the impact of the activity, and approaches for documenting the workflow.

The RID protocol described in RFC 6545 (Moriarty, 2012) was designed to transport IODEF cybersecurity information. RID is flexible enough to exchange other schemas or data models embedded in IODEF or independent of IODEF, with a transport binding using HTTP/TLS. RID is preferred for P2P models with higher levels of security and privacy.

4.7.3 Organizational Aspects of Tools Application

One should notice that with respect to tools, there is no "one size fits all" solution. Usually powerful solutions also need considerable resources to be operated, which small or medium-sized enterprise often cannot afford. On the other side, there is the strong need to secure critical infrastructures. Eventually, every organization needs to perform a careful consideration of the cost–benefit ratio.

However, in general we can conclude that some open-source solutions with a quite large user community (cf. Table 4.5) can be installed rather quickly and operated with manageable costs—even for SMEs. Regarding standards, those from IETF seem to be easier to learn and apply, whereas the OASIS standards are more complex, but also more powerful—and have a large community. Adoption of technical standards and the will to integrate them in products might be accelerated with the release of STIX 2.0 and the decision to use JSON instead of XML to model artifacts.

4.8 Review of Cyber Incident Information-Sharing Aspects

Incident information sharing is a vital effort for future infrastructures. However, quite diverse aspects need to be considered in order to implement and run effective systems; they have been addressed in this chapter. The following section sums up the most important findings, of both technical and nontechnical nature, derived from our survey, and provides recommendations for future developments.

4.8.1 *Public and Private Sector Cooperation*

European and the American regulations aim at achieving cyber resilience enhancing cooperation between public and private sectors in order to improve capacities, resources, and processes to address cyber threats in critical infrastructures. Details are provided in Chapter 7; here, we survey the most important initiatives.

The U.S. effort (White House, 2013a) points to expanding the Enhanced Cybersecurity Services (ECS) (Department of Homeland Security, 2013) information-sharing program, in order to enable near real-time sharing of cyber threat information between critical infrastructure companies and governmental entities. In particular, by implementing the CISA (The Senate of The United States, 2015), the U.S. government aims at facilitating the sharing of personal information for companies with the authorities, especially in cases of cybersecurity threats, as well as at enabling the process of notifying entities affected by malicious cyber activity. With respect to privacy, this bill includes provisions for preventing the act of sharing data known to be both personally identifiable and irrelevant to cybersecurity. These shared cyber threat indicators can be used to prosecute cybercrimes but may also be used as evidence for crimes involving physical force.

The European strategy (European Commission, 2013) intends to increase the international cooperation, (including exchanging best practices, sharing early warnings, enabling joint incident management exercises, and so on), intensifying the ongoing efforts to strengthen CIIP cooperation networks involving governments

---

FURTHER INFORMATION

The closer collaboration between private and public bodies shall be enforced by the European Cyber Security Organisation (ECSO).[27] ECSO is a fully self-financed not-for-profit organization under the Belgian law, established in June 2016. ECSO represents an industry-led contractual counterpart to the European Commission for the implementation of the cybersecurity contractual public–private partnership (cPPP). ECSO members include a wide variety of stakeholders such as large companies, SMEs and Start-ups, research centers, universities, end-users, operators, clusters, and association as well as European Member States' local, regional, and national administrations, countries part of the European Economic Area (EEA), the European Free Trade Association (EFTA), and H2020 associated countries. The main objective of ECSO is to support all types of initiatives or projects that aim to develop, promote, and encourage European cybersecurity.

---

[27] http://ecs-org.eu/ (last accessed in March 2017)

and private stakeholders. Moreover, the EU incentivizes the enhancement and subsequent exploitation of the synergies between civilian and military approaches in protecting critical cyber assets by the means of establishing research and development programs and closer cooperation among governments, private sector and academia in the EU.

No particular focus is reserved in these documents on sharing of information about vulnerabilities affecting the ICT "supply chain" itself. Legal frameworks regulating the discovery of traces of possible threats, such as the presence of hardware back doors (see Waksman and Sethumadhavan, 2011), "built-in" by IT systems manufacturers, are strongly required.

4.8.2 International Cooperation

Currently cooperation between incident-handling teams across the world occurs mainly in the form of sporadic physical meetings, conferences, mailing lists subscriptions, and the like (ENISA, 2006). However, more structured collaboration means are required to achieve tighter and more extensive cooperation. There are barriers that limit the possibilities to cooperate or even make cooperation impossible. Confidence between cooperating teams while handling sensitive information is usually prevented by international regulations that limit the exchange and usage of such information. Building a valuable level of cooperation is also a monetary issue: real life contacts between interested people are necessary, but the costs for achieving that are not always small. Team–Team cooperation is in many cases slowed down by the lack of service level agreements (SLAs) between cooperating entities; the incident-handing process, for instance, relies on tight request/response times that need to be strictly regulated by common rules. Teams working in different countries have to comply with different legal environments. This issue influences the way the teams provide their services and therefore the way they treat particular kinds of attacks (ENISA, 2003). This especially concerns international cooperation. Moreover, although CERT teams were established more than 20 years ago, there is no developed and adopted standard for CERT operations. This hugely impedes international cooperation, making the exchange of information barely possible.

Although cooperation between international stakeholders is hampered by many obstacles, it is beneficial for all sides. Cooperating international cyber incident response teams get most benefit in terms of joint incident handling, project conducting, resource and information sharing, and (social) networking.

Having an ecosystem of (international) interconnected sharing entities (critical infrastructure providers, governments, security organizations, etc.), such as the one proposed in Kaufmann et al. (2014) (and exemplarily elaborated in Chapter 9), would indeed ease the gaining of situational awareness, allowing consciousness on the current cybersecurity situation of all the monitored infrastructures. This is the initial step required to effectively perform cyber defense and incident response. Being part of such ecosystems enables the participating organizations to get access to a large amount of relevant security information that can be essential while defending against ongoing cyber threats. Best practices, resolved security issues, newly discovered vulnerabilities and any other relevant information included in this shared knowledge are fundamental for protecting the organizations' infrastructures and prevent future incidents. Eventually, coordinated incident response methods can produce more effective results, thanks to the diversity of available resources and skills within the sharing community.

4.8.3 Incident Information-Sharing Architecture

From an architectural standpoint, the European directive (European Commission, 2016) indicates the necessity for each Member State to create national CERTs that are responsible for handling incidents and national risks, interconnected with each other through a common interoperable secure information-sharing infrastructure.

The U.S. strategy (White House, 2013a), instead, foresees two national critical infrastructure centers operated by the DHS—one for physical infrastructures and another for cyber infrastructures. They are intended to work in a complementary way to serve as focal points for critical infrastructure stakeholders, in order to obtain situational awareness and integrated information to protect the physical and the cyber aspects of critical infrastructure.

Even though the aforementioned approaches both suggest a centralized architecture, a different option should also be taken into account when designing incident information-sharing architectures: P2P sharing models. From previous information-sharing research and studies (Golle et al., 2001; Parameswaran et al., 2001) emerge the strong need—from the perspective of the sharing organization—for a more reactive infrastructure layout capable of guaranteeing high responsiveness, availability, resilience, and trustworthiness. Moreover, establishing a P2P sharing infrastructure would enable ad-hoc incident response. In emergency situations (such as the case described by Shin and Gu, 2010), affected peers would be able to request tailored and anonymous security support approaching the most trusted and qualified peers in the sharing network. Having a centralized entity in charge of collecting data from the sharing parties, analyzing it, generating information about incidents, threats, and attacks, and distributing indicators back to the sharing nodes could lead to a slowly reacting architecture; moreover, the centrally collecting node would inevitably be a single point of failure.

Furthermore, private companies and organizations appear to be more willing to share sensitive information with trusted parties (Fernandez Vazquez et al., 2012; Skopik and Li, 2013) rather than with a centralized common entity. This is clearly inferred from the analysis on the cooperation between CERT teams. Although regional and international collaboration initiatives between CERTs exist and work effectively, more and more sector cooperation groups have recently been put in place (see Section 4.7). Teams tend to establish P2P collaboration infrastructures and exchange information with centers they can mutually trust (Abrams et al.,

2003; Gibson and Cohen, 2003). This type of approach, on the other hand, leads to increased value and sensitivity of the information shared and therefore requires a more secure and reliable communication infrastructure.

4.8.4 Data Collection, Information Analysis, and Intelligence Disclosure

The analysis reported in this chapter points out the necessity for cyber defense centers to consider different data-collection points when deploying their architecture. Interfaces that enable the collection of open-source intelligence information and unstructured data should be defined and employed. Situational awareness can be more readily achieved by correlating information gathered from "classic" data sources (e.g., CERTs providing reports and indicators of compromise) with OSINT information. Both the German and the Dutch cybersecurity centers examined in this work already adopt this approach and analyze both confidential and open-source information in order to continuously get an insight into current threats. Collecting large amounts of data requires, as already mentioned, more complex analysis methods and capabilities. For this reason, big data analytics techniques (Maltby, 2011) should be considered in facilitating the generation of situational awareness.

A crucial aspect to be considered, once data are collected and ready to be analyzed, is the sharing procedure. Automated sharing guarantees a high data transfer rate, but implies unsupervised transmission of information. This might raise serious liability concerns and might also be limited by regulation in international cooperative frameworks. Moreover, purely automated sharing is not favorable in certain situations, as security information might be too complex, ambiguous, or simply not fitting to any preexisting model to be shared automated (see Dandurand and Serrano, 2013). In these cases, free text reports written and read/interpreted by humans should be used. Nevertheless, to perform a comprehensive incident analysis, where possible, a combination of automated and manual information sharing should be established (see Settanni et al., 2015).

One of the main objectives of security-information sharing is to selectively warn targeted organizations about discovered bugs, vulnerabilities and threats. The process of disclosing such insights is critical and needs to be suitably designed. Reporting publicly a discovered vulnerability might expose organizations if no hot-fix or patch has been released yet. Information sharing requires trust among sharing partners, and it will not be effective if performed in a completely public manner. Complete public disclosure of sensitive security information must therefore not be applied as the first step in the sharing procedure, but a responsible disclosure should be put in place (Shepherd, 2003). As regulated by the EU NIS Directive Chapter V (European Commission, 2016), sensitive and critical information on bugs and vulnerabilities (as well as available exploits) can be disclosed to the public; however, the vendor needs to be contacted upfront to also provide a solution (bugfix, update, configuration change) together with the disclosure. Similarly, the Enhanced Cybersecurity Program, extended by the U.S. Executive Order (White House, 2013a), imposes the sharing of sensitive and classified government-vetted cyber threat information with qualified commercial service providers and operational implementers. The DHS, therefore, does not share threat indicators with CI entities directly but rather with participating CSPs.

4.8.5 Data Format and Exchange Protocols

The quality and the timeliness of the information and intelligence exchanged are of primary importance within the incident-sharing architecture among the expert centers, the organizations, the agencies, and the critical infrastructure owners and operators. Currently, sharing communities use a combination of standard and proprietary mechanisms to exchange indicators; as described in this chapter, numerous data types are exchanged using different protocols depending on the scope of the sharing system.

The European directive (European Commission, 2016) demands the Union's NIS cooperation plan provide a definition of the format and procedures for the collection and sharing of compatible and comparable information on risks and incidents by the competent authorities. Similarly, one of the U.S. PPD's goals is to enable efficient information exchange through the identification of baseline data and systems requirements, data formats, availability and accessibility, and ability to exchange various classifications of information.

The "Receipt Procedures" of the American Cybersecurity Information Sharing Act—CISA (The Senate of the United States, 2015) describe the processes for receiving, handling, and disseminating information that is shared, including through operation of the DHS Automated Indicator Sharing capability.[28] It explains that the DHS capability to receive, filter, analyze, and disseminate such information in real-time leverages STIX and TAXII specifications, along with the procedures and standards developed by the national cybersecurity centers. Any entity participating in the incident sharing capability must be able to communicate using these machine-to-machine specifications.

Moreover, the U.S. cybersecurity framework (NIST, 2014) encourages the development of standard approaches in the data exchange mechanism to incorporate successful practices to enable sharing within and among sectors. When organizations share indicators, security automated technologies should be able to detect past attacks in operational data archives, identify compromised systems and support detection of future attacks.

---

[28] Automated Indicator Sharing: https://www.us-cert.gov/ais (last accessed March 2017)

4.8.6 *Future Research and Development*

A common point highlighted in all the analyzed regulations, strategies, and international initiatives reported in the previous sections are the need for investment in innovation, research, and development. According to the EU strategy (European Commission, 2013), R&D will support a strong industrial policy, promote a trustworthy ICT industry, boost the internal market, and reduce European dependence on foreign technologies.

The U.S. POD (White House, 2013b) directs the competent authorities to develop a comprehensive research and development plan that shall provide input to align the Federal and federally funded R&D activities that seek to strengthen the security and resilience of U.S. critical infrastructures.

An exemplary implementation of this requirement is the Tallinn Manual Process (NATO Cooperative Cyber Defence Centre of Excellence, 2013). It was launched in 2009 and is a leading effort in international cyber law research and education. In collaboration with distinguished international law scholars and practitioners, the center develops programs based on two pillars: (1) a comprehensive research agenda and (2) practitioner-oriented training opportunities.

4.9 Further Readings

Cyber attacks are becoming increasingly sophisticated, targeted, and coordinated, resulting in so-called APTs (Farwell and Rohozinski, 2011; Tankard, 2011). Consequently, new paradigms are required for detecting and mitigating these kinds of attack (Virvilis and Gritzalis, 2013) and eventually to establish situational awareness (Jajodia et al., 2010; Sarter and Woods, 1991; Tadda et al., 2006). Many of these tasks are currently performed within individual organizations only, and—apart from the important works that national CERTs[29] do—there is little cross-organizational security-information sharing. However, information sharing is a crucial step to acquiring a thorough understanding of cyber attack situations and is necessary to warn others against (advanced) threats.

However, in practice, security information sharing is usually accomplished via ad-hoc and informal relationships (U.S. Homeland Security Cyber Security R&D Center, 2009). Often, national CERTs assume the role of national contact points for coordinating and aggregating security incidence reports via communication channels such as email, instant messaging, file exchange/storage, VoIP, IRC, and the Web (ENISA, 2011a). Internet forums, such as the Internet Storm Center from SANS,[30] collect and provide data about malicious activities on the Internet.

---

[29] http://www.cert.org; April 2016.
[30] http://isc.sans.org; April 2016
[31] http://www.arbornetworks.com; April 2016.

Commercial service providers, such as Arbor Networks,[31] offer networkwide threat information updates and analysis services. Usually there is a crucial economic trade-off to be considered between economic benefit of sharing (Agrawal et al., 2003; Skopik and Li, 2013) and potential disadvantages, such as harm of reputation and commitment of costly resources. The timing at which information is revealed and exchanged between the involved parties plays a crucial role in the mitigation phase, not only to an economic extent, but also with respect to the derived social costs (see Arora et al., 2008).

Cooperative cyber defense (Harrison and White, 2012; Hernandez-Ardieta et al., 2013; Zhao and White, 2012) has been studied in recent years, yet its broad adoption is still missing. In particular, sharing sensitive information among companies (Hausken, 2007) is still an unsolved issue as the risk for reputation damage is high. On the other side, several studies have shown that securing networks as a shared effort has clear economic advantages (Gal-Or and Ghose, 2005; Gordon et al., 2003). However, a major prerequisite to this is the creation of trust (Abrams et al., 2003; Golle et al., 2001; Skopik et al., 2010) among involved parties, specifically when it comes to the sharing of security-sensitive information (Fernandez Vazquez et al., 2012).

Standard bodies and the like have produced volumes about how to establish security information-sharing networks—the canonical examples being the NIST guideline "Framework for Improving Critical Infrastructure Cybersecurity" (NIST, 2014), the ENISA documents "Cyber Security Information Sharing: An Overview of Regulatory and Non-regulatory Approaches" (ENISA, 2015) and "Cybersecurity Cooperation: Defending the Digital Frontline" (Helmbrecht et al., 2013) or the ISO/IEC standard 27010 "Information technology—Security Techniques—Information Security Management for Inter-Sector and Inter-Organizational Communications" (ISO, 2015). While representing important work, these recommendations are not the complete picture, and important pieces are still missing. For instance, current recommendations largely take an architectural (and partly organizational) view of the problem and omit guidance on the operational aspects of enabling security information sharing. Little attention is given to the technologies and processes needed to maintain situational awareness for these potentially complex cyber systems.

4.10 Conclusion

In practice, security-information sharing is usually accomplished via ad-hoc and informal relationships. Often, national CERTs assume the role of a contact point for coordinating and aggregating security incidence reports. However, the information

---

[31] http://www.arbornetworks.com; April 2016.

that is provided is usually not targeted to particular vertical industry sectors. We suggest that sector-oriented views, along with rich information and experience reports, are required to make such platforms more effective. Furthermore, there is a crucial trade-off to be considered: existing platforms require information to be verified centrally (in order to avoid hoaxes); therefore, the speed of information distribution suffers. Timeliness of information is very important when protecting against aggressive attackers and zero-day exploits. Consequently, there is a need for new standards that employ suitable direct-sharing models, which allow the targeted exchange of specific information about discovered vulnerabilities of ICT systems utilized in critical infrastructure control systems, as well as current threats (such as new SCADA-targeted malware) and recent incidents. The application of these standards further implies the existence of a federated trust and reputation model to address the reservations of users and to attract a critical mass of users. This is also in line with the objectives of the recently introduced European NIS directive and its U.S. pendant. Both explicitly recommend the implementation of national cyberse-curity centers, which are not only informed about the security status of the national critical infrastructure providers but also play a coordinating role in the prevention of or protection from attacks.

List of Abbreviations

APCERT	Asia-Pacific CERT
APT	Advanced persistent threat
ASN	Autonomous System Number
CAPEC	Common Attack Pattern Enumeration and Classification
CCIRC	Canadian Cyber Incident Response Centre
CEENet	Central and Eastern European Networking Association
CERT	Computer Emergence Response/Readiness Team
CI	Critical infrastructure
CIIP	Critical Information Infrastructure Protection
CISA	Cybersecurity Information Sharing Act
CLARA	Cooperation of Advanced Networks in Latin America
COTS	Commercial off the shelf
CSIC	Computer Security Incident Coordination
CSIRT	Computer Security Incident Response Team
CTI	Cyber threat intelligence
CyBOX	Cyber Observable Expression
ENISA	European Network and Information Security Agency
EO	Executive Order
ETSI	European Telecommunications Standards Institute
FIRST	Forum for Incident Response and Security Teams
HTTPS	Hyper Text Transfer Protocol Secure (over SSL/TLS)

ICT	Information and Communication Technology
IDEA	Intrusion Detection Extensible Alert
IETF	Internet Engineering Task Force
IoC	Indicator of compromise
IODEF	Incident Object Description Exchange Format
ISO	International Organization for Standardization
ITU-T	International Telecommunication Union
JSON	JavaScript Object Notation
MAEC	Malware Attribute Enumeration and Characterization
MILE	Managed Incident Lightweight Exchange
NATO CCD CoE	NATO Cooperative Cyber Defence Centre of Excellence
NIS	The (European) Directive on Security of Network and Information Systems
NIST	(US) National Institute of Standards and Technology
PPD	Presidential Policy Directive
RID	Real-time Inter-network Defense
SCP	Secure Copy (protocol)
SIEM	Security Information and Event Management
SFTP	SSH/Secure File Transfer Protocol
STIX	Structured Threat Information eXpression
TAXII	Trusted Automated eXchange of Indicator Information
TF-CSIRT	Task Force on Computer Security Incident Response Teams
USCERT	United States Computer Emergency Readiness Team

References

Abrams LC, Cross R, Lesser E, Levin DZ. Nurturing interpersonal trust in knowledge-sharing networks. *Acad Manage Exec*, 2003;17(4):64–77.

Agrawal R, Evfimievski A, Srikant R. Information sharing across private databases. In: Proceedings *of the 2003 ACM SIGMOD International Conference on Management of Data*. ACM; San Diego, CA, June 9-12, 2003. pp. 86–97. ISBN 1-58113-634-X.

Anonymous. Port scanning/0 using insecure embedded devices. 2012. http://internetcensus2012.bitbucket.org/paper.html [accessed April 2016].

Arora A, Telang R, Xu H. Optimal policy for software vulnerability disclosure. *Manage Sci*, 2008;54(4):642–56.

Arstechnica. Spamhaus DDoS grows to internet-threatening size. 2013. http://arstechnica.com/security/2013/03/spamhaus-ddos-grows-to-internet-threatening-size/ [accessed April 2016].

BSA-The Software Alliance and Galexia. Asia-pacific cybersecurity dashboard—A path to a secure global cyberspace. 2015. http://www.bsa.org/APACcybersecurity [accessed April 2016].

Clarke R. China cyberassault on America. *Wall Street J*, June 15, 2011.

Dacey R. Homeland security: Information sharing responsibilities, challenges, and key management issues. US General Accounting Office. 2003. https://books.google.at/books?id=R2n-PQAACAAJ [accessed April 2016].

D'Amico A, Whitley K, Tesone D, O'Brien B, Roth E. Achieving cyber defense situational awareness: A cognitive task analysis of information assurance analysts. In: *Proceedings of the Human Factors and Ergonomics Society Annual Meeting*, vol. 49. SAGE Publications; Orlando, FL, September 26–30, 2005. pp. 229–33.

Dandurand L, Serrano O. Towards improved cyber security information sharing. In: *Proceedings of 5th International Conference on Cyber Conflict*. CyCon 2013, Tallinn, Estonia, June 4–7, 2013. pp. 1–16. IEEE 2013, ISBN 978-1-4799-0450-1.

Danyliw R, Meijer J, Demchenko Y. Rfc 5070: The incident object description exchange format (IODEF). 2007. http://www.ietf.org/rfc/rfc5070.txt [accessed April 2016].

Denise Z, James L. Cyber threat information sharing. 2015. Department of Homeland Security. Enhanced cybersecurity services program. 2013. http://www.dhs.gov/sites/default/files/publications/ecs_final_factsheet_08182014.pdf [accessed April 2016].

ENISA. CSIRT legal handbook. 2003. https://www.enisa.europa.eu [accessed April 2016].

ENISA. CERT cooperation and its further facilitation by relevant stakeholders. 2006. https://www.enisa.europa.eu [accessed April 2016].

ENISA. Incentives and challenges to information sharing. 2010. https://www.enisa.europa.eu/news/enisa-news/incentives-challenges-for-cyber-security-information-sharing-in-europe-identified [accessed April 2016].

ENISA. Practical guide/roadmap for a suitable channel for secure communication: secure communication with the CERTs and other stakeholders. 2011a.

ENISA. Proactive detection of network security incidents. 2011b. https://www.enisa.europa.eu/activities/cert/support/proactive-detection/survey-analysis [accessed April 2016].

ENISA. Detect, share, protect—Solutions for improving threat data exchange among CERTs. 2013a. https://www.enisa.europa.eu/activities/cert/support/data-sharing/detect-share-protect-solutions-for-improving-threat-data-exchange-among-certs/at_download/full-Report [accessed April 2016].

ENISA. Flash note: Can recent attacks really threaten internet availability? 2013b. https://www.enisa.europa.eu/publications/info-notes/flash-note-can-recent-attacks-really-threaten-internet-availability [accessed April 12, 2013].

ENISA. Enisa threat landscape 2016. February 2017. https://www.enisa.europa.eu/publications/enisa-threat-landscape-report-2016.

ENISA, Cyber security information sharing: An overview of regulatory and non-regulatory approaches. 2015. https://www.enisa.europa.eu/publications/cybersecurity-information-sharing [accessed April 2016].

European Commission. Cybersecurity strategy of the European Union: An open, safe and secure cyberspace. 2013. http://eeas.europa.eu/policies/eu-cyber-security/cybsec_comm_en.pdf [accessed April 2016].

European Commission. Directive (EU) 2016/1148 of the European Parliament and of the Council of 6 July 2016 concerning measures for a high common level of security of network and information systems across the Union. 2016. http://eur-lex.europa.eu/legal-content/EN/TXT/?uri=uriserv:OJ.L_.2016.194.01.0001.01.ENG&toc=OJ:L:2016:194:TOC [accessed February 2017].

Farwell JP, Rohozinski R. Stuxnet and the future of cyber war. *Survival (Lond)*, 2011;53(1):23–40.

Fernandez Vazquez D, Pastor Acosta O, Brown S, Reid E, Spirito C. Conceptual framework for cyber defense information sharing within trust relationships. In: *2012 4th International Conference on Cyber Conflict (CYCON)*. IEEE; CyCon 2012, Tallinn, Estonia, June 5–8, 2012. pp. 1–17. ISBN 978-1-4673-1270-7.

FireEye. Advanced targeted attacks. How to protect against the next generation of cyber attacks. White Paper. 2013. http://www.exebridge.com/landing%20pages/FireEye/docs/Exebridge-Advanced-Targeted-Attacks-White-Paper.pdf [accessed April 2016].

Gal-Or E, Ghose A. The economic incentives for sharing security information. *Inform Syst Res* 2005;16(2):186–208.

Gibson CB, Cohen SG. *Virtual Teams That Work: Creating Conditions for Virtual Team Effectiveness*. John Wiley & Sons; 2003.

Golle P, Leyton-Brown K, Mironov I, Lillibridge M. Incentives for sharing in peer-to-peer networks. In: *Electronic Commerce*. Springer; Tampa, FL, October 14–17, 2001. pp. 75–87. http://dl.acm.org/citation.cfm?id=501193

Gordon LA, Loeb MP, Lucyshyn W. Sharing information on computer systems security: An economic analysis. *J Account Public Policy*, 2003;22(6):461–85.

Harrison K, White G. Information sharing requirements and framework needed for community cyber incident detection and response. In: *2012 IEEE Conference on Technologies for Homeland Security (HST)*. IEEE; 2012. pp. 463–9.

Hausken K. Information sharing among firms and cyber attacks. *J Acc. Public Policy*, 2007;26(6):639–88.

Helmbrecht U, Purser S, Cooper G, Ikonomou D, Marinos L, Ouzounis E. et al. ENISA: Cybersecurity cooperation: Defending the digital frontline. October 18, 2013. https://www.enisa.europa.eu/publications/cybersecurity-cooperation-defending-the-digital-frontline.

Hernandez-Ardieta JL, Tapiador JE, Suarez-Tangil G. Information sharing models for cooperative cyber defence. In: *2013 5th International Conference on Cyber Conflict (CyCon)*. IEEE; 2013. pp. 1–28.

Herzog S. Revisiting the Estonian cyber attacks: Digital threats and multinational responses. *J Strateg Secur* 2011;4(2):4.

Howard JD, Longstaff TA. A common language for computer security incidents. Sandia National Laboratories; 1998.

Hudson A. Top German spy says Berlin under cyber attack from other states. Reuters; November 2014.

ISO. ISO/IEC27010: Information technology—Security techniques—Information security management for inter-sector and inter-organizational communications. 2015. November 10, 2015.

ITU-T. Recommendation ITU-T x.1500 cybersecurity information exchange techniques. 2012.

Jajodia S, Liu P, Swarup V, Wang C. *Cyber Situational Awareness: Issues and Research*, vol. 14. Springer; 2010. http://www.springer.com/de/book/9781441901392.

Kácha P. Idea: Security event taxonomy mapping. In: *18th International Conference on Circuits, Systems, Communications and Computers*. Santorini Island, Greece, Jul 17–21, 2014.

Kaufmann H, Hutter R, Skopik F, Mantere M. A structural design for a pan-European early warning system for critical infrastructures. In: *Elektrotechnik und informationstechnik*. Springer; 2014.

Langner R. Stuxnet: Dissecting a cyberwarfare weapon. *IEEE Secur Privacy*, 2011;9(3):49–51.

Maltby D. Big data analytics. In: Communication and information in society, technology and work, vol. 48. ASIST; 2011. Proceedings of the 74th ASIS&T Annual Meeting. Bridging the Gulf: Communication and Information in Society, Technology, and Work, New Orleans, LA, October 9–12, 2011. https://www.asist.org/events/annual-meeting/past/.

Micro T, Organization of American States. Report on cybersecurity and critical infrastructure in the Americas. 2015.

Miller C. The legitimate vulnerability market: The secretive world of 0-day exploit sales. In: *Proceedings of the Workshop on the Economics of Information Security (WEIS)*. Pittsburgh, PA, June 7– 8, 2007. pp. 1–10.

Moriarty K. Rfc 6545: real-time inter-network defense (RID), 2012. http://www.ietf.org/rfc/rfc6545.txt accessed April 2016].

NATO Cooperative Cyber Defence Centre of Excellence. International cyber incidents—Legal consideration. 2010.

NATO Cooperative Cyber Defence Centre of Excellence. Strategic cyber security. 2011.

NATO Cooperative Cyber Defence Centre of Excellence. National cyber security—Framework manual. 2012.

NATO Cooperative Cyber Defence Centre of Excellence. Tallinn manual on the international law applicable to cyber warfare. 2013.

NIST. Framework for improving critical infrastructure cybersecurity, Version 1.0, February 12, 2014. https://www.nist.gov/sites/default/files/documents/cyberframework/cyber-security-framework-021214.pdf.

NIST. Guide to cyber threat information sharing. NIST special publication 800-150. October 2016. http://nvlpubs.nist.gov/nistpubs/SpecialPublications/NIST.SP.800-150.pdf.

Olson P. We Are Anonymous: Inside the Hacker World of LulzSec, Anonymous, and the Global Cyber Insurgency. Little, Brown 2012;528. Back Bay Books, ISBN-10: 0316213527; ISBN-13: 978-0316213523, https://books.google.at/books?id=ncGVPtoZPHcC [accessed April 2016].

Parameswaran M, Susarla A, Whinston AB. P2P networking: An information-sharing alternative. *Computer*, 2001;34(7): 31–38.

Phillips CE Jr, Ting T, Demurjian SA. Information sharing and security in dynamic coalitions. In: *Proceedings of the Seventh ACM Symposium on Access Control Models and Technologies*. ACM; Monterey, CA, June 3–4, 2002. pp. 87–96. http://dl.acm.org/citation.cfm?id=507711&picked=prox.

Rinaldi SM. Modeling and simulating critical infrastructures and their interdependencies. In: *Proceedings of the 37th Annual Hawaii International Conference on System Sciences*. IEEE; Big Island, HI, January 5–8. 2004. p. 8. http://ieeexplore.ieee.org/document/1265029/.

Sarter NB, Woods DD. Situation awareness: A critical but ill-defined phenomenon. *Int J Aviat Psychol*, 1991;1(1):45–57.

Settanni G, Skopik F, Fiedler R, Shovgenya Y. A blueprint for a pan-European cyber incident analysis system. In: *Proceedings of 3rd International Symposium for ICS and SCADA Cyber Security Research*. Ingolstadt, Germany, September 17–18, 2015. pp. 84–88.

Shepherd S. Vulnerability disclosure: How do we define responsible disclosure? GIAC SEC practical repository. SANS Institute, 2003;9.

Shin S, Gu G. Conficker and beyond: A large-scale empirical study. In: *Proceedings of the 26th Annual Computer Security Applications Conference*. ACM; Austin, TX, December 06–10, 2010. pp. 151–60. http://dl.acm.org/citation.cfm?id=1920261.

Skopik F, Li Q. Trustworthy incident information sharing in social cyber defense alliances. In: *2013 IEEE Symposium on Computers and Communications*. ISCC; Split, Croatia, July 7–13, 2013. pp. 233–9.

Skopik F, Schall D, Dustdar S. Modeling and mining of dynamic trust in complex service-oriented systems. *Inform Syst*, 2010;35(7):735–57.

State of California Department of Justice Office of the Attorney General. Sony Pictures Entertainment notice letter. 2014.

Tadda G, Salerno JJ, Boulware D, Hinman M, Gorton S. Realizing situation awareness within a cyber environment. In: *Defense and Security Symposium*. International Society for Optics and Photonics. Orlando, FL, April 18–19, 2006. p. 624204.

Tankard C. Advanced persistent threats and how to monitor and deter them. *Network Security*, 2011;(8):16–19.

The Senate of The United States. Cybersecurity Information Sharing Act, 2015. https://www.congress.gov/114/bills/s754/BILLS-114s754es.pdf [accessed April 2016].

US Homeland Security Cyber Security R&D Center. A roadmap for cybersecurity research. 2009.

Virvilis N, Gritzalis D. The big four-what we did wrong in advanced persistent threat detection? In: *2013 Eighth International Conference on Availability, Reliability and Security (ARES)*. IEEE; Regensburg, Germany, September 2–6, 2013. pp. 248–54.

Waksman A, Sethumadhavan S. Silencing hardware backdoors. In: *2011 IEEE Symposium on Security and Privacy (SP)*. Oakland, CA, May 22–25, 2011. pp. 49–63.

White House. Executive order (EO13636): improving critical infrastructure cybersecurity. 2013a. http://www.whitehouse.gov/the-press-office/2013/02/12/executive-order-improving-critical-infrastructure-cybersecurity [accessed April 2016].

White House. Presidential policy directive—Critical infrastructure security and resilience. 2013b. http://www.whitehouse.gov/the-press-office/2013/02/12/presidential-policy-directive-critical-infrastructure-security-and-resil [accessed April 2016].

Zhao W, White G. A collaborative information sharing framework for community cyber security. In: *2012 IEEE Conference on Technologies for Homeland Security (HST)*. IEEE; Waltham, MA, November 13–15, 2012. pp. 457–62.

Chapter 5

Cyber Threat Intelligence Sharing through National and Sector-Oriented Communities

Frank Fransen and Richard Kerkdijk

Netherlands Organisation for Applied Scientific Research (TNO)

Contents

5.1 Introduction

Over the past years, the landscape of cyber threats has greatly evolved. High-end cyber attacks are now conducted by professional organizations that have substantial resources and (technical) capabilities at their disposal. Such attacks are often targeted in nature and may involve a great degree of persistence and (technical) sophistication (see Chapter 2). To deal with the nature and dynamics of present-day cyber threats, most large and ICT intensive organizations have fundamentally revised their cyber resilience strategies. Most prominently, it has become common to complement traditional (preventive) security controls with elaborate provisions for security monitoring and incident response. Underlying this development is a widespread notion that no preventive measure can avert a security incident if the adversary is sufficiently motivated and competent.

As depicted in Figure 5.1, the evolution of cyber resilience strategies is still ongoing. While monitoring and response provisions have greatly helped to reduce the damage resulting from cyber attacks, relying on such a reactive strategy is generally considered suboptimal. To regain some of the initiative, many organizations are now developing cyber threat intelligence (CTI) capabilities. In essence, such capabilities serve to *anticipate* (existing or emerging) cyber threats rather than awaiting an actual incident. To this end, organizations collect and process vast amounts of threat related data, some structured (i.e., in a standardized, machine-readable format) and some unstructured (narrative, e.g., threat investigation reports) in nature. Typically, this involves as follows:

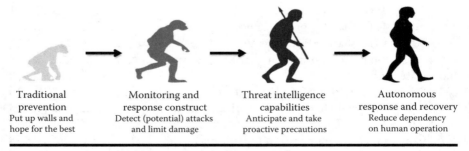

| Traditional
prevention
Put up walls and
hope for the best | Monitoring and
response construct
Detect (potential) attacks
and limit damage | Threat intelligence
capabilities
Anticipate and take
proactive precautions | Autonomous
response and recovery
Reduce dependency
on human operation |

Figure 5.1 Evolution of cyber resilience strategies.

- Indicators of compromise (IoCs). This refers to observable artifacts on hosts or networks that are indicative of malicious tools or known attacker methods and may thus reveal an ongoing intrusion.
- Tactics, techniques and procedures (TTPs). TTPs represent the typical tradecraft or modus operandi (MO) of cyber adversaries, i.e., how they operate in specific stages of an attack, the tools and techniques they employ, the resources (infrastructure, personas) they leverage in the target environment, etc.
- Threat actor profiles. This encompasses characterizations of cyber adversaries, e.g., identity or alias, objectives/motivators, typical TTP/MO, known (historical) attacks, suspected associations with other threat actors, etc.
- Attacker campaigns. Characteristics of mutually related attacks and intrusions through which an adversary pursues a larger (strategic) intent. This may for instance encompass attributes of the responsible threat actor(s), suspected objectives, TTPs employed, and related incidents.

Such cyber threat intelligence (CTI) can be acquired from a great variety of sources (see Chapter 3). Companies such as FireEye, AlienVault, and IBM, for instance, supply CTI on a commercial basis. Alternatively, CTI can be gathered from public sources (e.g., national CERTs, open source intelligence repositories) or even from company-internal processes and systems. The great wealth of sources presents security practitioners with an overwhelming amount of data in which it is hard to assess what is truly relevant for their specific organization and business. Apart from the sheer volume, much of this data are unqualified and lacks proper context.[1] Moreover, some of the most interesting threat intelligence (e.g., pertaining to *state actors* or zero-day exploits) might appear fairly late—if at all—through public or commercial channels.[2] Thus, while valuable in their own right, common sources of CTI tend to come with some intrinsic limitations.

Some of the aforementioned issues might be overcome through the concept of threat intelligence *communities*, i.e., networks of organizations that exchange CTI among one another. The remainder of this chapter will explore characteristics of such CTI communities and the value that might be gained from participating in them.

5.2 The Promise of Intelligence Communities

Exchanging CTI in a community context can offer several appealing benefits. Most prominently:

- *Reduction of sensitivity barriers.* Participants in a threat intelligence community can develop trusted relationships, thus stimulating openness in information sharing and offering access to intelligence that might not be shared with

---

[1] E.g., where has the threat been sighted, the identification of the attackers their motives, the exact nature of an IP address that was qualified as "bad," etc.
[2] Highly sensitive threat intelligence is often restricted to a selected audience (e.g., international intelligence agencies and major software companies) for a certain period.

broader audiences. In such a trusted environment, the information exchange might even extend to specific partner experiences such as actual incidents ("sightings") resulting from a certain threat or effects achieved through specific threat mitigation strategies.

■ *Meaningful vetting.* Individual participants can validate the authenticity and relevance of threat related information for the benefit of the entire community. Threat intelligence that was "vetted" (i.e., verified and designated as relevant[3]) by a trusted and competent partner can generally be treated with a high degree of confidence, thus accelerating decisions on (the need for) threat mitigation.

■ *Leveraging of expert capabilities.* Through the intelligence community, experts at individual organizations can effectively build on each other's analyses and insights, thus strengthening investigative work rather than duplicating it. Partners might, for instance, enrich specific threat information that they received from the community with insights (e.g., indicators or TTP characteristics) observed in their own infrastructures, thereby supplying all community participants with a better understanding of the threat under consideration.

Interestingly, benefits such as these have also been recognized at the level of national and regional politics. The U.S. government, for instance, recently introduced legislative provisions to stimulate threat information sharing within the private sector as well as between private companies and the federal government.[4] Similarly, the European NIS Directive (EU, Directive 2016/1148) (adopted by the European Parliament in July 2016) addresses the exchange of cyber threat intelligence (a.o. referred to as "early warnings") among national (Member State) CSIRT teams and CERT-EU.[5] These developments are addressed further in Chapters 7 and 8.

The concept of a threat intelligence community is not entirely new. Sharing threat-related insights is a common activity of CSIRT collaboration bodies such as FIRST[6] and TF-CSIRT[7] and also takes place through sector-oriented Information Sharing and Analysis Centers (ISACs[8]), Information Sharing and Analysis Organizations (ISAOs), and various other platforms and initiatives (e.g.,

---

[3] Community relevance of specific threat information can be appraised most accurately if partners have some familiarity with each other's business and infrastructure, e.g., because they operate in the same industry or geographic region. This will be addressed further in Section 5.6.

[4] https://en.wikipedia.org/wiki/Cybersecurity_Information_Sharing_Act; January 2017.

[5] CERT-EU, established in 2012, is the permanent Computer Emergency Response Team for EU institutions, agencies, and bodies.

[6] https://www.first.org/; January 2017.

[7] https://www.terena.org/activities/tf-csirt/; January 2017.

[8] Countries such as the United States and the Netherlands have established such ISACs for each of their vital industries, e.g., water, energy, telecommunications, finance, and health care.

the information exchanges maintained by CPNI UK). For the actual exchange of threat-related information, such communities have traditionally relied on fairly conventional channels and instruments. Threat intelligence might for instance be shared through e-mail distribution lists or discussed among experts and coordinators via physical meetings, conference calls or IRC[9] channels.

The dynamics of present-day cyber threats are quickly pushing traditional community channels to their limits. Malware families, zero-day exploits, phishing schemes, DDoS campaigns and numerous other threat manifestations emerge at such a tremendous pace that it is simply impossible to capture every piece of (seemingly) relevant intelligence in an e-mail thread or IRC chat. To complicate matters further, threat information acquired via human dialogue or as narrative text in an e-mail body is typically not suited for any form of automated processing. Thus even the most basic forms of analysis (e.g., cross-referencing community data with internal or public intelligence sources) or mitigation (e.g., converting threat indicators into a detection signature) will immediately put a strain on (usually scarce) expert resources.

Since traditional channels for exchanging threat intelligence are limited in both speed and efficiency, they will ultimately not suffice to keep pace with the unremittent stream of threat information. To overcome this, communities are increasingly streamlining the exchange of threat intelligence through dedicated technical platforms. Such platforms not only facilitate an efficient exchange of threat information (e.g., Indicators of Compromise, see above), but also optimize the practicality of such information in company-internal security processes (e.g., patch management and incident monitoring). The latter is fortified by the advent (and industry adoption) of standardized technology for threat intelligence exchange such as the framework of protocols developed by the MITRE Corporation (see Section 5.5). The remainder of this exploration will focus on CTI communities that exchange threat information via such dedicated automation solutions.

5.3 CTI Community Structures

Established threat intelligence communities (see previous section) are gradually embracing the concept of standardized and automated information exchange. In parallel, the advent of intelligence sharing technology is catalyzing the creation of entirely new community structures. Table 5.1 presents some prominent examples of CTI communities that exchange threat information via automated channels.

As this table reveals, CTI communities often comprise organizations with similar (business) profiles and technical infrastructures. In such a context, threats deemed relevant by an individual participant will usually be of interest to the entire

---

[9] Internet Relay Chat.

Table 5.1 CTI Communities That Employ Automated Channels

Community	Est.	Region	Constituents	Description
CIRCL MISP[38]	2012	Europe	Private companies in Luxemburg, security vendors and researchers, national CERTs	Operated by CIRCL, the national CERT in Luxemburg. Efforts focus on exchanging malware indicators (IoCs). Separate community environments for private organizations and national CERTs with selective mutual synchronization via an intermediate clearing house
Cyber security information Sharing Partnership[39] (CiSP)	2013	UK	Diverse	Joint industry and government initiative to exchange (broad scope of) cyber threat information via secure technical platform. Operated by UK's National Cyber Security Center (NCSC). Initially Focused on providers of critical national infrastructure but gradually expanded to broader audience. Team of analysts maintains situational awareness at national level
Cyber Threat Alliance[40] (CTA)	2014	Global	Security solution providers	Exchange of threat information on "advanced cyber adversaries" among vendors of security solutions. Objective is to raise overall situational awareness and allow members to better protect their commercial customers. Activities focus on malware manifestations and malicious sites that have not been reported via public channels
ETIS CERT-SOC Telco Network[41]	2015	Europe	Telecoms providers	Exchange of threat information among telco CERT and CSIRT teams. Efforts encompass "vetting" and enriching malware indicators (IoCs) from public sources and sharing unique CTI stemming from telco internal investigations. Initial pilot involved four European telcos

(Continued)

38 https://www.circl.lu/services/misp-malware-information-sharing-platform/; January 2017.
39 https://www.ncsc.gov.uk/cisp; January 2017.
40 http://cyberthreatalliance.org/; January 2017.
41 http://www.etis.org/?page=CERT_SOC; January 2017.

Table 5.1 (Continued) CTI Communities That Employ Automated Channels

Community	Est.	Region	Constituents	Description
FS-ISAC[42]	2013	Global	Financial services firms	Global exchange of threat information among financial institutions via vendor-operated platform. Information flow a.o. encompasses threat indicators, incidents and vulnerabilities. Dedicated analysis team collects and validates threat information from variety of sources (including member submissions) and disseminates alerts to the participants
National Detection Network[43] (NDN)	2014	NL	Vital infrastructure providers and national government bodies	Operated by Dutch National Cyber Security Center (NCSC). NCSC collects and validates threat information and disperses it to separate community platforms for private and governmental organizations, respectively. Efforts initially focused on exchanging malware indicators (IoCs) and are now shifting to contextual CTI
NATO MISP[44]	2012	NATO member nations	National and military CERTs	Operated by NATO Computer Incident Response Capability (NCIRC). Efforts focus on exchanging samples and indicators (IoCs) of malware encountered by community participants. Context of incidents is explicitly excluded to reduce sensitivity. Participation is open to cyber defense and government related constituents of NATO Member States

(Continued)

[42] https://www.fsisac.com/; January 2017.
[43] https://www.ncsc.nl/english/Cooperation/national-detection-network.html; January 2017.
[44] https://www.ncia.nato.int/Documents/Agency%20publications/MISP%20leaflet.pdf; January 2017.

Table 5.1 (Continued)   CTI Communities That Employ Automated Channels

Community	Est.	Region	Constituents	Description
NICP MISP	2016	NATO member nations	Diverse	Exchange of threat information among members of the NATO Industry Cyber Partnership (NICP). Efforts focus on unique threat indicators (IoCs) that resulted from investigations at individual partners. Initial pilot involved NATO itself and a selection of security solution providers and telecommunications firms
ThreatExchange[45]	2015	Global	Diverse	Operated by Facebook. Initially comprised of technology companies (a.o. Twitter, Pinterest, Tumblr, Yahoo) but gradually expanded to a more diverse partner base. The platform builds on existing Facebook infrastructure and social media concepts[46]

[45] https://www.facebook.com/threatexchange/; January 2017.

[46] As an example, connections between threat actors and their methodologies are determined through the same technology that helps Facebook track friendships and "likes."

membership. To achieve the desired focus and ensure a sufficient degree of mutual trust, most such CTI communities are—at least to a certain degree—*closed* in nature. This means that admission is restricted by specific criteria or even subject to invitation (see Section 5.4). The technical solutions employed for exchanging threat information vary per individual community, as does the extent to which such exchange is based on standardized technical protocols (see Section 5.5). Notably, automated channels for threat information sharing rarely stand on their own. Communities typically use their technical solution of choice to disperse (and process) machine readable data as efficiently as possible while employing fairly conventional methods (e.g., mailing lists or periodic conference calls) to share supporting material (e.g., threat investigation reports) or exchange in-depth insights.

The communities outlined in Table 5.1 are all operated by the constituents themselves, a representing body or a designated service provider. A separate class of communities revolves around cloud-based CTI sharing services offered by vendors of commercial CTI platforms. Prominent examples of such vendor-driven CTI communities are presented in Table 5.2.

Contrary to the communities outlined in Table 5.1, these vendor-driven communities are generally *open* to any interested security practitioner or researcher (specific terms or conditions may apply). Essentially they apply the concept of "crowdsourcing" to CTI sharing and collaboration. While this offers benefits in terms of scale, such environments do not encompass the trusted relationships typical of private CTI communities. Rather than engaging with known and trusted peers, participants collaborate with entities that have at best been vetted by the vendor operating the platform. Thus, these vendor-driven communities differ in nature from the private CTI communities described above. That does not detract from the fact that these are viable platforms for exchanging CTI that can offer access to some interesting threat information (not least that supplied by the vendor itself). A particularly interesting characteristic is they allow participants to engage in ad hoc (temporary) collaborations, typically driven by shared interest in a contemporary threat.

As explained in the table, cloud-based sharing services usually offer means to exchange threat information within a predefined (closed) user group. Thus, they can also be employed by private CTI communities.[10] The obvious benefit of using a cloud service is that it removes the need to maintain dedicated technical infrastructure for exchanging CTI. The inevitable downside is that communities will have less control over their (potentially sensitive) threat information. For starters, all such information resides "in the cloud," and community members must rely on the vendor to protect it from third-party abuse. On top of this, the vendor itself may require access to all CTI that is exchanged via its public intelligence platform.

---

[10] The U.S. based Information Technology ISAC in fact employs HP Threat Central for exchanging intelligence among its members; see http://www8.hp.com/us/en/hp-news/press-release.html?id=2184147.

Table 5.2 Cloud-Based Services for CTI Sharing

Community	Est.	Operator	Description
HPE Threat Central[47]	2014	Hewlett Packard	Aggregates intelligence from public sources, security vendors and community members into thread feeds for communities with a common interest (e.g., of a common industry or geography). Users can access, create, and share threat information via a web portal. Dedicated research teams validate data before community dissemination and contribute specific threat information
Open Threat eXchange (OTX)[48]	2012	Alienvault	OTX enables members to share, discuss, and research security threats. Users can share threat information themselves or subscribe to the ongoing analysis of a specific threat (a so called "pulse"). All data submitted are validated and anonymized by automated tools. Participants can create private communities for in-depth discussions on specific threats
ThreatConnect[49]	2013	ThreatConnect	Distributes latest threats via social media-type feeds and allows users to contribute their own analysis where they see fit. Collaboration can take place with the general user base or within specific (industry-oriented or privately created) communities. Supports both attributable (named) and anonymous information sharing. A dedicated research team contributes threat information and participates in moderated communities
X-Force Exchange[50]	2015	IBM	Combines community intelligence with the full repository of IBM security intelligence and several third-party sources. Users can create custom collections of indicators, vulnerabilities, and contextual data, access other (public) collections or exchange them more selectively in a private group. The platform tracks trending indicators and displays current threat activity. It also serves as a distribution point for X-Force advisories

[47] http://www8.hp.com/us/en/software-solutions/cyber-threat-analysis/index.html; January 2017.
[48] https://www.alienvault.com/open-threat-exchange; January 2017.
[49] https://www.threatconnect.com/; January 2017.
[50] https://exchange.xforce.ibmcloud.com/; January 2017.

This is in fact a likely element in the vendor's business model.[11] Thus, communities that exchange highly sensitive threat information (and require a corresponding degree of trust) will often prefer a dedicated solution. Here we note that some of the aforementioned vendors offer "private cloud" alternatives to their public service that might prove equally viable as a self-managed platform for particular communities.

5.4 Organizational Context of a CTI Community

Establishing and maintaining a CTI community is not solely a technical matter. A certain degree of organization is required to ensure a smooth operation and (ultimately) guarantee that participation offers actual (and lasting) value to the constituency. Typically, the following issues require attention:

1. *Community objectives.* The foundation of any CTI community lies in a clear definition of its mission and objectives. Most importantly, communities should clearly demarcate the type and nature of threat information that is to be exchanged. This demarcation primarily involves the following factors:

   a. *Manifestations of threat information.* CTI comes in many shapes and formats (see Section 5.1) and communities should choose which particular manifestations they wish to focus on. Some communities revolve solely around Indicators of Compromise (IoCs) that members can use to trace malicious activity in their infrastructures while others focus on higher grade threat information, e.g., concerning (new) attacker methods or mid- to long-term attacker campaigns. Communities could enrich their information exchange even further by including such things as IoC sightings,[12] recommended actions, or malware samples.

   b. *Vetting versus unicity.* As explained in Section 5.2, a core benefit of sharing CTI in a community context is that members can validate threat information for the benefit of the entire membership. The concept of "vetting" can in fact be the sole driver for sustaining a CTI community. In such a setup, the threat information that members exchange is not novel in itself, but the community acts as a filter that separates (and possibly enriches) relevant insights from the vast amount of publicly available CTI. An alternative approach is to focus on truly unique threat information. In communities that pursue this objective, members typically share

---

[11] Vendors might want to use such threat information to enhance their broader security offering, e.g., compile detection signatures for customers of their SIEM product.

[12] In this context, the term "sighting" refers to an actual "hit" on indicators obtained via the community exchange.

insights that stem from their internal investigations (e.g., forensic analysis conducted by a company internal CSIRT or Red Team) that would often not be disclosed via public channels.

Note that the choices outline above are not mutually exclusive—communities can focus on very distinct information types but might also have a broader orientation if that is somehow more suitable for the member base. It is essential, however, that the objectives of the community are unambiguously clear since these not only determine the value that might be obtained from participating but also the competence required to supply a meaningful contribution.

2. *Membership conditions.* Among the defining characteristics of any CTI community is its membership. Thus, communities need to determine upfront which target audience best suits their objectives. This may result in distinct criteria concerning the profile of member organizations. A community might for instance only be open to organizations in a particular industry or region. Alternatively, some communities might only admit organizations that have an acknowledged CTI or incident response capability (i.e., a CERT or CSIRT) in place. Such criteria are often instrumental to the community's performance and should thus be unambiguously clear. Another factor to consider is the required member contribution. Some communities maintain strict (even quantitative) requisites concerning the supply of threat information by individual members. The criteria maintained by the Cyber Threat Alliance (see Figure 5.2) are illustrative of this approach. While such criteria might discourage certain companies from joining, they do ensure an ongoing level of community activity and may thus be worth considering.

   Note that the duration of membership is also factor that can be tuned. While not particularly common, some CTI communities maintain the

❓ What are the minimum requirements to join the Alliance?

Each member must share at least 1000 samples of new Portable Executable (PE) malware per day that are not observed on VirusTotal over the preceding forty-eight (48) hours at the time of sharing, **and** meet at least one (1) of the following three (3) criteria:

1. **Mobile Malware:** At least fifty (50) samples of new mobile malware per day in the APK, DEX, or other popular mobile malware file formats that are not observed on VirusTotal over the last forty-eight (48) hours at time of sharing.
2. **Botnets C2 Servers:** At least one hundred (100) botnet command and control servers (C2), and/or peer to peer nodes, per week beyond those listed on public forums such as ZeusTracker, must be different than the previous week's dump from the contributing member; and must be active upon sharing.
3. **Vulnerabilities & Exploits Sites:** At least one hundred (100) attack sites per week beyond those listed on public forums, must be different than the previous week's dump from the contributing member, and must be active upon sharing.

Figure 5.2   Contribution requirements of cyber threat alliance.[1]

---

[1] http://cyberthreatalliance.org/faq.html; January 2017.

principle of temporary membership. Such communities periodically review their member affiliations and only renew a membership if specific criteria (e.g., concerning the degree of activity) have been met.

3. *Confidentiality arrangements.* As explained in Section 5.1, a core benefit of CTI communities is that they can reduce sensitivity barriers and stimulate exchange of threat information that is not typically not accessible to a broad audience. To exploit this benefit in full, it is essential that communities maintain proper confidentiality arrangements. Here a key issue to address is the extent to which threat information acquired from community partners may be disclosed to other entities and the specific circumstances that might or might not warrant such disclosure.

The most common method for earmarking the sensitivity of information in a community context is the Traffic Light Protocol (TLP).[13] TLP essentially allows the originator of threat information to clarify how widely this information can be circulated beyond immediate recipients. To achieve this, the originator simply marks the threat information with one of four colors, each representing specific sharing boundaries (see Table 5.3).

Notably, TLP has been incorporated in technical protocols for cyber threat intelligence sharing as well as several CTI sharing platforms (see Section 5.6) and is thus fairly easy to adopt. Alternatives, however, do exist. The Forum of Incident Response and Security Teams (FIRST), for instance, developed the Information Exchange Policy (IEP)[14] framework to facilitate CSIRTs even further with sensitive information sharing. IEP revolves around four so-called policy types: handling, action, sharing, and licensing (HASL—see Table 5.4).

The IEP framework extends beyond defining the permitted redistribution of (threat) information and thus allows more refinement in conveying

Table 5.3 TLP Scheme Definitions

RED	Not for disclosure. Restricted to immediate recipients
AMBER	Limited disclosure. Recipients may only share information with members of their own organization and with clients or customers who need to know the information to protect themselves or prevent further harm
GREEN	Limited disclosure. Recipients may share information with peers and partner organizations within their sector or community, but not via publicly accessible channels
WHITE	Disclosure is not limited .

---

[13] https://www.first.org/tlp; November 2016.
[14] https://www.first.org/iep; November 2016.

Table 5.4 IEP Policy Types

HANDLING	Policy statements that define any obligations or controls on information received, to ensure the confidentiality of information that is shared
ACTION	Policy statements that define the permitted actions or uses of theinformation received that can be carried out by a recipient
SHARING	Policy statements that define any permitted redistribution of information that is received
LICENSING	Policy statements that define any applicable agreements, licenses, or terms of use that governs the information being shared

confidentiality requisites. The HANDLING policy, for instance, allows the originator of threat information to indicate whether data should be encrypted during retransmission or storage while the SHARING policy may state that threat information must be anonymized before it is redistributed.

Frameworks such as TLP and IEP offer useful means of streamlining confidentiality arrangements in a CTI community. While TLP will often suffice, IEP offers a viable alternative for communities that wish to govern the confidentiality of threat information with a higher degree of granularity.

Note that the confidentiality arrangements of a CTI community may also extend to security controls in member infrastructures. Member organizations might for instance be required to encrypt all threat information received from the community or implement specific access control policies on community related IT systems.

4. *Legal constraints.* The exchange of threat information within CTI communities can be bounded by legal and regulatory constraints. Privacy and data protection laws, for instance, may limit the exchange of certain information. What's more, a freedom of information act may cause reluctance among members to share (e.g., incident related) information with government organizations due to the potential of public disclosure (see Section 5.6.3 for an example). When establishing a CTI sharing community it is thus necessary to discuss legal and regulatory issues and ensure that the information sharing takes place within the constraints of applicable laws. Notably this may also have an affect on the aforementioned confidentiality arrangements. The legal implications of information sharing are further elaborated in Chapter 7.

5. *Governance and operations.* Maintaining a CTI community involves a degree of planning and decision making. Experienced (mature) communities often maintain a formal board or steering committee to this end. Such governing

bodies are generally comprised of delegates from the participating organizations and deal with issues such as member admission, community policies, and the community's overall performance. At the operational level, the task of compiling and sharing threat information may solely reside with individual partners, but the community could also put a dedicated analysis team in place. Such dedicated teams are, for instance, seen in the FS-ISAC community (see Table 5.1) and in the Dutch NDN (see case studies in Section 5.6). Whether specific communities feel the need and have the means to establish a dedicated operations team will obviously vary from case to case. It is a provision worth considering, since it can ensure a base level of community activity. What's more, dedicated operations teams can moderate the feeds supplied by individual partners to enhance the overall quality of threat information that is circulated within the community.

Organizational issues and constraints such as those outlined above are usually specified in a community's formal policy or Terms of Reference (ToR). Such terms essentially demarcate the rules of play for members of a CTI community (explicitly or implicitly).

5.5 Tooling and Infrastructure

5.5.1 Introduction

To enhance the speed and efficiency of CTI sharing there is a growing need for automation. Over the last couple of years several software applications have emerged that can be used for automated CTI exchange within a community. The Malware Information Sharing Platform (MISP)[15] is a platform specifically developed for exchange of CTI among community partners. In addition, general CTI platforms have emerged to provide automated acquisition, analysis, management of CTI, and support for community-based CTI sharing. Also, the cloud-based CTI sharing services, as described in the previous section, also provide the capability to establish automated CTI exchange within a specific community. These CTI sharing solutions can typically be used to setup different CTI sharing infrastructures.

In this section, CTI sharing infrastructures are described in more detail. Next, the typical functions of a CTI sharing platform are described. Last, the CTI sharing platform MISP is described in more detail, since it was the platform used in both CTI sharing cases described in Section 5.6.

---

[15] https://github.com/MISP/MISP; December, 2016.

5.5.2 CTI Sharing Infrastructure

CTI community sharing infrastructures can be categorized as either hub–spoke, or peer-to-peer (Johnson et al., 2016). In the hub–spoke model, there is a central CTI service (the *hub*), to which all participants are connected (the *spokes*). CTI information is shared via the central CTI service that acts as a clearinghouse and may also store the CTI information. Participants either connect using a browser to access the CTI service to retrieve or upload CTI information or use an automated exchange protocol to retrieve and/or upload CTI information in a machine-readable format. In the latter case, the participant will have its own local CTI sharing platform. In Figure 5.3, the concept of a hub–spoke CTI sharing community is depicted. The figure also depicts the notification service that is typical for CTI sharing service to inform participants of newly shared CTI. Note that participants with their own CTI sharing platforms do not rely on the notification service from the central CTI service, but their local CTI sharing platform will typically also provide such service. An example of a CTI sharing community that was setup as a hub–spoke model is the Dutch National Detection Network (NDN; see Section 5.6.2). Also, most of the cloud-based CTI sharing services are examples of hub–spoke CTI sharing communities.

In the peer-to-peer model, all members have their own CTI sharing platform with a local CTI store. Using an automatic exchange protocol, the CTI information that is made available for sharing with the other members is exchanged. This is depicted in Figure 5.4. An example of a peer-to-peer CTI sharing community is the ETIS CERT-SOC Telco Network (see Section 5.6.1).

Often an organization does not only participate in one community but shares CTI with multiple communities simultaneously. This is depicted in Figure 5.5. The CTI sharing platform then has to ensure that CTI shared in one community will not end up in another CTI sharing community, unless explicitly allowed. Note that an organization can participate in multiple types of sharing communities simultaneously. In the call out box below, this CTI information community spillover is described by means of an example.

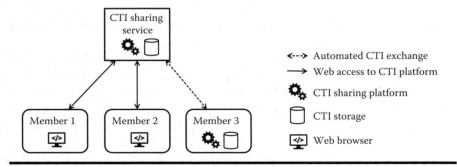

Figure 5.3 Hub–spoke CTI sharing infrastructure.

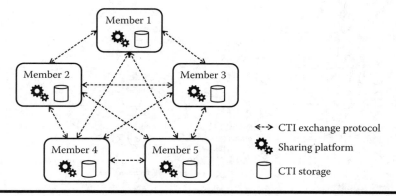

Figure 5.4   Peer-to-peer CTI sharing infrastructure.

EXAMPLE OF CTI INFORMATION COMMUNITY SPILLOVER

The following case is based on the CTI sharing communities depicted in Figure 5.5. Member 1 shares CTI information within three communities. Each community could be a different type, such as different sector, national/international, private/public, or classification. When member A shares CTI information with members 1, B, C, D, and E, member 1 can also share this CTI information received from member A within the other two communities, for instance with members 2, 3, 4, and 5. This is referred to as a spillover from one community to another. This may happen intentionally or unintentionally (e.g., member 1 has not configured its CTI sharing platform correctly).

This spillover may not immediately be a problem, but if the CTI information shared by member A was marked as TLP Amber or even Red, then information should not have been shared with other organizations.

Managing multiple CTI sharing communities in a single platform is not trivial and should be carefully configured. Moreover, the platform should automatically support sensitive information sharing markings and polices, such as the Traffic Light Protocol (TLP) and the Information Exchange Policy (IEP). In some cases, it may be better to set up one or more CTI sharing platforms toward the outside world and synchronize with your own internal general CTI platform to better manage the different sharing policies.

Cloud-based CTI sharing communities are typical examples of the hub–spoke model. But many other centrally coordinated communities follow the hub–spoke model, such as those run by ISACs or national CERTs. Advantages compared to the

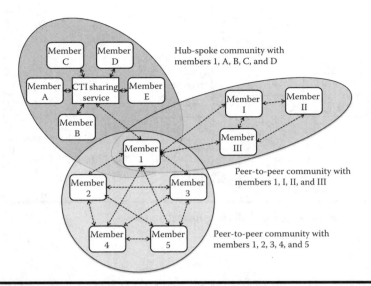

Figure 5.5 Example of simultaneously participating in multiple CTI sharing communities.

peer-to-peer model are that the participants do not need to set up their own CTI sharing platforms and do not need to set up trust relations with all the other partici- pants individually. Moreover, a central CTI service could provide additional services such as customizable filtering, anonymization toward other members (e.g., hiding the source of the CTI information or reporting of sightings). On the other hand, peer-to-peer communities can share CTI information on a more equal trust basis without having to trust or rely on a central entity. This is, e.g., relevant in the case of commercial CTI sharing providers that will use the shared CTI for the commu- nity for their own commercial services. Moreover, some organizations are typically less reluctant to share CTI information with their peers than a government agency, such as the national CERT. A novel approach for creating secure and trustworthy CTI sharing without relying on a central authority may be created using blockchain technology. The use of blockchain technology for intelligence sharing has been sug- gested by Jerry Cuomo, IBM's vice president of blockchain, during his testimony for the USA President's Commission on Enhancing National Cybersecurity, on May 16, 2016[16]. This, however, is currently a topic for scientific research.

The Trusted Automated eXchange of Indicator Information (TAXII) standard sup- ports both the hub–spoke and the peer-to-peer sharing models. By using standardized CTI exchange data formats and protocols, such as TAXII and STIX, members should be able to choose their own (vendor-independent) CTI sharing platform to participate

[16] https://www.nist.gov/sites/default/files/documents/2016/09/16/ibm_rfi_executive_sum- mary.pdf; January, 2017.

in a CTI sharing community. This is unfortunately, nowadays, not yet possible due to the use of proprietary exchange protocols and CTI data formats, and the lack of full support of standards. Many vendors have started adopting STIX and TAXII[17, 18]. The technical implementation, however, often does not fully support all fields and constructs of the STIX data model. If a CTI sharing platform does not support a particular STIX construct (e.g., TTP, Incident, Campaign) it will discard that information when it receives STIX documents containing that information formatted in that construct. The developers of STIX recognized this issue and developed a mechanism to support interoperability by means of the so-called STIX profiles.[19] In a STIX profile, one describes what STIX fields and constructs MUST, SHOULD, MAY, SHOULD NOT, or MUST NOT be in the exchanged STIX document. A STIX profile is exchanged out-of-band. A community can describe in a so-called *community profile* how it will use STIX. A member of the community can use the community profile to determine whether a CTI sharing platform supports all required STIX fields and constructs, both as consumer and as producer. At the moment of writing this chapter, the OASIS CTI working group is drafting a new approach for STIX interoperability for STIX version 2.0. Note that vendors do not always implement all TAXII capabilities. When only the TAXII server is implemented (e.g., inbox), the platform can only receive CTI. This is typically sufficient if the CTI platform is only intended to receive CTI information from a CTI feed. For CTI feeds TAXII provides the one-way source/subscribe mechanism. In order to also share CTI information with other members, a TAXII client is necessary. The TAXII client pushes CTI information to the TAXII server in the central hub, or directly to TAXII servers of other members in a peer-to-peer community.

5.5.3 CTI Sharing Platforms

CTI sharing platform typically support the creation and exchange of CTI within one or more communities. The CTI sharing platform does not have to be the main or general CTI platform of an organization. A general CTI platform supports an organization with the automation of the capabilities to collect, store, and analyze CTI from different sources and disseminate actionable CTI (including appropriate courses of actions) within the organization to prevent or detect cyber attacks. It may even be beneficial to have a separate CTI sharing platform. Sharing of CTI with community partners requires a conscious decision to release information that is sensitive for the organization. The separation between a general CTI platform and the dedicated CTI sharing platform could facilitate such a decision. Table 5.5 provides examples of some CTI (sharing) platforms.

As the CTI field is still in development, the functionality and features of these CTI sharing platforms may change in the coming years. Many of these CTI sharing platforms have their own philosophy, terminology, features, and focus on particular cyber threat data. Instead of describing specific CTI sharing products, this chapter

---

[17] https://stixproject.github.io/supporters/; January, 2017.
[18] https://wiki.oasis-open.org/cti/Products; January, 2017.
[19] http://stixproject.github.io/documentation/profiles/; January 2017.

Table 5.5   Examples of CTI (Sharing) Platforms

Product	Vendor	Description
Blueliv Threat Intelligence Platform[51]	Blueliv	General CTI platform with community sharing capabilities
Cyber Threat Exchange[52]	NC4	CTI sharing platform. Previously called Soltra Edge is used by a.o. the FS-ISAC
EclecticIQ Platform[53]	Eclectic IQ	General CTI platform with community sharing capabilities
Malware Information Sharing Platform (MISP)[54]	Open source	Free and open source community-sourced CTI sharing platform
ThreatConnect[55]	ThreatConnect	General CTI platform with community sharing capabilities

[51] https://www.blueliv.com/our-platform/; December 2016.
[52] http://nc4.com/Pages/cyber-threat-exchange.aspx; December 2016.
[53] https://www.eclecticiq.com/platform; December 2016.
[54] https://github.com/MISP/MISP; December, 2016.
[55] https://www.threatconnect.com/; December 2016.

gives an overview of the main components and function of a CTI sharing platform. In order to clearly describe these functions some distinctions need to be made in the type of CTI information stored by a CTI sharing platform. In this chapter, distinction made among CTI data, CTI context information, and CTI meta data is described in Table 5.6. The term CTI record is introduced to refer to the combined

Table 5.6   Type of CTI Information Stored on a CTI Sharing Platform

Function	Description
CTI data	CTI data are used to refer to the data, such as an IP address, filename, name of malware, and CVE number that combined with contextual information creates the actual cyber threat intelligence
CTI context information	The contextual information enables community members to understand what the CTI data are about and to make informed decisions on how to treat the CTI data. CTI context information can be provided by means of additional content, such as title, tags, and comments and by means of the markup language that implicitly provides the context to the CTI data
CTI meta data	A CTI platform typically also uses meta data, such as source, author, contact details, time and date of creation, time and date received, etc.

set of CTI data, CTI context information, and CTI meta data that is to be shared. The reason is that CTI sharing platforms use different terms for a CTI record (e.g., it is an Event in MISP, a Pulse in OTX, and an Activity in IBM X-Force Exchange). The basic functions of a CTI sharing platform are:

- *View, create, and edit function*: This enables the user to create new CTI records. In addition, the user should be able to view and edit CTI records.
- *Import CTI data function*: This supports the creation of new CTI records and contributes to shared CTI records with, e.g., additional indicators; typically an import function is provided to ingest CTI data from external sources, such as an intrusion detection system (IDS), security information and event management (SIEM) solution or other CTI platform. Typical formats for ingestion of CTI data are OpenIOC, STIX or comma-separated values (CSV). Some tools even allow the import of pdf and plain text files and support extracting Indicators from these files.
- *CTI storage and search function*: The CTI records are stored in a database with a search function.
- *CTI exchange function*: This enables the user to securely share created CTI events with community members. The way the exchange takes place depends on the type of CTI sharing infrastructure (see Section 5.5.2). The security requirements are confidentiality protection and integrity protection including source authentication.
- *Community management function*: This provides the capability to add and remove members and to configure the secure exchange.
- *Notification function*: When new CTI records are shared, this function provides a configurable notification to the user, for instance, by means of e-mail.
- *CTI export function*: To support the members to act upon the received CTI, a CTI export function may be provided to enable exporting of the CTI data in different formats. Typical formats are STIX, OpenIOC, and CSV. To make the application of CTI for security monitoring even more simple, some vendors provide export as in a specific IDS rule format (e.g., snort[20], Suricata[21], Bro[22]).

Examples of advanced functions are the following:

- *Correlation, fusion, and analysis functions*: CTI platforms are typically capable of automatically correlating CTI data and identifying relations between CTI records. A CTI sharing platform could provide such advanced functionality.

---

[20] https://www.snort.org/; December 2016.
[21] https://suricata-ids.org/; December 2016.
[22] https://www.bro.org/; December 2016.

Analysis functions, such as statistical and graphical, can be beneficial for the analyst.

■ *Automatic enrichment*: Some CTI data can automatically be enriched, to assist the analyst in making more informed decisions. For instance, geolocation and IP address can automatically be retrieved.

■ *Contributing, liking, and commenting*: For active interaction between members of a community, a function to contribute and comment on CTI records from other members can be provided; even social media type of interactions, such as liking the CTI record of another member. In the next section more examples of collaboration are given that require specific advance functions from the CTI sharing platform.

■ *Consuming CTI feeds*: This can be of value for correlation and fusion with the community-shared CTI data. Consuming CTI feeds is, however, more a feature of a general CTI platform.

■ *Moderation and anonymous sharing function*: For the hub–spoke type of CTI infrastructure, the CTI platform could provide a moderation function and anonymous sharing of CTI records.

5.5.4 Malware Information Sharing Platform

The Malware Information Sharing Platform (MISP)[23] is an open source software platform[24] to share information about malware and their indicators. It was initially developed by Belgian Defense and NATO Computer Incident Response Capability (NCIRC). Nowadays, MISP is a community-driven project on GitHub led by a core team of developers, of whom most are working at the Computer Incident Response Center Luxembourg (CIRCL). CIRCL is the CERT for the private sector, communes and nongovernmental entities in Luxembourg, and hosts several CTI sharing communities using MISP (e.g., CIRCL MISP private sector).

As the name indicates, MISP was developed for sharing malware related indicators (Wagner et al., 2016). As there was no standard data model for CTI when the MISP developments started, a data model was defined. It had to be simple and convenient while enabling complex requirements. The data model consists of the following objects: (1) Event, (2) Attribute, and (3) Tag. In Figure 5.6, a simplified data model is depicted. When a user creates a new entry in MISP, a new Event is created. The fields of an Event include date, event info, threat level, and organization (source). The specific Indicator data are added to an Event by adding Attribute objects. An Attribute is characterized by the field's category and type, and the data are contained in the value field. An Event can also contain a Tag object to further

---

[23] http://www.misp-project.org/; accessed December 23, 2016.
[24] https://github.com/MISP/MISP; accessed December 23, 2016.

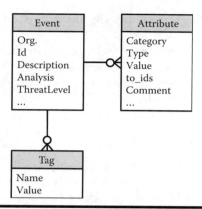

Figure 5.6 **Simplified data model of an event in MISP. (From Wagner et al., The design and implementation of a collaborative threat intelligence sharing platform. In:** *Proceedings of the 2016 ACM Workshop Information Sharing and Collaborative Security,* **ACM, New York, pp. 49–56, 2016.)**

characterize the Event; for instance, to tag the TLP level of the Event. Over the years, the MISP data model was extended.

MISP is a community sharing platform. It depends fully on community-generated content. The MISP platform supports both types of CTI community sharing infrastructures. Via the web interface a hub–spoke sharing community can be set up. In addition, MISP has its own protocol to synchronize the events between different MISP instances in a JSON format. MISP supports several mechanisms: pull, push, and cherry picking. The pull mechanism enables MISP to discover available events on another MISP instance and download a new or modified event. The push mechanism sends an event to another MISP instance. The cherry picking mechanism allows users to select events from another MISP instance to be pulled to the local MISP instance. These synchronization mechanisms are typically used for setting up a peer-to-peer CTI sharing infrastructure. To control the distribution of events, MISP traditionally differentiates among organization only, community only, connected communities, and all sharing levels. Newer versions of MISP allow the user to define sharing groups more granularly.

To integrate with other tools, MISP supports the export of events and attributes in different formats (e.g., OpenIOC, CVS, STIX in XML, and JSON) and as intrusion detection systems (IDS) signatures (e.g., Bro, Suricata, and Snort). For the export as IDS rule, MISP allows the user to determine whether an attribute is eligible to be automatically included in an IDS rule. Some attributes may, for instance, create an inappropriately large number of false positives or only include information for a human analyst. In addition, MISP provides support to automatically generating IDS signatures to automate the distribution of the received indicators to an IDS.

As the developers of MISP intend to accommodate the changing and evolving requirements of the IT community, the capabilities of MISP will change over time to better support incident analysis, mitigation, and response.

5.6 Case Studies

This section discusses practical experiences and lessons learned in two actual CTI communities with which the authors have been involved. The first is the ETIS CERT-SOC Telco Network that encompasses CERT and CSIRT teams of European telecoms providers. The second is the National Detection Network (NDN) operated by the Dutch National Cyber Security Center (NCSC). Both communities exchange threat information via the Malware Information Sharing Platform (MISP) covered in Section 5.4, and at first glance their (technical) setups might seem fairly similar. As shown in Table 5.7, however, there are some fundamental differences between these community structures, and these have greatly affected the specific challenges that each encountered.

The remainder of this section addresses the setups of these communities, their expected advancements, and some essential lessons learned.

5.6.1 ETIS CERT-SOC Telco Network

ETIS,[25] the community for telecom professionals, is a membership-based organization that facilitates collaboration among European telecom providers. Its member base covers a substantial portion of the European telco landscape. Early 2013, ETIS established the so-called CERT-SOC Telco Network, comprised of security operations and incident response specialists in the various member organizations. A key activity of this group is the exchange of threat information and incident response experiences. Originally, this took place via biweekly conference calls, online forum

Table 5.7 European Telco Network vs. Dutch NDN

ETIS CERT-SOC Telco Network	National Detection Network
International (Europe)	National (the Netherlands)
Single sector (telecommunications)	Multisector (critical industries)
Industry initiative	Government coordinated
Peer-to-peer exchange	Hub–spoke model

---

[25] www.etis.org; February 2017.

discussions, and biannual meetings. While this dialogue offered valuable insights and stimulated mutual familiarity and trust, the group gradually recognized that it needed an enhanced setup to fully exploit its potential. Thus, the members set out to explore the merits of structured automation in their mutual exchange of threat information. A small-scale pilot was launched to establish and try the base infrastructure. The pilot involved four of the group's member organizations and took place in the first half of 2015. TNO[26] was involved as a facilitator and independent advisor. The pilot was exploratory in nature, and the group expressly embraced a practical approach that would not be burdened by disproportionate governance or overhead. The idea was to assess the feasibility of automated CTI exchange in the telco community, thus paving the way for a more elaborate and formal operational setup.

In the early stages of the pilot project, the participants selected the specific manifestations of threat information they wished to exchange via the automated channel. They decided to focus primarily on the following elements:

- *Malware indicators.* The group agreed to focus on indicators with a certain degree of unicity, either because they were not included in standard monitoring configurations (detection signatures) of solution vendors[27] or because the underlying threat was not elaborately documented in public sources. Such indicators typically stemmed from telco internal investigations and might include malware specifically targeting the telco industry[28] (if such were to occur). An essential constraint was to only share indicators that were "vetted" (validated), meaning that they were actually observed in the infrastructure of a community participant. Through this approach, the group intended to ensure that indicators received from the community always came with a high degree of relevance (thus making them suitable for further automation downstream, see below).

- *Vulnerabilities in telco-relevant equipment.* To some extent, this was positioned as an extension of the "vetting" concept also employed for malware indicators. Reporting presence (or exploitation) of publicly known vulnerabilities in telco infrastructures would alert participants of their relevance and potential urgency. The prime driver for including this element, however, was to acquire access to *unique* vulnerability discoveries. Telcos with a mature security capability often have teams in place that conduct security testing or forensic investigations on telco-specific equipment. Vulnerabilities discovered through such activities are typically not disseminated to a broad audience, but other telcos would greatly benefit from an early warning.

---

[26] www.tno.nl; February 2017.

[27] The group designated VirusTotal (https://virustotal.com/) as the applicable reference. This on-line service reflects the detection signatures of a great many anti-virus solutions.

[28] The extent to which the CTI exchange included telco-specific threats was in fact explicitly monitored during the pilot.

The group explicitly positioned the above as a nonrestrictive baseline. Participants were free to share other manifestations of threat information (e.g., concerning attacker strategies or campaigns) as they saw fit, as long as the "vetting" criterion was met. Notably, the actual trials revolved almost exclusively around malware indicators (IoCs). This will be addressed further in the "lessons learned" Section 5.6.3.

As mentioned above, the telco group used the MISP platform[29] to establish its automated threat exchange channels. Using an open source solution was considered appealing (certainly for the pilot stage), and MISP was a reputable platform that seemed to offer most of the desired functionality. At the architectural level, it was decided that each telco would maintain a separate instance of the MISP platform in its own infrastructure. This resulted in a peer-to-peer CTI sharing infrastructure as depicted in Figure 5.4 (see above), where individual platform instances exchanged threat information in the proprietary XML format employed by the MISP application. This setup was preferred over a shared (centralized) MISP installation because it allowed each telco to integrate the community exchange with internal security solutions and other threat information feeds according to its own individual desires. Some of the pilot participants made extensive use of this possibility, among others by automatically processing IoCs received from the ETIS community into signatures for their security monitoring solutions. The underlying reasoning was that threat indicators received from the telco community should always be considered relevant *and* trustworthy and could thus be transferred to operational security processes without manual intervention. In many ways, these particular telcos were quick to recognize (and exploit) the benefits of CTI communities outlined in Section 5.2.

The actual task of compiling and sharing threat information with community partners fully resided with the telco CERT and CSIRT teams. The group did not see a need (nor did it have the means) to establish a dedicated operations team to run or moderate the community exchange. Also, as explained above, the telcos chose not to establish any formal governance body since it was felt that this would not be beneficial to the pilot's objectives and pragmatic setup. The telcos did define distinct "rules of play" concerning community participation. These rules essentially address the behavior community partners expect from one another. For the purpose of the pilot, it was agreed to limit these rules to a concise 10-point manifesto. Among the issues addressed was the extent to which threat information received from community partners could be shared with other parties. This was of particular interest because security is not only a business requisite but also a commercial product for most Telecom providers. In light of this, the ETIS partners explicitly stated that threat information exchanged within their community was not intended to serve any commercial purpose. What this illustrates is that community rules can be very specific to the context of the member base.

---

[29] Specifically, the pilot employed MISP version 2.3.40 issued on January 29, 2015. This version has since been succeeded by several (fairly fundamental) updates.

The rules of play for the telco CTI community also dictated that sharing threat information was strictly voluntary and that participants were free to act upon such information as they saw fit. Thus, the telcos did not embrace the concept of "supply quota" as for instance employed by the Cyber Threat Alliance (see Section 5.4).

5.6.2 National Detection Network

In 2012, the Dutch NCSC[30] (in collaboration with Dutch intelligence services) launched a CTI sharing initiative among organizations involved in critical infrastructures and national government bodies. Following various legal and ministerial preparations and a successful pilot, the concept of a "National Detection Network" (NDN) was part of the second National Cyber Security Strategy[31] for The Netherlands and went into operation by the end of 2014.

NDN focuses on two distinct target groups:

■ Private companies in industries that are considered crucial for the proper functioning of Dutch society. Examples of such industries are energy, water, and telecommunications.
■ Departments and agencies of the Dutch national government, e.g., the ministries and executive bodies such as the tax and customs administration.

Notably, NCSC was already exchanging threat information with these target groups well before NDN was conceived. With the NDN, however, came a technical environment that supports automation and (correspondingly) larger information volumes. NDN started with a small number of participants but has the ambition to grow quite considerably in the near future.

NDN was originally positioned as a platform where NCSC could disseminate unique *high-profile* threat information—e.g., concerning state actor methods and campaigns—to stakeholders in critical industries. CTI of this nature is often bound by restrictions, at least for a certain period. NDN was seen as a means to convey such high-value threat information at an appropriate speed to organizations that needed it most. Over time, the scope was expanded to include cyber threat information from public sources. At this level, the added value of NDN lies in consolidating a great variety of sources and selecting threat information that is actually relevant for its member base. Thus, similar to the telco community addressed in the previous section, NDN embraced the concept of "vetting."

NDN also employs the MISP platform for all automated exchange of (technical) threat information. Contrary to the telco community outlined above, however, NDN was set up as a centralized service facilitated by centralized technical infrastructure (i.e., a hub–spoke architecture as depicted in Figure 5.4). This approach

---

[30] https://www.ncsc.nl/English; February 2017.
[31] https://www.ncsc.nl/english/current-topics/national-cyber-security-strategy.html; October 2013.

was chosen to ensure that the uptake of the community would not be hindered by practical obstacles. Figure 5.7 depicts the NDN architecture in more detail.

NDN actually encompasses three distinct instances of the MISP platform. The *internal* (see figure) MISP platform serves to collect, enrich, and correlate source information. The outcome of such processing is fed to separate, dedicated MISP instantiations for each of the aforementioned target groups. This setup was chosen because it allows the NCSC to

- Compile separate (customized) threat information feeds for private and governmental community participants and avoid undesired spillover between the two and
- Offer each target group specific means of interfacing with the community platform that suit the corresponding agreements and relationships.

Concerning the latter, both target groups have similar (browser-based) web access to their respective MISP environments. Specialists in the respective partner organizations can use this channel to log on to the appropriate MISP instantiation and review the threat information that is in store. On top of this, NDN encompasses specific technical interfaces that facilitate automation. Here the following applies:

- The platform for private partners is equipped with an API[32] through which native security solutions can be integrated with the NDN's threat information feed. Partners can for instance use this to automatically feed detection signatures into their SIEM solutions, similar to the setup seen in the telco community (see previous section). The extent to which such integration is indeed established is currently left at the discretion of each partner.

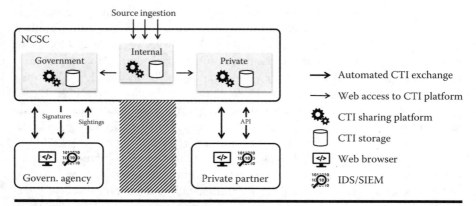

Figure 5.7   Simple schematic of NDN architecture.

---

[32] Application Programming Interface.

■ The MISP instance maintained for government bodies can interface directly with IDS sensors in governmental ICT networks. These sensors are offered by the NCSC but installed and maintained by the government agencies themselves. They interact with the NCSC's MISP environment (see Figure 5.7) on a bidirectional basis. Specifically, IDS sensors are automatically fed with detection signatures (deduced from threat information), and the IDS reports so called "sightings" (i.e., actual "hits" on a particular threat indicator) back to the centralized CTI platform. Such "sightings" alert the NCSC of potential incidents and strengthen its overall situational awareness.

This differentiated setup stems from the fact that the NCSC is itself part of the national government, and as such is considered the same legal entity as other government bodies.[33] Having said this, the NCSC would like to extend the NDN with threat information (voluntarily) supplied by private partners. The aforementioned API was in fact already prepared for such collection. At present, however, the interaction with private partners is largely one-way. This will be addressed further in the "lessons learned" section.

Participation in NDN is strictly voluntary, for both private organizations and the government. In its daily practice, NDN is operated by a dedicated team of analysts. For governance purposes, the community established a formal steering committee comprised of the NCSC itself and a selection of public and private partners. This steering committee serves to govern the NDN road map (e.g., platform functionality, member expansion) and resolve any operational or organizational issues.

5.6.3 Lessons Learned

The case studies described above resulted in several "lessons learned" concerning the establishment and optimization of CTI communities that employ automated information exchange channels. This section presents some of the most prominent findings.

■ *Automated exchange of CTI in a community context is viable and offers demonstrable value.* Both the European telco group and the Dutch NDN observed that community participation brought tangible value to their members. Some material evidence thereof is shown in Table 5.8, which depicts the extent to which (1) the NDN platform supplied threat indicators ("IoCs") to the IDS sensors in government infrastructures and (2) such indicators raised an actual alarm ("sighting"). As the table shows, threat information dispersed via the community channel led to substantial numbers of "sightings" in partner infrastructures. Arguably, this allowed these organizations to act

---

[33] The NCSC's role toward government bodies a.o. includes security monitoring and (coordination of) incident response and thus extends well beyond the supply of threat information.

Table 5.8   Effects of IoC Sharing in the Dutch NDN Community

	Aug. 2016	Sep. 2016	Oct. 2016	Nov. 2016
Active IoCs	5819	3356	4738	6669
Sightings	764	1297	341	487

upon (potential) incidents that they might not have seen—at least not in quite as timely a manner—had they not taken part in the community. On a deeper level, these "sightings" indicate that community effort can indeed act as an effective filter for identifying threat information with actual relevance (see Section 5.2).

■ *Active participation in a CTI community requires a capability that is not always in place.* The CTI working area is fairly new, and many organizations are still exploring what would constitute a mature CTI practice in their particular context. The performance of a CTI community, however, is greatly affected by the competence of its members. Organizations with limited CTI capabilities may for instance have trouble supplying meaningful threat information to their community partners. This was evident in the early stages of the telco pilot (see above), where some participants shared lengthy sets of threat indicators with no or limited contextual information (e.g., "malicious IPs" with no explanation of their exact nature). This left the recipients with little foundation to evaluate the threat and initiate an appropriate course of action. The need for reasonably mature CTI provisions also extends to the receiving end of the community concept. If participants are insufficiently able to follow up on intelligence received and create tangible value from it (i.e., demonstrably avoid incidents), the need to be present in the community might become subject to debate.

Both communities outlined above have the experience that participation in a CTI community actually stimulates the maturity of CTI provisions of individual members. Arguably, if organizations join a CTI community that is functioning well, they will be subjected to a steep learning curve that is beneficial for all involved parties. To achieve this, however, the community needs a foundation of members with (reasonably) mature CTI capabilities. This is a factor to consider when founding a CTI community or moving from a small pilot into a more elaborate operational setting. Based on the above experiences, a viable expansion strategy is to start the community with selected organizations that have relatively mature CTI capabilities (e.g., on an invitational basis) and consider less-developed candidates in a second stage (when a base level of community activity has been achieved). The message to take away in this respect is that more participants will not necessarily imply more participation.

■ *CTI communities cannot solely revolve around* "unique" *threat information.* Both communities considered above found that truly unique CTI is hard to obtain and generally comes in low volumes. A community that solely exchanges CTI of this nature will end up exhibiting little activity. This offers a limited basis for building threat information sharing into the daily routine of the involved specialists. A more effective foundation lies in the "vetting" of cyber threat information that was acquired from public sources. As explained above, threat information that was verified and designated as relevant by a trusted partner can be treated with a high degree of confidence, potentially allowing fully automated follow-up. This fulfills an evident need and ensures that working procedures are in fact running routinely whenever a more unique event does occur.

■ *Optimizing a CTI community means overcoming intrinsic and external barriers.* As explained throughout this chapter, the value of any CTI community is greatly catalyzed by the presence of trusted relationships among the participating organizations and specialists. Such trust not only involves the *intentions* but also the *competence* of community partners. Based on the experiences outlined above, it seems fair to say that trust is easiest to achieve in a community (1) that consists of natural peers and (2) has relatively few participants. The telco community has these characteristics, and in fact it did not encounter any material trust issues that might hinder the exchange of valuable threat information. In other constellations, however, establishing the desired level of trust is not always trivial. In the case of NDN, many private organizations were initially hesitant to contribute threat information to a community that was supervised by a government body. As a reason for their caution, many mentioned that government agencies might be forced to disclose the information shared by their organization through a request under the Freedom of Information Act (FoIA[34]). This issue has since been resolved, mostly[35] through legislative guarantees that FoIA directives will not apply to threat information that can be deduced to the originating community partner(s). What this example shows is that trust within a CTI community needs to be actively managed and may require rather particular arrangements.

■ *Resourcing and incentive affect the long-term sustainability of CTI communities.* In most organizations, CTI-related duties presently reside with the CERT or CSIRT team. For such teams, handling a (severe) incident will always have higher priority than sharing or processing threat information. Thus, under particular circumstances, the community contribution of such participants may come to an abrupt (albeit temporary) halt. Both the telco group and the NDN community encountered this phenomenon, which imposes a degree of

---

[34] In The Netherlands, this act is known as the "Wet Openbaarheid Bestuur" or WOB.

[35] In addition, the retention period of community intelligence was limited to a minimum (after which only statistics remain).

uncertainty upon the community's sustainability. Another relevant factor in this context is the *incentive* for organizations to actively share and collaborate with community partners. Here it is essential to pursue a proper balance between contributing and receiving threat information for all community members. As outlined above, this is not trivial because the maturity of CTI provisions (and thus the ability to offer a meaningful contribution) may vary greatly across individual partners. An easier provision (and one that is often overlooked) is to establish recipient-to-source feedback. Such feedback could for instance reveal if threat information shared was generally found useful and/or if any community partner acted upon it. Both the telco group and several NDN participants indicated that such feedback was greatly rewarding and acted as a stimulus for community activity.

5.7 Community Enrichment and Enhancements

Apart from sharing CTI information such as IoCs, TTPs, and campaigns among community members, there are several potential approaches to enriching the value of the CTI information shared within the community. In this section, some of these community enrichment approaches are discussed. In addition, an approach to securely and privately share IoCs and sightings is briefly described.

5.7.1 Feedback and Additions

The simplest form of community enrichment is providing feedback on the shared CTI Information. A basic example is a Like button for shared CTI. This does provide some indication on how the shared information was received by the community members but not much more. A more valuable form of feedback is reporting that the shared indicator of compromise resulted in a successful detection of an attack. This is typically referred to as a sighting. Also, reporting negative feedback on the shared CTI information can be of value, for instance, reporting that the shared indicator resulted in false positive detections. The latter two examples clearly support other community members' ability to better interpret the value of the shared CTI. Several of the CTI sharing communities and CTI sharing platforms already provide such feedback functions (e.g., MISP and OTX).

Suggesting the addition of certain information to previously shared CTI information is also a basic form of community enrichment. An example is the suggestion of adding some indicators. When a community member detects an incident based on indicators from previously shared CTI information, during the incident response new indicators may be identified. It makes sense to propose these new indicators be added to the already shared CTI information instead of creating and sharing a new CTI record on basically the same threat. Such additions typically need to be moderated to ensure that the suggested information is actually related and relevant to the previously shared CTI information.

5.7.2 Reporting Sightings and Incidents for Creating Situational Awareness

As described in the previous section, sharing sightings can be valuable for community members as they provides an indication that the CTI information was of value to another community member. Sharing sightings or shared IoCs can, however, also be used for the creation of situational awareness. In Fransen et al. (2015) and Settanni et al. (2016) a concept is presented for leveraging CTI sharing infrastructures to gain early insight into the large scale effects of cyber threats and incidents, in particular, those incidents that might have a disruptive effect on society either due to the cascading effect of an incident (e.g., a power outage impacts many other services) or the large scale of a cyber attack that targets and impacts many organizations simultaneously.

Both papers assume a CTI sharing infrastructure centrally coordinated by a national CERT (i.e., hub–spoke sharing model) with CSIRTs or Security Operation Centers (SOCs) from organizations responsible for critical infrastructure. The national CERT will typically coordinate the distribution of CTI, including Indicator, to the community members. The community members may report back to the national CERT on the following:

- *Number of sightings of one or more of the received IoCs*: This will provide the national CERT with information on the active use of the attack method or malware.
- *Potential impact of the threat for the organization*: This will create insight at the national CERT with respect to the severity of the threat for the organizations. The national CERT can use this information to assess the potential level of damage this threat could cause.
- *Incident related to the particular threat and/or IoC*: This will inform the national CERT of successful use of the attack method and will thereby increase the situational awareness at the national CERT on the active usage of the attack method.
- *Incident related to the particular threat and/or IoC and the impact to the organization*: In addition to the previous, this will inform the national CERT of the damage and/or disruptions caused by the incident.

Current initiatives such as the NDN (see Section 5.6.2) are already working toward the exchange of indicators of compromise and reporting back the "count" of the number of sightings. This is a very good first indicator that something is happening, but what the effect is on services rendered by individual organizations is not immediately clear. The ability to share the effects (or impact) is needed to get an insight as to the (potential) impact.

To illustrate the differences, the analogy of weather radar can be used. In this analogy, an indicator of compromise is the type of downpour (e.g., rain). The sighting is the actual downpour (e.g., amount of rain) and the impact is the related damage at a certain location (e.g., damage to a server due to leakage). The trick with cybersecurity is that there is an ever-increasing type of downpour and not a lot of experience in what the average impacts are when the downpour materializes. There needs to be a "translation" from sightings to impact information.

Reporting incidents and information on the impact of these incidents in particular is not something an organization will easily do. Breach notification laws (e.g., those in the Directive on Privacy and Electronic Communications (E-Privacy Directive) from 2009, and in the EU's General Data Protection Regulation) introduce mandates to report certain types of incidents to an authority, but this will not necessarily create a good basis for sharing sightings and incident information for the purpose described above. Mandates to report on breaches will drive organizations to create a formal compliance-oriented process for reporting to the authorities. When an organization can directly benefit from sharing this type of information, the hesitance to share the information may reduce.

5.7.3 Collaborative Analysis

Community members could also actively collaborate in the analysis and creation of CTI information. A CTI sharing platform could for instance enable two or more community members to setup a working space for discussing and collaboratively creating new CTI information. When, e.g., several members of a community become the victim of a particular threat, they can share their experiences within the workspace and collaboratively develop CTI information to be shared with the other community members. Such workspace can also be used to collaboratively analyze new threat information. When a new threat emerges, often not all details are completely clear. Moreover, typically not all initial information on the threat has to be correct. A group of community members can join in a collaborative workspace to share information that each collected and try to create trustworthy CTI information to be shared with the whole CTI sharing community. Such forms of collaboration can be very valuable, as many organizations have limited resources and expertise to analyze and draft good cyber threat intelligence. This type of collaboration can also helpful when a community wants to move beyond sharing indicators and move toward sharing higher value CTI (i.e., tactics, techniques and procedures (TTP) used by adversaries, campaigns, course of actions, and threat actors). This type of CTI is much more difficult and time consuming to establish but has more value in the defense against adversaries. This was first described by David Bianco in a blog post on the pyramid of pain.[36] He explained that adversaries can easily adapt to disclosure of indicators like file hashes and IP addresses. The disclosure of the TTP will require significantly more effort on the part of the adversary. By collaboratively analyzing and discussing the shared CTI information, and working

---

[36] http://detect-respond.blogspot.nl/2013/03/the-pyramid-of-pain.html; accessed January 2017.

toward creating insight in the TTP, campaigns, and possible courses of actions, the community can potentially achieve more value out of the collaboration.

5.7.4 *Private and Secure Sharing of Indicators and Sightings*

CTI data are often very sensitive. When law enforcement is involved in an investigation with the intention of catching attackers red-handed, it is not wise to share indicators or other information that could hint to the attackers that they have been discovered. Also, organizations are typically not willing to publicly communicate about cybersecurity incidents—particularly not when it is an ongoing attack. Quickly sharing indicators, TTPs, and other CTI information of ongoing attacks can, however, provide the most value for other CTI sharing community members. A valuable enhancement for a CTI sharing platform would therefore be the capability to share indicators of compromise without revealing details and anonymously sharing sightings and incidents. Note that a sighting is already sensitive as people could interpret it as a cybersecurity incident. There's no smoke without a fire.

Van de Kamp et al. (2016) describe two complementary cryptographic techniques to allow community members to share information without the need to immediately reveal the information: first, a mechanism to hide the details of an indicator of compromise so that it can be shared with community members but still allow the information to detect compromises. This is achieved by hashing the indicator. A community member receiving such a hashed Indicator can perform detection by hashing the observables and match those to the hashed IoC. The authors only consider "simple" IoCs that consist of formulas in disjunctive normal form (DNF), without negations, in which the propositional variables can be evaluated using an equality match. As an example, the paper described an IoC consisting of a destination IP address (destIP) and a destination port number (destIP =198.51.100.43 Δ destPort = 80). The values of the indicator can be hashed with function H to hide the actual value. To ensure the search space of the indicator is sufficiently large, the authors propose hashing the concatenation of the values and sharing the indicator as follows: destIP||destPort = H(198.51.100.43||80). The security can further be improved by using a nonsecret salt, chosen at random for each IOC, in the computation of the hash. Indeed, a community member will learn the values of the indicator when it successfully detects a compromise. Also, an adversary that was capable of stealing the hashed indicators can actively test whether its values used are among the hashed indicators.

Second, the paper described a mechanism to privately report back the number of sightings to the source by means of a construction for privacy-preserving aggregation (Shi, 2011). The authors assume that a sufficiently large number of community members collaboratively report the number of sighting for an indicator over a certain timespan to the source of the Indicator, e.g., a national CERT as described in Section 5.7.2. Each community member encrypts the number and sends it to the source. The source can only perform an AggregateDecrypt over all collected encrypted values and thereby only learns the total number of sightings reported.

In Settanni et al. (2016), an approach is described to limit the distribution of CTI information within a community to specific community members based on specific characteristics. The mechanism is based on attribute-based encryption (ABE) that provides a mechanism to cryptographically enforce access policies that are formulated using attributes describing the parties that should be able to decrypt (see Bethencourt et al., 2007). The access policy becomes part of the encrypted data and can only be decrypted if the access policy is satisfied. In other words, only those members that fit the description in the access policy used to decrypt the CTI information can decrypt it.

5.8 Conclusions

Driven by recent technological developments, CTI communities increasingly share information via standardized and automated communication channels. Case studies reveal that this approach not only facilitates an efficient exchange of threat information but also optimizes follow-up in the security processes of individual community participants.

Establishing an effective and sustainable CTI community comes with several challenges. While some of these are technical, special attention should be devoted to organizational aspects and the CTI capabilities of community partners. Prominent issues include demarcation of community objectives and membership conditions, establishment of appropriate confidentiality arrangements and fulfillment of applicable regulatory constraints.

While current solutions suffice for the basic exchange of threat information, technical advancements could enhance the value of CTI communities even further. Promising concepts include the establishment of recipient-to-sender feedback, inclusion of "sightings" and impact information in the community exchange, and provisions to share "sightings" and incidents anonymously.

Acknowledgments

The authors would like to thank the experts and coordinators of the Dutch National Cyber Security Center (The Hague), Proximus CSIRT (Brussels), and Swisscom CSIRT (Zurich) that kindly contributed to this chapter.

List of Abbreviations

ABE	Attribute-based encryption
API	Application Programming Interface
CERT	Computer Emergency Response Team
CIRCL	Computer Incident Response Center Luxembourg
CPNI	Centre for the Protection of National Infrastructure
CSIRT	Computer Security Incident Response Team
CSV	Comma-separated value
CTI	Cyber threat intelligence
CVE	Common vulnerabilities and exposures
DDoS	Distributed denial of service
FIRST	Forum of Incident Response and Security Teams
HASL	Handling, action, sharing, and licensing
ICT	Information and communications technology
IDS	Intrusion detection system
IEP	Information Exchange Policy
IoC	Indicator of compromise
IRC	Internet Relay Chat
ISAC	Information Sharing and Analysis Center
ISAO	Information Sharing and Analysis Organizations
JSON	JavaScript Object Notation
MISP	Malware Information Sharing Platform
MO	Modus operandi
NCIRC	NATO Computer Incident Response Capability
NCSC	National Cyber Security Center
NDN	National Detection Network
NICP	NATO Industry Cyber Partnership
OTX	Open Threat eXchange
SIEM	Security information and event management
SOC	Security Operation Center
STIX	Structured Threat Information eXpression
TAXII	Trusted Automated eXchange of Indicator Information
TF-CSIRT	Task Force-Computer Security Incident Response Teams
TLP	Traffic Light Protocol
TNO	Nederlandse Organisatie voor Toegepast Natuurwetenschappelijk Onderzoek (TNO; English: Netherlands Organisation for Applied Scientific Research)
TTP	Tactics, techniques, and procedures
XML	Extensible Markup Language

References

J. Bethencourt, A. Sahai, B. Waters, Ciphertext-policy attribute based encryption. In: *SP'07 Proceedings of the 2007 IEEE Symposium on Security and Privacy.* 2007, pp. 321–334.

European Union, Directive 2016/1148 of the European Parliament and of the Council concerning measures for a high common level of security of network and information systems across the Union, 2016. (Accessed June 20, 2017). Available at: http://eur-lex.europa.eu/legal-content/EN/TXT/?uri=uriserv:OJ.L_.2016.194.01.0001.01.ENG&toc=OJ:L:2016:194:TOC.

F. Fransen, A. Smulders, R. Kerkdijk, Cyber security information exchange to gain insight into the effects of cyber threats and incidents. *e & i Elektrotechnik und Informationstechnik,* 2015, 132: 106–112.

C. Johnson, L. Badger, D. Waltermire, J. Snyder, C. Skorupka, Guide to cyber threat information sharing. NIST special publication 800-50, 2016. (Accessed June 20, 2017). Available at: http://dx.doi.org/10.6028/NIST.SP.800-15.

G. Settanni, F. Skopik, Y. Shovgenya, R. Fiedler, M. Carolan, D. Conroy, K. Boettinger, M. Gall, G. Brost, C. Ponchel, M. Haustein, H. Kaufmann, K. Theuerkauf, P. Olli, A collaborative cyber incident management system for European interconnected critical infrastructures. *Elsevier Journal of Information Security and Applications (JISA),* 2017, 34, Part 2, pp. 166–182.

E. Shi, T.H. Chan, E.G. Rieffel, R. Chow, D. Song, Privacy-preserving aggregation of time-series data. In: *NDSS.* The Internet Society, 2011.

T.R. van de Kamp, A. Peter, M.H. Everts, W. Jonker, Private sharing of IOCs and sightings. In: *WISCS '16.* Vienna, Austria, October 24, 2016. New York: ACM, 2016, pp. 35–38.

C. Wagner, A. Dulaunoy, G. Wagener, A. Iklody, MISP: The design and implementation of a collaborative threat intelligence sharing platform. In: *Proceedings of the 2016 ACM on Workshop on Information Sharing and Collaborative Security.* New York: ACM, 2016, pp. 49–56.

Chapter 6

Situational Awareness for Strategic Decision Making on a National Level

Maria Leitner, Timea Pahi, and Florian Skopik
Austrian Institute of Technology

Contents

6.1 Introduction

The example scenarios in Chapter 2 demonstrated that cyber incidents, such as the power outage in the Ukraine, can have an impact on citizens. Power outages themselves can have a significant impact on health and life, environment, institutions, lifestyle, or economy as shown in (Praktiknjo et al., 2011). It is incontestable that a similar incident like this or a series of incidents can have an impact on national health, public safety and security, economy or other areas that are typically overseen or controlled by governments (and governmental authorities). In this chapter, "government" specifies a group of people who control a country and make decisions—to be referred to in this chapter as decision makers. These decisions include resolutions (on e.g., law, taxes, or policies). These resolutions can entail recommendations, guidelines, or obligations that have to be adapted in public and private organizations within the economic system. Modern economic systems enable allocating production, resources, and goods and services within, e.g., a society or country. High-impact incidents in critical infrastructures that lead to, e.g., power outages, water shortages, or the shutdown of Internet communication can put modern economic systems at risk. For example, without electricity, production is stopped; without cell phone service clients might not be able to call hotlines (e.g., emergency hotlines or hotline support), or without Internet access many services that use information and communication technologies (ICT) cannot be provided to or used by customers. Depending on the severity of the incidents, national decision makers have to inform citizens or provide measures to diminish the incidents. If national authorities are informed about incidents that might affect citizens, they can make decisions to mitigate or diminish the impact.

FURTHER INFORMATION: CYBERSPACE

National Security Presidential Directive 54/Homeland Security Presidential Directive 23 (NSPD-54/HSPD23) defines cyberspace as the interdependent network of information technology infrastructures, including the Internet, telecommunications networks, computer systems, and embedded processors and controllers in critical industries. Commonly the term also refers to the virtual environment of information and interactions between people.

As cyber incidents can have an impact on many areas of economic systems, national governments aim at gaining and providing situation awareness (situational awareness will be interchangeably used in this chapter) in cyberspace. The definition of situational awareness is mainly based on Endsley, 1988a,b, p. 792: "… the perception of the element in the environment within a volume of time and space, the comprehension of their meaning, and the projection of their status in the near future." Following this definition, national governments require

1. To perceive events and environmental elements within time and space. Activities for perception are, e.g., to establish a national cybersecurity policy, to identify high-impact incidents of critical infrastructure, to enable and provide a notification system between public authorities, or to provide an information sharing system between national stakeholders.

2 To comprehend their meaning. Understanding who attacked whom and why is challenging as it can become very complex to identify and determine the real attacker (cf. Chapter 2). National governments rely on critical infrastructure and other stakeholders to share information in order to establish a common operating picture.

3 To project their status in future. This entails, e.g., providing communication procedures and an information exchange between national stakeholders in case of large-scale incidents.

This description also shows that governments are acting as a point of exchange between national stakeholders (e.g., critical infrastructure) and as a link to international organizations as shown in Figure 6.1.

This chapter will focus on how to establish cyber situational awareness for national governments. Section 6.2 will provide an overview on how nations and international organizations establish cybersecurity policies. Furthermore, the implementation of cybersecurity centers at the national level is analyzed in Section 6.3. Section 6.4 examines situational awareness models for decision makers and how they can be adapted to national cybersecurity centers. How information and sources can contribute to common operating pictures is outlined in Section 6.5. Section 6.6 concludes this chapter.

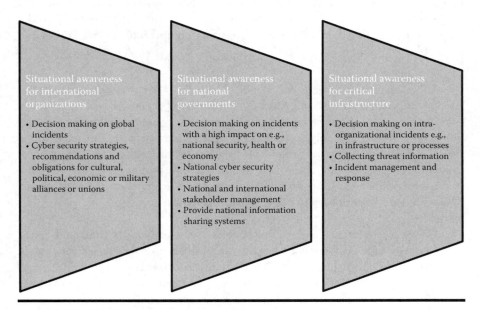

Figure 6.1   Situational awareness: overview.

6.2 An Overview of National and International Cybersecurity Strategies

This section describes how cybersecurity strategies (e.g., standards, policies, obligations, recommendations, or strategies) are defined by international organizations and national governments to maintain a level of security of and operations in cyberspace. Both perspectives provide interesting insights and results. For example in international organizations, Member States elaborate on and cooperate to identify cybersecurity strategies. Their findings are often the outcome of hours of work, discussion, and international cooperation. Three example countries provide an insight into how certain countries draft and implement cybersecurity policies.

> **FURTHER INFORMATION: CYBERSECURITY POLICY**
>
> Based on the White House (2009), a cybersecurity policy as used in this document includes strategy, policy, and standards regarding the security of and operations in cyberspace and encompasses the full range of threat reduction, vulnerability reduction, deterrence, international engagement, incident response, resiliency, and recovery policies and activities, including computer network operations, information assurance, law enforcement, diplomacy, military, and intelligence missions as they relate to the security and stability of the global information and communications infrastructure. The scope does not include other information and communications policy unrelated to national security or securing the infrastructure.

6.2.1 Cybersecurity Strategies of International Organizations

In this century, most international organizations have acknowledged the importance of cybersecurity and cyber resilience in existing and new technologies. Therefore, many organizations have started working groups to discuss and provide cybersecurity strategies. Their development often takes longer than the development of national strategies as there are typically more stakeholders involved (e.g., UN nations or European Union). Many organizations have developed guidelines, recommendations, or resolutions that provide at an international level a certain level of consensus. However, its implementation is often differently handled. In the following, three selected examples of international organizations are described: the European Union, the United Nations, and the North Atlantic Treaty Organization (NATO). However, many other international organizations have started to define and specify international agreements. For example, an overview is given in the International Cyber Developments Review (INCYDER)[1] database.

---

[1] NATO CCD CoE, INCYDER, https://ccdcoe.org/incyder.html; Last visited on 28.12.2016.

6.2.1.1 European Union

The European Union (EU) has been actively working on specifying strategies for cybersecurity and cybercrime. The EU published the Cybersecurity Strategy of the EU (European Commission et al., 2013) and the European Agenda on Security (European Commission, 2015) to provide a strategic framework for the EU entities on cybersecurity and cybercrime. In addition, the Digital Single Market strategy specifies trust and security as important aspects. The key goals for cybersecurity for the European Commission[2] are:

1. Increasing cybersecurity capabilities and cooperation. Enabling capabilities and information sharing for all Member States at equal levels. In this area, the Directive on Security of Network and Information Systems (NIS Directive European Union, 2016, see Chapter 7) is the main instrument for the protection of IT networks and systems.
2. Making the EU a strong player in cybersecurity. Increasing competitiveness by enabling a high digital security technology and standard for citizens, enterprises, and public organizations.
3. Mainstreaming cybersecurity in EU policies. Incorporate cybersecurity in future EU policy initiatives such as for new technologies or emerging sectors [e.g., connected cars or Internet of Things (IoT)].

The EU aims at engaging stakeholders from public and private sectors to increase cyber resilience. Further cybersecurity activities are supported by ENISA and the Computer Emergency Response Team for the EU institutions (CERT-EU). The EU is also linked to international organizations and other Nations to collaborate in matters concerning cyberspace.

6.2.1.1.1 European Network and Information Security Agency (ENISA)

ENISA is a center for cybersecurity in Europe. It is actively involved in improving and protecting network and information security (NIS) within the EU and its Member States. ENISA's[3] activities are manifold and can be assigned to the following areas: recommendations, activities that support policy making and implementation as well as hands-on work, in collaboration with operational teams. ENISA consults and works closely with Member States and the private sector; therefore ENISA

- Organizes pan-European cybersecurity exercises.
- Develops national cybersecurity strategies.

---

[2] EU, Cyber security, https://ec.europa.eu/digital-single-market/en/cybersecurity; Last visited on 28.12.2016.

[3] ENISA, What does ENISA do, https://www.enisa.europa.eu/about-enisa; Last visited on 28.12.2016.

- Enables cybersecurity capability building, computer security incident response teams (CSIRTs) cooperation.
- Develops studies on various topics in cybersecurity such as threats and vulnerabilities, cloud computing, data protection, privacy enhancing technologies, and others.

6.2.1.1.2 European Defence Agency

The European Defence Agency (EDA) has defined cybersecurity/cyber defense as a priority action[4] in the Capability Development Plan.[5] The EDA addresses thereby the *Cyber Defence Policy Framework* (Council of the European Union, 2014) that was published by the Council of the European Union in November 2014. The framework contains five priorities:

- Supporting the development of Member States' cyber defense capabilities related to the Common Security and Defence Policy (CSDP)
- Enhancing protection of the CSDP information and communication networks that are used by EU entities
- Supporting civil-military cooperation and synergies with wide-ranging EU cyber policies, relevant for EU bodies and agencies as well as for the private sector
- Improving training, education, and exercises opportunities
- Enhancing cooperation with relevant international partners

Based on this framework, EDA is active in the following areas:

- *Training and exercises:* EDA organizes and hosts several exercises in the area of cybersecurity and cyber defense with different target groups (e.g., from operational experts to decision makers).
- *Cyber situational awareness:* EDA is working on cyber defense situational awareness for CSDP activities and ways cyber defense can be integrated into military planning processes.
- *Cyber Defence Research Agenda (CDRA):* Research aims at developing "dual use" technologies, technologies relevant for the civil and military domain. The CDRA develops a R&D roadmap for the next 10 years.
- *Advanced persistent threats (APT) Detection:* APT detection is a key topic in various projects as targets can be EU entities or other organizations. EDA is currently leading a project to develop solutions.
- *Protection of information, cryptography:* Several initiatives have been started to work on this area within the European Framework Cooperation.

---

[4] EDA, Cyber Defence, http://www.eda.europa.eu/what-we-do/activities/activities-search/cyber-defence; Last visited on 29.01.2016.

[5] EDA, Capability Development Plan, http://www.eda.europa.eu/docs/default-source/eda-publications/futurecapabilities_cdp_brochure; Last visited on 29.01.2016.

6.2.1.2 United Nations

There have been several activities regarding cybersecurity in the UN. So far, most resolutions issued by UN entities have been passed in the UN General Assembly (UNGA) or the Security Council (UNSC). Many resolutions, with the exception of those adopted by the UNSC, are recommended and not legally binding for Member States. Until 2016, no resolutions regarding cybersecurity have been adopted by UNSC.

The UNGA held the *World Summit on the Information Society* (WSIS) in 2003 and 2005. At the WSIS, the International Telecommunication Union (ITU),[6] a UN specialized agency for issues regarding ICT, was entrusted with the role of facilitator of action line C5 [i.e., *Building confidence and security in the use of ICTs in* (UN, 2015)] by heads of states and world leaders. For a complete list of action lines, refer to UN (2015). In 2007, the ITU launched a Global Cybersecurity Agenda as a framework for international cooperation in this domain. In 2014, the WSIS+10 High-Level Event was an extended version of the WSIS Forum and reviewed the outcomes of the past 10 years based on the WSIS stakeholder reports and developed new proposals for the WSIS action lines.

In addition, several groups of governmental experts (GGE) have been established (in 2004, 2009,[7] 2011,[8] and 2014[9]) that focused on topics in the area of cybersecurity. Except for 2004, all GGEs have produced consensus reports showing the need for international cooperation and consensus in cybersecurity.

6.2.1.3 NATO

NATO adopted an enhanced policy and action plan[10] for cyber defense, which was endorsed by the Allies in September 2014. This policy establishes that cyber defense is part of NATOs core task on collective defense, acknowledges that international law applies in cyberspace, and ensures partnerships with industry. The action plan includes activities for capability development, education, training, and exercises and partnerships.

In July 2016, NATO recognized cyberspace as a domain of operation NATO must defend, as in the air, on land, or at sea. Furthermore, developing cyber defense

---

6 ITU Cybersecurity activities, http://www.itu.int/en/action/cybersecurity/Pages/default.aspx; Last visited on 28.12.2016.
7 UN General Assembly, Group of Governmental Experts on Developments in the Field of Information and Telecommunications in the Context of International Security, http://www.un.org/ga/search/view_doc.asp?symbol=A/65/201; Last visited on 28.12.2016.
8 UN General Assembly, Group of Governmental Experts on Developments in the Field of Information and Telecommunications in the Context of International Security, http://www.un.org/ga/search/view_doc.asp?symbol=A/68/98; Last visited on 28.12.2016.
9 UN General Assembly, Group of Governmental Experts on Developments in the Field of Information and Telecommunications in the Context of International Security, http://www.un.org/ga/search/view_doc.asp?symbol=A/70/174; Last visited on 28.12.2016.
10 NATO Cyber defence, http://www.nato.int/cps/en/natohq/topics_78170.htm; Last visited on 27.12.2016.

capabilities is one of the main cyber defense activities of NATO. For example, the NATO Computer Incident Response Capability (NCIRC) aims at protecting NATOs networks and systems by providing 24/7 cyber defense support. Further, it has the key role in responding in cases of collective defense. In addition, cyber-defense capabilities are defined for NATO member countries via the NATO Defence Planning Process.

Furthermore, NATO aims at increasing cyber-defense capacity by improving and advancing cyber-defense education, training, and exercises. The NATO Cooperative Cyber Defence Centre of Excellence (CCD CoE) in Tallinn, Estonia, hosts the research and training center for cyber-defense education, consultation, lessons learned, research, and development. The CCD CoE hosts regular NATO exercises such as the annual Cyber Coalition Exercise that allows re-enacting cyber-defense scenarios on virtual environments simulating IT networks and systems. In 2016, CCD CoE has 16 sponsoring nations (NATO Member States) as well as 2 contributing participants (Austria and Finland). The NATO Communications and Information Systems School (NCISS) in Latina, Italy, provides training to staff from member countries as well as non-NATO countries relating to NATO communication and information systems. The NATO School in Oberammergau, Germany, conducts cyber defense-related education and training to support NATO operations, strategy, policy, doctrine, and procedures. The NATO Defense College in Rome, Italy, fosters strategic thinking on political-military matters.

NATO cooperates with partners such as the EU, the UN, or the Organization for Security and Co-operation in Europe (OSCE) as well as other relevant countries to support and strengthen international security. In addition, it provides a NATO Industry Cyber Partnership (NICP) to foster relationships to industry as well as other entities such as CERTs.

The policy on cyber defense is implemented by multiple NATO bodies and members. Any collective defense response, however, would be managed by the North Atlantic Council (NAC). The NAC is the principle authority in cyber defense crisis and incident response management. Subordinate to NAC, the Cyber Defence Committee (CDC) is the lead committee for cyber defense policy and governance that provides also consultation in these matters to NATO allies. Furthermore, the NATO Cyber Defence Management Board (CDMB) is responsible for coordinating cyber defense throughout NATO civilian and military bodies and consists of stakeholders in cybersecurity within NATO. Moreover, the NATO Communications and Information Agency (NCIA) deals with cyber activities. The NCIRC is incorporated into NCIA.

6.2.2 National Cybersecurity Strategies

Due to highly interconnected stakeholders, IT networks and systems, international cooperation, and coordination are gaining in importance for the protection of global and local networks and services. Conventional strategies require a global view for the stabilization and protection of IT networks and systems. This paradigm shift has been identified in national and international cybersecurity strategies within the past 10 years (Franke and Brynielsson, 2014). In fact, the long-term protection of IT networks and systems can be ensured only by the cooperation of governments, industry (such as vendors, owners, and operators), and society.

Nowadays, many national countries develop their own cybersecurity strategies. Several reports have assessed national cybersecurity strategies. For example, Luiijf et al. (2013) compare 19 national cybersecurity strategies of Australia, Canada, Czech Republic, Estonia, France, Germany, India, Japan, Lithuania, Luxembourg, Romania, the Netherlands, New Zealand, South Africa, Spain, Uganda, the United Kingdom (2009 and 2011), and the United States. The authors compare the strategies' commonalities and weaknesses. For example, they assess the visions, strategic objectives, guiding principles, and stakeholders. They further propose a structure for a national cybersecurity strategy:

1. Executive summary
2. Introduction
3. Strategic national vision on cybersecurity
4. Relationship of the national cybersecurity strategy with other strategies (national, international, and legal frameworks)
5. Guidance principles
6. Relationship with other strategies (national, international, and legal frameworks)
7. Cybersecurity objective(s) (between one and four)
8. Outline of the tactical action lines
9. Glossary
10. Annex (optional). Envisioned operational activities

Another example is the EU Cybersecurity dashboard in BSA (2015) that compares cybersecurity strategies within the EU countries. In particular, legal foundations, operational entities (e.g., CERTs), public–private partnerships, sector-specific cybersecurity plans, and educational aspects were compared (see the website[11] for the comparison results). The results showed that most of the EU countries are working toward national cybersecurity strategies and the protection of the critical infrastructure. However, differences exist in the policies, legal frameworks, and operational capabilities. For example, the range of capabilities and mission of national CERTs vary greatly. The study also announces that the implementation of the NIS Directive (European Union, 2016) will contribute to closing gaps in cybersecurity among Member States. Another study by ENISA compares the national cybersecurity strategies of 18 EU Member States, for example in goals, input indicators, outputs, and participation of stakeholders (e.g., CERTs, CI) (ENISA, 2014).

---

[11] BSA EU Cybersecurity Dashboard, http://cybersecurity.bsa.org/index.html; Last visited on 27.12.2016.

Other examples include handbooks such as the *Crisis and Risk Network* (CRN) and the International *Critical Information Infrastructure Protection* (CIIP) handbook. The CIIP handbook 2008/2009 (Brunner and Suter, 2008) focuses on national governmental efforts to protect critical infrastructure. It summarizes the strategies and plans for national CIIP of Australia, Austria, Brazil, Canada, Estonia, Finland, France, Germany, Hungary, India, Italy, Japan, Republic of Korea, Malaysia, the Netherlands, Norway, Poland, Russia, Singapore, Spain, Sweden, Switzerland, United Kingdom, and United States.

Following are four selected examples of national cybersecurity strategies. Please refer to the studies mentioned above to investigate further national cybersecurity strategies. Although each nation provides its own strategy, overall similarities can be identified. For example, governments need to protect and defend their national economy, safety, and security as well as public health with adequate measures.

6.2.2.1 Germany

Germany published its national cybersecurity strategy (Federal Ministry of the Interior) in 2011. The strategy aims at ensuring cybersecurity, enforcing rights, and protecting critical information infrastructures at a national level and in cooperation with international partners. The strategic objectives and measures for the cybersecurity strategy are based on the critical infrastructure protection (CIP) implementation that focuses on 10 strategic areas:

1. Protection of critical information infrastructures
2. Secure IT systems in Germany
3. Strengthening IT security in the public administration
4. National Cyber Response Center
5. National cybersecurity council
6. Effective crime control in cyberspace
7. Effective coordinated action to ensure cybersecurity in Europe and worldwide
8. Use of reliable and trustworthy information technology
9. Personnel development in federal authorities
10. Tools to respond to cyber attacks

In the following, only the fourth and fifth strategic areas will be discussed. Please refer to Federal Ministry of the Interior (2011) for more details. The fourth strategic area "National Cyber Response Center" (NCRC) aims at establishing a national cybersecurity center (NCSC) for enhanced cooperation and coordination among all state authorities in case of cyber incidents. In particular, it will enable information sharing of vulnerabilities in devices or products, attacks, and Threat Actors and analyze and recommend mitigation measures. In addition, stakeholders will incorporate adequate measures to contribute to cybersecurity. The NCRC will provide recommendations to the National Cyber Security Council for early warnings and prevention on a regular or incident-specific basis.

The fifth strategic area is about setting up a national cybersecurity council that includes representatives of governmental and federal authorities as well as associate members from business and academia. It aims to coordinate interdisciplinary and preventive cybersecurity measures between the private and public sectors.

6.2.2.2 Switzerland

In 2012, Switzerland defined a cybersecurity strategy in Eidgenössisches department für Verteidigung, Bevölkerungsschutz and Sport VBS (2012) for the protection of information and communication infrastructures against cyber threats. It aims for the following three long-term goals, based on Eidgenössisches department für Verteidigung, Bevölkerungsschutz and Sport VBS (2012, p. 3):

- Early recognition of cyber threats and dangers
- The increase of the resilience of critical infrastructure
- The effective reduction of cyber risks, in particular cybercrime, cyber espionage, and cyber sabotage

In this context, seven spheres of actions and measures were proposed (see Table 6.1).

Table 6.1 Sphere of Actions and Measures

Sphere of Action 1		Measures
Research and Development	1	New cyber risks connected with related problems must be researched.
Sphere of Action 2		**Measures**
Risk and vulnerability analysis	2	Independent evaluation of systems Risk analyses to minimize risks in collaboration with authorities, ICT-service or system providers
	3	Examine ICT infrastructure for systematic, organizational or technical vulnerabilities.
Sphere of Action 3		**Measures**
Analysis of the threat landscape	4	Establish a picture of the situation and its development.
	5	Review of incidents for the development of measures
	6	Overview of cases and coordination of inter-cantonal complex cases

(Continued)

Table 6.1 (*Continued*) Sphere of Actions and Measures

Sphere of Action 4	Measures	
Competence building	7	Establish an overview of competence building offers and identification of deficiencies.
	8	Fill in gaps in competence building and increased use of high-quality offers.
Sphere of Action 5	**Measures**	
International relations and initiatives	9	Active participation of Switzerland in Internet governance
	10	Cooperation at the international security policy level
	11	Coordination of actors involved in initiatives and best practices, relating to security or assurance processes
Sphere of Action 6	**Measures**	
Continuity and crisis management	12	Strengthening and improvement of resilience toward disturbances and incidents
	13	Coordination of activities, primarily with directly involved actors and support of decision-making processes with expertise
	14	Active measures to identify the perpetrator and possible impairment of its infrastructure in the event of a specific threat
	15	Elaboration of a concept for management procedures and processes to resolve problems in good time
Sphere of Action 7	**Measures**	
Legal basis	16	Evaluation of existing legislation on the basis of measures and implementation concepts and prioritization of immediate adjustment needs

Source: Eidgenössisches Departement für Verteidigung, Bevölkerungsschutz and Sport VBS, National Strategy for Switzerland's Protection against Cyber Risks, Schweizerische Eidgenossenschaft, https://www.melani.admin.ch/dam/melani/en/dokumente/2013/05/nationale_strategiezumschutzder-schweizvorcyber-risiken.pdf.download.pdf/national_strategyforswitzer-landsprotectionagainstcyberrisks.pdf, 2012.

Furthermore, measures can be classified into four categories based on the Federal Department of Finance (FDF) et al. (2015):

■ Prevention: risk and vulnerability analysis for critical infrastructure operators and the Federal Administration
■ Response: threat situation, incident analysis, and identification of perpetrators
■ Continuity: continuity and crisis management
■ Support processes: research and competence building, international cooperation, and legal bases

6.2.2.3 United Kingdom

The cybersecurity strategy of the United Kingdom has been developed in HM Government (2010, 2016). This section will further discuss only the latter as it provides a strategy through 2021. In the 2016 cybersecurity strategy, five potential Threat Actors are identified: First, *cyber criminals* are criminals that commit cyber-dependent crimes (such as stealing, destroying, or damaging data) or cyber-enabled crimes (such as CEO fraud tactics or data theft). Second, *states and state-sponsored threats* are typically larger groups of people that aim to penetrate or infiltrate networks and services. These groups often have large sets of cyber capabilities and therefore can launch more sophisticated attacks. Third, *terrorists* are groups of people that aim to conspire to damage and potentially harm national interests. Depending on the level of expert knowledge, terrorists can use cyber-related activities to attract media and society. Fourth, *hacktivists* are people that are decentralized and focus on specific issues. They select potential targets based on a set of criteria related to the issue. They often aim at disrupting business processes or value chains (e.g., DDoS attacks) or attract media attention (e.g., website defacements). Last, *script kiddies* are typically individuals that use scripts and programs developed by others to perform cyber attacks.

Also, several vulnerabilities are identified, such as an expanding range of devices, poor cyber hygiene and compliance, insufficient training and skills, legacy and unpatched systems, and availability of hacking resources.

In the cybersecurity strategy in HM Government (2016), three categories are defined to tackle the challenges that lie ahead in cybersecurity. DEFEND aims at defending systems, enabling incident response planning and management procedures, and ensuring that systems are protected and resilient. DETER centers on the detection and understanding of cyber incidents and not only how they can be persecuted legally, but also how one can take offensive actions. DEVELOP is about fostering and growing innovation and research to enable cybersecurity capabilities for individuals as well as organizations and industry.

6.2.2.4 United States of America

In the United States, several documents can be linked to cybersecurity strategies. The cyberspace policy review in the White House (2009) consists of a set of strategies to assure the resilience of information and communication infrastructures. A near-term and mid-team action plan is suggested to engage society, industry, and public authorities in cybersecurity activities, sharing responsibility in a partnership between government and private sectors, managing and planning detailed incident-response plans, and empowering innovation by increasing research and development activities for cybersecurity. In particular

- Leading from the top
  - Anchor leadership at the White House.
  - Review laws and policies.
  - Strengthen federal leadership and accountability for cybersecurity.
  - Elevate state, local, and tribal leadership.
- Building capacity for a digital nation
  - Increase public awareness.
  - Increase cybersecurity education.
  - Expand federal information technology workforce.
  - Promote cybersecurity as an enterprise leadership responsibility.
- Sharing responsibility for cybersecurity
  - Improve partnership between private sector and government.
  - Evaluate potential barriers impeding evolution and public–private partnership.
  - Partner effectively with the international community.
- Create effective information sharing and incident response
  - Build a framework for incident response.
  - Enhance information sharing to improve incident-response capabilities.
  - Improve cybersecurity across all infrastructures.
- Encourage innovation
  - The future.
  - Link R&D frameworks to infrastructure development.
  - Establish identity management as an option.
  - Integrate globalization policy with supply chain security.
  - Maintain national security/emergency preparedness capabilities.

The international strategy for cyberspace in the White House (2011) analyzes and defines the basic principles for using cyberspace, thereby relying on open and interoperable, secure and reliable, and stable (through standardization) technologies. Furthermore, it addresses how diplomacy, defense, and development can be handled in cyberspace in the future, and policy priorities are specified. In 2013, the President issued Executive Order 13636, "Improving Critical Infrastructure Cybersecurity" that aimed at improving the security and resilience of critical infrastructure providers in the United States and outlining responsibilities of federal departments and agencies. The order states "It is the policy of the United States to enhance the security and resilience of the Nation's critical infrastructure and to maintain a cyber environment that encourages efficiency, innovation, and economic prosperity while promoting safety, security, business confidentiality, privacy, and civil liberties" in the White House (2013, Sect. 1). The Cybersecurity Framework was developed in response to the Executive Order and issued in Version 1.0 in (National Institute of Standards and Technology, 2014) by the National Institute of Standards and Technology (NIST) in 2014. The voluntary Cybersecurity Framework consists of a set of industry standards and best practices to support organizations in assessing and evaluating their cybersecurity risks.

The Department of Defense (DoD) (2015) defined a cyber strategy in 2015. The department is responsible for defending the U.S. homeland and U.S. interests from attack, including attacks that may occur in cyberspace. The strategy aims at guiding the development of cyber forces, strengthen cyber defense and cyber deterrence posture. The DoD has three primary missions in cyberspace (based on DoD (2015):

- Defend its own networks, systems, and information
- Must be prepared to defend the United States and its interests against cyber attacks of significant consequence
- (If directed by the President or the Secretary of Defense) must be able to provide integrated cyber capabilities to support military operations and contingency plans

Furthermore, the DoD specifies five strategic goals and implementation measures in DoD (2015):

1. Build and maintain ready forces and capabilities to conduct cyberspace operations.
2. Defend the DoD information network, secure DoD data, and mitigate risks to DoD missions.
3. Be prepared to defend the U.S. homeland and U.S. vital interests from disruptive or destructive cyber attacks of significant consequence.
4. Build and maintain viable cyber options and plan to use those options to control conflict escalation and to shape the conflict environment at all stages.
5. Build and maintain robust international alliances and partnerships to deter shared threats and increase international security and stability.

6.3 Cybersecurity Centers and Their Responsibilities and Tasks

While the section above discussed national and international strategies, one of the common themes is to establish (national) cybersecurity centers (CSCs or NCSCs) to increase cyber resilience of nations as well as the coordination and provision of information sharing systems between national stakeholders and governments and other related activities. CSCs are often called situation centers or IT incident response and management centers depending on the nation or intended functionality. This section will use the term CSCs and further elaborate on their stakeholders, tasks, and responsibilities. Selected examples are given at the end of the section.

6.3.1 Stakeholders

CSCs aim to coordinate (cybersecurity) activities with different stakeholders—from vendors and critical infrastructure providers to political parties and organizations. CSCs can enable and provide measures to ensure the information exchange of cyber threat information between stakeholders. Doing that, CSCs aim to collect and interpret this information in order to detect potential threats and attacks and provide countermeasures. Figure 6.2 displays how CSCs interact with decision makers and other stakeholders from various domains (such as energy, oil and gas, or ICT).

CSCs interact for example with decision makers that require a certain Cyber Common Operating Picture (cf. Section 6.5.1) to make decisions. Further

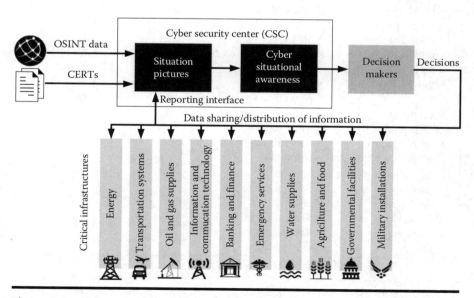

Figure 6.2 Cybersecurity center and stakeholders (Skopik, 2016).

stakeholders are organizations (such as critical infrastructure providers such as banks, energy or water suppliers, and Internet providers). These organizations are shown in the figure by domains. In addition, national computer emergency response teams (CERTs) or CSIRTs are often the first contact for organizations about cyber incidents (such as DDOS attacks or CEO fraud scams) and distribute information on publicly known vulnerabilities (Skopik et al., 2012).

6.3.2 Tasks and Responsibilities

Table 6.2 contains recommendations of ENISA for possible services and tasks of national CSIRTs. The tasks are split in four categories: reactive services, proactive services, artifact handling, and security quality management.

Table 6.2   Possible Services of CSIRTs (based on ENISA[12])

Reactive Services	Proactive Services	Artifact Handling	Security Quality Management
• Alert and warning • Incident handling • Incident analysis • Incident response on site • Incident response coordination • Vulnerability handling • Vulnerability analysis • Vulnerability response • Vulnerability response coordination • Forensic evidence collection • Tracking or tracing	• Announcements • Technology watch • Security audits or assessments • Configuration and maintenance of security tools, application, infrastructures, and services • Development of security tools • Intrusion detection services • Security-related information dissemination • Infrastructure review • Best practice review • Scanning • Penetration testing	• Artifact analysis • Artifact response • Artifact response coordination	• Risk analysis • Business continuity and disaster recovery • Security consulting • Awareness building • Education/Training • Product evaluation or certification

---

12 ENISA, https://www.enisa.europa.eu/activities/cert/support/guide/appendix/csirt-services; Last visited on 04.02.2016.

6.3.3 Selected Examples of CSCs

This section provides an overview of selected examples of CSCs based on publicly available information. Note that there is limited information on CSCs available (to protect national security measures). Hence, it can be assumed that there is far more (confidential) information available concerning the competencies and progress of the centers.

6.3.3.1 Germany

Germany has established several centers relating to cybersecurity that are coordinated by the Federal Office for Information Security (abbreviated BSI, Bundesamt für Sicherheit und Informationstechnik). In the following, the three centers are outlined:

■ *BSI IT-Lage und Analysezentrum*[13] (IT Situation and Analysis Center) was established based on the national cybersecurity strategy (see Section 6.2.2.1). The center is the primary 24/7 contact for public authorities, critical infrastructure providers, and partners. On a daily basis, open sources on the Internet are skimmed in order to determine the current state of the Internet and to identify potential threats and vulnerabilities that are summarized in regular reports.
■ *BSI IT-Krisenreaktionszentrum*[14] (IT Crisis and Response Center) aims primarily at providing fast response to and countermeasures against major incidents in order to minimize damages and impact. In the center, cyber incidents are analyzed, rated, and forwarded to relevant offices.
■ *Nationales Cyber-Abwehrzentrum*[15] (National Cyber Defense Center) has the objective to optimize the operational cooperation among all relevant offices and public authorities and to coordinate protection and defense measures for cyber incidents.

6.3.3.2 Switzerland

Die *Melde- und Analysestelle Informationssicherung (MELANI)*[16] (Reporting and Analysis Centre for Information Assurance) is a center where partners collaborate

---

[13] BSI, IT-Lagezentrum, https://www.bsi.bund.de/DE/Themen/Cyber-Sicherheit/Aktivitaeten/IT-Lagezentrum/itlagezentrum_node.html (in German); Last visited on 15.12.2015.
[14] BSI, IT-Krisenreaktionszentrum, https://www.bsi.bund.de/DE/Themen/Cyber-Sicherheit/Aktivitaeten/IT-Krisenreaktionszentrum/itkrisenreaktionszentrum_node.html (in German); Last visited on 15.12.2015.
[15] BMI Deutschland, Nationales Cyber-Abwehrzentrum, http://www.bmi.bund.de/DE/Themen/IT-Netzpolitik/IT-Cybersicherheit/Cybersicherheitsstrategie/Cyberabwehrzentrum/cyberabwehrzentrum_node.html (in German); Last visited on 15.12.2015.
[16] MELANI, https://www.melani.admin.ch/melani/de/home.html (in German); Last visited on 15.12.2015.

from areas of computer systems security, Internet security, and the protection of critical infrastructure. In particular, the center's tasks align with the four pillars of the information assurance system are as follows: (1) prevention, (2) early detection, (3) minimizing the impact of cyber attacks and crisis, and (4) alleviating the causes of crisis. Please refer to Informatikstrategieorgan Bund ISB (2002) and Cavelty (2014) for more details on the pillars.

The tasks of MELANI are, based on Rytz and Römer (2003):

- *Reporting office for technical events* (e.g., incidents) in Switzerland that affect networks and computer systems. Such tasks are typically handled by CERTs (i.e., it requires the operation of a national CERT).
- *Reporting office for the impact of business disruptions in information and communication technologies.* Examples include traffic systems, mobile networks, or other ICT-related infrastructure.
- *Cybersecurity center.* The incoming incident reports and the activities of the CERT will be brought together to establish situational awareness.
- *Notification of public authorities and relevant offices* such as SONIA, a special task force on information assurance.
- *Communication and distribution of information* has to be performed depending on the target audience (SONIA, public authorities, industry, citizens).
- *Prevention:* Lessons learned and best practices are documented and added as recommendations or strategies that can be used for industry, public authorities, or citizens.

MELANI generates reports every half year in order to assess the current situation of information assurance in Switzerland and internationally.

6.3.3.3 United Kingdom

As part of Government Communications Headquarters (GCHQ), a British intelligence and security organization, the *National Cyber Security Center* (NCSC) is United Kingdom's authority on cybersecurity. Starting in October 2016, it brings together the Information Security arm of GCHQ—the Center for the Protection of National Infrastructure, CERT-UK, and the Center for Cyber Assessment. According to HM Government (2016), the NCSC handles national cyber incidents, provides an authoritative voice and center of expertise on cybersecurity, and delivers mitigation strategies and advice to government and industry. It will be a center for incident management and detection, analysis and evaluation of threats, and the addressing of systemic vulnerabilities.

6.3.3.4 United States of America

In the United States, the Department of Homeland Security (DHS) is responsible for protecting critical infrastructure from physical or cyber threats. It operates the

National Cybersecurity and Communications Integration Center (NCCIC)[17], a center where several partners involved in cybersecurity and communications protection coordinate and synchronize their efforts. Its mission is to "operate at the intersection of the private sector, civilian, law enforcement, intelligence, and defense communities, applying unique analytic perspectives, ensuring shared situational awareness, and orchestrating synchronized response efforts while protecting the Constitutional and privacy rights of Americans in both the Cybersecurity and communications domains."

The NCCIC is comprised of four branches:

■ *NCCIC Operations & Integration* (NO&I) develops operational planning, training, and exercises for the NCCIC. This includes also managing cyber exercises (from small to large scale) such as the DHS Cyber Storm[18] exercises.

■ *United States Computer Emergency Readiness Team* (US-CERT) aims at providing cybersecurity by analyzing threats and vulnerabilities, responding to major incidents, and sharing information with national and international partners.

■ *Industrial Control Systems Cyber Emergency Response Team* (ICS-CERT)[19] has a mission to guide a collaboration between the government and industry to improve cybersecurity posture of control systems within the critical infrastructure. It aims to identify vulnerabilities and develop mitigation strategies to reduce risks within and across all critical infrastructure sectors in cooperation with system vendors and operators.

■ *National Coordinating Center for Communications* (NCC)[20] continuously monitors national and international incidents and events that impact emergency communications. Incidents include not only acts of terror but also catastrophes such as floods or earthquakes. In 2000, the White House designated the NCC as Information Sharing and Analysis Center (ISAC) for Telecommunications, in accordance with Presidential Decision Directive-63.

6.4 Situational Awareness Models Supporting Strategic Decision-Making Processes

In the early 1980s and 1990s, situational awareness (SA) was about how a person perceived and understood his or her environment, in particular a dynamic and evolving

---

[17] US-CERT NCCIC, https://www.us-cert.gov/nccic; Last visited on 27.12.2016.

[18] Cyber Storm: Security Cyber Space, https://www.dhs.gov/cyber-storm; Last visited on 27.12.2016.

[19] ICS-CERT, https://ics-cert.us-cert.gov/; Last visited on 27.12.2016.

[20] NCC, https://www.us-cert.gov/nccic/ncc-watch; Last visited on 27.12.2016.

environment. The concept had its origins in the military domain. For example, pilots have to be aware of their current situations, assess and evaluate ongoing events, and predict future developments. In their ongoing situation assessments, they have to include and value different parameters (e.g., their location, flight direction, mission plan, and fuel consumption) and entities (e.g., opponents or civilians). In this context, several definitions were specified and are summarized in Table 6.3.

Table 6.3 Definitions of Situational Awareness

Year	Citation	Reference
1987	"Situation awareness is knowledge of current and near-term disposition of both friendly and enemy forces within a volume of airspace."	Hamilton (1987)
1988	"Where, what, when, and who. Where refers to spatial awareness, what characterizes identity awareness, who is associated with responsibility or automation awareness, and when signifies temporal awareness."	Harwood et al. (1988)
1991	"Situational awareness is principally (though not exclusively) cognitive, enriched by experience."	Hartman and Secrist (1991)
1992	"SA is a pilot's (or aircrew's) continuous perception of self and aircraft in relation to the dynamic environment of flight, threats, and mission, and the ability to forecast, then execute tasks based on that perception. It is problem solving in a three-dimensional spatial relationship complicated by the fourth dimension of time compression, where there are too few givens and too many variables."	Carroll (1992)
	"Situation Awareness refers to the ability to rapidly bring to consciousness those characteristics that evolve during a flight." "Notice that the 'evolve' part of this definition excludes other information, like declarative and procedural knowledge, that may be rapidly brought to mind. Notice too that 'the ability to bring' allows SA to refer to things that may not at that moment be in consciousness (or working memory, if you choose). But you have to be able to grab them when you need them."	Wickens (1992)
	"One's ability to remain aware of everything that is happening at the same time and to integrate that sense of awareness into what one is doing at the moment."	Haines and Flateau (1992)

(Continued)

Table 6.3 (*Continued*) Definitions of Situational Awareness

1995	SA is "an abstraction that exists within our minds, describing phenomena that we observe in humans performing work in a rich and usually dynamic environment."	Billings (1995)
	"SA provides 'the primary basis for subsequent decision making and performance in the operation of complex, dynamic systems…' At its lowest level the operator needs to perceive relevant information (in the environment, system, self, etc.), next integrate the data in conjunction with task goals, and, at its highest level, predict future events and system states based on this understanding." "…the perception of the elements in the environment within a volume of time and space, the comprehension of their meaning, and the projection of their status in the near future."	Endsley (1995)
	"Situation awareness is adaptive, externally-directed consciousness that has as its products knowledge about a dynamic task environment and directed action within that environment."	Smith and Hancock (1995)
1997	"SA means that a human appropriately responds to important informational cues. This definition contains four key elements: (1) humans, (2) important informational cues, (3) behavioral cues, and (4) appropriateness of the responses. Important informational cues refer to environmental stimuli that are mentally processed by the human."	Dalrymple and Schiflett (1997)
1998	"SA is 'the pilot's internal model of the world around him at any point in time.' It is derived from the aircraft instrumentation, the out-the-window view, and his or her senses. Individual capabilities, training, experience, objectives, and the ability to respond to task workload moderate the quality of the operator's SA."	Endsley (1998)

Of all of these definitions above, only that of Endsley (1995) has been widely adopted in literature and research (see Section 6.4.1.1). In particular, research and development have adopted the notion of cyber situational awareness (CSA), i.e., how to be aware of the current situation in cyberspace. Furthermore, being aware of the cyber domain (such as the ongoing situation in computer networks and services) is a challenging and complex task. Methods, tools, and algorithms will be developed to understand and evaluate the current situation within the systems, for example, to understand current network traffic or sensor interaction in a system of systems.

In the following, cognitive as well as technical models for situational awareness are assessed. Both classes of models can be relevant for today's situational awareness depending on the application scenario. While cognitive models try to assess and model the cognitive processing of situation assessments, technical models try to realize the cognitive models with technological means; i.e., they try to enrich or enhance the cognitive processes of the operators (e.g., the pilots) with technology.

6.4.1 Cognitive Models on Situational Awareness

This section analyzes two cognitive models for situational awareness that were originally developed for pilots or soldiers in the army. Their intention was to capture the cognitive thinking and acting within dynamic situations. Their primary goal was to identify factors within situations first, analyze them, and make decisions based on these assessments. These build the foundation for CSA models (see Section 6.4.2) and are often cited. Therefore, they shall not be missing.

6.4.1.1 Situational Awareness Model (1995)

SA is specified in Endsley (1988a,b, p. 792) as: "Situation awareness is the perception of the element in the environment within a volume of time and space, the comprehension of their meaning, and the projection of their status in the near future." SA presents a level of focus that goes beyond traditional information-processing approaches in attempting to explain human behavior while operating complex systems, e.g., pilots. Based on the SA definition provided by Endsley (1995), SA gaining consists of three levels (as shown in Figure 6.3):

- *Level 1: Perception of the Elements in the Environment* is the first step in achieving SA. This level covers the perception of status, attributes, and dynamics of relevant elements in the environment.
- *Level 2: Comprehension of the Current Situation* is based on outputs of Level 1. Level 2 includes the understanding of the significance of relevant elements.
- *Level 3: Projection of Future Status* covers the ability to predict the future actions of the elements in the environment. This is achieved through knowledge of the status and dynamics of the elements and comprehension of the situation.

As can be seen from the figure, the situational awareness model (SAM) includes the components Decision, Performance of Action, Feedback, and the variables that can influence the development and maintenance, such as environmental (above) and individual factors (below).

- *Decisions* are strongly influenced by SA, because it provides input to making decisions. These decisions can be affected by individual factors (e.g., goals, experience, or abilities) task and environmental factors (e.g., workload, stressors, or complexity), for example.

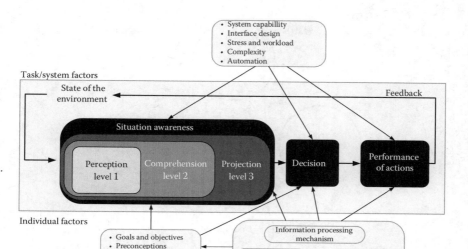

Figure 6.3   Situational awareness model (Endsley, 1995, p.4).

- The relationship between SA and *Performance of Actions* can also be predicted (Endsley, 1995). Appropriate SA increases the probability of good performance and course of actions but cannot guarantee it. The actions are also influenced by the same factors as the decisions.
- *Feedback* covers state of the environment or the system affected by the decision and by the performance of the selected actions.

Time plays an important role in the SAM. As SA is a dynamic construct affected by the surrounding environment and various factors, it therefore serves as input in the model.

6.4.1.2 OODA Loop (1976)

The OODA Loop was originally developed in an attempt to explain why American fighter pilots were more successful than their adversaries in the Korean War (Boyd, 1996). Compared to the SAM, the OODA Loop is originally made for supporting decision-making processes. Many decisions are required in dynamic environments, especially in ever-changing cyberspace. Therefore, one of the main requirements is to obtain and maintain an accurate SA. Kaempf et al. (1993) confirm the relevance of SA in decision-making processes. They claim that the recognition of the situation is a challenge for the decision makers.

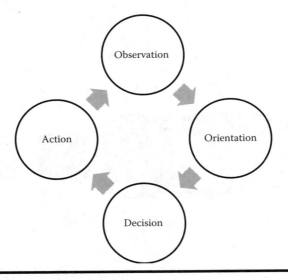

Figure 6.4   OODA loop (Boyd, 1976).

Figure 6.4 displays the four major stages of the OODA Loop (see Brehmer, 2005):

- *Observe* involves the perception of features of the environment.
- *Orient* refers to orienting within a specific environment.
- *Decide* involves deciding what the next steps are.
- *Act* is about implementing what has been decided.

The SAM and the OODA Loop describe the cognitive processes of decision making in complex environments. These models are often used as the basis for SA gaining and application (e.g., decision making) in literature.

6.4.2 Cyber Situational Awareness Models

Cyber situational awareness (CSA) models adapt the notion of situational awareness to the cyberspace. They provide tools and methods to simulate cognitive models with technical means, i.e., to establish awareness of a situation in cyberspace. These situations can comprise computer networks and services, local (within an organization) or distributed (over multiple organizations or nations), concerning a wide target audience (e.g., social media or Internet providers) or a small target group (e.g., confidential interest groups, SMEs, etc.) and operated on a critical or non-critical infrastructure. Already these examples show that capturing and assessing a technical situation in cyberspace can be complex. However, several models suggest ways to establish cyber-situational awareness based on technical methods, tools, and techniques.

6.4.2.1 JDL Data Fusion Model (1980)

Contrary to the focus on the cognitive processes in the SAM and the OODA Loop, this model describes the technical information processes of SA gaining. The Joint Directors of Laboratories (JDL) Subgroup developed the Data Fusion Model (JDL DFM) (White, 1988) as an approach to refine data collected from various systems (Figure 6.5). The JDL DFM was designed to take data from any aspect of the world, e.g., flight information or network traffic, and process it in a way to make the output more useful. The output is supposed to better estimate, predict, or assess the environment under observation (Raulerson, 2013). The JDL model has six different levels of data processing, from 0 to 4. The levels of the JDL DFM outlined in Figure 6.5 are described as follows (Giacobe, 2010; Steinberg et al., 1998):

- 0: The *Source Processing* is responsible for the sensor-based data collection.
- 1: The *Object Refinement* combines the data from Level 0 with sensor data to detect security events. The main objective of the level is to identify, detect, and characterize entities, such as computers, adversaries, data flows, or network connections. The output of Level 1 is a list of entities and their properties.
- 2: The *Situation Refinement* combines various entities to provide an overview of the current state of the system or environment.
- 3: The *Threat Refinement* predicts future states of the system or possible attacks against the system.
- 4: The *Process Refinement* manages the system's capability for sensors and their health.
- 5: The *Cognitive Refinement* represents the link between the security analysts and the JDL DFM. In this process, the analyst (performing the human cognitive processes) receives the technological support from the JDL system.

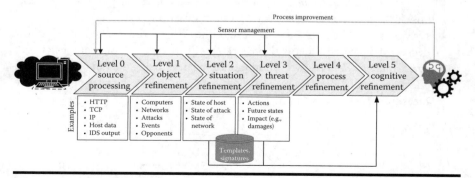

Figure 6.5   JDL data fusion model (Giacobe, 2010).

The result of these data processing levels serves as a basis for gaining accurate and present SA such as in CSCs. Inaccurately designed data processing steps could lead to incorrect situational awareness and possibly to wrong decisions.

6.4.2.2 Cyber Situational Awareness Model (2009)

The cyber situational awareness model (CSAM) (Okolica, 2009) proposes a methodology for building an automated discovery engine for CSA. Okolica (2009) argue that any SA system must perform the three functions perception, comprehension, and projection as described in the SAM in Section 6.4.1.1. These three functions can be aligned to Sense, Evaluate, and Assess in the CSAM (see Figure 6.6). The system senses its environment; it takes its raw sense data, assembles them into a meaningful understanding of the environment, and uses its current understanding to predict future developments.

- Sense: The function includes data gathering through sensors.
- Evaluate: The system compiles the gathered information into a concept that matches already existing threat concepts.
- Assess: The system predicts possible future activities and attacks.

All of these functions are essential in CSCs to foresee emerging threats and be able to prevent future attacks.

6.4.2.3 Effective Cyber Situational Awareness (2014)

The Effective Cyber Situational Awareness (ECSA) model by Evancich et al. (2014) focuses on a particular type of CSA: SA within a computer network by applying network monitoring. The ECSA model includes four main phases as outlined in Figure 6.7:

- *Network awareness* includes the analysis and enumeration of assets and defense capabilities.
- *Threat or attack awareness* establishes a current situation picture of possible attacks and vectors against the network in question.
- *Operational or mission awareness* establishes SA of the operation, e.g., how decreased or degraded network operations will affect the mission of the network
- *Prediction and data fusion* is about obtaining and fusing data in order to make adequate predictions and project the future (e.g., network states or responsive measures).

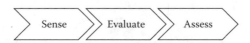

Figure 6.6 Cyber situational awareness model (Okolica, 2009).

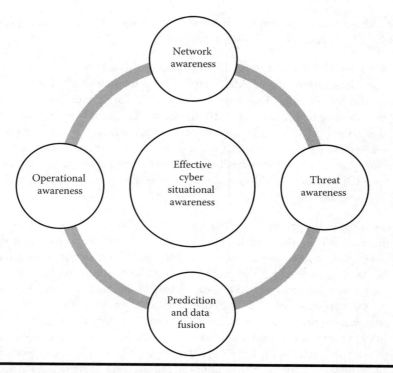

Figure 6.7   ECSA model (Evancich et al., 2014).

ECSA aims at providing better intelligence about the status of the network than regular CSA.

The ECSA is CSA that improves decision making, collaboration, and resource management (Evancich et al., 2014). Moving from CSA to ECSA requires that the CSA created by the system allow the analysts to acquire knowledge about the status of the network. Therefore, the ECSA model provides actionable intelligence on the current situation within a network.

6.4.2.4 CSA Model for National Cybersecurity Centers (2017)

Governments worldwide are adopting security strategies and capabilities (Franke and Brynielsson, 2014) or national incident response plans to protect critical information infrastructures (CII) within the new threat landscape in the cyber age. Most of the initiatives are based on National Cyber Security Strategies (NCSS). In the NCSS (Luiijf et al., 2013), governments identify essential national cyber capabilities and often assign ownership of these capabilities and responsibilities to a centralized NCSC (or a set of NCSCs). These procedures are often reactive and focus on the recovery processes and not necessarily on prevention. The model illustrated in

Figure 6.8 proposes a preventive CSA model for National Cyber Security Centers (CSA NCSC) that addresses several requirements:

- CSA for NCSCs is a versatile, dynamic, and complex process that should consider different stakeholders (national and international). The CSA model should have a collaborative approach based on data correlation and information sharing by providing suitable interfaces, i.e., Reporting Interface.
- The complete CSA model should focus on prevention, i.e., implementing an early-warning system that can prevent and detect national incidents.
- The CSA model should be flexible and open to future threats and Threat Actors.
- The CSA model should provide capabilities for cognitive and technical SA Gaining and Application.

Figure 6.8 shows the general SA gaining and application processes in NCSCs based on Pahi et al. (2017). The model contains CSA in three different levels with different information sources: *organizations,* the *National Cyber Security Center,* and the level of the *decision makers.* The gained CSA at the organization level serves as a basis for creating an accurate and holistic picture of the status of critical infrastructures in the national scope (see the *SA Gaining Information Flow* in Figure 6.8). The participating organizations and their reporting activity through the *Reporting Interface* are important information sources for the SA gaining processes, such as Perception, Comprehension, and Projection, in the NCSC. CSA is applied at every level; it is presented in the figure only on the decision makers level because of the high relevance for national (cyber) security. The organizations and the NCSC make decisions and perform actions on a daily basis. Actions relevant for national security are for instance the reporting of noticed cyber incidents and the measures undertaken to protect their own systems. The SA information flow, the decisions,

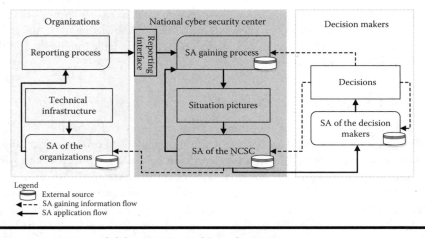

Figure 6.8 CSA model for NCSCs (Pahi et al., 2017).

and the actions of the decision makers have an influence on the other levels (see *SA Application Information Flow* in the figure). A decision from the political level could have serious consequences in a large-scale espionage campaign, such as releasing documents containing sensitive information (for instance the analysis of the espionage at RUAG, see GovCERT.ch, 2016). One piece of legislation could entirely shape the cyber capability of the state, such as introducing mandatory reporting of cyber incidents, for instance, in the United States or Estonia.

Figure 6.8 displays the stakeholders and entities that are involved in the SA gaining and application processes in the NCSCs. As the government and the NCSC play an essential role in establishing and maintaining cybersecurity at the national level, the model must include the private sector, especially the providers of the critical infrastructures (CI). The governments and the private sectors need to establish formal partnerships, because the technical information from the CI domains serve as primary information source for the NCSCs. These centers are often formed as CERTs or CSIRTs. The stakeholders are the following in our simplified model: high-level decision makers, the NCSC, and participating public and private organizations. The *decision makers* include the government and other relevant private or public stakeholders. The *NCSC* focuses on collecting, interpreting, and evaluating cybersecurity relevant information at the national level. This is required for translating the cyber incidents within the CI domains into strategic and tactical actions at the national level. A NCSC can consist of National Incident Response Teams (NIRTs), i.e., the expert team of the NCSC. The NCSC supports decision making by creating various situation pictures and gaining SA at their level. SA is current and predictive knowledge of the environment, as well as all factors, activities, and events (Conti et al., 2013). Therefore, CSA includes the holistic and current knowledge about the CI at the national level. The situational pictures, also known as common operating pictures (COPs), support the stakeholders and decision makers to have an appropriate CSA about the current situation. The main tasks of these centers are information gathering from the CI domains and external sources (see *external sources* in Figure 6.8, such as national CERTs and open source information, information processing, and sharing among the participating organizations about cyber incidents. The experts of the NCSCs generate situation pictures with various focal points. These situation pictures establish the decision maker's CSA about the status of the national CI.

The *organizations* include all participating public or private CI (or CII) service providers (see Section 6.3.1). The key approach to CI protection is the identification and modeling of the relevant activities, resources, and services in each organization. These activities form the basis for the analysis and assessment to determine current impacts of assets and missions and to derive plausible future trends and their future impacts or effects on assets and missions (Tadda and Salerno, 2010).

The CSA model for NCSCs includes proactive cyber capabilities in order to prevent cyber attacks through information sharing and multilevel monitoring related to cyber attacks. This modern CSA model helps to close the gap between the capabilities of the public and private sector related to cybersecurity.

6.4.3 *Overview and Analysis of Situational Awareness Models*

This section analyzes the functions and capabilities of the SA models. The interpretation of the SA changes according to the application area. SA gaining processes need different information depending on the scope, for instance ECSA requires particularly network information, while the CSA in the NCSCs model uses a wide range of information types. Despite the broad application range, most of the models for SA gaining share one similarity: they are based on the general definition and most cited model, the SAM. Based on the six components of the SAM (see Section 6.4.1.1), the models are analyzed and assessed regarding their applicability in NCSCs. The processes of the models are divided into two main categories, in SA gaining (with Perception, Comprehension, and Projection) and in SA application (with decision making, performance of actions, and feedback). The analysis of the models is based on two main aspects: on the *focus* of the models (i.e., strong or weak coverage of SA gaining and application) and on the *operator* (i.e., a person or a machine/program that establishes SA with technical means or cognitively). Both aspects are displayed in the figure above. Automated processes are displayed with a gear icon, while processes using cognitive skills of human operators are marked with a person icon.

6.4.3.1 Focus

To define the focus and the scope of each relevant model for gaining and applying SA, the models are compared to the components of the most cited SA model (see the description of the model in Section 6.4.1.1). Establishing SA is a major, complex task. Therefore, two main processes, *SA gaining* and *SA application*, are required. Figure 6.9 illustrates the phases of SA gaining (Perception, Comprehension, and Projection) and SA application (Decisions, Performance of actions, Feedback).

	SA gaining			SA application		
	Perception	Comprehension	Projection	Decision making	Performance of actions	Feedback
SAM	Strong	Strong	Strong	Strong	Strong	Strong
OODA	Strong	Strong	Strong	Strong	Strong	Weak
JDL DFM	Strong	Strong	Strong	Weak	Weak	Strong
CSAM	Strong	Strong	Strong	Weak	Weak	Weak
ECSA	Strong	Strong	Strong	Strong	Strong	Weak
CSA NCSC	Strong	Strong	Strong	Strong	Strong	Strong

Legend: Operator: ⚙ Technical process 👤 Cognitive process
Focus: Strong or weak coverage of SA gaining/SA application

Figure 6.9 Extended overview of SA models (Pahi et al., 2017).

The *SA gaining* phase contains the three levels based on the SAM: Perception, Comprehension, and Projection. Based on the early models, SA is useful present knowledge about, and understanding of, the environment. This process is covered in all models. See the Perception and Comprehension Level in the SA model or the Observe and Orient Stage in the OODA Loop. In the remaining models are sensors and algorithms responsible for the perception and comprehension of the environment. The component projection is essential in models, because SA is typically forecasting, projecting what is plausible to happen in order to inform effective decision processes (Kaber and Endsley, 2004).

SA application contains the Decision, Performance of actions, and Feedback phases. Figure 6.9 identifies the models that incorporate and respond to decision making by providing a performance of actions, i.e., the SAM, OODA, ECSA, and CSA NCSC. The OODA Loop describes the steps for decision making in detail, while the ECSA provides technical features for decision making by predicting possible scenarios. The models provide assistance by creating SA or additionally by providing options for action for the decision maker. Ideally, the SA gaining process contains a feedback cycle between the environment and the decision maker. For example, the Feedback component by the SAM is complemented with a process refinement function. The operator can have for instance the possibility of verifying or modifying the SA gaining processes or even their results. The feedback loops could vary enormously depending on the application area. Therefore, this component is not a focus in most of the models.

6.4.3.2 Operators

The operator aspect analyzes how SA is established by humans or machines (e.g., programs) in the SA models. The early definitions and models, such as the SAM and the OODA Loop, include the human aspect in crisis situations. They describe SA as cognitive knowledge that can be enriched by experience. In the 1980s and 1990s, the operator was mainly a human, e.g., a pilot or a soldier. Then, technical sensors and data complemented human perception; see, for instance the JDL Data Fusion Model. This approach defines the need for human and machine information processes in SA gaining and application. Each presented CSA model tries to reproduce and improve the cognitive SA gaining processes with the integration of technical solutions. The CSAM proposed to be an automated data processing system to sense the environment. Other models, such as the ECSA Model and the CSA for NCSCs, have different approaches. They integrate the human operator in the SA creating processes with a verifier and improver role, while the SA gaining processes are totally automated. All these approaches need to be integrated into the CSA model to combine the advantages of the different models in order to enhance the cyber defense capability at the national level.

These results indicate that appropriate awareness could be developed with both the cognitive data comprehension capability and technical solutions, such as data processing algorithms. Technology appropriately complements limited cognitive capabilities, with technical data correlation techniques. Based on this understanding, modern CSA models combine the technical processes with the required human aspect. The automatized processes are usually the SA gaining processes, while the human capabilities play a significant role in the application of the SA.

6.5 Information and Sources for Situational Awareness at the National Level

Establishing SA at the national level is a challenging task. One way would be to create a national cyber common operating picture (CCOP; also referred to as a situation picture) that provides the current state on major national incidents and responses at the national level. To do that, information has to be acquired, processed, and visualized so that national decision makers can interpret the situation in a realistic way and make adequate decisions. However, this is often very difficult as obtaining a comprehensive (live) national CCOP is very difficult and complex. As outlined in Section 6.2.2, the protection of critical infrastructure and IT networks and systems depends on the coordination and cooperation of government, industry, and society. Chapter 5 has explained emerging threat intelligence communities and standards that facilitate information sharing and exchange activities. Building these information sharing and exchange communities is complex in most countries. Furthermore, establishing a CCOP is often only possible if industry and other actors strongly cooperate and share information on incidents and mitigation strategies via reporting. This (often voluntary) information is vital for ensuring a comprehensive assessment of the situation at the national level. Private organizations, for example, act as sources to provide information on major incidents. In this chapter, both orthogonal dimensions—which information can be used to create a CCOP at the national level—as well as which sources can be used to establish SA are discussed. Both dimensions are becoming more important in order to establish a comprehensive picture of the current situation at the national level.

6.5.1 Information for Cyber Common Operating Pictures

A classification of information for CCOPs can be established in many ways. In this chapter, a classification was chosen that has two categories as shown in Figure 6.10:

- *Core information* focuses on incident response management based on the standard STIX.
- *Contextual information* gained from stakeholders that enables an extended view on incidents at the national level (e.g., to determine the impact or damages on national economy or national security).

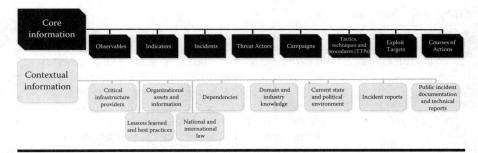

Figure 6.10 Overview of information for CCOPs.

This classification is not exhaustive and may be extended or adapted for the intended purpose. It can be used as a starting point to add, extend, or remove information for CCOPs. In the following, both categories are described.

6.5.1.1 Core Information

CCOPs can be generated by using and correlating basic elements such as observables, indicators, incidents, or Threat Actors. Recent efforts have created standards that enable the sharing and exchanging of incident information. For example, the standard *STIX* (Structured Threat Information eXpression) enables the structured representation of threat information and supports the automated and structured exchange of information (see http://stixproject.github.io/ for further project details and information). Currently, the STIX architecture has version 1.2 (Version 2.0 is currently under Review). As version 1.1 is the official current release in Barnum (2014), it will serve as the basis for this chapter. In particular, the core elements of the STIX architecture are used to classify the core information for CCOPs. STIX is a community-driven standard and builds on an international community of experts in the fields of threat intelligence; hence, it can further serve as a basis for structuring threat information. Table 6.4 describes the core elements of CCOPs based on STIX.

6.5.1.2 Contextual Information

A CCOP can contain more information than just the core elements. Additional context information can be used for example to establish SA (e.g., to identify critical infrastructures and its impact, to provide reactive measures, or define countermeasures). Depending on the CCOPs objectives and focus, part of the picture could be to establish awareness of the current state of critical infrastructure providers, certain domains, or the whole system of systems (nationwide). Hence, the context information for CCOPs should include relevant and useful information that gives an additional value or perspective to the CCOP (such as political situation, geographical position, geological resources, power distribution). These information assets can span from information of organizations or companies, including

Table 6.4   STIX Elements

Element	Definitions based on Barnum (2014, p.14ff)
Observables	Observables are the "base" construct within the STIX architecture. Observables are stateful properties or measurable events pertinent to the operation of computers and networks. Information about a file (name, hash, size, etc.), a registry key value, a service being started, or an HTTP request being sent are all simple examples of observables.
Indicators	Indicators convey specific Observable patterns combined with contextual information intended to represent artifacts and/or behaviors of interest within a cybersecurity context. They consist of one or more observable patterns potentially mapped to a related TTP context and adorned with other relevant meta-data on things like confidence in the indicator's assertion, handling restrictions, valid time windows, likely impact, sightings of the indicator, structured test mechanisms for detection [...].
Incidents	Incidents are discrete instances of Indicators affecting an organization along with information discovered or decided during an incident response investigation. They consist of data such as time-related information, parties involved, assets affected, impact assessment, related Indicators, related Observables, leveraged TTP, attributed Threat Actors, intended effects, nature of compromise, response Course of Action requested, response Course of Action taken, confidence in characterization, handling guidance, source of the Incident information, log of actions taken [...]
Threat Actors	Threat Actors are characterizations of malicious actors (or adversaries) representing a cyber attack threat including presumed intent and historically observed behavior. In a structured sense, Threat Actors consist of a characterization of identity, suspected motivation, suspected intended effect, historically observed TTP used by the Threat Actor, historical campaigns believed associated with the Threat Actor, other Threat Actors believed associated with the Threat Actor, handling guidance, confidence in the asserted characterization of the Threat Actor, source of the Threat Actor information

(Continued)

Table 6.4 (*Continued*)   STIX Elements

Campaigns	Campaigns are instances of Threat Actors pursuing an intent, as observed through sets of Incidents and/or TTP, potentially across organizations. In a structured sense, Campaigns may consist of the suspected intended effect of the adversary, the related TTP leveraged within the campaign, the related Incidents believed to be part of the campaign, attribution to the Threat Actors believed responsible for the campaign, other campaigns believed related to the campaign, confidence in the assertion of aggregated intent and characterization of the campaign, activity taken in response to the campaign, source of the campaign information, handling guidance[...].
Tactics, Techniques and Procedures (TTP)	TTPs are representations of the behavior or modus operandi of cyber adversaries. It is a term taken from the traditional military sphere and is used to characterize what an adversary does and how, in increasing levels of detail. To give a simple example, a tactic may be to use malware to steal credit card credentials. A related technique (at a lower level of detail) may be to send targeted e-mails to potential victims; the e-mails have documents attached containing malicious codes that execute upon opening, capture credit card information from keystrokes, and use http to communicate with a command and control server to transfer information. A related procedure (at a lower level of detail) may be to perform open source research to identify potentially gullible individuals, craft a convincing socially engineered e-mail and document, create malware/exploit that will bypass current antivirus detection, establish a command and control server by registering a domain called mychasebank.org, and send mail to victims from a Gmail account called accounts-mychasebank@gmail.com TTPs consist of the specific adversary behavior (attack patterns, malware, exploits) exhibited, resources leveraged (tools, infrastructure, personas), information on the victims targeted (who, what, or where), relevant ExploitTargets being targeted, intended effects, relevant kill chain phases, handling guidance, source of the TTP information [...].

(*Continued*)

Table 6.4 (*Continued*)   STIX Elements

Exploit Targets	Exploit Targets are vulnerabilities or weaknesses in software, systems, networks, or configurations that are targeted for exploitation by the TTP of a Threat Actor. In a structured sense, Exploit Targets consist of vulnerability identifications or characterizations, weakness identifications or characterizations, configuration identifications or characterizations, potential Courses of Action, source of the Exploit Target information, handling guidance [...].
Courses of Action	Courses of Action (COA) are specific measures to be taken to address threats, whether they are corrective or preventative, to address Exploit Targets, or responsive to counter or mitigate the potential impacts of Incidents. In a structured sense, COA consist of their relevant stage in cyber threat management (e.g., remedy of an Exploit Target or response to an Incident), type of COA, description of COA, objective of the COA, structured representation of the COA (e.g., IPS rule or automated patch/ remediation), the likely impact of the COA, the likely cost of the COA, the estimated efficacy of the COA, observable parameters for the COA, handling guidance [...].

Source: Barnum, S., Standardizing cyber threat intelligence information with the Structured Threat Information eXpression (STIX), Version 1.1, Revision 1, http://www.standardscoordination.org/sites/default/files/docs/STIX_ Whitepaper_v1.1.pdf, 2014.

critical infrastructure providers, to information about what services they have and what impact a shutdown would have. It can be assumed that the exchange with relevant organizations and the organizations themselves are essential information sources for contextual information for CCOPs. Provided information can be static or dynamic and has to be updated (if possible) regularly. In the following list, the contextual information for CCOPs is summarized; this list is not exhaustive or sorted; it can be adapted to the CCOP's needs and requirements.

6.5.1.2.1 List of Critical Infrastructure Providers

Many countries worldwide have started to establish a list of critical infrastructure providers in order to manage and handle risks as well as threats in a coordinated manner. For example, in the United States the Department of Homeland Security (DHS) has specified a national infrastructure protection plan (Homeland Security, 2013) that identifies 16 sectors with critical infrastructure: chemical, commercial facilities, communications, critical manufacturing, dams, defense industrial base, emergency services, energy, financial services, food and agriculture, government facilities, healthcare and public health, information technology, nuclear reactors, materials and waste, transportation systems, and water and wastewater systems. The NIS Directive (European Union, 2016) categorizes CI into operators of critical infrastructure providers and so-called digital service providers (e.g., online market-places, search engines, and providers of cloud computing services).

6.5.1.2.2 Organizational Assets and Information

For each organization (for example that is part of the CI providers), further infor-mation on assets or threats can give support to establish SA with CCOPs. This information can consist of key data as well as operating figures of organizations (e.g., market share, asset classes, customers, provided services, contact person for incidents, investment figures). However, it is currently rather unlikely that CSCs will be able to obtain such detailed information on organizational assets (in par-ticular from the private sector). Mostly, they will be able to obtain information from public sources (e.g., management reports or other documentation). ENISA provides in Dekker and Karsberg (2015) a categorization that can be a starting point for organizations to examine and assess their assets.

FURTHER INFORMATION: ASSETS

Assets can be basically anything of value to an organization [based on ENISA (Dekker and Karsberg, 2015)]. Assets can be abstract (e.g., processes or repu-tation), virtual (e.g., data), physical (e.g., power plants, equipment, or cables), human resources, or money.

In the case of ENISA, only assets that are in the scope of ICT that provide (elec-tronic) communication networks and services are analyzed. Three ways to classify assets are suggested in Dekker and Karsberg (2015):

- *Asset type:* An asset type describes a class of assets. Examples of classes include subscriber equipment, switches and routers, mobile user and location registers, mobile base stations and controllers, power supplies, and cooling systems.
- *Asset group:* Asset groups can be used to describe which role and functional-ity the assets have within the provider's networks. For example, assets can be classified by their location within a provider's network.
- *Asset component:* Asset components classify assets by their type of compos-ing parts. For example, assets can be categorized into a software layer (i.e., software assets), hardware layer (i.e., hardware assets), or supplies layer (i.e., supplies such as power supply).

6.5.1.2.3 Dependencies

Information about dependencies between organizations and domains of CI can be relevant for CCOPs. However, this task is very complex and challenging and requires for example a fundamental understanding and knowledge of the national economy. Intra-organizational and inter-organizational research is still working to define and evaluate models that can cope with this complexity and structural dynamics (Fombrun, 1986).

6.5.1.2.4 Domain and Industry Knowledge

Knowledge about current trends, threats, attacks, and countermeasures is key to establishing SA in CSCs or organizations. It is an advantage to gather knowledge extensively from many areas such as on current trends in cybercrime or cyberterrorism, knowledge on technology loopholes and countermeasures by ICT security experts, and knowledge on industry (e.g., incident response plans or risk assessments).

6.5.1.2.5 Current State and Political Environment

Situational awareness requires knowing the current political environment and health of the nation of the targets as well as the nation where the attackers are located. Here, diplomatic ties or incidents may relate to cyber threats and attacks.

6.5.1.2.6 Incident Reports

Incident reports from CI providers to CSCs can be used for CCOPs. Depending on the country, organizations such as CI providers can have an obligation to inform or report certain authorities in case of cyber incidents. For example, within the EU, the NIS Directive (European Union, 2016) consists of an obligation to notify pre-defined national organizations (such as NCSCs) in case of cyber incidents (see Chapters 7 and 8 or more information). Incident reporting requires well-defined specifications on when, how, and with whom to share incident information. In particular, it has to be specified which level of detail and which level of granularity of information should be reported or the use of standards (e.g., STIX).

6.5.1.2.7 Public Incident Documentation and Technical Reports

Although the documentation of cyber incidents and technical reports cannot contribute to a dynamic and daily updated CCOP, they can contribute to the long-term understanding of threats, Threat Actors and countermeasures. For example in GovCERT.ch (2016) the advanced persistent threat (APT) case of the RUAG company is examined and evaluated. The processes and measures used within the case can be useful to similar organizations or managers (e.g., CISOs) to handle similar APT cases. In addition, white papers and technical reports can be used to assess current trends in cybersecurity and other related topics such as damage control.

6.5.1.2.8 Lessons Learned and Best Practices

Lessons learned are often condensed learnings of experience with cyber incidents and attacks that were made by target organizations. These learnings consist often of assessments, measurements, errors, and notes that were made during incident handling and management processes. Often, the documentation of this hands-on experience contributes to the general know-how of handling incidents but also allows other organizations to learn from and to avoid errors when handling future incidents. Best practices can be derived from these lessons as they have proven to be a method or technique that achieve adequate results. Often, best practices become standards or reference works such as the ISO 27000 family, ITIL, or NIST 800 series.

6.5.1.2.9 National and International Law

Providing legal foundations contributes to establishing situational awareness, in particular at national and international levels. Legal foundations are described in Chapters 7 and 8.

6.5.2 Sources for Cyber Common Operating Pictures

While the last section focused on information for CCOPs, this section centers on sources that can be used to collect and extract information. With the Internet, a wide set of well-known as well as hidden information sources emerged, apart from the typical information sources (e.g., daily newspapers, informants, or wiretaps). With the increase of publicly available information on the Internet and the use of social media or the Dark Web (see Chapter 2), the selection process for sources has become more complex. Challenges include, for example, distinguishing information sources with a high level of quality or integrity from potentially fake information sources, skimming information sources, automatically selecting new sources, or managing and combining complex data models behind information sources in order to augment other information sources. Furthermore, the use and selection of information sources impacts the further aggregation of information to establish SA. Information sources should be selected very carefully so as to not miss or misinterpret information. The selection of adequate sources also influences the potential decisions that are made based on the information the sources provide. In the following, potential sources for CCOPs are described and categorized by accessibility, by information modeling and by ownership (see Figure 6.11). These categories enable different views on sources and do not claim to be exhaustive. Additional categories might exist for classifying sources. In this section, information sources are assessed from different viewpoints in order to identify a potentially complete list of sources for CCOPs.

6.5.2.1 Classification by Accessibility

Information sources can be distinguished in the simplest way—their accessibility. There are open, public sources as well as nonpublic sources. Public sources are often referred to as Open Source Intelligence (OSINT) in the intelligence domain. These sources are accessible by the public. Classic examples of public sources are public city libraries. In most of the public libraries, all people can get in (although, sometimes you have to apply for a membership to join) and go through books and magazines. Other examples are television, news (papers and magazines), magazines, blogs, web pages (that do not require a membership or login), or other publications that are accessible. Nonpublic sources, on the other hand, are typically intended for a specific target audience that is eligible to access the information of these nonpublic sources. For example, only book club members receive mailings of summaries of books or special offers by a local bookstore. The information is only intended for the members of the book club. Nonpublic sources can be confidential; they can be part of intelligence services (such as a confidential informant in an ongoing investigation or information on the next raids). Typically, intelligence services use methods and tools to receive, transmit, and interpret nonpublic information from sources. However, ICT have provided technologies that enable home users with a few simple clicks to receive and transmit confidential information using cryptography or other techniques.

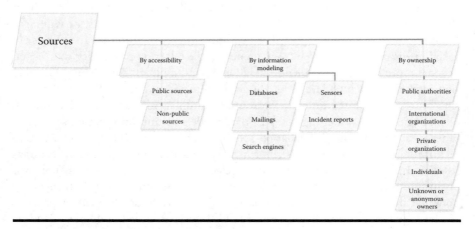

Figure 6.11 Overview of sources for CCOPs.

6.5.2.2 Classification by Information Modeling

Another classification can be the type of information modeling and structuring. The information model is a representation of concepts, their dependencies, operations, and rules as data semantics. Data semantics are important in the processing of data of different information sources for CCOPs. Each information source typically has an underlying information or data model. Different sources typically have varying data models. For example, a blog on vulnerabilities might be differently structured than a database containing common vulnerabilities and exposures (CVEs). Please refer to Chapter 3 for more examples. However, recent efforts try to overcome these differences by providing standards for information sharing, for example, the STIX language defines a model to define cyber threat intelligence, and the Trusted Automated eXchange of Indicator Information (TAXII) standard supports the automated exchange of threat information (see http://taxiiproject. github.io/about/ for more information on TAXII). In the following, selected, public information sources for threat information are described.

6.5.2.2.1 Databases

Databases are a collection of structured data. Databases typically contain tables, queries, schemas, reports, and views that can be searched and retrieved. Cyber threat information can be collected in databases. Currently, there are two groups of databases that can be found on the Internet:

- *Vulnerability databases* provide descriptions, classifications, and attack vectors as well as references to commercial products. Popular examples include the MITRE CVE database (https://cve.mitre.org/) and the National Vulnerability Database (NVD) (see https://nvd.nist.gov/).
- *Exploit databases* contain descriptions and tools for making use of (such as enter, analyze, or disturb) unpatched systems. They can be a starting point for organizations for IT security penetration tests. Examples are exploit-db (https://www.exploit-db.com/) or Metasploit (https://www.metasploit.com/).

6.5.2.2.2 Mailings

Mailings are sent from one sender to one or more receivers and share messages.

- *Mailing lists* can contain public as well as confidential information. They are often used to quickly distribute information of threats (such as vulnerabilities, phishing, or scamming cases) before they are actually registered in one of the previously named databases. Typical mailing lists are for example CERT mailing lists or phishing mailing lists (e.g., http://www.antiphishing.org/, a mailing list to discuss phishing and cybercrime issues).

■ *Newsletters* can be provided as a service by vendors or other organizations to inform customers about potential vulnerabilities, problems in devices or services, new patches, or maintenance information. Examples can be found from vendors worldwide.

6.5.2.2.3 Search Engines

Specific search engines have emerged that make potentially (unwanted) functionality of devices and services visible. For example, the search engine Shodan (https://www.shodan.io/) can be used to search and retrieve information on the Internet of things. Shodan collects data of different web servers and protocols that can be used to give insight into potentially unsecure systems (some might call it the use of not secure enough standard settings).

6.5.2.2.4 Sensors

Sensors may collect data that can be used to analyze and detect changes in their environment. For example, sensors in ICT networks such as SCADA can be used to monitor and control the production processes and support operators with information on latency or other meta-information for a healthy network. In addition, sensors can be used to gather information for CCOPs in CSCs. For example, the use of sensors in critical infrastructures can be used to directly provide live feeds of information (e.g., the power distribution, Internet connections).

6.5.2.2.5 Incident Reports

One way to share threat information with NCSCs is by incident reporting. This information can be submitted in a structured (e.g., with STIX) or unstructured mode (e.g., text or e-mail). Recent efforts (see Chapter 7) oblige, for example, critical infrastructure providers to report major incidents). These reports can include automated reports generated by monitoring tools within the organization (such as security information and event management (SIEM) tools). These submissions can be used as input for CCOPs. In addition to threat information of organizations, incident reports from home users can be also another option (such as cybercrime incidents, spamming). These incidents however, often are summarized by the authorities and incorporated into periodic reports and other documents (e.g., statistical reports).

6.5.2.3 Classification by Ownership

From the legal perspective, the ownership of information can be an important aspect. Depending on the country's legislation, the owner of information can represent a person that is (legally) responsible for creating, processing, and using the information, including providing access to this information. The quality level of information can be influenced by the owner of the information. For example, an organization might analyze the quality level of information (such as cost, completeness, confidentiality, technicality, legal rights) beforehand to minimize the risk of financial losses. Public institutions might be bound legally to be objective, for example. In the following, five information owners are distinguished: (1) Public authorities are state-based and are often bound to a certain level of quality of information. Information can be guaranteed and verified. (2) In a similar manner, international organizations are often driven by representatives of various countries; they can be political (e.g., ENISA or UN) or domain associations (e.g., Information Systems Audit and Control Association (ISACA)). Also, here, information is often authenticated and guaranteed. (3) Private organizations are often profit driven (such as critical infrastructure providers, small and medium enterprises (SMEs), or others). (4) In addition, individuals can be the owner of certain data on the Internet. (5) Unknown or anonymous owners of information can be found for example in the deep web where the information provenance is often uncertain. Therefore, the origin and the authenticity of information cannot be guaranteed.

6.6 Conclusion

CSA is about assessing and understanding a dynamic situation in cyberspace with technical means such as methods and tools. National governments face many challenges when establishing CSA at the national level. Governments typically establish cybersecurity policies and aim at achieving a close collaboration with different stakeholders (e.g., critical infrastructure, national CSIRTs/CERTs, or international partners) to maintain and ensure a certain level of security and running operations. In addition, they often initiate NCSCs to handle critical incidents with a high impact on the economic system. This is important for maintaining a stable national security, health, or economy.

This chapter analyzed how national governments and decision makers can establish CSA at the national level and which tools and practices they commonly share. Therefore, cybersecurity strategies of national governments and international organizations were examined in Section 6.2. While cyber policies in international organizations often focus on information sharing and exchange of related threat information, national governments focus on establishing cybersecurity centers and units, processes, and structures that manage and facilitate an information exchange at the national level.

Furthermore, national cybersecurity centers and their typical responsibilities were described in Section 6.3. These centers often incorporate or closely work with national CSIRTs or CERTs and focus on the close collaboration to facilitate incident information exchange (that has a high impact on society, national security, health, or the economy, for example) between national stakeholders.

In addition, in Section 6.4, an investigation of situation awareness models was conducted—from cognitive models that originate from the military domain to technical models that adapt ideas of cognitive models to technology (e.g., algorithms and data structures). The evaluation and comparison of models showed that early models were specified to mimic the cognitive processes of individuals. Technical models use the idea but focus often on situational awareness at the organization level (e.g., companies using SIEM tools). Only one model exists that suggests different aggregated layers of situational awareness and stimulates the situational awareness for national decision makers.

In Section 6.5, information and sources for situational awareness at the national level were examined. A variety of threat information and sources is openly provided and can be downloaded from public sources (e.g., CVE databases). In addition, non-public sources (e.g., traditional hidden communication channels, the Dark Web) have recently emerged that are increasingly used to exchange and sell threat information and tools (e.g., zero days, toolkits) as well as identify potential threats. With the amount and complexity of information sources, national stakeholders need to select and aggregate relevant sources and information in order to derive cyber common operating pictures. As this sounds facile, it will be one of the most complex challenges, along with coping with new and advanced technology paradigms such as big data, data mining, and machine learning, as well as the dynamics of these systems.

In conclusion, key factors for establishing CSA for national governments and decision makers are (1) to choose adequate and viable solutions that enable facile sharing of threat and other relevant information to identify, detect, mitigate and resolve cyber attacks, (2) to define practicable cybersecurity strategies and standards, (3) to establish common operating pictures that include dynamic (e.g., attack maps or impact analysis) and static elements (e.g., reports and statistics), and (4) cooperation with national stakeholders. These measures can contribute to national communication and information sharing processes and enable national stakeholders to act more quickly and authorities to respond in time to threats and attacks.

List of Abbreviations

APT	Advanced persistent threats
BSA	Business Software Alliance
BSI	(German) Bundesamt für Sicherheit und Informationstechnik
CCD CoE	Cooperative Cyber Defence Centre of Excellence
CCOP	Cyber common operating picture
CDC	Cyber Defence Committee
CDMB	Cyber Defence Management Board
CDRA	Cyber Defence Research Agenda
CEO	Chief executive officer

CERT	Computer Emergency Response Teams
CII	Critical information infrastructures
CIIP	Critical Information Infrastructure Protection
CIP	Critical infrastructure protection
COA	Courses of Action
CRN	Crisis and Risk Network
CSA	Cyber situational awareness
CSAM	Cyber situational awareness model
CSDP	Common Security and Defence Policy
CVE	Common vulnerabilities and exposures
DDOS	Distributed denial of service
ECSA	Effective Cyber Situational Awareness
EDA	European Defence Agency
ENISA	European Network and Information Security Agency
FDF	Federal Department of Finance
GCHQ	Government Communications Headquarters
GGE	Groups of governmental experts
HTTP	Hypertext transfer protocol
ICS	Industrial control systems
ICT	Information and communication technologies
IPS	Intrusion Protection System
ISAC	Information Sharing and Analysis Center
ISACA	Information Systems Audit and Control Association
ISB	Informatikstrategieorgan Bund
ISO	International Organization for Standardization
ITIL	IT Infrastructure Library
JDL DFM	JDL Data Fusion Model
NAC	North Atlantic Council
NATO	North Atlantic Treaty Organization
NCC	National Coordinating Center for Communications
NCCIC	National Cybersecurity and Communications Integration Center
NCIA	Communications and Information Agency
NCIRC	NATO Computer Incident Response Capability
NCISS	NATO Communications and Information Systems School
NCRC	National Cyber Response Center
NCSC	National Cyber Security Center
NCSS	National Cyber Security Strategies
NICP	NATO Industry Cyber Partnership
NIS	Network and information systems
NIST	National Institute of Standards and Technology
NSPD	National Security Presidential Directive
NVD	National Vulnerability Database
OODA	Observe-Orient-Decide-Act

OSCE	Organization for Security and Co-operation in Europe
OSINT	Open Source Intelligence
SA	Situational awareness
SAM	Situational awareness model
SCADA	Supervisory control and data acquisition
SIEM	Security information and event management
STIX	Structured Threat Information eXpression
TAXII	Trusted Automated eXchange of Indicator Information
TTP	Tactics, techniques, and procedures
UNGA	UN General Assembly
UNSC	UN Security Council
US DHS	US Department of Homeland Security
WSIS	World Summit on the Information Society

References

Barnum, S. 2014. Standardizing cyber threat intelligence information with the Structured Threat Information eXpression (STIX). Version 1.1, Revision 1. http://www.standard-scoordination.org/sites/default/files/docs/STIX_Whitepaper_v1.1.pdf.

Billings, C. E. 1995. Situation awareness measurement and analysis: A commentary. In *Proceedings of the International Conference on Experimental Analysis and Measurement of Situation Awareness (Vol. 1)*. Daytona Beach, FL: Embry-Riddle Aeronautical University Press.

Boyd, J. R. 1995. The Essence of Winning and Losing. Unpublished lecture notes. June 28, 1995, http://danford.net/boyd/essence.htm.

Brehmer, B. 2005. The dynamic OODA loop: Amalgamating Boyd's OODA loop and the cybernetic approach to command and control. In *Proceedings of the 10th International Command and Control Research Technology Symposium*, McLean, VA, June 13–16, 2005, 365–368.

Brunner, E. M. and Manuel, S. 2008. *International CIIP Handbook 2008/2009*. Zurich: Center for Security Studies, ETH Zurich. http://www.css.ethz.ch/content/dam/ethz/special-interest/gess/cis/center-for-securities-studies/pdfs/CIIP-HB-08-09.pdf.

BSA. 2015. EU Cybersecurity dashboard. http://cybersecurity.bsa.org/assets/PDFs/study_eucybersecurity_en.pdf.

Carroll, L. A. 1992. Desperately seeking SA. *TAC Attack (TAC SP 127-1)*, 32(3), 5–6.

Cavelty, M. D. 2014. Reporting and analysis center for information assurance (MELANI) (phase 2: 2004–2010). *Cybersecurity in Switzerland*, Myriam Dunn Cavelty (ed.) 39–55. SpringerBriefs in Cybersecurity. Springer International Publishing, Cham, Switzerland. doi:10.1007/978-3-319-10620-5_4.

Conti, G., Nelson, J., and Raymond, D. 2013. Towards a cyber common operating picture. In *2013 5th International Conference on Cyber Conflict (CyCon)*, 1–17. IEEE, Tallinn, Estonia, May 26–29, 2015.

Council of the European Union. 2014. EU Cyber Defence Policy Framework. 15585/14. Brussels. www.europarl.europa.eu/meetdocs/2014_2019/documents/sede/dv/sede160315 eucyberdefencepolicyframework_/sede160315eucyberdefencepolicyframework_en.pdf.

Dekker, M. and Christoffer, K. 2015. Guideline on threats and assets—Technical guidance on threats and assets in article 13a. V1.1, March 2015. ENISA. https://resilience.enisa.europa.eu/article-13/guideline_on_threats_and_assets/Guideline_on_Threats_and_Assets_v_1_1.pdf.

Department of Defense. 2015. *The DoD Cyber Strategy.* Washington, DC: Department of Defense. https://www.defense.gov/Portals/1/features/2015/0415_cyber-strategy/Final_2015_DoD_CYBER_STRATEGY_for_web.pdf.

Eidgenössisches Departement für Verteidigung, Bevölkerungsschutz and Sport VBS. 2012. National Strategy for Switzerland's Protection against Cyber Risks. Schweizerische Eidgenossenschaft. https://www.melani.admin.ch/dam/melani/en/dokumente/2013/05/nationale_strategiezumschutzderschweizvorcyber-risiken.pdf.download.pdf/national_strategyforswitzerlandsprotectionagainstcyberrisks.pdf.

Endsley, M. R. 1988a. Design and evaluation for situation awareness enhancement. *Proceedings of the Human Factors and Ergonomics Society Annual Meeting* 32(2): 97–101. doi:10.1177/154193128803200221.

Endsley, M. R. 1988b. Situation awareness global assessment technique (SAGAT). In *Aerospace and Electronics Conference*, 1988. NAECON 1988, Proceedings of the IEEE 1988 National (pp. 789–795). IEEE, Dayton, OH, May 23–27, 1988.

Endsley, M. R. 1995. Toward a theory of situation awareness in dynamic systems. *Human Factors: The Journal of the Human Factors and Ergonomics Society* 37(1): 32–64.

ENISA. 2014. *An Evaluation Framework for National Cyber Security Strategies.* Heraklion, Greece: European Union Agency for Network and Information Security. https://www.enisa.europa.eu/publications/an-evaluation-framework-for-cyber-security-strategies.

European Commission. 2015. *The European Agenda on Security. Communication from the Commission to the European Parliament, the Council, the European Economic and Social Committee ·and the Committee of the Regions, COM(2015) 185 Final.* Strasbourg: European Commission. https://ec.europa.eu/home-affairs/sites/homeaffairs/files/e-library/documents/basic-documents/docs/eu_agenda_on_security_en.pdf.

European Commission and High Representative of the European Union for Foreign Affairs and Security Policy. 2013. *Cybersecurity Strategy of the European Union: An Open, Safe and Secure Cyberspace. Joint Communication to the European Parliament, the Council, the European Economic and Social Committee and the Committee of the Regions JOIN(2013) 1 Final.* Brussels: European Commission. http://ec.europa.eu/newsroom/dae/document.cfm?doc_id=1667.

European Union. 2016. Directive (EU) 2016/1148 of the European Parliament and of the Council of 6 July 2016 concerning measures for a high common level of security of network and information systems across the Union, OJ L 194. http://data.europa.eu/eli/dir/2016/1148/oj.

Evancich, N., Zhuo L., Jason L., Yi C., Joshua T., and Peng X. 2014. Network-wide awareness. In *Cyber Defense and Situational Awareness*, edited by Kott, A., Wang, C., and Erbacher, R. F. 63–91. Advances in Information Security 62. Springer International Publishing, Cham, Switzerland. doi:10.1007/978-3-319-11391-3_5.

Federal Department of Finance FDF, Federal IT Steering Unit FITSU, and MELANI. 2015. NCS Factsheet 2014. The national strategy for the protection of Switzerland against cyber risks (NCS). MELANI. https://www.isb.admin.ch/dam/isb/en/dokumente/themen/NCS/Factsheet%20NCS%202014.pdf.download.pdf/Factsheet_NCS-2014-ENGL.pdf.

Federal Ministry of the Interior. 2011. *Cyber Security Strategy for Germany.* Berlin: Federal Ministry of the Interior. https://www.bsi.bund.de/SharedDocs/Downloads/EN/BSI/Publications/CyberSecurity/Cyber_Security_Strategy_for_Germany.pdf?__blob=publicationFile.

Fombrun, C. J. 1986. Structural dynamics within and between organizations. *Administrative Science Quarterly* 31(3): 403–421. doi:10.2307/2392830.

Franke, U. and Brynielsson, J. 2014. Cyber situational awareness—A systematic review of the literature. *Computers & Security* 46: 18–31. doi:10.1016/j.cose.2014.06.008.

Giacobe, N. A. 2010. Application of the JDL data fusion process model for cyber security. In *Proceedings of SPIE 7710, Multisensor, Multisource Information Fusion: Architectures, Algorithms, and Applications*, 7710:77100R-77100R-10, Orlando, FL, April 28, 2010. doi:10.1117/12.850275.

GovCERT.ch. 2016. APT Case RUAG. Technical Report. MELANI:GovCERT. https://www.melani.admin.ch/dam/melani/de/dokumente/2016/technical%20report%20ruag.pdf.download.pdf/Report_Ruag-Espionage-Case.pdf.

Haines, R. F. and Flatau, C. 1992. *Night Flying*. Practical Flying Series. 1st edition. Tab Books, Blue Ridge Summit, PA, September 1992. ISBN 978-0-8306-3780-5.

Hamilton, W. L. (1987). Situation Awareness Metrics Program (SAE Technical Paper Series No. 871767). Warrendale, PA: Society of Automotive Engineers.

Harwood, K., Barnett, B., and Wickens, C. D. 1988. Situational awareness: A conceptual and methodological framework. In *Proceedings of the 11th Biennial Psychology in the Department of Defense Symposium* (pp. 23–27), Colorado Springs, CO.

Hartman, B. O. and Secrist, G. E. 1991. Situational awareness is more than exceptional vision. *Aviation, Space, and Environmental Medicine* 62(11), 1084–1089.

HM Government. 2010. *A Strong Britain in an Age of Uncertainty: The National Security Strategy*. Cm 7953. London: UK Government. https://www.gov.uk/government/uploads/system/uploads/attachment_data/file/61936/national-security-strategy.pdf.

HM Government. 2016. *National Cyber Security Strategy 2016–2021*. UK Government, London. https://www.gov.uk/government/uploads/system/uploads/attachment_data/file/567242/national_cyber_security_strategy_2016.pdf.

Homeland Security. 2013. *NIPP 2013—Partnering for Critical Infrastructure Security and Resilience*. USA: Department of Homeland Security. https://www.dhs.gov/sites/default/files/publications/NIPP%202013_Partnering%20for%20Critical%20Infrastructure%20Security%20and%20Resilience_508_0.pdf.

Informatikstrategieorgan Bund ISB. 2002. Verletzliche Informationsgesellschaft—Herausforderung Informationssicherung. https://www.isss.ch/events/ft2003.03/pia_d.pdf.

Kaempf, G. L., Wolf, S., and Miller, T. E. 1993. Decision making in the AEGIS combat information center. *Proceedings of the Human Factors and Ergonomics Society Annual Meeting* 37(16): 1107–1111. doi:10.1177/154193129303701615.

Kaber, D. B. and Endsley, M. R. 2004. The effects of level of automation and adaptive automation on human performance, situation awareness and workload in a dynamic control task. *Theoretical Issues in Ergonomics Science* 5(2): 113–153. doi:10.1080/1463922021000054335.

Luiijf, E., Besseling, K., and de Graaf, P. 2013. Nineteen national cyber security strategies. *International Journal of Critical Infrastructures* 9(1–2): 3–31. doi:10.1504/IJCIS.2013.051608.

National Institute of Standards and Technology. 2014. Framework for improving critical infrastructure cybersecurity. Cybersecurity Framework Version 1.0. https://www.nist.gov/sites/default/files/documents/cyberframework/cybersecurity-framework-021214.pdf.

Okolica, J., McDonald, J. T. Peterson, G. L., Mills, R. F., and Haas, M. W. 2009. Developing systems for cyber situational awareness. In 2nd Cyberspace Research Workshop, 46, Shreveport, LA, June 2009.

Pahi, T., Leitner, M., and Skopik, F. 2017. Analysis and assessment of situational aware-
ness models for national cyber security centers. In *Proceedings of the 3rd International
Conference on Information Systems Security and Privacy (ICISSP)*. SCITEPRESS, Porto,
Portugal, February 19–21, 2017.

Praktiknjo, A. J., Hähnel, A., and Erdmann, G. 2011. Assessing energy supply security:
Outage costs in private households. *Energy Policy, Clean Cooking Fuels and Technologies
in Developing Economies*, 39(12): 7825–7833. doi:10.1016/j.enpol.2011.09.028.

Raulerson, E. L. 2013. Modeling cyber situational awareness through data fusion (No. AFIT-
ENG-13-M-41). AIR FORCE INST OF TECH WRIGHT-PATTERSON AFB OH
GRADUATE SCHOOL OF ENGINEERING AND MANAGEMENT. March
2013, Masters Thesis, http://www.dtic.mil/docs/citations/ADA576193, last accessed
on 31-07-2017.

Rytz, R. and Römer, J. 2003. MELANI-Ein Lagezentrum Zum Schutz Kritischer
Infrastrukturen Im Informationszeitalter. In GI Jahrestagung (Schwerpunkt Sicherheit-
Schutz Und Zuverlässigkeit), 57–65.

Smith, K. and Hancock, P. A. 1995. The risk space representation of commercial airspace. In
Proceedings of the 8th International Symposium on Aviation Psychology, Columbus, OH,
April 24–27, 1995.

Skopik, F., Bleier, T., and Fiedler, R. 2012. Information management and sharing for national
cyber situational awareness. In *ISSE 2012 Securing Electronic Business Processes*, edited
by Reimer, H., Pohlmann, N., and Schneider, W. 217–227. Wiesbaden: Springer
Fachmedien Wiesbaden. doi:10.1007/978-3-658-00333-3_21.

Skopik, F., Leitner, M., and Pahi, T. 2016. CISA: Establishing national cyber situational
awareness to counter new threats. ERCIM News, Special Theme: Cyber Security, no.
106: 52–53.

Steinberg, A. N., Bowman, C. L., and White, F. E. 1998. Revisions to the JDL model. In
Joint NATO/IRIS Conference Proceedings, Quebec, Canada, October.

Tadda, G. P. and Salerno, J. S. 2010. Overview of cyber situation awareness. In *Cyber Situational
Awareness*, edited by Jajodia, S., Liu, P., Swarup, V., and Wang, C. 15–35. Advances
in Information Security 46. Springer, New York. doi:10.1007/978-1-4419-0140-8_2.

National Cybersecurity and Communications Integration Center (NCCIC). 2013. Resources
and Capabilities Guide. Department of Homeland Security. https://info.publicintel-
ligence.net/NCCIC-CapabilitiesGuide.pdf.

White House. 2009. Cyberspace policy review. https://www.whitehouse.gov/assets/docu-
ments/Cyberspace_Policy_Review_final.pdf.

White House. 2011. International strategy for cyberspace. https://www.whitehouse.gov/
sites/default/files/rss_viewer/international_strategy_for_cyberspace.pdf.

White House. 2013. Improving critical infrastructure cybersecurity. Executive Order.
https://www.whitehouse.gov/the-press-office/2013/02/12/executive-order-improving-
critical-infrastructure-cybersecurity.

United Nations. 2015. Implementing WSIS outcomes: A ten-year review. UNCTAD/DTL/
STICT/2015/3. *United Nations Conference on Trade and Development*. Geneva, Switzerland,
April 2015. http://unctad.org/en/PublicationsLibrary/dtlstict2015d3_en.pdf.

Wickens, C. D. 1992. Workload and situation awareness: An analogy of history and implications. *Insight: The Visual Performance Technical Group Newsletter* 14(4), 1–3.

White, F. E. 1988. A model for data fusion. In *Proceedings of the First National Symposium on
Sensor Fusion*, Orlando, FL, April 5–8, 1988.

Chapter 7

Legal Implications of Information Sharing

Jessica Schroers and Damian Clifford
Katholieke Universiteit Leuven

Contents

7.1 Introduction

The sharing of information can help the operators of critical infrastructures increase security and identify threats and attacks more effectively. Shared information helps governments to gain an overview of risks at a national level and evaluate potential threat scenarios. Such insights are therefore necessary for developing and adjusting strategies, policies, legislation, and the allocation of resources (ENISA, 2016a, p. 33). Information can be shared between entities. For instance, critical infrastructure (CI) operators can share information with each other or indeed with national competent authorities [computer emergency response teams/computer security incident response teams (CERTs/CSIRTs), law enforcement, etc.]. Such information can also be exchanged between similar authorities in other Member States, with the EU Commission, and with international organizations such as Interpol.

As has been explained in previous chapters, there has been significant technological development to improve information sharing. Nevertheless, numerous legal issues and regulatory constraints must be considered when setting up information sharing structures at both the national and international levels. Countries take very different approaches regarding critical information infrastructure protection, which often result in different legislative outcomes.[1] Accordingly, the national approaches and the applicable legislation can vary extensively. It is not feasible to provide an examination of all applicable legislation, as this depends on the country,

---

[1] A 2016 ENISA study identified three different Critical Information Infrastructure Protection (CIIP) governance profiles: a decentralized approach, a centralized approach, and co-regulation with the private sector. The decentralized approach follows the principle of subsidiarity, and therefore generally speaking sector-specific legislation exists. Examples are Sweden, Austria, and Ireland (ENISA, 2016a, p. 29). The centralized approach includes a comprehensive legislative framework including obligations and requirements for all operators of critical information infrastructure and often a central authority. The main example of this approach is France, but the Czech Republic and Germany are mentioned in the ENISA report (p. 30). Finally, the coregulatory approach with the private sector often takes the form of public private partnerships, generally based on contractual agreements. An example of this approach can be found in the Netherlands (p. 32).

sector, capabilities of the actors, and several other factors. As it is impossible to provide overviews of every country and sector in this chapter, this analysis focuses on the cross-sectoral legislation at the EU level and hence on the legislative requirements that are not exclusive to one particular domain.

Furthermore, although the Cybersecurity Strategy spans three key pillars, "Network and Information Security," "Law Enforcement," and "Defense," the focus of this chapter is on Network and Information Security. Information sharing with "Law Enforcement" will only be briefly considered in this analysis and Defense entirely omitted. This decision has been made given that the focus of this book is on information sharing by predominantly private parties and also that cyber defense is still an evolving topic (with often very different legislative rules applying), which would therefore exceed the scope of this chapter and indeed book.

As such, this chapter gives an overview of the different horizontal legislation that is potentially applicable to information sharing in relation to NIS. The research will focus on a descriptive and evaluative analysis of the EU legislative framework in order to provide the background and general information regarding legislative requirements and hurdles for information sharing in order to set the scene for the more applied analysis, considering several cases, which will be the focus of Chapter 8.

However, although the focus of the chapter is to set the scene for the later analysis, in doing so it aims to provide a fundamental critique of the barriers to information sharing and thus provide normative legal insights into the mitigation of such obstacles. The legal instruments have been selected based on the relevance of their substantive and material scope. The chapter is divided in four parts, namely mapping the EU cybersecurity legal framework; information sharing: breaches, threats and best practices; legal certainty, information sharing, and potential legal barriers to data transfer; and, finally, moving beyond breach notification and the limitations of reactive sharing.

7.2 Mapping the EU Cybersecurity Legal Framework

Various dangers exist for network and information systems as a result of natural disasters, human errors, or malicious attacks. At the same time, the functioning of these systems has become increasingly important for society. As explained in Chapter 4, given that more and more sectors rely on the proper functioning of these systems, any disturbance can have a major influence on the functioning of the economy and indeed well-being of the society. As such, the purpose of this section of the analysis is to first outline the recognition of the need for and subsequently the moves toward a coordinated EU cybersecurity strategy. The second part of this section then scopes the applicable horizontal framework in order to set the scene for the later analysis of information sharing requirements, initiatives, and obstacles (i.e., Sections 7.3 and 7.4 respectively).

7.2.1 Plotting the Moves toward a More Coordinated EU Cybersecurity Strategy

As mentioned previously, information sharing is important for cyber resilience, situation monitoring, and policy development. A general goal is to increase the security of network and information systems against attacks. This goal is of particular importance for critical infrastructures. To improve security, it is also important to facilitate the investigation and prosecution of criminal attacks. As such, it is necessary to have legislation prohibiting such criminal activities and rules specifying information sharing obligations following criminal attacks in order to facilitate police investigations. For successful information sharing practices, many elements are prerequisites for effectiveness. Some basic examples include that it must be clear who should be contacted/provided with information in each context, it should be clear what information should be shared, and it is important that the same or comparable information classifications are utilized.

At a European level, the security of network and information systems has already been on the European agenda for some time. The EU approach to cybercrime developed parallel to the information security strategies (Christou, 2016, p. 90), and the protection of critical infrastructures is considered an area coming within the realm of cybersecurity (ENISA, 2015a, p. 25). The eEurope initiative in 1999 and the EU's "Communication on Network and Information Security: Proposal for a European Policy Approach" in 2001 are both early examples highlighting the importance of information infrastructure protection (Christou, 2016, p. 121). At a broader international level, the Council of Europe adopted the Convention on Cybercrime[2] in 2001. This convention is the first international treaty on crimes committed via the Internet and other computer networks, including violations of network security.

There were several communications from the European Commission[3] on aspects of cybercrime and network and information security including recommendations vis-à-vis improving cooperation between stakeholders and encouraging industry and community-led initiatives (Christou, 2016, p. 91). In 2004, ENISA was established with the aim of collaborating with relevant

---

[2] Council of Europe, ETS 185, Convention on Cybercrime/Budapest convention.

[3] For example: European Commission, "Creating a Safer Information Society by Improving the Security of Infrastructures and Combating Computer-Related Crime," COM (2000) 890, January 26, 2001 and European Commission Communication from the Commission to the Council, the European Parliament, the European Economic and Social Committee and the Committee of the Regions on Network and Information Security: Proposal for A European Policy Approach, COM (2001) 298 Final, Brussels, June 6, 2001, Communication from the Commission of May 31, 2006: A strategy for a Secure Information Society—"Dialogue, partnership and empowerment" [COM(2006) 251 final].

stakeholders in the public and private sector and providing advice and recommendations vis-à-vis best practices (Christou, 2016, p. 120). As a response to terrorism, the European Council called for the preparation of an overall strategy to protect critical infrastructures in 2004. The European Programme for Critical Infrastructure Protection (EPCIP) (COM, 2006) and the establishment of a Critical Infrastructure Warning Information Network (CIWIN)[4] were subsequently endorsed.

In 2005, the Commission's Green Paper on EPCIP provided policy options on how the Commission could establish EPCIP and CIWIN, and in 2006 the Communication from the Commission on EPCIP was provided (COM, 2006). As outlined in Chapter 6 of this book, trust and security are specifically mentioned as important in the Digital Single Market Strategy, and the European Agenda on Security calls for more cooperation and information sharing in different areas. In 2013, the Commission released the Cybersecurity Strategy of the EU ("An open, Safe and Secure Cyberspace") (JOIN, 2013). Almost every strategic priority of the 2013 Cybersecurity Strategy highlights the importance of sharing cybersecurity information (ENISA, 2015a, p. 10).

7.2.2 Scoping the Applicable Framework

As alluded to in the introduction, when considering information sharing many different actors can potentially be involved in different forms of mandatory or voluntary mechanisms. For example, a Critical Infrastructure Provider (CI provider) may share information on cyber attacks with other CI providers, within sectorial or other cooperation groups, and with CERTs (cf. Chapter 4). The CI provider may also be obliged to share information with national competent authorities and may wish or be obligated to share such information with Law Enforcement in the event of a criminal attack. These different actors again may share information with *inter alia* other CERTs, national authorities, and European organizations such as ENISA or Europol. Furthermore, it has to be taken into account that many CI providers are private; CERTs can be private or public, while National Competent Authorities and Law Enforcement agencies are public bodies. The precise interplay among these types of information exchange and the law varies given that countries have different approaches and national legislation on this matter. As one can imagine this clearly complicates matters especially in the context of cross-border information sharing.

---

4 See https://ec.europa.eu/home-affairs/what-we-do/networks/critical_infrastructure_warning_ information_network_en and https://europa.eu/sinapse/sinapse/index.cfm?fuseaction=login. redirect&redirect=cmtyrestricted.home&CMTY_ID=A0F55C70-0E9E-32D9- E5A7822B96D84471&request=1 [last accessed on 28.2.2017]

At a European level, three directives are worth mentioning, namely

- Directive 2013/40/EU on attacks against information systems[5] (hereafter referred to as the "Cybercrime Directive")
- Council Directive 2008/114 on European critical infrastructure (ECI)[6]
- The new Directive 2016/1148[7] (NIS Directive)

Specifically in relation to information sharing, the Cybercrime Directive provides common definitions of cybercrimes and includes provisions on the improvement of cooperation, obliging EU countries to have *inter alia* an operational national point of contact and to collect statistical data on cybercrime. Directive 2008/114/EC focuses on the identification of ECI. This Directive does not directly relate to information systems but focuses instead on the energy and transport sectors.[8] The NIS Directive aims at improving cybersecurity across the EU with a particular focus on essential services and specific digital services.

In general it should be noted that Art. 5 of the Treaty on European Union (TEU) provides that the EU can only act within the limits of the competences that were conferred upon it by the Member States. The use of these competences is governed by the principles of subsidiarity and proportionality. In particular, the principle of subsidiarity is important in this context. This principle provides that the Union should only act in areas that do not fall within the exclusive competence of the EU, if the objectives of the proposed action cannot be sufficiently achieved by the Member States and can be better achieved at the Union level due to the scale or effects of the proposed action.

Accordingly, the main legislation regarding cybersecurity remains at the national level. At the European level, approaches are fragmented with some directives providing a minimum harmonization approach often restricted to specified areas and limited to cross-border issues. This becomes especially visible in Directive 2008/114/EC. This was a first European regulatory step toward the protection of critical infrastructures. The Directive focuses on ECI in the transport

---

[5] Directive 2013/40/EU of the European Parliament and of the Council of August 12, 2013 on attacks against information systems and replacing Council Framework Decision 2005/222/JHA, OJ L 218, 14.8.2013.

[6] Council Directive 2008/114/EC of December 8, 2008 on the identification and designation of ECI and the assessment of the need to improve their protection, OJ L345/75, 23.12.2008.

[7] Directive (EU) 2016/1148 of the European Parliament and of the Council of July 6, 2016 concerning measures for a high common level of security of network and information systems across the Union, OJ L 194, 19.7.2016.

[8] However, already in the recitals it is stated that the directive should be reviewed with a view to assessing the need to include other sectors, specially mentioning the information and communication technology sector.

and energy sector. ECIs are critical infrastructures located in Member States that, if disrupted or damaged, have a significant impact on at least two Member States (Art. 2(b) Council Directive 2008/114/EC). The principle of subsidiarity is thus clearly visible in the scope of this Directive.

In addition, the Directive states that the ultimate responsibility to manage arrangements for the protection of critical infrastructures within the respective national borders falls within the competence of the relevant Member State (recital 4 Directive 2008/114/EC). The Member States are rather cautious regarding the delegation of activities in the field of security as they have a legitimate interest in keeping national security under their direct control (Lazari, 2014, p. 53). Therefore, the requirements introduced by the Directive have been fulfilled in 28 different ways, with varying interpretations of the definitions and cross-cutting and sectoral criteria (Lazari, 2014, p. 53).

In relation to information sharing, the Directive requires each ECI to have a Security Liaison Officer and each Member State to implement an appropriate communication mechanism between the relevant national authority and the Security Liaison Officer so as to facilitate the exchange of relevant information concerning identified risks and threats (Art. 6(4) Directive 2008/114/EC). Furthermore, the Directive also requires each Member State to appoint a European critical infrastructure contact point (ECIP) to coordinate European critical infrastructure protection issues within the Member State, with other Member States, and with the Commission (Art. 10 Directive, 2008/114/EC).

The issue of varying interpretations and the necessity to have a common framework with comparable terminology in order to exchange information was one of the driving forces behind the Cybercrime Directive. The European Council adopted the Directive on attacks against information systems in July 2013 in order to harmonize domestic approaches in national criminal laws. The Directive entirely replaces the provisions of Council Framework Decision 2005/222/JHA of February 24, 2005, and aims to allow for the consistent penalization of illegal access and system and data interference, thereby reinforcing the protection of critical infrastructures.

The "Directive establishes minimum rules concerning the definition of criminal offences and sanctions in the area of attacks against information systems. It also aims to facilitate the prevention of such offences and to improve cooperation between judicial and other competent authorities" (Art. 1 Cybercrime Directive, 2013). The Directive aims at harmonizing minimum standards by ensuring that these types of crimes are punishable by effective, proportionate, and dissuasive criminal penalties. Art. 5(4)(c) states that attacks against critical infrastructures should be punishable by a term of imprisonment of at least 5 years. Furthermore, the Directive also aims to improve the cooperation among the competent authorities, agencies, and bodies (such as national authorities), Eurojust, Europol (and its European Cybercrime Centre), and ENISA.

However, both of these Directives (i.e., Directive 2008/114/EC and the Cybercrime Directive, 2013) have been judged to fall short of any real improvement vis-à-vis the level of protection against network and information security incidents. More specifically, points of critique include that Directive 2008/114/EC only covers the energy and transport sector, the number of ECIs that were identified was limited, and no obligations to report security incidents or mechanisms for Member States to cooperate were included in the Directive (COM 2013, p. 4). The Cybercrime Directive on the other hand only covers "the criminalization of specific conducts, but does not address the prevention of NIS risks and incidents, the response to NIS incidents and the mitigation of their impact" (COM, 2013, p. 4). The insufficient sharing of information on incidents, risks, and threats was considered one of the two main problems leading to an insufficient level of protection against network and information security incidents (COM, 2013).[9]

As a consequence, therefore, the NIS Directive[10] was adopted. Member States have 21 months (until May 9, 2018) to transpose the Directive into their national legislative framework. The NIS Directive aims to achieve a high common level of security of network and information systems within the EU. In order to achieve this goal, the Directive specifies certain obligations for Member States. Member States must adopt a national strategy on the security of network and information systems, designate one or more national competent authorities, a national single point of contact, and CSIRTs.

The main goal of the NIS Directive is to increase the security of network and information systems of "operators of essential services." While the proposal had a broader scope (including for example public authorities) the final directive specifies that "operators of essential services" are public or private entities in the energy, transport, banking, financial market infrastructure, health, drinking water supply and distribution, and digital infrastructure sectors which fulfill three criteria (see Box).

The Member States are obligated to identify operators of essential services in their territories (Art. 5(1) NIS Directive 2016). The determination of what constitutes a "significant disruptive effect" will be defined at the national level. However, the Member States are not completely free in their definition. Indeed Member States are required to take certain factors into account, namely, the number of users relying on the service, the dependency of other essential services on the service, and the possible impact of incidents in degree and duration on economic and societal activities or public safety (Art. 6 NIS Directive 2016). Furthermore, they should take the market share of the entity, the area that could be affected by

---

[9] The other problem was the uneven level of capabilities at the national level across the EU, which hinders the creation of trust among peers.

[10] Directive (EU) 2016/1148 was adopted on July 6, 2016, and it entered into force in August 2016.

OPERATORS OF ESSENTIAL SERVICES:

Annex II of the NIS Directive specifies types of public or private entities in the sectors:

1. Energy (electricity, oil, and gas)
2. Transport (air, rail, water, and road)
3. Banking
4. Financial market infrastructures
5. Health
6. Drinking water supply and distribution
7. Digital Infrastructures (IXPs, DNS providers, TLD name registries)

To be considered operators of essential services, these entities must fulfill *three criteria* (Art. 5(2) NIS Directive 2016) as follows:

1. They provide a service that is essential for the maintenance of critical societal and/or economic activities.
2. The provision of their services depends on network and information systems.
3. An incident would have a significant disruptive effect on the provision of that service.

an incident, the importance of the entity for maintaining a sufficient level of the essential service and/or the availability of alternative means for the provision of that service, into account (Art. 6 NIS Directive 2016). In many countries, it is likely that there will be an overlap between identified operators of essential services and nationally defined critical infrastructure providers. However, Member States are only required to send a list of the identified operators to the Commission with the nationally defined critical infrastructure providers (by remaining outside of the Directive's scope) considered a matter for national security (i.e., unless they are also classified as ECIs, thereby coming within the scope of Directive 2008/114/EC as discussed above).

The NIS Directive specifies some obligations for identified operators of essential services, namely, that they must take appropriate and proportionate technical and organizational measures for risk management and to prevent and minimize the impact of incidents (Art. 14 NIS Directive 2016). Similar obligations are introduced for digital service providers (providers of online marketplaces, online search engines, and cloud computing services) to ensure the security of their network and information systems (Art. 16 NIS Directive 2016).

7.3 Information Sharing: Breaches, Threats, and Best Practices

Having scoped the security framework, the analysis now turns to an examination of information sharing requirements. This analysis is divided in two parts: breach notification obligations/damage limitations and proactive information sharing.

7.3.1 Breach Notification Obligations and Damage Limitations

A general problem associated with information sharing is that private companies are often reluctant to participate given the perceived threat to reputation and thus profit. Since 2009, obligations to send notifications of incidents have been increasingly enshrined in legislation in order to counteract this hesitancy. This move toward obligatory information sharing began in the telecommunication sector. Directive 2009/140/EC[11] (which amended the Framework Directive 2002)[12] introduced Articles 13a and 13b containing *inter alia* the obligation to notify the competent national regulatory authority where a "breach of security or loss of integrity" results in "a significant impact on the operation of networks or services."

Following this notification, the competent regulatory authority could then (if necessary) inform the relevant national regulatory authorities in other Member States, ENISA, and the public if deemed in the public interest. Information is also collected and exchanged in summary documents resulting in reports compiled by ENISA, which include analysis and recommendations and anonymized national reports that are made available to the national authorities. National reports are also shared with the operators who agree to provide incident information (ENISA, 2015b).

Generally speaking, in transposing the Directive, Member States included the provisions in their national telecommunications legislation (e.g., Germany: §109 (5) German telecommunications act; the Netherlands: Art. 11a2 Dutch Telecommunications Act; and Belgium: Art. 114 Belgian Electronic Communications Act). The national legislation is often further specified by secondary legislation (e.g., in the Netherlands "Besluit continuïteit openbare elektronische communicatienetwerken en—diensten").

Of particular importance in the adoption of such secondary legislation were ENISA recommendations. For example, in Belgium in Art. 114/1, §2 Electronic

---

[11] Directive 2009/140/EC of the European Parliament and of the Council of November 25, 2009 amending Directives 2002/21/EC on a common regulatory framework for electronic communications networks and services, 2002/19/EC on access to, and interconnection of, electronic communications networks and associated facilities, and 2002/20/EC on the authorisation of electronic communications networks and services.

[12] Directive 2002/21/EC (Framework Directive).

Communications Act it was provided that "The undertakings providing public communications networks or publicly available electronic communications services shall immediately notify the Institute of a breach of security or loss of integrity that has had a significant impact on the operation of networks or services. Following the prior consent of the Minister, the Institute shall specify in which hypotheses the breach of security or loss of integrity has a significant impact in the sense of this paragraph." Accordingly, the national regulatory authority BIPT (Belgisch Instituut voor Postdiensten en Telecommunicatie) provided a decision.[13] The decision lays down the practical rules regarding the notification of security incidents that do not involve personal data, as inspired by ENISA's Technical Guidelines on Incident Reporting (ENISA, 2013a), and also aims to ensure consistency between the operator notifications to the BIPT and the BIPT summary report sent to ENISA. In its decision, BIPT defines the criteria for a breach of security or loss of integrity having a significant impact on the operation of networks or services. ENISA defines the threshold based on the duration and the number of affected users as a percentage of the national user base of the service (ENISA, 2013a). The BIPT clearly based its decision upon the criteria defined by ENISA. However, instead of using percentages it specifies six different thresholds per service adjusted to the number of end users in Belgium.

According to ENISA, Art. 13a and the evaluation brought a certain amount of uniformity and contributed to increasing the resilience and security of the telecommunication infrastructure in Europe (ENISA, 2016b, p. 41). Given their success, notification obligations were increasingly also used for other sectors (see for an overview of different notification provisions, Table 7.1). Examples include Art. 19 of the new European Regulation 910/2014 (eIDAS Regulation, 2014)[14] that provides a notification obligation with a 24-hour time limit after becoming aware of the incident for qualified and nonqualified trust service providers, which is almost identically to the above provisions in the telecoms sector. Another example is the Directive 2015/2366 (PSD II Directive, 2015),[15] which includes incident reporting obligation for payment service providers (Art. 96 PSD II Directive 2015). Finally,

---

[13] Decision of the BIPT council of April 1, 2014, laying down the circumstances in which the operators have to notify BIPT of a security incident and the terms and conditions of this notification, available at http://www.bipt.be/en/operators/telecommunication/security/network-security/decision-of-the-bipt-council-of-1-april-2014-laying-down-the-circumstances-in-which-the-operators-have-to-notify-bipt-of-a-security-incident-and-the-terms-and-conditions-of-this-notification (last accessed 20.3.2017).

[14] Regulation (EU) No 910/2014 of the European Parliament and of the Council of July 23, 2014 on electronic identification and trust services for electronic transactions in the internal market and repealing Directive 1999/93/EC.

[15] Directive (EU) 2015/2366 of the European Parliament and of the Council of November 25, 2015 on payment services in the internal market, amending Directives 2002/65/EC, 2009/110/EC and 2013/36/EU and Regulation (EU) No 1093/2010, and repealing Directive 2007/64/EC.

also the NIS Directive specifies notification obligations for operators of essential services and for digital service providers. If an incident has a significant/substantial impact on their service, such providers are required to notify the competent authority appointed by the Member State or the CSIRT without undue delay. The NIS Directive explicitly excludes service providers falling within the more targeted scope of the notification provisions contained in the Framework Directive and the eIDAS Regulation from its requirements. In addition, the Directive provides an exception for the operators of essential services and providers of digital services in cases where a sector specific Union legal act (such as PSD II) already establishes obligations to notify that are at least equivalent to the NIS Directive (Art. 1(7) NIS Directive 2016).

Furthermore, it should be noted that there are specific notification obligations for personal data breaches. While the frameworks analyzed in the previous paragraphs provide obligations focused on the nature of the service being provided, the personal data breach notification mechanism hinges on the scope of the definition of personal data: any information relating to an "identified or identifiable natural person" (Art. 4(1) General Data Protection Regulation (GDPR)). The term "identifiable" here refers to natural person who can be directly or indirectly be identified.

To assess whether a person is identifiable all the reasonable means that may be used, either by the controller or a third party, need to be taken into account (recital 26 GDPR). Importantly, "identified" is not limited to an individual's name and instead refers to "singling out" through the use of an identifier (Art. 4(1) GDPR) with pseudonymous data still classified as coming within the scope of the personal data definition (see Art. 4(5) GDPR). Therefore, personal data may include for example a name, an identification number, location data, an online identifier, or one or more factors specific to the physical, physiological, genetic, mental, economic, cultural, or social identity of that natural person.

An important point of analysis in this regard is the status of IP addresses, which in some countries were considered personal data while in others not.[16] Indeed, although the CJEU previously found that IP addresses were personal data,[17] some uncertainty remained given that the previous case law only referred to static and not dynamic IP addresses. In the 2016 *Breyer Case* the Court of Justice of the European Union (CJEU) decided on the status of dynamic IP addresses (albeit by limiting this somewhat to the facts in the case).[18] The background of the case involved the operation of websites by the Federal Republic of Germany and more specifically the storing of the dynamic IP addresses of visitors. Patrick Breyer wanted the Federal Republic of Germany to refrain from collecting IP addresses when not technically

---

[16] Also mentioned as a point of concern for information sharing between CERTs in ENISA 2013b, p. 8.

[17] For example, the CJEU Judgement Case C-70/10, November 24, 2011 (Scarlet SABAM), ECLI:EU:C:2011:771.

[18] CJEU Judgement Case C-582/14 October 19, 2016 (Breyer), ECLI: EU:C:2016:779.

necessary in terms of functionality. Following two lower court hearings, the case ended up in front of the German Federal Court of Justice, the *Bundesgerichtshof* (BGH). On October 28, 2014, the *Bundesgerichtshof* referred questions to the Court of Justice of the European Union (CJEU) for a preliminary ruling.

Importantly for our current analysis, the first question related to whether the classification of IP addresses as personal data extends to dynamic IP addresses in situations where the website operator who processes the IP addresses does not have the identifying information necessary to link them to individual users. In such cases, the identifying information is instead held by a third party (i.e., the ISP) and is therefore beyond the reach of the website operator without direct cooperation between the parties.[19]

In responding to this question, the CJEU considered that the possibility of combining a dynamic IP address with additional data held by the Internet service provider could constitute a means "likely reasonably" to be used to identify the data subject given that (as in the case of Germany) legal channels exist to obtain such information. The Advocate General in his opinion pointed out that a dynamic IP address would not be considered personal data if the identification of the data subject was prohibited by law or practically impossible due to its requiring a disproportionate effort in terms of time, cost, and man-power, thereby resulting in an insignificant risk of identification.

Consequently, given that ISPs keep a record of the persons to whom dynamic IP addresses have been assigned, and as legal means to access the information exist, dynamic IP addresses in such circumstances are considered personal data.[20] The reasoning of the court regarding the "likely reasonably" means can also be applied in relation to information other than dynamic IP addresses.

From the previous few paragraphs, it is clear that the definition of personal data is broad, and this obviously renders the notification obligations for personal data breaches significantly important. This notification obligation applies to both data controllers and data processors. Consequently, this requirement applies to a broader audience and can coincide with notification obligations aimed at specific services as long as personal data is processed. This is provided for by also obliging notification to other relevant bodies and highlighting the need for close cooperation (e.g., Art. 19 eIDAS Regulation 2014, Art. 15(4) NIS Directive 2016).

The telecommunication sector introduced specific obligations in 2009 as part of the Telecommunications reform package via an amendment to Art. 4 of Directive

---

[19] It is important to note that this is more significant in the context of dynamic IP addresses given that they change, for static IP addresses as they remain fixed such additional information becomes less important.

[20] Article 29 Working Party, Opinion 4/2007 on the concept of personal data, WP 136, June 20, 2007; WP 37: Privacy on the Internet—An integrated EU Approach to On-line Data Protection—adopted on 21.11.2000; CJEU Judgement Case C-582/14 October 19, 2016 (Breyer).

2002/58/EC (ePrivacy Directive 2002).[21] This Article requires the provider to notify the competent national authority and, in certain circumstances, the subscriber or individual concerned in case of a personal data breach without undue delay. In order to ensure implementation consistency, the Commission adopted technical implementing measures through Regulation No 611/2013.[22] This regulation requires that where feasible the provider must provide notification of all personal data breaches to the competent national authority no later than 24 hours after detection (Art. 2 Regulation 611/2013). This may also be merely an initial notification if the required information is unavailable at the time of the initial notification and must then be followed by a second notification within three days after the initial notification with the further details.

The Commission Regulation 611/2013 defines certain circumstances in which a personal data breach is likely to adversely affect the personal data of a subscriber or individual, namely

1. The nature and content of the personal data concerned, in particular where the data concerns financial information, special categories of data, as well as location data, Internet log files, web browsing histories, e-mail data, and itemized call lists;
2. The likely consequences of the personal data breach for the subscriber or individual concerned, in particular where the breach could result in identity theft or fraud, physical harm, psychological distress, humiliation, or damage to reputation; and
3. The circumstances of the personal data breach, in particular where the data has been stolen or when the provider knows that the data are in the possession of an unauthorized third party (Art. 3(2) Regulation 611/2013).

The Data Protection Directive 95/46/EC did not include a specific data breach notification obligation. However, obligations of this kind were often included in national law or the Data Protection Authorities recommended it, by inferring good practice standards to notify from other provisions of the Directive.[23] In contrast,

---

[21] Directive 2002/58/EC of the European Parliament and of the Council of July 12, 2002 concerning the processing of personal data and the protection of privacy in the electronic communications sector (Directive on privacy and electronic communications) OJ L 201, 31/07/2002 pp. 37–47.

[22] Commission Regulation (EU) No 611/2013 of June 24, 2013 on the measures applicable to the notification of personal data breaches under Directive 2002/58/EC of the European Parliament and of the Council on privacy and electronic communications, 26.6.2013, OJ L 173/5.

[23] For example, in Germany and the Netherlands a notification obligation was enshrined in law; in Belgium and Italy the DPAs deduced an obligation to notify from the principles of security or fairness.

the new GDPR[24] does include a notification obligation in case of a personal data breach in Art. 33 GDPR. The controller is required to provide notification of the personal data breach without undue delay and, where feasible, no later than 72 hours after having become aware of it (if the notification is made later, reasons for the delay must be given). Where a data processor becomes aware of a personal data breach, this entity is obligated to notify the controller without undue delay who in turn must notify the supervisory authority. As distinct from the other notification obligations, the data protection provision does not focus on the impact of the service to trigger a notification obligation. Instead, breaches must notified in general with the exception of a personal data breach that is unlikely to result in a risk to the rights and freedoms of natural persons. In situations where the personal data breach is likely to result in a high risk to the rights and freedoms of natural persons, the controller is required to inform not only the supervisory authority but also the data subject without undue delay.

In contrast with Art. 13a Frameworks Directive, the data protection authorities are not required to report the received notifications to the European Commission or ENISA on an annual basis. Art. 59 GDPR requires data protection authorities to draw up an annual report on its activities, which must be transmitted to different authorities and made available to the public, the European Commission, and the European Data Protection Board. The Article does not specifically mention that the DPAs should also include the received notifications.

It should be noted, however, that, given that much of the EU framework has been adopted in the form of directives, one is required to examine the specific national implementations for a more specific analysis of each Member State's legal framework. In addition, in areas that are not legislated at the EU level (or areas in which Member States have the competence to enact diverging substantive rules due to a minimum harmonization legislative approach), some Member States may have specific legislation of relevance. For example France [French Military Programming Law (LPM)] and Germany (German IT Security) both oblige specific operators to report cybersecurity incidents, implement technical and organizational security measures, and undergo cybersecurity audits (ENISA, 2016a, p. 18f).

7.3.2 Proactive Information Sharing

Although the developments outlined in the previous section are important, breach notification has some disadvantages. In particular, differences between the national legislation may hinder cross-border information sharing (ENISA, 2015a, p. 34), the notifications happen only after a breach, and companies tend to be

---

[24] Regulation (EU) 2016/679 of the European Parliament and of the Council of April 27, 2016 on the protection of natural persons with regard to the processing of personal data and on the free movement of such data, and repealing Directive 95/46/EC (General Data Protection Regulation), OJ L 119, 4.5.2016, pp. 1–88.

Table 7.1 Overview of Different Notification Provisions

Legislation	Art. 13a Directive 2009/140/EC	Art. 19 eIDAS Regulation	Art. 96 PSD II Directive	Art. 33/34 General Data Protection Regulation	Art. 14 NIS Directive
Who has to notify?	Undertakings providing public communications networks or publicly available electronic communications services	Qualified and nonqualified trust service providers	Payment service providers	Controller	Operators of essential services + digital service providers
What?	A breach of security or loss of integrity that has had a significant impact on the operation of networks or services	Any breach of security or loss of integrity that has a significant impact on the trust service provided or on the personal data maintained therein	Major operational or security incident	Personal data breach that results in a risk for the right and freedom of individuals	Incidents having a significant impact on the continuity of the essential service
When?	*[not specified in the Directive]*	Without undue delay but in any event within 24 hours of having become aware of it	Without undue delay *[possibly specified in national legislation]*	Without undue delay and, where feasible, not later than 72 hours of having become aware of it	Without undue delay *[possibly specified in national legislation]*
To whom?	Competent national regulatory authority	The supervisory body and, where applicable, other relevant bodies, such as the competent national body for information security or the data protection authority	Competent authority in the home Member State of the payment service provider	Competent supervisory authority [in case of high risk for rights and freedoms of individuals also to the data subject]	Competent authority/CSIRT appointed by Member State

careful with notifications due to reputational worries or fear of liability (see *infra* Section 7.5). To achieve resilience, a broader, proactive exchange of information is also important.

However, proactive information sharing is a matter closely protected by the Member States. Even in the context of public sector information, EU Member States have guarded their authority over Freedom of Information and access tightly and essentially decide which data sets become public. The area of freedom of information legislation focuses on the public sector bodies' rights and obligations in relation to making "public information" available upon request (but also encouraging proactive release) to the general public in order to support accountability and transparency. Although there is an EU-level legal framework on the reuse of public sector data in the form of Directive 2003/98/EC (PSI Directive, 2003)[25] designed to stimulate the European information services market, the release of this information remains a determination in the sole competence of the Member States, thus facilitating clear disparities.[26]

As noted by the ENISA report on encouraging information sharing between CERTs:

> For CERTs, this [PSI Directive] can be relevant when requesting permission to re-use information which is made available by public sector bodies, or inversely when they themselves are public sector bodies and make their own information available for re-use. In these circumstances, the PSI Directive provides a common framework for the rights of re-users, which could theoretically support the exchange of information. In practice, however, the impact of this framework is likely to be very limited for CERTs, primarily because the information which directly relates to security incidents that fall within their remit is unlikely to be made available for re-use.
>
> *ENISA, 2011*

Moreover, in our current analysis it is also important to again emphasize that this Directive only applies to public sector information. Therefore, given that many of the CI operators are private entities, the Directive would remain largely inapplicable to the information held by such operators (the consequences/fear of sharing this information with public sector bodies and its potential subsequent release will be dealt with in Section 7.5).

---

[25] Directive 2003/98 of November 17, 2003 on the re-use of public sector information [2003] OJ L 345/90, amended in 2013 by Directive 2013/37/EU of June 26, 2013 amending Directive 2003/98/EC on the re-use of public sector information [2013] OJ L 175/1.

[26] For more see: http://journalism.cmpf.eui.eu/maps/freedom-of-information/.

As such, for a more accurate overview of hard law requiring proactive information sharing, one must refer to the national level. That being said, many different soft law initiatives exist to improve information sharing. ENISA has worked on and provided many recommendations for information sharing among different stakeholders. Examples of different information sharing communities and networks are given in Chapters 4 and 5. As explained there, information sharing communities have the benefit of increasing trust and therefore stimulating openness in information sharing. Additionally, they also provide meaningful vetting and leverage expert capabilities.

The NIS Directive not only introduces new entities in order to increase the national level of network and information security, but it also includes some approaches to increase and improve information sharing. The Cooperation Group and the CSIRTs network are two such groups established by the NIS Directive, which should increase the exchange of information. The Cooperation Group is composed of representatives of the Member States, the European Commission, and ENISA and has a more strategic role, focusing on exchanging information regarding best practice (e.g., on the exchange of information related to incident notification). On the other hand, the CSIRT network consists of representatives of the Member States' CSIRTs and CSIRT-EU. The aim of the network is to exchange information on CSIRTs' services, operations and cooperation capabilities and discuss noncommercially sensitive information (at the request of a representative of a CSIRT), and voluntarily make available nonconfidential information concerning individual incidents.

As becomes visible from the restrictions, the sharing is purely voluntary. It is further provided that Member State CSIRTs may refuse to contribute to discussions if there is a risk of prejudice to the investigation of an incident. Moreover, the sharing only involves nonconfidential and noncommercially sensitive information.

7.4 Legal Certainty, Information Sharing, and Potential Legal Barriers to Data Transfer

The analysis now turns to an examination of the legal frameworks that protect certain categories of data at the EU level and thus may act as barriers to more effective information sharing. In order to facilitate the analysis, the section has been divided in two parts, namely: recognizing national security and private economic interests and individual rights, data protection, and fair balancing protections. The first of these sections will outline the classification of certain information as classified by public authorities and the economic interests associated with keeping information hidden (thus trade secrets and confidentiality clauses). The second aims to outline the role of data protection and thus the individual fundamental right to the protection of personal data.

7.4.1 Recognizing National Security and Private Economic Interests

7.4.1.1 Intellectual Property, Trade Secrets, and Confidentiality

Intellectual property law is an ancillary area of law that may have an impact on information sharing. Intellectual property grants rights holders exclusive rights, meaning that they have the exclusive power to perform certain categories of actions in relation to their works (e.g., dissemination and duplication). At an international level, attempts at harmonizing the protection of intellectual property rights have resulted in the adoption of a combination of international treaties, EU legislation, and national provisions. Although there is some degree of harmonization, this is far from complete and clear disparities exist between Member States.

IP rights can theoretically provide hurdles for information sharing. Indeed, although it is unlikely that there would be an infringement of certain IP rights such as computer program copyright, patent law, or trademark law[27] it is however, necessary to consider potential IP issues associated with the information in itself and indeed its organization in a database. The key Directives[28] in the context of cybersecurity information sharing are Directive 2001/29/EC on the harmonization of certain aspects of copyright and related rights in the information society[29] and Directive 96/9/EC on the legal protection of databases (Database Directive).[30]

The EU Database Directive (1) harmonizes the treatment of databases under copyright law and (2) establishes a *sui generis* right for the creators of databases that do not qualify for copyright protection. As such, there are three divisions to consider, namely: ordinary copyright, database copyright, and the *sui generis* database

---

[27] This is based on the assumption that the insights that would be shared would be unlikely to constitute anything other than information to be processed by a computer program. However for absolute certainty, regard must be had for all relevant IP rights.

[28] Other EU legislation includes: Directive 2006/115/EC of the European Parliament and of the Council of December 12, 2006 on rental right and lending right and on certain rights related to copyright in the field of intellectual property, OJ L 376, pp. 28–35; Directive 2009/24/EC of the European Parliament and of the Council of April 23, 2009 on the legal protection of computer programs, OJ L 111, pp. 16–22; Council Directive 87/54/EC of December 16, 1986 on the legal protection of topographies of semiconductor products, OJ L24, 36; Directive 2004/48/EC of the European Parliament and of the Council of April 29, 2004 on the enforcement of intellectual property rights, OJ L 195, pp. 16–25; Council Directive 93/83/EEC of September 27, 1993 on the coordination of certain rules concerning copyright and rights related to copyright applicable to satellite broadcasting and cable retransmission, OJ L 248, pp. 15–21.

[29] Directive 2001/29/EC of the European Parliament and of the Council of May 22, 2001 on the harmonization of certain aspects of copyright and related rights in the information society (OJ 2001 L 167, p. 10).

[30] Directive 96/9/EC of the European Parliament and of the Council of March 11, 1996, on the legal protection of databases (Database Directive).

right. Generally copyright (i.e., ordinary copyright and database copyright) as a legal concept grants the creator/author of an original work exclusive rights for a limited period of time (usually 70 years after the death of the creator/author). In contrast, the *sui generis* database right does not protect the original result of an intellectual creation but instead the *sweat of the brow* of the database creator. According to recital 7 of the Database Directive this right was developed as "the making of databases requires the investment of considerable human, technical and financial resources while such databases can be copied or accessed at a fraction of the cost needed to design them independently."

Both ordinary and database copyright grant the rights holder an exclusive power over the "reproducing," "communicating to the public," "distributing," "lending," and "renting" of the work. Therefore, IP infringements may occur if the information that is protected is shared without the permission of the rights holder. Although these difficulties can in principle be solved via licenses, as noted by the ENISA report on encouraging information exchange between CERTs,

> The scope of application of these rights can be very broad, with the line between protection and unprotected information being particularly blurred in the case of copyrights... and sui generis database rights... as these do not require any prior registration.
>
> *ENISA, 2011*

Importantly, however, there are certain exceptions to IP rights, for example for purely temporal reproduction, lawful users, or public security.[31]

Building on the above, complementary to IP rights is the protection of trade secrets. Trade secrets are pieces of information of an economic value (despite not granting exclusivity of rights) that are not publically known and are treated as confidential within a company (SWD, 2013). As part of the 2011 IPR strategy on June 8, 2016, Directive 2016/943[32] on trade secrets was adopted (Tradesecrets Directive, 2016). This Directive aims to harmonize the national laws in EU countries against the unlawful acquisition, disclosure, and use of trade secrets. In order for information to be considered a trade secret, the key requirement is that the person in

---

[31] As provided for by Article 5(3)(e) the Information Society Directive and Articles 6(1)(c) and 9(1)(c) of the Database Directive. Member States such as Germany (Section 45, 2, German Copyright Law) and the UK (Sections 45–50 UK Copyright) have implemented such an exception in contrast to Belgium and Ireland. However, in their review of the current implementation in Ireland the Copyright Review Committee recommended such a provision (Modernising Copyright A Report prepared by the Copyright Review Committee for the Department of Jobs, Enterprise and Innovation www.enterprise.gov.ie/en/Publications/CRC-Report.pdf).

[32] Directive (EU) 2016/943 of the European Parliament and of the Council of June 8, 2016, on the protection of undisclosed know-how and business information (trade secrets) against their unlawful acquisition, use, and disclosure. OJ L 157, 15.6.2016, pp. 1–18.

control of the information take reasonable steps to keep it secret. At a business level, it should be noted that there might also be confidentiality obligations toward third parties, which may have a restricting impact on the sharing of information. For example, a third party may make its voluntary cooperation subject to a confidentiality agreement in the form of a nondisclosure agreement.

7.4.1.2 Classified Information and the Public–Private Overlap

It is clear that information relating to critical infrastructures can potentially be security sensitive. Given the importance of critical infrastructures however, such information may also be classified as secret at a national level thereby blurring the public–private dividing lines. There is a large degree of disparity between the Member States in this regard. For example, in Ireland no framework currently exists for the classification of data. However, the Official Secrets Act 1963 does stipulate the definition for an official secret. This contrasts sharply with the situation in many other countries.

For instance in Germany, national security secrets are defined in § 93 of the German Criminal Code (StGB), while the Safety Assessment Act (SÜG)[33] regulates the requirements for people who do security relevant tasks, including the accessing of classified information. § 4 SÜG defines four levels of classification for information or items considered necessary to be kept secret in the public interest. Similar classification systems are evident in the UK, Italy, Belgium, and France.[34] The key issue however, relates to the fact that the precise criteria and oversight of such classifications are not always apparent.

The EU itself does not have specific legislation on the classification of security information. As described supra, this is due to the fact that the EU has no competence as national security, according to Art. 4 TEU, is "the sole responsibility of each Member State" (Galloway, 2014). Nevertheless, as the Maastricht and Amsterdam treaties included the development of a common foreign and security policy and the commitment to take action to prevent and combat crime as an objective, security classification rules were seen as a necessary prerequisite for the EU to cooperate in a meaningful way with third-country states and international organizations (Galloway, 2014).

Accordingly, in order to develop a regulatory framework for security classification the EU's institutions have taken a procedural approach largely based on internal rules.[35] In 2001, the Council adopted a decision detailing comprehensive security

---

[33] Gesetz über die Voraussetzungen und das Verfahren von Sicherheitsüberprüfungen des Bundes (Sicherheitsüberprüfungsgesetz—SÜG).

[34] See: http://cybersecurity.bsa.org/countries.html.

[35] Galloway (2014). This approach has been criticized by some authors, e.g., Deirdre Curtin, "Overseeing Secrets in the EU: A Democratic Perspective: Overseeing Secrets in the EU," *JCMS: Journal of Common Market Studies* 52, no. 3 (May 2014): 684–700, doi:10.1111/jcms.12123.

rules on protecting EU classified information. This decision defined "EU classified information" (EUCI) as a legally distinct category from "national classified information."[36] The Commission followed this with the adoption of equivalent provisions in the same year[37] and the European Parliament adopted rules on the treatment of confidential information in 2011.[38]

FURTHER INFORMATION

The Council and the Commission define EUCI as "any information or material designated by an EU security classification, the unauthorised disclosure of which could cause varying degrees of prejudice to the interests of the European Union or of one or more of the Member States."[39] EUCI is separated into four levels distinguished on the basis of the effect an unauthorized disclosure could have on the interests of the European Union or one or more of the Member States:

■ TRES SECRET UE/EU TOP SECRET: could cause exceptionally grave prejudice to the essential interests
■ SECRET UE/EU SECRET: seriously harm the essential interests
■ CONFIDENTIEL UE/EU CONFIDENTIAL: harm the essential interests
■ RESTREINT UE/EU RESTRICTED: be disadvantageous to the interests

---

Aside from the fact that revealing classified information is punishable in many Member States, the necessary technical and organizational requirements coming

---

[36] Council of the European Union (2001), 'Council Decision of 19 March 2001 adopting the Council's security regulations', 2001/264/EC, OJ L 101, April 11, 2001.

[37] Commission Decision 2001/844/EC,ECSC,Euratom of November 29, 2001, amending its internal Rules of Procedure, OJ L 317, December 3, 2001. After its first decision in 2001, the Council updated its internal rules with Council Decision 2001/264/EC of March 19, 2001 adopting the Council's security regulations (OJ L 101), Council Decision 2011/292/EU of March 31, 2011 on the security rules for protecting EU classified information (OJ L 14)1 and Decision 2013/488/EU, which was amended by Council Decision 2014/233/EU of April 14, 2014, amending Decision 2013/488/EU on the security rules for protecting EU classified information. Furthermore, there are internal guidelines [Council of the European Union, Handling of documents internal to the Council, 1136/11 (9.6.2011) and 10384/13 (31.5.2013)] and the Commission also updated their Commission Decision (EU, Euratom) 2015/444 of March 13, 2015, on the security rules for protecting EU classified information, OJ L72/53, March 17, 2015.

[38] European Parliament (2011), "Decision of the Bureau of the European Parliament concerning the rules governing the treatment of confidential information by the European Parliament," OJ C 190, June 20, 2011.

[39] Art. 3 Commission decision, Art. 2 Council decision.

along with the handling of classified information can provide a barrier for information sharing. For example, the Council Directive 2008/114 requires that any person handling classified information (also in case of nonwritten information exchanged during meetings at which sensitive subjects are discussed) must have gone through an appropriate level of security vetting (Art. 9, recital 18 Directive 2008/114).

The NIS Directive also includes exceptions regarding confidential information in Art. 1(5) and (6). These provide that confidential information based on Union or national rules (including rules on business confidentiality) shall only be exchanged with the European Commission and other relevant authorities if the exchange is necessary for the application of the Directive. Such information must be kept confidential, used to protect the interest of the operators of essential services, and be limited to what is relevant and proportionate to achieve the purpose of the exchange. The Directive does not however, require the disclosure of information Member States consider contrary to their national security interests.

7.4.2 Individual Rights, Data Protection and Fair Balancing Protections

Probably the most referenced potential hurdle to data sharing is data protection. Indeed, in a 2013 ENISA report on information exchange among CERTs, it was observed from interviews that there were doubts regarding the particular sets of data that can be shared with privacy and data protection perceived as particularly problematic in large part due to the lack of harmonization and the different interpretations of the law by different bodies (ENISA, 2013b, p. 8).

The adoption of the GDPR on May 24, 2016, aims to provide a higher level of harmonized protection. Distinct from its predecessor, the Data Protection Directive 95/46/EC,[40] the GDPR as a Regulation is directly applicable, does not require transposition into national law, and will apply from May 25, 2018. The GDPR thus constitutes a single set of rules for all Member States regulating the processing of personal data.

Importantly, however, according to Art. 2(2)(b), the GDPR is not applicable in circumstances where Member States carry out activities falling "within the scope of Chapter 2 of Title V of the TEU" thereby excluding matters pertaining to national security from the scope of application. Furthermore, Art. 2(2)(d) provides that the GDPR does not apply to personal data processing conducted "by competent authorities for the purposes of the prevention, investigation, detection or prosecution of criminal offences or the execution of criminal penalties, including the safeguarding against and the prevention of threats to public security." In such

---

[40] Directive 95/46/EC of the European Parliament and of the Council of October 24, 1995 on the protection of individuals with regard to the processing of personal data and on the free movement of such data, OJ L 281, 23.11.1995, pp. 31–50.

circumstances, one is required to refer to Directive 2016/680/EU and its national implementing measures.[41]

Nevertheless, and as repeated on several occasions already, CIs are often operated by private entities, therefore ruling out the application of these exemptions. As such, it is necessary to comply with the requirements in the GDPR if personal data is being processed. As described *supra* (see Section 7.3.1), personal data is defined as any information related to "identified or identifiable natural person." It should also be noted that "processing" is construed broadly to include almost anything that can be done with personal data.

> **DEFINITION: PROCESSING**
>
> *Processing*: according to Art. 4(2) GDPR "processing" means any operation or set of operations performed on personal data or on sets of personal data, whether or not by automated means, such as collection, recording, organization, structuring, storage, adaption or alteration, retrieval, consultation, use, disclosure by transmission, dissemination or otherwise making available, alignment or combination, restriction, reassure or destruction.

The GDPR outlines certain basic principles relating to the processing of personal data in Art. 5 GDPR. These include, *inter alia* the requirement that personal data must be processed fairly, lawfully, and in a transparent manner, only be collected for specified, explicit, and legitimate purposes, and not further processed in a way incompatible with that purpose (i.e., network and information security or possible even more specified, e.g., enforcing access restrictions, mitigating DDoS attacks); that personal data processing should be limited to what is adequate, relevant, and not excessive in relation to the purposes of the processing (data minimization); and that personal data must be processed in a secure manner through the use of appropriate technical or organizational measures. Furthermore, the data should be accurate and kept up to date and only be stored as long as is necessary for the purpose. This means that it might be necessary to provide deletion timeframes and that it is therefore unacceptable to keep personal data for an undefined timeframe *just in case*.

Data subjects (i.e., those to whom the personal data relate) are also awarded certain rights such as the right to information; the right to access, rectify, and erase personal data; the right to data portability; the right to restrict a processing operation; the right to object to such processing and the right not to be subject to

---

[41] Directive (EU) 2016/680 of the European Parliament and of the Council of April 27, 2016, on the protection of natural persons with regard to the processing of personal data by competent authorities for the purposes of the prevention, investigation, detection, or prosecution of criminal offences or the execution of criminal penalties and on the free movement of such data and repealing Council Framework Decision 2008/977/JHA.

an automated individual decision. The data controller has an obligation to inform data subjects as to how they may exercise these rights.

However, Member States may restrict these rights by legislative measures in certain circumstances, more specifically, for example, to safeguard national security, public security, or important objectives of general public interest. These legislative measures must respect the essence of the fundamental rights and freedoms at stake and be necessary and proportionate in a democratic society. In order to gain a more accurate understanding of the implementation of such an exemption, one is required to refer to national law. Although such an analysis is outside the scope of this chapter, it should be noted that the equivalent exception in Directive 95/46/EC was not extensively used by many Member States (Korff, 2002, p. 142).

Compliance with these limitations and requirements are the responsibility of the data controllers (i.e., the person who determines the purposes and the means of the processing of personal data, Art. 4(7) GDPR) as provided for by the principle of accountability contained in Art. 5(2) GDPR. Where personal data is shared with a data processor, the controller needs to ensure the adherence to the provisions via a contract. In addition, the data controller must ensure that the processing of personal data is based on lawful grounds for processing.

LAWFUL GROUNDS FOR PROCESSING

Art. 6 GDPR provides *six lawful grounds for processing*:

Art. 6(1)(a)—the data subject has given consent to the processing of his or her personal data for one or more specific purposes;
Art. 6(1)(b)—processing is necessary for the performance of a contract to which the data subject is party or in order to take steps at the request of the data subject prior to entering into a contract;
Art. 6(1)(c)—processing is necessary for compliance with a legal obligation to which the controller is subject;
Art. 6(1)(d)—processing is necessary in order to protect the vital interests of the data subject or of another natural person;
Art. 6(1)(e)—processing is necessary for the performance of a task carried out in the public interest or in the exercise of official authority vested in the controller;
Art. 6(1)(f)—processing is necessary for the purposes of the legitimate interests pursued by the controller or by a third party, except where such interests are overridden by the interests or fundamental rights and freedoms of the data subject that require protection of personal data, in particular where the data subject is a child.

Of particular relevance for our current purposes are that the processing is necessary for compliance with a legal obligation to which the controller must adhere;

that it is necessary for the performance of a task carried out in the public interest or in the exercise of official authority vested in the controller; or finally, that the processing is necessary for the purposes of the legitimate interests pursued by the controller or by a third party.

More specifically in relation to legitimate interests as lawful grounds, the GDPR clarifies that the processing of personal data necessary to ensure network and information security by public authorities, CERTs, CSIRTs, providers of electronic communications networks and services, and providers of security technologies and services constitutes a legitimate interest of the controller (recital 49 GDPR).[42] When relying on legitimate interests as lawful grounds, however, one is required to satisfy the fair balancing test imbued in this provision. Indeed, Art. 6(1)(f) requires that the processing must be necessary and proportionate vis-à-vis the purposes of the legitimate interests pursued by the controller (i.e., ensuring network and information security). Therefore, this means that the lawfulness of such processing must be balanced and, as such, respect the fairness principle contained in Art. 5(1)(a) GDPR.

Furthermore, it should also be noted that although CI operators (as data controllers)[43] can avail themselves of legitimate interests as lawful grounds vis-à-vis the collection of NIS information of their own systems, public entities cannot generally rely on Art. 6(1)(f) GDPR if the processing is carried out in performance of their task. This appears to contradict recital 49 GDPR, which, as mentioned *supra*, provides that the processing of personal data for network and information security constitutes a legitimate interest and then explicitly mentions public authorities as a type of controller that can avail themselves of the lawful grounds. It is probable that the overlap here will depend on whether the processing for network and information security purposes lies within the specific task of the public authority. In such circumstances, the authority will not be able to avail itself of Art. 6(1)(f) GDPR.[44]

In such situations, alternative lawful grounds are required. In particular Art. 6(1)(c) (processing is necessary for either the compliance with a legal obligation) or Art. 6(1)(e) GDPR (processing is necessary for the performance of a task carried out in the public interest or in the exercise of official authority vested in the controller). For processing based on a legal obligation or performance of a task in

---

[42] Network and information security is considered "i.e., the ability of a network or an information system to resist, at a given level of confidence, accidental events or unlawful or malicious actions that compromise the availability, authenticity, integrity and confidentiality of stored or transmitted personal data, and the security of the related services offered by, or accessible via, those networks and systems, by public authorities, by computer emergency response teams (CERTs), computer security incident response teams (CSIRTs), by providers of electronic communications networks and services and by providers of security technologies and services" Recital 49 GDPR.

[43] The one who determines the purposes and means of the processing of personal data [Art. 4 (7) GDPR] and who is responsible to comply with the data protection obligations.

[44] This appears to be similar to the distinction made between consent and contract as respective lawful grounds.

the public interest, the Member States may maintain or introduce more specific provisions by determining particular obligations. The basis for the processing to which the controller is subject must be laid down by Union or Member State law, which must meet a public interest objective and be proportionate to the legitimate purpose pursued. The legal basis should determine the purpose of the processing, or the purpose must be necessary for the performance of the task.

In contrast to the above, where the network and information security purpose is not within the scope of the task of the public authority, it may be possible for the public authority to rely upon legitimate interests of the controller as lawful grounds. The type of network and information system security measure and the reason for enacting it can provide clues in this regard. While it might be debatable whether a public authority should provide a website if it is not in the scope of its task and whether retaining IP addresses is the right security measure, it is reasonable for example that public authorities can rely upon the legal interest of the controller to keep their internal computer systems secure and process different types of data in order to do this (of course keeping in mind the balancing exercise in Art. 6(1)(f) GDPR).

In this context, one can refer to the recent CJEU judgement in the *Breyer Case* as discussed above (see Section 7.3.1). Although the case primarily dealt with the definition of personal data in relation of dynamic IPs, the second question referred to the CJEU inquired as to whether §15 of the German Telemedia Act, which requires data subject consent for the collection and other processing of personal data by online media service providers and restricts this information processing to that which is necessary to ensure functionality, is legitimate in light of Directive 95/46/EC and hence whether the grounds for processing contained in Art. 7(f) Directive 95/46/EC could be relied upon in lieu of consent for the processing of such personal data (in this case IP addresses). In its judgement, the CJEU found the § 15 of the German Telemedia Act was too restrictive and therefore found that legitimate interests could act as lawful grounds in such circumstances.

Consequently, it appears that the division made above vis-à-vis the lawful grounds for processing is reflected in the Breyer judgment. It should be noted however, that the *Breyer Case* referred to Directive 95/46/EC and not the GDPR. Nevertheless, given that the lawful grounds for processing have remained unaltered in the GDPR, this interpretation seems directly transferable. Building on the above, in situations where the personal data have originally been collected for a purpose other than one related to network and information security, any further processing for such purposes must be based on lawful grounds. Although it is clear that Articles 6(1)(c) and 6(1)(e) may be applicable here as lawful grounds, this is potentially significant where they are not.

In such situations, therefore, it must be assessed whether the processing for NIS is compatible with the purpose for which the personal data was originally collected.[45] In such circumstances, any link between the original purpose and the

---

[45] Art 6 (4) GDPR.

new purpose, the context in which the data was originally collected and the nature or the personal data should be considered. This is especially important in case of special categories of data (data relating to racial or ethnic origin, political opinions, religious or philosophical beliefs, or trade union membership, and the processing of genetic data, biometric data for the purpose of uniquely identifying a natural person, data concerning health or data concerning a natural person's sex life or sexual orientation) and data related to criminal convictions and offences.

In addition to the above, it should also be noted that such considerations may be applicable in relation to the transfer of personal data as such an action would also be clearly classified as processing. Therefore, if the transfer of information was not included within the original purpose, the above discussion relating to the determination of lawful grounds for secondary purposes is also potentially relevant (also again where Articles 6(1)(c) and 6(1)(e) do not cover such processing).

More generally, in relation to information transfer is it important to take into account whether the recipient is located within the EU or in a third country/international organization. In situations where the recipient is located outside the EU, specific requirements apply to such transfers.[46] In circumstances where the recipient is located within the EU, the data protection legislation applies directly, and therefore the recipient (a processor or controller) is required to respect the requirements in the GDPR. The GDPR specifically aims at facilitating the "free flow of personal data" in the EU.

In determining whether the recipient of the personal data is a processor or controller, one is required to analyze the factual circumstances in light of the respective definitions contained in the GDPR. Hence, where the recipient merely receives and processes the data in line with the original controller's instruction (e.g., the controller instructed the recipient but the results are for the controller, and the recipient will not process the personal data for its own purposes), the recipient will be considered a processor. As mentioned *supra*, in such circumstances this must be reflected in a contractual agreement as defined in the GDPR. In contrast, in circumstances where the recipient of the personal data processes (also) for its own purposes (i.e., it determines the purposes), the recipient will be considered a data controller. The controllers could then be categorized as joint controllers or indeed separate controllers. Joint control arises "when different parties determine with regard to specific processing operations either the purpose or those essential elements of the means which characterize a controller" (Art.29WP, 2010, p. 18). On the other hand the sharing of data between two controllers without mutual purposes or means in a common set of operations is considered only as transfer of data between separate controllers (Art.29WP 2010).

It should be noted that the assessment of the status is based upon a factual assessment, depending on who determines the purposes and means, contractual arrangements can only provide an indication and always need to be checked against

---

[46] For example, if the Commission gave an adequacy decision for the third country or if the transfer is subject to appropriate safeguards, for example in the form of binding corporate rules, standard data protection clauses or an approved certification mechanism.

the factual circumstances (Art.29WP 2010). Therefore, it depends on how the information sharing takes place and whether or not the information sharing can be considered one "set of operations" with a joint purpose or jointly defined means, in order to assess the status of the participants (Art.29WP 2010).

Linked with the above discussion in terms of grounds it should be noted that establishing which entity is classified as a controller is important because if the recipient is a processor, the processing will be done under the original legal ground for processing whereas if the recipient falls under the definition of a controller, it will need to ensure the applicability of one of the lawful grounds for processing.

7.5 Moving beyond Breach Notification and the Limitations of Reactive Sharing

Having now sketched the origins of the legal framework, the specific information sharing obligations and initiatives at an EU level and specific frameworks that may impede or act as barriers to information sharing the analysis now turns to an examination of the broader placing of the failure to encourage more meaningful proactive information sharing practices. Indeed, as specifically indicated in Section 7.3.2 and inherently hinted at throughout the analysis thus far, there is a clear reluctance on behalf of operators to share information beyond what is legally required vis-à-vis breach notification.

Accordingly, the purpose of this section of the analysis is to, first, examine some of the broader socioeconomic obstacles to sharing including examples of some indirect legal obstacles before then examining an example of how such obstacles may be overcome (i.e., via a discussion of US law) while at the same time nuancing such normative suggestions in light of the division of competence issues inherent in law making in this domain.

7.5.1 Economic Interests, Secrecy and Indirect Obstacles to a More Coordinated Approach

Although avoiding the sharing of information for fear of running afoul of the legal requirements discussed in the previous section certainly occurs, it is argued that such framework may also present convenient shields to hide behind when a policy moves in such a direction. It seems obvious to suggest that no business wants its trade secret to be disclosed. Similarly, classified public information is kept hidden for a purpose, i.e., public safety/security. Data protection is somewhat different in certain respects as this is largely related to a perceived fear of exposure to liability for breaches of the data protection framework.

Aside from the restrictions on personal data processing contained in the GDPR there are also more indirect barriers associated with the perceived potential risk associated with sharing. Indeed, such legal barriers can indirectly prevent a sharing of certain information, and this is evidenced by the concern and doubts vis-à-vis the sharing of personal data and its impact on privacy and data protection as discussed in Section 7.4.1.2 (ENISA, 2013b, p. 8). However, this argumentation can be extended to other areas of law. Examples of these are competition law and freedom of information legislation.

For instance, specifically in the context of freedom of information the fear that shared data might become public under national information access legislation has been mooted as a deterrent for critical infrastructure operator information sharing with public bodies. The extent to which these legal provisions are indeed perceived as barriers to information sharing is not clear and might depend on each country individually. For example, experiences in the Netherlands have shown that they are indeed perceived as barriers (see NDN pilot in Chapter 5), while in an ENISA survey of 2010 it was found that the respondents of the survey ranked this as of relatively low importance (ENISA, 2010, p. 35).

Similarly, for the fear of breaching competition law, which is sometimes mentioned in the literature (and in particular the US literature), no empirical evidence was found, and it was even ranked last in the ENISA survey; it was not reported as being a problem in the interviews (ENISA, 2010, p. 37). That being said although such frameworks in themselves do not restrict the sharing of information, they can sometimes discourage critical infrastructure operators from participating in such sharing.

7.5.2 Proactive Incident Reporting: Overcoming the Fear of Data Sharing

In the US, the issue of legal uncertainty has been expressed as a barrier for information sharing (McKeown & Storm-Smith, 2016). The US answer to this concern was the passing of the Cybersecurity Information Sharing Act of 2015 (CISA). CISA was designed to create a voluntary cybersecurity information sharing process. The Act includes provisions regarding the sharing of information by the Federal Government and also private entities with the Federal Government. When complying with the provisions of CISA, private entities are broadly protected from liability under any Federal or State law while monitoring and protecting their information systems or disclosing or receiving information regarding cyber threats (McKeown & Storm-Smith, 2016).

Moreover, CISA addresses the concerns vis-à-vis the potential disclosure of information to the public. More specifically, CISA classifies all information shared with the government as proprietary and thereby exempts such information from disclosure under the Freedom of Information Act or any other federal or state law (McKeown & Storm-Smith, 2016; Sec 105 (d) CISA). Furthermore, Sec. 104(d) (4) (B) provides that a cyber-threat indicator shared with the government under Sec. 104 shall be considered voluntarily shared information and exempt from disclosure under any state, tribal, or local law requiring disclosure of information or records.

Considering the concern that the sharing of information may result in companies themselves becoming the focus of investigations, CISA provides that the shared information may not be used for unrelated regulatory or investigative purposes (albeit with certain exceptions applying depending on the circumstances (McKeown & Storm-Smith, 2016). Section 104 (d) (4) (C) provides that a cyber-threat indicator or defensive measure shared with the state, tribal, or local regulatory authorities shall not be directly used to regulate, including an enforcement action, the lawful activity of any entity,[47] including an activity relating to monitoring, operating a defensive measure, or sharing of a cyber-threat indicator.

However, the information may be used for the development or implementation of a regulation relating to such information systems. Furthermore, CISA includes Section 106 regarding protection from liability that declares that neither for the monitoring of information systems and information under Section 104(a), nor the sharing or receipt of cyber-threat indicators or defensive measures under Section 104(c), a cause of action shall lie or be maintained in any court if it has been done in accordance with the title (of course excluding acts of gross negligence and willful misconduct).

CISA also provides protection regarding competition law (in the US called antitrust) concerns mentioned earlier. Section 104(e) constitutes an antitrust exemption, which provides that the exchange or provision of cyber-threat indicators or assistance relating to the prevention, investigation, or mitigation of a cybersecurity threat shall not be considered a violation of any provision of antitrust law. This provision only refers to measures relating to cybersecurity, Sec. 108(e) explicitly declares that nothing in CISA should be construed to permit competition-damaging behavior such as boycotting, exchanges, or price or cost information, customer lists, or information regarding future competitive planning. Furthermore, CISA includes several provisions regarding the sharing of personal data/personally identifiable information.

The sharing of information by the Federal Government requires procedures to, prior to the sharing of a cyber-threat indicator, review the indicator in order to assess whether it contains any personal information and to remove such information; to implement and utilize a technical function configured to remove any personal information; and to notify US persons whose personal information has been shared by a Federal entity in violation of the Act.

A private entity that shares a cyber-threat indicator has similar responsibilities. However, CISA does not include the requirement of informing US persons whose information has been shared. In general, CISA requires the development of different policies and procedures, including guidelines by the Attorney General regarding privacy and civil liberties governing the receipt, retention, use, and dissemination of cyber-threat indicators by a Federal entity.[48] As obvious from the earlier explanations, a difference exists between the sharing of information by private entities and the sharing of information by Federal entities. Nonfederal entities can use the Department of Homeland Security's (DHS) free Automated Indicator Sharing (AIS)

---

[47] Entity means any private entity, nonfederal government agency or department, or state, tribal, or local government (including a political subdivision, department, or component thereof).

[48] https://www.us-cert.gov/sites/default/files/ais_files/Privacy_and_Civil_Liberties_ Guidelines_(Sec%20105(b)).pdf.

capability, which enables the exchange of cyber-threat indicators between the Federal Government and the private sector and must refer to the Guidance[49] provided there and can find further information in the Privacy Impact Assessment.[50] Federal entities must comply with the guidelines as provided by the Attorney General.

But are the above US experiences directly transferable to the EU? In short, they are in part and with some considerable difficulty. As has been alluded to throughout the analysis in this chapter, EU policy making in this context is based on, at best, joint and sometimes coordinating competence. This reflects the fact that security and policing remain matters closely guarded by the Member State. As such, a very practical obstacle in adopting legislation similar to the US approach would be simply the complex construction that is the EU and hence the potential political objections that would inevitably come from such broad-level reform.

It should therefore be recognized that these potential political objections and the more disjointed nature of the EU are indicative of just that, a union or collection of Member States, with diverging (yet comparable) concerns. However, any such developments would need to not only find a compromise across the Member States but also reflect the potentially different concerns experienced in the EU (i.e., where it seems that data protection rather than competition law or the disclosure of information appears to be the most prominent concern).

Aside from this more practical concern, one must realize that although simply affording proprietary rights in information shared by CI operators may seem like a simple solution, in an EU context this would potentially present extremely complex legal issues. More specifically, if one accepts that the information shared will at least in principle contain personal data, affording such information a proprietary nature would appear to contradict the fundamental rights framework and thus arguably dilute the status of data protection as a fundamental right in Art. 8 of the Charter of Fundamental Rights of the EU.

7.6 Conclusion

Therefore, in conclusion this chapter has outlined the legal implication of information sharing in the context of network and information security. By doing so, the chapter has laid the groundwork for Chapter 8, which aims to assess the operation of this framework in practice. However, through the discussion of the framework the analysis has also aimed to provide some insights into the limitations of a reliance on reactive breach notification-orientated information sharing, outlined the barriers to more proactive sharing, and made a short attempt at highlighting some normative insights into the move towards a more proactive, coordinated, and effective information sharing ecosystem.

---

[49] https://www.us-cert.gov/sites/default/files/ais_files/Non-Federal_Entity_Sharing_Guidance_%28Sec%20105%28a%29%29.pdf.

[50] https://www.us-cert.gov/sites/default/files/ais_files/PIA_NPPD-AIS.pdf.

List of Abbreviations

AIS	Automatic Indicator Sharing
BGH	Bundesgerichtshof
BIPT	Belgisch Instituut voor Postdiensten en Telecommunicatie
CISA	Cyber Information Sharing Act
CIWIN	Critical Infrastructure Warning Information Network
CJEU	Court of Justice of the European Union
CSIRT	Cybersecurity Incident Response Team
DDoS	Distributed denial of service (attack)
DHS	Department of Homeland Security
DNS	Domain name service
ECI	European critical infrastructure
ECIP	ECI contact point
ENISA	European Network and Information Security Agency
EPCIP	European Programme for Critical Infrastructure Protection
EUCI	EU classified information
GDPR	General data protection regulation
IPR	Intellectual property rights
ISP	Internet service provider
LPM	French Military Programming Law
NDN	(Dutch) National Detection Network
NIS	The (European) Directive on security of network and information systems
PSD	Payment service directive
PSI	Public sector information
SÜG	Sicherheitsüberprüfungsgesetz
TEU	Treaty on European Union
TLD	Top level domain

Bibliography

Books

Christou, G. 2016. *Cybersecurity in the European Union*, Basingstoke, UK: Palgrave MacMillan.
Lazari, A. 2014. *European Critical Infrastructure Protection*, Cham, Switzerland: Springer.

Journals

Curtin, D. 2014. Overseeing secrets in the EU: A democratic perspective: overseeing secrets in the EU. *Journal of Common Market Studies* 52, no. 3 (2014): 684–700, doi:10.1111/jcms.12123.

Galloway, D. 2014. Classifying secrets in the EU. *Journal of Common Market Studies* 52, no. 3 (2014): 670, doi:10.1111/jcms.12122.

McKeown, E. and E. Storm-Smith. 2016. New legislation strengthens legal protection for cybersecurity information-sharing. *Intellectual Property & Technology Law Journal* 28, no. 5 (2016): 17–19.

Reports/Studies

Korff, D. 2002. EC study on implementation of data protection directive, Cambridge UK, September 2002.

ENISA

ENISA 2010: Robinson, N. and E. Disley. Challenges and barriers to information sharing, September 8, 2010.

ENISA 2011: Portesi, S., N. Robinson, and H. Graux. A flair for information sharing-encouraging information exchange between CERTs, November 2011.

ENISA 2013a: ENISA, M. Dekker, and C. Karsberg. Technical guidance on the incident reporting in Article 13a. Version 2.0, January 2013.

ENISA 2013b: Bourgue, R., J. Budd, H. Homola, M. Wladenko, and D. Kulawik. Detect, SHARE, protect: Solutions for improving threat data exchange among CERTs, October 2013.

ENISA 2015a: Bedrijfsrevisoren, D., J. De Muynck, and S. Portesi. Cyber security information sharing: An overview of regulatory and non-regulatory approaches, final, v1.0, December 2015.

ENISA 2015b: Moulinos, K., C. Karsberg, and M.A.C. Dekker. Proposal for Article 19 incident reporting-proposal for an incident reporting framework for eIDAS Article 19, 2015.

ENISA 2016a: Anna, S. and M. Konstantinos. Stocktaking, analysis and recommendations on the protection of CIIs, January 2016.

ENISA 2016b: Tofan, D., K. Moulinos, and C. Karsberg. ENISA impact evaluation on the implementation of Article 13a incident reporting scheme within EU, March 18, 2016, 5.

EU Documents

Communication from the Commission: A strategy for a Secure Information Society: Dialogue, partnership and empowerment, COM (2006) 251 Final, May 31, 2006.

COM2006: Communication from the Commission on a European Programme for Critical Infrastructure Protection, COM (2006) 786 Final, Brussels, December 12, 2006.

COM2013: Commission Staff Working Document, Executive summary of the impact assessment, Strasbourg, SWD (2013) 31 Final, February 7, 2013.

European Commission, Creating a Safer Information Society by Improving the Security of Infrastructures and Combating Computer-Related Crime, COM (2000) 890 Final, January 26, 2001.

European Commission Communication from the Commission to the Council, the European Parliament, the European Economic and Social Committee and the Committee of the Regions on Network and Information Security: Proposal for A European Policy Approach, Brussels, COM (2001) 298 Final, June 6, 2001.

JOIN2013: Joint Communication to the European Parliament, the Council, The European Economic and Social Committee and the Committee of the Regions, 'Cybersecurity Strategy of the European Union: An Open, Safe and Secure Cyberspace', Brussels, JOIN (2013) 1 Final, February 7, 2013.

SWD2013: Commission Staff Working Document Impact Assessment accompanying the document proposal for a Directive of the European Parliament and of the Council on the protection of undisclosed know-how and business information (trade secrets) against their unlawful acquisition, use and disclosure Brussels, SWD (2013) 471 Final, November 28, 2013.

Art. 29 WP

Article 29 Working Party, Working Document Privacy on the Internet: An integrated EU Approach to On-line Data Protection, WP 37, adopted on November 21, 2000.

Article 29 Working Party, Opinion 4/2007 on the concept of personal data, WP 136, June 20, 2007.

Article 29 Working Party, Opinion 1/2010 on the concepts of "controller" and "processor", 00264/10/EN WP 169, February 16, 2010.

Regulation

Commission Regulation (EU) No 611/2013 of June 24, 2013 on the measures applicable to the notification of personal data breaches under Directive 2002/58/EC of the European Parliament and of the Council on privacy and electronic communications. OJ L 173/5, June 26, 2013.

Council Directive 2008/114/EC of December 8, 2008 on the identification and designation of European critical infrastructures and the assessment of the need to improve their protection. OJ L 345/75, December 23, 2008.

Council of Europe, European Treaty Series-No. 185, Budapest, November 23, 2001, Convention on Cybercrime/Budapest convention.

Directive 95/46/EC of the European Parliament and of the Council of October 24, 1995 on the protection of individuals with regard to the processing of personal data and on the free movement of such data. OJ L 281, November 23, 1995, pp. 31–50.

Directive 96/9/EC of the European Parliament and of the Council of March 11, 1996 on the legal protection of databases.

Directive 2001/29/EC of the European Parliament and of the Council of May 22, 2001 on the harmonisation of certain aspects of copyright and related rights in the information society. OJ L 167, 2001, p. 10.

Directive 2002/21/EC of the European Parliament and of the Council of March 7, 2002 on a common regulatory framework for electronic communications networks and services. OJ L 108, April 24, 2002, pp. 33–50.

Directive 2002/58/EC of the European Parliament and of the Council of July 12, 2002 concerning the processing of personal data and the protection of privacy in the electronic communications sector (Directive on privacy and electronic communications) OJ L 201, July 31, 2002 pp. 37–47.

Directive 2003/98 of November 17, 2003 on the re-use of public sector information [2003] OJ L 345/90, amended in 2013 by Directive 2013/37/EU of June 26, 2013 amending Directive 2003/98/EC on the re-use of public sector information [2013] OJ L 175/1.

Directive 2009/140/EC of the European Parliament and of the Council of November 25, 2009 amending Directives 2002/21/EC on a common regulatory framework for electronic communications networks and services, 2002/19/EC on access to, and interconnection of, electronic communications networks and associated facilities, and 2002/20/ EC on the authorisation of electronic communications networks and services.

Directive 2013/40/EU of the European Parliament and of the Council of August 12, 2013 on attacks against information systems and replacing Council Framework Decision 2005/222/JHA. OJ L 218, August 14, 2013.

Directive (EU) 2015/2366 of the European Parliament and of the Council of November 25, 2015 on payment services in the internal market, amending Directives 2002/65/EC, 2009/110/EC and 2013/36/EU and Regulation (EU) No 1093/2010, and repealing Directive 2007/64/EC.

Directive (EU) 2016/680 of the European Parliament and of the Council of April 27, 2016 on the protection of natural persons with regard to the processing of personal data by competent authorities for the purposes of the prevention, investigation, detection or prosecution of criminal offences or the execution of criminal penalties, and on the free movement of such data, and repealing Council Framework Decision 2008/977/JHA.

Directive (EU) 2016/943 of the European Parliament and of the Council of June 8, 2016 on the protection of undisclosed know-how and business information (trade secrets) against their unlawful acquisition, use and disclosure. OJ L 157, June 15, 2016, pp. 1–18.

Directive (EU) 2016/1148 of the European Parliament and of the Council of July 6, 2016 concerning measures for a high common level of security of network and information systems across the Union. OJ L 194, July 19, 2016.

Regulation (EU) No 910/2014 of the European Parliament and of the Council of July 23, 2014 on electronic identification and trust services for electronic transactions in the internal market and repealing Directive 1999/93/EC.

Case Law

CJEU Judgement Case C-70/10, November 24, 2011 (Scarlet SABAM), ECLI:EU:C:2011:771.
CJEU Judgement Case C-582/14, October 19, 2016 (Breyer), ECLI:EU:C:2016:779.

Chapter 8

Implementation Issues and Obstacles from a Legal Perspective

Erich Schweighofer and Vinzenz Heussler
University of Vienna

Walter Hötzendorfer
Research Institute – Digital Human Rights Center

Contents

8.1 Introduction

The role of criminal justice in fighting cybercrime remains insufficient, and prevention and mitigation have always been effective means to counteract crime. In particular, as already discussed in Chapter 4, the sharing of information regarding critical information infrastructure and potential cyber threats (CT) remains an essential part of a successful strategy. Operators must be supported in increasing cybersecurity.

Collecting information about potential cyber threats helps authorities gain critical information about the national risk situation and potential threat scenarios. Whereas cyber threat intelligence information should be free and available to all, in practice, many restrictions make sharing of information difficult (refer to the description of legal and indirect barriers in Chapter 7). While information not containing personal data, trade secrets, copyrighted materials, or restricted information can be shared with everybody, such as news distributed worldwide, it is obvious that information about fighting against cyber threats rarely fits into this category. Information about the existence of a threat may be shared but not its details. Strategies against cyber threats and information security may be restricted information or contain trade secrets. Thus, the balancing between needs of sharing for avoiding danger—in particular for third parties—and keeping confidentiality requires high sensibility and care.

8.2 Case Study 1: Distribution of Security-Relevant Information Containing Personal Data and Anonymization

8.2.1 Case Description

The collecting, processing, and sharing of security-relevant information that contains personal data must abide by data protection law. A private entity shares the Internet Protocol address (IP address) of a command and control server of a botnet with another private entity to warn it. Is such an IP address security-relevant information that contains personal data according to data protection law? If so, is the sharing of such information violating data protection law? What are the options to lawfully share security-relevant information containing personal data?

8.2.2 Introduction

The first question regarding this case study is whether the IP address exchanged is personal data under data protection law, which would entail that the provisions of data protection law would apply to the exchange of the IP address. Notice that applying anonymization or pseudonymization of the IP address is not an option in this case study because the IP address is only useful if it is shared in plain numbers (Cormack, 2016, p. 281). The value of the information lies in knowing the specific IP address of the command and control server (C&C server) in order to be able to detect incoming or outgoing traffic with this server and/or to block it, etc.

8.2.3 Legal Analysis—Data Protection Law

Information constitutes personal data under data protection law if it relates to a natural person who is identified or identifiable (Art. 2 (a) Directive 95/46/EC (Data Protection Directive)[1]). Identifiable means that the identity of the data subject does not arise directly from the information; additional information is required in order to determine the identity. According to recital 26 of the, "to determine whether a person is identifiable, account should be taken of all the means likely reasonably to be used either by the controller or by any other person to identify the said person."

---

[1] Directive 95/46/EC of the European Parliament and of the Council of October 24, 1995 on the protection of individuals with regard to the processing of personal data and on the free movement of such data, OJ L 281, 23.11.1995, pp. 31–50.

In its recent case *Breyer*[2] (refer to Chapter 7 for a more extensive description of the case), the European Court of Justice (ECJ) had to decide on the question "whether Article 2(a) of Directive 95/46 must be interpreted as meaning that a dynamic IP address registered by an online media services provider when a person accesses a website that that provider makes accessible to the public constitutes, with regard to that service provider, personal data within the meaning of that provision."[3] The court came to the conclusion that the dynamic IP address constitutes personal data in relation to that provider, "where the latter has the legal means which enable it to identify the data subject with additional data which the internet service provider (ISP) has about that person."[4]

This means that, first, for answering the question whether a piece of information is personal data, a subjective view has to be taken, i.e., the view of the data holder, and that the answer can be different for different data holders. Second, data is personal data for a data holder not only if information enabling the identification of the data subject is in the hands of the data holder, but also if the data holder can obtain that information with the assistance of other persons.

From this it can be concluded that, generally, an IP address can constitute personal data. Does this apply also to the particular IP address in this case study? This would require a relation of the IP address to a particular natural person and that the entities in question that share the IP address do have legal means enabling them to identify this person. One important difference in the Breyer case is that the IP address is not that of a client but of a server. The obvious relation of the IP address of a server to a natural person is the relation to the server's owner or operator. In general, a means to identify this natural person would be a Domain Name System (DNS) reverse lookup to determine the domain name associated with that IP address—if any—and to use the WHOIS protocol to determine the owner of that domain. If this led to an identified natural person, the particular IP address in question would constitute personal data. The same is true if another lawful way to establish a relation between the IP address of the server in question and the owner or operator of the server can be found. In this case, the question is whether data protection law allows the sharing of the IP address, considering the right to data protection of the operator of a command and control server on the one hand and the safety of potential victims of a malicious botnet operated by that command and control server or of the public on the other hand.

However, regarding a command and control server of a botnet, the server operator has strong motivation to prevent the establishment of a link between him or her and the IP address of the server. Either the IP address would simply not be associated with a domain name so that the relation cannot be established as it was described above or the operator would misuse the server of a third entity to run the command and control server software.

---

[2] CJEU Judgement Case C-582/14, October 19, 2016 (Breyer), ECLI:EU:C:2016:779.
[3] ECJ 19 October 2016, C-582/14, Breyer, no. 31.
[4] ECJ 19 October 2016, C-582/14, Breyer, no. 49.

Hence, besides the case described previously where a relation between the IP address and the operator of the command and control server can be established, we have to distinguish two more cases: one in which practically no relation between the IP address and a natural person can be established and the other in which a relation between the IP address and a third person can be established who is him-or herself a victim as being the owner or operator of the server that is misused by the attacker.

Consequently, in the following, we distinguish the following three cases:

1. Relation between the IP address and the malicious operator of the server
2. Practically no relation between the IP address and a natural person
3. Relation between the IP address and a third person

In contrast to the first case outlined previously, where a relation between an IP address and an attacker can be established, in the second case, it is, by any means reasonably likely to be used (cf. recital 26 of the General Data Protection Regulation (GDPR)[5]), not possible to establish a relation between the IP address and a natural person, and therefore the particular IP address would not constitute personal data. The important issue here is that in practice it is not immediately clear whether, by any means reasonably likely to be used, such a relation between the IP address and a natural person can be established or not. The entity willing to share the IP address would have to try and find such a relation. If it fails to do so this does not necessarily mean that it is impossible. In that sense, the burden of proof that the shared IP address does not constitute personal data practically lies upon the entity that shares the address.

In the third case, where a relation between the IP address in question and a third person can be established, the IP address clearly constitutes personal data. Here, unlike in the first case, the interests of potential victims of the command and control server have to be balanced with the interests of a third person who is in the position of a victim (Figure 8.3).

Let us consider the first case (Figure 8.1), where a relation between the IP address and the operator of the command and control server can be established. Here, the sharing of the IP address constitutes processing of personal data of the operator of the server. For doing so, a legal basis is required, which can be laid down in EU law or in Member State law (Art. 6 Sec. 3 GDPR). Such a statutory legal basis can be found particularly in reporting obligations, which will be discussed below. First, the general situation is considered, where such an explicit statutory legal basis for the processing by the specific data controller in question does not exist.

Pursuant to Art. 6 Sec. 1 (f) GDPR, processing is lawful if it is necessary for the purposes of the legitimate interests pursued by the controller, except where such

---

[5] Regulation (EU) 2016/679 of the European Parliament and of the Council of 27 April 2016 on the protection of natural persons with regard to the processing of personal data and on the free movement of such data and repealing Directive 95/46/EC (General Data Protection Regulation), OJ L 119, 4.5.2016, pp. 1–88. For an overview on GDPR see Paal and Pauly (2017) and Knyrim (2016).

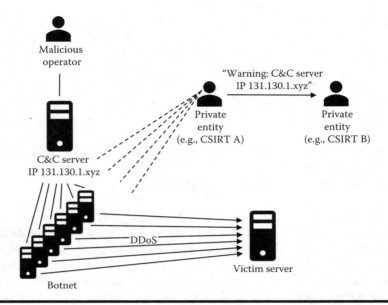

Figure 8.1 Security-relevant information IP address—Case 1: relation with the malicious operator of the server.

interests are overridden by the interests or fundamental rights and freedoms of the data subject (Art29WP 2014). Hence, a balancing test of these interests has to be conducted (Cormack, 2016, p. 271).

According to recital 49 GDPR the "processing of personal data to the extent strictly necessary and proportionate for the purposes of ensuring network and information security, i.e. the ability of a network or an information system to resist, at a given level of confidence, accidental events or unlawful or malicious actions that compromise the availability, authenticity, integrity and confidentiality of stored or transmitted personal data, and the security of the related services offered by, or accessible via, those networks and systems, by public authorities, by Computer Security Incident Response Teams (CSIRTs), also known as Computer Emergency Response Teams (CERTs), by providers of electronic communications networks and services and by providers of security technologies and services," constitutes such a legitimate interest of the data controller concerned.

It can be argued that the interests of the operator of a command and control server that would potentially harm the parties exchanging the IP address cannot override their legitimate interests to share this information in order to protect themselves. Therefore, in this case, the exchange of the IP address is lawful under Art. 6 Sec. 1 (f) GDPR. However, this is restricted to the transfer of data to recipients located within the EU. As explained in Chapter 7, according to Art. 44 et seq. GDPR for the transfer of personal data to recipients located outside the EU

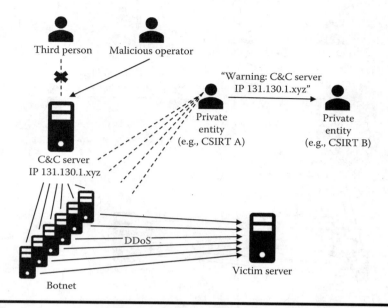

Figure 8.2 Security-relevant information IP address—Case 2: practically no relation with a natural person.

(EEA) additional requirements must be fulfilled, such as an adequacy decision by the European Commission for the given country or institutionalized safeguards between the controller who is transferring the data and the recipient, the existence of which depends on the individual case. Therefore, within this chapter only transfers to recipients within the EU are assessed.

The second case where the IP address does not constitute personal data because no link can be established between the IP address and a natural person (Figure 8.2), has a straightforward solution. Data protection law only applies to personal data and hence does not apply to the IP address in this case. The exchange of the IP address is therefore lawful. Oftentimes exploited servers will belong to companies, in which case the IP addresses do not constitute personal data.

The most difficult one is the third case (Figure 8.3) where a third person comes into play (neither the malicious party nor the victim but the owner or operator of the server that is misused by the malicious party to run the command and control server in question). If the server is owned by a company and not by a natural person, the result is the same as in the second case because there is no link between the IP address and a natural person. However, if the server is owned by a natural person, the IP address clearly constitutes personal data, but unlike in the first case, it is the personal data of a data subject who is herself a victim of the malicious operator of the command and control server. Again, the sharing of the IP address constitutes a processing necessary for the purposes of the legitimate interests pursued by the

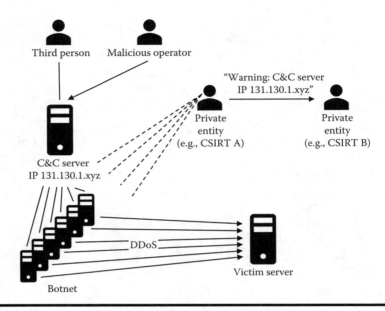

Figure 8.3 Security-relevant information IP address—Case 3: relation with a natural person.

controller pursuant to Art. 6 Sec. 1 (f) GDPR. However, in this case it is much more difficult to answer whether these interests of the controller are outweighed by the interests or fundamental rights and freedoms of the data subject. But still, it can be argued that the IP address of a server on the Internet is a piece of information deserving a relatively low level of protection whereas the exchange of the IP address in order to mitigate the risk stemming from the command and control server is an important interest (cf. recital 49 GDPR); hence, the interests of the data subject do not outweigh the interests of the processor in this case.

8.2.4 Legal Analysis—Information Duties

As described in Chapter 7 different incident notification obligations exist in European legislation. The exchange of information prescribed by such legislation is lawful under data protection law because processing of data necessary for compliance with a legal obligation is lawful pursuant to Art. 6 Sec. 1 (c) GDPR. In the following, different notification obligations introduced in Chapter 7 are discussed in the context of this case study.

8.2.4.1 General Data Protection Regulation

The notification duty under Art. 33 GDPR applies to any infringement of the protection of personal data, unless this violation does not presumably lead to a risk to the rights and freedoms of natural persons. Risk assessment shall take into account physical, material, and nonmaterial damage such as loss of control over their personal data or limitation of their rights, discrimination, identity theft or fraud, financial loss, unauthorized reversal of pseudonymization, damage to reputation, loss of confidentiality of data protected by professional secrecy, any or other significant economic or social disadvantage to the natural person concerned (see recital 85 GDPR).

In the event of such a personal data breach the controller has to notify the supervisory authority (Data Protection Authority) without undue delay. When the personal data breach is likely to result in a high risk to the rights and freedoms of natural persons, the controller shall also communicate the personal data breach to the data subject without undue delay (Art. 34 GDPR). However, it seems unlikely that the exchange of an IP address of the command and control server of a botnet would be related to a personal data breach. In addition, the minimum content of a notification under these obligations is laid down in Art. 33 Sec. 3 and Art. 34 Sec. 3 GDPR and does not include information on the cause of the data breach such as information on the attacker (if applicable), on the modus operandi, on a possible vulnerability that was exploited, etc. Therefore, it can be concluded that there is no overlap between the scenario in this case study and the data breach notification obligations laid down in the GDPR. The obligation under this regime would not encompass the exchange of an IP address or other personal data of third parties.

8.2.4.2 Telecommunication Framework Directive

In the telecommunications sector, Directive 2009/140/EC[6] (which amended the Framework Directive[7]) introduced the obligation that undertakings providing public communications networks or publicly available electronic communications services notify the competent national regulatory authority of a breach of security or loss of integrity that has a significant impact on the operation of networks or services. However, this does not apply to the exchange of an IP address or other personal data with third parties other than the competent authorities.

In addition, there are specific personal data breach notification duties in the telecommunications sector. Like the GDPR notification duties mentioned previously, they would, however, most likely not be applicable to the scenario in this case study.

---

[6] Directive 2009/140/EC of the European Parliament and of the Council of November 25, 2009 amending Directives 2002/21/EC on a common regulatory framework for electronic communications networks and services, 2002/19/EC on access to, and interconnection of, electronic communications networks and associated facilities, and 2002/20/EC on the authorization of electronic communications networks and services, OJ L 337, 18.12.2009, pp. 37–69.

[7] Directive 2002/21/EC of the European Parliament and of the Council of March 7, 2002 on a common regulatory framework for electronic communications networks and services (Framework Directive), OJ L 108, 24.4.2002, pp. 33–50.

8.2.4.3 eIDAS Regulation

Similarly, the eIDAS Regulation[8] contains provisions on electronic identification and trust services (electronic seals, electronic time stamps, electronic registered delivery services, website authentication). Art. 19 defines security requirements for trusted service providers including a notification obligation for qualified and non-qualified trust service providers. These entities shall, without undue delay, notify the supervisory body of any breach of security or loss of integrity that has a significant impact on the trust service provided or on the personal data maintained therein. The notification shall also be sent, where applicable, to other relevant bodies, such as the competent national body for information security or the data protection authority. In addition, the notification shall be reported without delay, but in any event within 24 hours of notification of the relevant incident. Furthermore, where the breach of security or loss of integrity is likely to adversely affect a natural or legal person to whom the trusted service has been provided, the trust service provider must also notify this person. Also in this case, the obligation under this provision would not apply to the exchange of an IP address or other personal data with third parties other than the competent authorities.

8.2.4.4 NIS Directive

Under Art. 14 Sec. 3 NIS Directive,[9] the operators of essential services are obliged to report immediately to the competent authority or the CSIRT security incidents that have a significant effect on the availability of essential services provided by them. A similar obligation exists for digital service provider under Art. 16 Sec. 3 NIS Directive. Under Art. 16 Sec. 5 NIS Directive, operators of essential services have an additional obligation to report.

Notifications shall have an information content enabling the competent authority or the CSIRT to determine whether the security incident has cross-border effects. The Directive also sets out a number of parameters to be taken into account to determine the extent of the impact of a safety incident. But other parameters can also be taken into account, in particular the number of users affected by the interruption in the provision of the essential service, the duration of the security incident, and the geographical spread of the area affected by the security incident.

Where it is possible for the competent authority or the CSIRT to do so, it shall make available to the reporting operator relevant information for the further

---

[8] Regulation (EU) No 910/2014 of the European Parliament and of the Council of July 23, 2014 on electronic identification and trust services for electronic transactions in the internal market and repealing Directive 1999/93/EC, OJ L 257, 28.8.2014, pp. 73–114.

[9] Directive (EU) 2016/1148 of the European Parliament and of the Council of July 6, 2016 concerning measures for a high common level of security of network and information systems across the Union, OJ L 194, 19.7.2016, pp. 1–30.

handling of the notification. Such information may be, e.g., information that could be useful for the effective management of the security incident.

The competent authority or the CSIRT may also inform the public of individual security incidents. However, this information is dependent on a concrete added value for the public. The competent authority or the CSIRT may only inform the public if it is necessary to raise awareness on the prevention of incidents or to deal with the current incident. The reporting operator must be consulted.

The regulation does not stipulate the content of a notification under this regime. It is upon the national legislators to define that more specifically in the national legislation which is going to be enacted in the ongoing process of the transposition of the NIS Directive into national law. It would be very important for effective cybersecurity that national legislators add reasonable legal bases for the exchange of threat information including, if necessary for the specific purpose, personal data, to this new legislation. This should cover both the notification of threat information to the competent authorities and the exchange of threat information between (potentially) affected private parties as in this case study.

8.2.4.5 Other Reporting Obligations

The Payment Services II Directive (PSD II)[10] introduces strict security requirements for the triggering and processing of electronic payments and the protection of consumers' financial data. Pursuant to Art. 96 Sec. 1 PSD II, payment service providers must immediately inform the competent authority in the Member State of the payment service provider in the event of a serious operational or security incident. Furthermore, the payment service providers must immediately notify their payment service users if the incident has or may have an impact on the financial interests of the payment service users. Users shall be informed of the incident and of any action that payment service providers can take to limit the negative impact of the incident.

Further information obligations can be found in laws concerning supervision of certain branches (banking, electricity, etc.) but also in the duty to reduce damage to third parties or resulting from contractual obligations. However, if not specifically stated they will not serve as a proper legal basis for the exchange of personal data.

8.2.5 Conclusion

Coming back to the scenario of the case study, to conclude, it can easily be the case that the IP address has to be considered personal data to which data protection law

---

[10] Directive (EU) 2015/2366 of the European Parliament and of the Council of November 25, 2015 on payment services in the internal market, amending Directives 2002/65/EC, 2009/110/EC and 2013/36/EU and Regulation (EU) No 1093/2010, and repealing Directive 2007/64/EC, OJ L 337, 23.12.2015, pp. 35–127.

applies. In most cases the exchange of the IP address in this scenario will be lawful, either because in specific instances there exists a reporting obligation or—more likely when the recipient of the information is a private entity—because carefully considering the interests of the parties involved leads to the conclusion that the interest for sharing the information outweighs the interests of the data subject. However, it should be very clear beforehand on what legal basis a specific exchange of data is performed as the consequences of a violation of the GDPR can be severe. In contrast to the current legal situation, a violation of the provisions of the GDPR results in fines up to 20 million EUR or up to 4% of the annual turnover achieved by companies, whichever is higher (Art. 83 Sec. 5 GDPR). National penal provisions also apply.

8.3 Case Study 2: Harm to Reputation of Third Parties

8.3.1 Case Description

This section will elaborate the reputational damage of third parties by the example of the following case study: The existence of a product vulnerability is reported to a CSIRT, cyber situation center, or competent authority that subsequently informs certain entities or the public as a whole (Figure 8.4). We assume that the reported fact is true, i.e., the vulnerability actually exists. What is the right balance between the interest of the public in being informed about vulnerabilities and the possible reputational and commercial damages the operator, manufacturer, or developer of the product incurs because the information is shared?

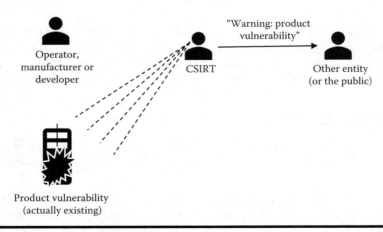

Figure 8.4   Harm to reputation of third parties.

8.3.2 Introduction

The key characteristic of this case study is that the information concerned is true. Therefore, as will be described below in more detail, most legal provisions in question do not apply because they penalize only situations where knowingly false information is spread. The relevant problem therefore in this case study is similar to what is known as responsible disclosure in computer security and hacker ethics. For example, the policy of the CERT Coordination Center (CERT/CC) states that vulnerabilities reported to it are forwarded to the affected vendors "as soon as practical" but are disclosed to the public only 45 days after the initial report (CERT/CC 2017). This gives the vendor time to respond adequately and ideally fix the vulnerability before it becomes known to the public. The 45-day period can be shortened or extended due to "[e]xtenuating circumstances, such as active exploitation, threats of an especially serious (or trivial) nature, or situations that require changes to an established standard" (CERT/CC 2017).

This should be kept in mind when reading the following legal analysis. Law is not the only and oftentimes not the most important factor to determine how to behave in a certain situation. Nevertheless, this is a chapter on the legal situation. What follows is a legal analysis on the example of Austrian criminal and civil law. Since criminal and civil law are not harmonized in the EU it is not possible to present an analysis that is applicable in all EU Member States. However, the fundamental principles discussed in the following will hold for most EU Member States.

8.3.3 Legal Analysis—Criminal Law

The same goes for Sec. 152 Austrian Criminal Code, which penalizes the damaging of a person's credit or professional advancement by making false claims. Relating to Sec. 297 para. 1 Austrian Criminal Code ("libel"), the information in question must be false and the person spreading the information must be aware of that; in addition, the information must constitute the accusation of a criminal act.

Regarding all of these statutory offenses, the result would be the same even if the relevant information were not true. As long as false information is not spread knowingly and intentionally these provisions do not apply, with the exception of defamation pursuant to Sec. 152 Austrian Criminal Code when the defamatory information is spread to a wide public. In this case the defamation remains unpunished only when it can be proven that there were good reasons to believe that the defamatory information was true.

8.3.4 Legal Analysis—Civil Law

Under private law, the situation is more nuanced. Under Sec. 1330 General Civil Code of Austria, material damages that arise from an insult of a person's honor or reputation can be claimed in two different forms. Sec. 1330 para. 2, like the criminal provisions described above, is applicable only when false information is spread. Sec. 1330 para. 1 protects the dignity of a person and applies when a person's honor is insulted either by pejorative value judgments or by a factual claim (true fact) (Welser and Zöchling-Jud, 2015, p. 415). However, the spreading of a legitimate information of a product vulnerability (true fact) cannot insult a person's honor in a way that dignity is affected.

Another field of law that could be applicable to this case study is competition law, in particular Sec. 7 or Sec. 1 Federal Act against Unfair Competition. However, neither applies. Sec. 7 does not apply because this provision only applies when the information in question is not true; Sec. 1 does not apply because a legitimate disclosure of an existing product vulnerability cannot constitute an unfair business practice. In addition, the entity spreading the vulnerability information and the manufacturer of the product concerned are not in competition with each other, which is another requirement for the applicability of competition law.

A practical problem in this context should be noted: While in this hypothetical case study it is known for sure that the information concerned is true, in practice truth of information can be contested. In some cases, it can be difficult to prove that particular vulnerability information is true, and under most of the relevant provisions in this regard the burden of proof lies with the person that spreads the information. This is another reason that responsible disclosure as described above is recommendable because by getting in touch with the affected vendor the existence of the claimed vulnerability can be confirmed or ruled out.

Further legal issues need to be considered when the CSIRT, cyber situation center, or competent authority that shares the information is a public authority. Under several constitutional systems—like the Austrian—a legal basis is required for every act by a public authority that interferes with the rights of a legal entity. The sharing of a product vulnerability is such an act that interferes with the legally protected reputational and financial interests of the manufacturer, and therefore a statutory legal basis is required pursuant to Art. 18 para. 1 of the Austrian Federal Constitutional Law. This may differ largely from country to country depending on the particular legal tradition, but in the Austrian example the case would be unlawful unless a legal provision exists that permits the sharing of the vulnerability information by the respective authority.

So far the legal analysis assumed that the CSIRT and the company affected by the product vulnerability have not entered into a contract as this is the situation found in most cases. Where there is no contract, the affected company must try to seek indemnification *inter alia* based on the legal grounds described above. However, a contract between the CSIRT and the company might exist. According to the NIS Directive, one of the tasks of CSIRTs is to establish cooperative relationships with the private sector (Annex I (2) (b) NIS Directive). To facilitate such cooperation, CSIRTs shall promote the adoption and use of common or standardized practices for incident and risk-handling procedures and incident, risk, and information classification schemes (Annex I (2) (c) NIS Directive). One way to enable efficient cooperative relationships between CSIRTs and the private sector is to establish CSIRTs responsible for a specific sector ("sector CSIRTs"). In particular, a sector CSIRT established and financed by the sector stakeholders themselves ensures efficient and mutual cooperation. In order to share confidential material, knowledge, or information, such as a product vulnerability (refer to case study 5 for the qualification of vulnerabilities in IT systems as trade secrets), with the sector-CSIRT as well as the other stakeholders from the sector for the purpose of incident handling, the parties may sign an nondisclosure agreement (NDA). This legal contract allows for confidential relationships by restricting access to confidential and proprietary information or trade secrets by any third party outside the affected stakeholders of the sector. In the majority of cases, NDAs contain specific provisions concerning to whom the information may be disclosed under what circumstances and which measures and efforts have to be taken to keep the information secure. If sharing certain information such as product vulnerabilities infringes on provisions of the NDA and, particularly, if the NDA contains a penalty for breach of contract, a CSIRT may be liable. Hence, if the CSIRT wants to inform potentially affected companies or the public of a product vulnerability, it must ensure compliance with the NDA and, in cases of doubt, obtain consent.

8.3.5 Conclusion

As it turns out, the spreading of true information about a third party encounters only very limited restrictions under general criminal and civil law. This holds at least under Austrian law when the information is spread by a private entity. The legal principles described here on the example of Austrian criminal and civil law will be very similar in other jurisdictions and hence the conclusion will be very similar in most EU Member States. However, nothing can be said about specific provisions regulating this scenario in different Member States, in particular when the CSIRT, cyber situation center, or competent authority that shares the information is a public authority as discussed in the last section above.

It should also be noted it was assumed here that the CSIRT, cyber situation center, or competent authority does not underlie any contractual restrictions, nondisclosure agreements (NDA) or the like imposed by the entity from which the information stems. Such restrictions, of course, would override the general legal situation described here. See case study 3 for a similar scenario where an NDA is involved and also case study 5, which deals with vulnerabilities as trade secrets.

Finally, it should be stressed again, while there are hardly any legal boundaries for spreading correct information, that such information should, nevertheless, be spread wisely. As discussed, ethical considerations of responsible disclosure are important in this case.

8.4 Case Study 3: Information Leakage of Threat Intelligence, Incident Data, and Status Data

8.4.1 Case Description

Case study 3 deals with the legal consequences of an information leakage of threat intelligence, incident data, and status data. For example, the data from case study 1 or 2 was initially reported to a CSIRT by a private entity and was leaked by this CSIRT. Is there a difference in the legal consequences if the information leakage is the result of a cyber attack or the misconduct of a civil servant or employee? Are there legal remedies available to an entity or individual in such a case on the grounds of commercial, reputational, or damage of different kind?

8.4.2 Introduction

First of all, it must be noted that this case study deals with information leakage whilst case study 2 elaborates on the legal consequences of informing certain entities or the public as a whole. The act of informing carried out by a CSIRT must be understood as a "conscious" act that was intentional. In contrast, there is no such intentional act when it comes to information leakage. An information leakage may be the result of a cyber attack or the misconduct of a civil servant or employee. Hence, one should bear in mind that the CSIRT is a victim itself.

When dealing with the legal consequences of an information leakage in general, certain differentiations must be made first. For instance, the legal consequences may vary depending on whether the CSIRT is a public or a private entity. Since the NIS Directive stipulates in Art. 9 Sec. 1 that a CSIRT may be established within a competent authority, it is up to the national legislator whether a CSIRT is established as a public or a private entity. To give a comprehensive legal analysis, information leakage in both public and private CSIRTs will be treated.

8.4.3 Legal Analysis—IP Address Leakage

In this case study, data from case study 1 or 2 was initially reported to a CSIRT by a private entity and was leaked by this CSIRT. Starting with data from case study 1, the scenario may look like the following (Figure 8.5): An operator of essential services is victim of a DDoS attack and notifies the CSIRT of this incident in accordance with Art 14 Sec. 3 NIS Directive. In the course of the incident handling process, the operator of essential services shares the IP address of a command and control server with the CSIRT. Such an IP address

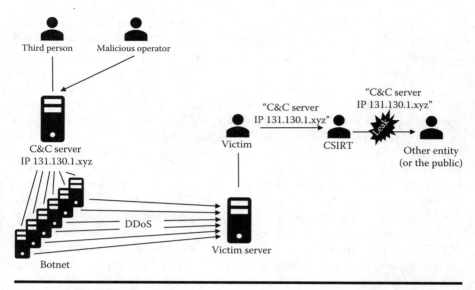

Figure 8.5 IP address leakage.

is security-relevant information that may qualify as personal data according to data protection law (see case study 1). Since stopping DDoS attacks and damage to computer and electronic communication systems constitutes a legitimate interest as stated in recital 49 GDPR, processing of such personal data by a CSIRT for that purpose can be considered as lawful (see case study 1). The occurrence of a leakage causes the IP address to go public. If the IP address qualifies as personal data, i.e., can be related to a natural person (see case study 1), a leakage must be considered a personal data breach and, consequently, a violation of data protection law.

A personal data breach means a breach of security leading to the accidental or unlawful destruction, loss, alteration, or unauthorized disclosure of or access to personal data transmitted, stored, or otherwise processed (Art. 4 Sec. 12 GDPR). An information leakage leading to a personal data breach may trigger the obligatory notification to the supervisory authority according to Art. 33 GDPR (see case study 1). As soon as the controller, the CSIRT, becomes aware that a personal data breach has occurred, the controller must report the personal data breach to the supervisory authority without undue delay and, where feasible, not later than 72 hours of having become aware of it, unless the controller is able to demonstrate, in accordance with the accountability principle, that the personal data breach is unlikely to result in a risk to the rights and freedoms of natural persons. The controller must also document any personal data breaches, comprising the facts relating to the personal data breach, its effects, and the remedial action taken.

Apart therefrom, an information leakage may also trigger the notification duty according to Art. 34 GDPR, obliging the controller to communicate the personal data breach to the data subject (i.e., the natural person to whom the personal data relates) without undue delay (see case study 1). The knowledge about the personal data breach should allow the data subject to take the necessary precautions (recital 86 GDPR). Therefore, the communication should describe the nature of the personal data breach as well as recommendations for the natural person concerned to mitigate potential adverse effects (see Art. 34 Sec. 2 GDPR). Here, too, the notification duty is only triggered when the personal data breach is likely to result in a high risk to the rights and freedoms of natural persons. Since this only applies to natural persons, the leakage of an IP address is unlikely to entail such high risk. Communication to the affected data subjects should be made as soon as reasonably feasible and in close cooperation with the supervisory authority, respecting guidance provided by it or by other relevant authorities such as law-enforcement authorities. For example, the need to mitigate an immediate risk of damage would call for prompt communication with data subjects whereas the need to implement appropriate measures against continuing or similar personal data breaches may justify more time for communication (recital 86 GDPR). The supervisory authority will also have the corrective power to order the controller to communicate a personal data breach to the data subject (Art. 58 Sec. 2 (e) GDPR). The communication to the data subject is not required if it would involve disproportionate effort. In such a case, a public communication or similar measure—whereby the data subjects are informed in an equally effective manner—is sufficient (Art. 34 Sec. 2 (c) GDPR). The case of the IP address could trigger this exemption because it could turn out to be a disproportionate effort to determine the identity of the data subject "behind" the IP address. However, such an announcement must not itself contain personal data protected by data protection law. To publicly communicate an IP address that is part of an ongoing attack would have a more negative impact on the data subject than the initial breach.

Certain infringements of the GDPR are subject to administrative fines that may be imposed by the supervisory authority (Art. 58 Sec. 2 (i) and Art. 83 Sec. 1 GDPR). Infringements of the obligation to report a personal data breach to the supervisory authority (Art. 33 GDPR) as well as of the obligation to communicate a personal data breach to the data subject (Art. 34 GDPR) can be sanctioned with administrative fines up to 10 million EUR, or in the case of an undertaking, up to 2% of the total worldwide annual turnover of the preceding financial year, whichever is higher (Art. 83 Sec. 4 (a) GDPR). The imposition of administrative fines must in each individual case be effective, proportionate, and dissuasive (Art. 83 Sec. 1 GDPR). When deciding whether to impose an administrative fine and deciding on the amount of the administrative fine, the supervisory authority must take due regard of the parameters listed in Art. 83 Sec. 2 GDPR.

The GDPR also stipulates a right to compensation and liability in Art. 82. Any person who has suffered material or nonmaterial damage as a result of an infringement of the GDPR has the right to receive compensation from the controller (or processor) for the damage suffered (Art. 82 Sec. 1 GDPR). Thereby, any controller involved in processing is liable for the damage caused by processing that infringes the GDPR (Art. 82 Sec. 2 GDPR). However, a controller is exempt from liability if it proves that it is not in any way responsible for the event giving rise to the damage (Art. 82 Sec. 3 GDPR).

At this point, it is necessary to examine whether it makes a difference in the legal consequences if the information leakage is caused by a cyber attack or the misconduct of a civil servant or employee. Information lost due to a cyber attack puts the question of the CSIRTs' culpability on the measures (not) taken against outside intruders, whereas information loss as the consequence of misconduct of a civil servant or an employee puts the focus on the internal security measures.

Because a CSIRT is dealing with potentially highly sensitive security-relevant information on a daily basis, it should be regarded as an attractive potential victim of cyber attacks. High-profile cyber attacks (refer to the numerous scenarios in Chapter 2) are usually performed by "outsiders," meaning that the actual delinquents are not active or former employees of the attacked organization. Motives, goals, and background of the cyber attacker are not important for further elaboration. Thus, the attacker in this scenario may act on behalf of a competing (foreign) company or may just be an ordinary criminal seeking to blackmail a company. In this example, the cyber attack targets the computer systems and networks by installing spyware on the PC of an employee of the CSIRT with the intent to obtain valuable information (refer to Chapter 2 for more details on data exfiltration). Such malicious acts must be considered illegal in at least the 52 states[11] which ratified or accessed the Convention on Cybercrime of the Council of Europe (CETS No. 185, see Chapter 7), known as the Budapest Convention, that was agreed on in 2001. According to the Conventions' Chapter II (Measures to be taken at the national level) Sec. 1 (Substantive criminal law) Title 1 (Offences against the confidentiality, integrity and availability of computer data and systems) Art. 2, the parties must adopt legislative and other measures to make access to a computer system without right, when committed intentionally, a criminal offence under its domestic law ("Illegal access"). In Austria, e.g., Art. 2 was implemented in § 118a Austrian Criminal Code[12] and in Belgium in Art. 550bis Strafwetboek. Chapter II Sec. 1 Title 1 Art. 3 of the Budapest Convention prohibits the interception without right of nonpublic transmissions of computer data to, from, or within a computer system. Art 3 was implemented in § 119a Austrian Criminal Code and in § 202b German

---

[11] See chart of signatures and ratifications of Treaty 185 at http://www.coe.int/en/web/conventions/full-list/-/conventions/treaty/185/signatures?p_auth=UrNOpl8I (accessed March 26, 2017).

[12] For an overview on the legal situation concerning cybercrime in Austria, see Reindl-Krauskopf (2009); for the legal situation in Germany, see Hilgendorf and Valerius (2012).

Criminal Code. Illegal access as well as illegal system and data interference had to be implemented into national criminal law not only because of the Budapest Convention but also in regard to the Council Framework Decision 2005/222/JHA of 24 February 2005 on attacks against information systems[13] that was replaced by the Directive 2013/40/EU[14] (Cybercrime Directive 2013/40/EU) (refer to Chapter 7). Thus, the installer of spyware on the PC of an employee of a CSIRT with the intent to obtain data is, at least in Europe, committing a criminal offence. However, the prosecution of such criminal offences will prove very hard (if not impossible, see Chapter 2). Very often, it is not possible to attribute the attack to a specific machine and to find the actual perpetrator; even if it is possible, the perpetrator might be based in a jurisdiction outside the EU where the enforcement of claims might be very difficult. Hence, a company negatively affected by a leak from a CSIRT in the course of a cyber attack will try to seek indemnification from the CSIRT. The CSIRT is itself a victim of the cyber attack. Consequently, a CSIRT can only be blamed if it didn't take adequate security measures with regard to the given risks. As mentioned above, a CSIRT should be regarded as an attractive victim of cyber attacks because it is dealing with potentially highly sensitive security-relevant information that is valuable to the owner of the information and, thus, to blackmailers. The processing of information on risks and incidents within a CSIRT and the sharing thereof with other CSIRTs, authorities, and stakeholders might require the processing of personal data. Hence, such processing must comply with data security requirements imposed by data protection law. The Data Protection Directive contains provisions concerning the security of processing stipulating that the controller must implement appropriate technical and organizational measures to protect personal data against accidental or unlawful destruction or accidental loss, alteration, and unauthorized disclosure or access, in particular where the processing involves the transmission of data over a network, and against all other unlawful forms of processing. Having regard for the state of the art and the cost of their implementation, such measures must ensure a level of security appropriate to the risks represented by the processing and nature of the data to be protected. The GDPR regulates the security of personal data in Art. 32 stating that the controller and the processor must implement appropriate technical and organizational measures to ensure a level of security appropriate to the risk, thereby taking into account the state of the art, the costs of implementation, and the nature, scope, context and purposes of processing as well as the risk of varying likelihood and severity for the rights and freedoms of natural persons. The GDPR further specifies that in assessing the appropriate level of security,

---

[13] OJ L 69, 16.3.2005, pp. 67–71.
[14] Directive 2013/40/EU of the European Parliament and of the Council of August 12, 2013 on attacks against information systems and replacing Council Framework Decision 2005/222/JHA, OJ L 218, 14.8.2013, pp. 8–14.

account shall be taken in particular of the risks that are presented by processing, especially from accidental or unlawful destruction, loss, alteration, unauthorized disclosure of, or access to personal data transmitted, stored, or otherwise processed (Art. 32 Sec. 2 GDPR). There shall also be a process for regularly testing, assessing, and evaluating the effectiveness of security measures (Art. 32 Sec.1 (d) GDPR). Summarizing, the data security provisions demand for security measures that comprise technical as well as organizational measures, take the state of the art into account and follow a risk-based approach. The security measures should ensure an appropriate and not an "absolute" level of security. If the CSIRT has taken appropriate measures and a data breach occurs nonetheless, the CSIRT cannot be held liable for the breach. Of course, the CSIRT will have to act accordingly to comply with the duty to mitigate damages. If the CSIRT fails to take appropriate measures and thereby contributes to the data breach, it is at risk of being held liable. The nature and details of actions for damages vary depending on the legal system.

The kind of technical and organizational measures deemed to be appropriate specifically depends on various factors, as listed above, and must be assessed on a case-to-case basis following a risk management approach. First of all, not all CTI is personal data. IP addresses may qualify as personal data, but there is much less severity for the rights and freedoms of natural persons when an IP address is leaked in contrast to the leakage of special categories of personal data such as biometric or genetic data (see Art. 9 GDPR). However, when assessing the likelihood of a security breach in a CSIRT, special regard should be given to the fact that CSIRTs process potentially highly sensitive security-relevant information that is valuable to its owner.

The loss of information as a result of misconduct of a civil servant or an employee is a different form of security breach. Where a cyber attack asks the question of the CSIRTs' culpability on the measures (not) taken against outside intruders, information loss as the consequence of misconduct of a civil servant or an employee puts the focus on internal security measures.

The differentiation between a civil servant and an employee is due to the fact that CSIRTs may be established within authorities (Art. 9 Sec. 1 NIS Directive). The misconduct of an employee can be the result of various forms of misbehavior. For instance, an employee may carelessly forget to encrypt sensitive information or send it to the wrong recipient. On the other hand, an employee may copy sensitive information on his own device and sell it to the best bidder. It is barely possible to preempt such security breaches because the human error potential can only be minimized and never fully eliminated. To minimize the human error factor, appropriate security measures must be taken. The GDPR, e.g., stipulates that the controller and processor must take steps to ensure that any natural person acting under their authority who has access to personal data does not process them except on instructions from the controller (Art. 32 Sec. 4 GDPR). Instructing the employees about their duties according to data protection law and the internal data protection regulations, including data security regulations, may help to minimize negligent conduct. Moreover, the right to operate data processing devices should be specified and every device should be secured against unauthorized operation by taking precautions.

8.4.4 Legal Analysis—Product Vulnerability Leakage

In addition to data from case study 1, this case study treats the leakage of information from case study 2, but unlike in case study 2 the CSIRT does not intend to make the information public. The scenario may look like the following: a provider of security technologies and services becomes aware of the existence of a vulnerability in its own product and reports it to a CSIRT where the information gets leaked (Figure 8.6).

As the information about a product vulnerability relates to a company rather than to a natural person, data security requirements imposed by data protection law do not protect this information. However, the CSIRT and the company affected by the product vulnerability may have entered into a contract. In particular, an NDA may be signed by the CSIRT and the company in order to share confidential material, knowledge, or information, such as a product vulnerability (refer to case study 5 for the qualification of vulnerabilities in IT systems as trade secrets). If the NDA contains specific provisions concerning to whom the information may be disclosed, under what circumstances, and which measures and efforts have to be taken to keep the information secure, the CSIRT may be liable if the leakage violates such provisions.

As the NIS Directive makes it possible for a CSIRT to be established within a competent authority (Art. 9 Sec. 1 NIS Directive), a CSIRT would need to abide by the legal provisions addressing the authority. Such legal provision may be the obligation of official secrecy. If information was leaked from a CSIRT established

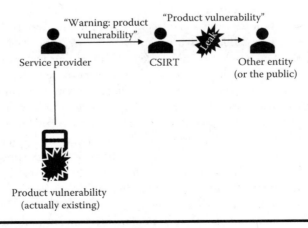

Figure 8.6 Product vulnerability leakage.

within an authority, the information leakage may violate the obligation of official secrecy and, thus, allow for claims arising from possible public liability. In this context, it is also worth mentioning that a CSIRT might also be established within a security or military authority. Security or military authorities may deal with classified information and share classified information with certain nonstate actors. International law, particularly in relation to NATO,[15] and European law[16] govern the security rules of classified information. In particular, national laws implementing such security rules[17] may contain special duties of secrecy, information security provisions, rules about access to and usage, transmission and disclosure of classified information, and administrative and criminal penalties. It should be noted that a CSIRT dealing with classified information must comply with such relevant applicable legal provisions.

An employee abusing confidential information that has been entrusted to or made accessible to him or her solely because of professional reasons will not only commit an administrative and very likely even a criminal offence but will also violate his or her employment contract and, if not included in the employment contract and signed separately, the NDA. A civil servant's misconduct will likely constitute criminal offences like abuse of authority or violation of official secrecy.

The owner of leaked information seeking indemnification can claim damages from the employee. The nature and details of actions for damages vary depending on the legal system. Also, there are differences in the type of damage (material vs. immaterial damage; commercial or reputational damage) and the cause of action. As elaborated above, there are various manifestations of an employee's misbehavior causing the information leakage. Depending on whether the leakage was caused by slight or gross negligent behavior or committed deliberately, different administrative or criminal offences come into consideration. The degree of fault will also influence the type of damage and the extent of compensation claims.

Seeking indemnification from the CSIRT instead of the employee is another possibility because the CSIRT may have to take responsibility for the employee's misbehavior depending on various circumstances. The admissibility, concrete nature, and details of actions for damages vary depending on the legal system. There will be a difference depending on whether the affected company and the CSIRT have entered into a contract. For instance, an NDA between the company and the CSIRT may contain a contractual penalty and a clause according to which

---

[15] Agreement between the Austrian Federal Government and NATO on the protection of information, Federal Law Gazette No. 18/1996.

[16] For example, Council Decision of September 23, 2013 on the security rules for protecting EU classified information (2013/488/EU), OJ L 274, 15.10.2013, pp. 1–50.

[17] In Austria: Federal Law on the implementation of international obligations for the safe use of information (Information Security Act), Federal Law Gazette I No. 23/2002 as amended by Federal Law Gazette I No. 10/2006.

the CSIRT has to take full responsibility for its employees. It must be considered though that a CSIRT may inform the public about individual incidents, where public awareness is necessary in order to prevent an incident or to deal with an ongoing incident (Art. 14 Sec. 6 NIS Directive). Still, the interest of the public in being informed about threats must be duly balanced with possible reputational and commercial damages (recital 59 NIS Directive). Thus, an information leakage not containing more information than the public was given by the CSIRT in a balanced act and in accordance with the NIS Directive is unlikely to cause further legal consequences.

8.4.5 Conclusion

The IP address of a command and control server is reported to a CSIRT. Such an IP address may qualify as personal data according to data protection law. The leakage of personal data must be considered a personal data breach and, consequently, a violation of data protection law.

An information leakage leading to a personal data breach may trigger the notification duty to the supervisory authority (Art. 33 GDPR) as well as the obligation to communicate the personal data breach to the data subject (Art. 34 GDPR). A violation thereof can be sanctioned with administrative fines. The GDPR also stipulates a right to compensation and liability in Art. 82.

There is a difference in the legal consequences if the information leakage is caused by a cyber attack or the misconduct of a civil servant or employee. Information lost due to a cyber attack puts the question of the CSIRTs' culpability on the measures (not) taken against outside intruders, whereas information loss as the consequence of misconduct of a civil servant or an employee puts the focus on the internal security measure. A CSIRT can be held liable if it fails to take appropriate measures as required by data protection law and thereby contributes to the personal data breach. The nature and details of actions for damages vary depending on the jurisdiction. An employee abusing confidential information that has been entrusted to or made accessible to him or her solely for professional reasons will not only commit an administrative and very likely even a criminal offence but will also violate his or her employment contract and NDA. A civil servant's misconduct will likely constitute a criminal offence like abuse of authority or violation of official secrecy. The owner of leaked information seeking indemnification can claim damages from the employee. The nature and details of actions for damages vary depending on the legal system. Seeking indemnification from the CSIRT may also be a possibility as the CSIRT may have to take the responsibility for the employee's misbehavior depending on various circumstances. Here too, the concrete nature and details of actions for damages vary depending on the jurisdiction. There will also be a difference depending on whether the affected company and the CSIRT have entered a contract containing specific rules or a contractual penalty.

8.5 Case Study 4: Harm due to Disproportionate Mitigation Measures

8.5.1 Case Description

This case study assumes that the mitigation measures taken to react to an attack turn out to be disproportionate and/or to affect not only the attacker. For example, an IP address is blocked by an ISP because DDoS traffic from botnet clients originates from that IP address. It turns out to be the IP address of a large organization so that this measure blocks this organization's access to the Internet. Also, the quality of service might be impaired when the ISP introduces "rate limits." This subchapter will treat the questions of what kind of mitigation measures are disproportionate and what are the consequences of the use of disproportionate mitigation measures (Figure 8.7).

8.5.2 Introduction

To deal with this case study properly, it must be asked first who is taking the mitigation measure. The reason for posing this question lies in the legal basis and consequences of the mitigation measure. Mitigation measures taken by military entities may qualify as military defense measures with very different legal consequences compared to the situation where "ordinary" civil enterprises take mitigation measures.

That being said, it must be determined on what legal basis mitigation measures can or have to be taken. In this scenario, an IP address is blocked as a reaction to a DDoS attack.

In the course of a denial-of-service (DoS) attack (refer to Chapter 2 for more details on such attacks), an attacker attempts to prevent legitimate users from

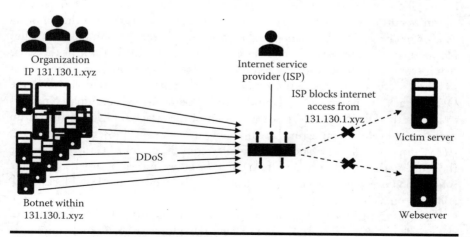

Figure 8.7   Disproportionate mitigation measures.

accessing information or services. In the most common and obvious type of DoS attack, the attacker overloads the server with requests to such an extent that the server can no longer process the legitimate users' requests. In a distributed denial-of-service (DDoS) attack, the attack is "distributed" because the attacker is using multiple computers, usually from multiple exploited owners, to launch the denial-of-service attack (McDowell, 2009). A company's computers that have been infected by a botnet become part of such a botnet.

FURTHER INFORMATION: DDOS ATTACKS BASED ON BOTNETS

Botnet originates from the term "roBOT NETwork" and can be defined as computers infected with malware without the owners' knowledge and controlled by a third party. These remote-controlled botnet clients are often referred to as "zombies" (Rouse, 2012). Recently, Internet of Things (IoT) devices have been used to create large-scale botnets. IoT is an emerging network of devices (e.g., printers, routers, video cameras, smart TVs) that connect to one another via the Internet, often automatically sending and receiving data. These networks of devices are infected with self-propagating malware that can execute crippling DDoS attacks (U.S. DHS US-CERT 2016). Refer to Scenario 4 in Chapter 2 for more details.

In the case of a DDoS attack, there are two possible ways of being a victim. The attacker uses the exploited companies' computers to attack victim computers by forcing the exploited companies' computers to send huge amounts of requests to a victim website or send spam to particular email addresses. This makes the company who owns the exploited machines, taken over by a botnet for instance, a victim. However, in this scenario, a company is a victim of a DDoS attack in the sense that its computers or network connections are targeted by mentioned botnet clients so that its services are inaccessible, making the company the actual victim of the DDoS attack. In the course of a DDoS attack, the attacker uses multiple computers to launch the DDoS attack. This distribution of the attack thus forces the victim company to deal with numerous, usually thousands of, IP addresses. In such a case, this victim company may block the IP addresses of the exploited companies (where the requests that amount to an attack come from) as mitigation to encounter the information overload. The victim company may also request that ISPs block the IP addresses on its behalf.

Notice, as outlined here, that in a DDoS attack the IP addresses are not the attacker's IP addresses. They are rather the address of exploited companies or individuals who are also victims of this very same botnet operator—just in another role. By blocking their IP addresses, they are excluded from the services provided by the victim company as a consequence of this particular mitigation measure. It should also be noted that company clients usually share IP addresses, which means that there are hundreds of computers that appear as one IP address. If this particular IP address gets cut off or blocked, all of the computers sharing this IP address get cut off or blocked too. By introducing "rate limits," the company will not be cut off but the quality of service may be impaired.

In this regard, it must be considered that the legal consequences mainly depend on the relationship between the providing company and the consumer of the service as well as on the kind of service provided by the company. For instance, if the service only consists of providing information about the company on a website, the unavailability of this information due to exclusion does not infringe on anyone's right because there is no duty to provide information to anyone online in general. However, if a company runs an online shop, certain information must be provided directly and be permanently accessible according to Art. 5 Directive 2000/31/EC (Directive on Electronic Commerce 2000)[18] (Zankl, 2016, p. 71). Also, the Directive 2011/83/EU (Consumer Rights Directive, 2011)[19] requires that traders provide the consumer with certain information for distance contracts (Hall et al., 2012, p. 142). When excluding particular IP addresses and, thereby, consumers from accessing this information, the information is still permanently accessible for the general public. Only those whose computers are part of a DDoS attack are excluded. If the attacked company does not take any action to stop DDoS attacks on their servers, the website will go down and no information can be provided to anyone. Excluding certain IP addresses and, thereby, a certain amount of (potential) consumers ensures that the information is available to the general public. Most individual users have dynamic IP addresses, an excluded individual user to whom a new IP address is allocated will, however, not necessarily be able to access the website again because his or her computer is still part of the botnet leading to the blocking of the newly allocated IP address. Still, if a company is violating legal provisions or infringing someone's rights by excluding IP addresses, the company will be justified under the legal mechanism of self-defense (see below).

As noted above, the legal consequences depend on the relationship between the company that provides a service and the consumer. For example, a company may provide cloud services to the consumer. In this case, the legal relationship

---

[18] Directive 2000/31/EC of the European Parliament and of the Council of June 8, 2000 on certain legal aspects of information society services, in particular electronic commerce, in the Internal Market (Directive on electronic commerce), OJ L 178, 17.7.2000, pp. 1–16.
[19] Directive 2011/83/EU of the European Parliament and of the Council of October 25, 2011 on consumer rights, amending Council Directive 93/13/EEC and Directive 1999/44/EC of the European Parliament and of the Council and repealing Council Directive 85/577/EEC and Directive 97/7/EC of the European Parliament and of the Council, OJ L 304, 22.11.2011, pp. 64–88.

between the service provider and the service user is primarily defined by a contract. Certain aspects of the service, including quality, availability, and responsibilities are typically part of a service-level agreement (SLA). An SLA may define the terms of mean time between failures (MTBF) and mean time to repair or mean time to recovery (MTTR). If a DDoS attack on a cloud service is carried out via a cloud user's IP address, the cloud provider's reaction must take into account the contract and the SLA.

Getting back to the case where a company is victim of a DDoS attack, one of the primary defense measures will be to block the "attacking" IP addresses of the exploited companies. The question is if there is a legal basis to do so and if such mitigation measures are proportionate.

8.5.3 Legal Analysis—Network and Information Security Legislation

Obviously, the legal basis for such mitigation measures must primarily be identified in laws protecting the security of networks, services, and data. To begin with, the situation is that a private provider of critical services is taking mitigation measures. When dealing with critical services, Directive 2008/114/EC comes to mind. However, the Directive 2008/114/EC focuses on the identification of European critical infrastructures in the energy and transport sectors and does not directly relate to information systems (see Chapter 7). The NIS Directive, on the other hand, aims at improving cybersecurity across the EU with a particular focus on essential services and specific digital services. There might be an overlap in the sense that companies are critical infrastructures in regard to the Directive 2008/114/EC as well as operators of essential services according to the NIS Directive. For the purposes of this case study, however, particularly Chapter IV of the NIS Directive is of relevance. Chapter IV lays down specifications for the security of the network and information systems of operators of essential services and states in Art. 14 Sec. 1 that operators of essential services have to take appropriate and proportionate technical and organizational measures to manage the risks posed to the security of network and information systems they use in their operations. Having regard to the state of the art, those measures must ensure a level of security of network and information systems appropriate to the risks posed. Further, according to Art. 14 Sec. 2 NIS Directive operators of essential services must take appropriate measures to prevent and minimize the impact of incidents affecting the security of the network and information systems used for the provision of such essential services, with a view to ensuring the continuity of those services.

Regarding ISPs, it must be noted that pursuant to Art. 1 Sec. 3 NIS Directive security and notification requirements provided for in the NIS Directive do not apply to undertakings that are subject to the requirements of Art. 13a and 13b of Directive 2002/21/EC (Framework).

FURTHER INFORMATION: SECTOR-SPECIFIC UNION LEGAL ACTS AND THE NIS DIRECTIVE

Art. 1 Sec. 7 NIS Directive stipulates that where a sector-specific Union legal act requires operators of essential services or digital service providers either to ensure the security of their network and information systems or to report incidents, provided that such requirements are at least equivalent in effect to the obligations laid down in the NIS Directive, those provisions of that sector-specific Union legal act apply (see also recital 9). As Art. 1 Sec. 3 NIS Directive refers to Art. 13a and 13b Directive 2002/21/EC and Art. 19 Regulation (EU) No 910/2014 (see case study 1), the shape of such sector-specific Union legal provisions can be derived. Art. 96 Sec. 1 Payment Services II Directive (PSD II) might qualify as such a sector-specific Union legal provision.

According to Art. 13a Framework Directive undertakings providing public communications networks or publicly available electronic communications services have to take appropriate technical and organizational measures to appropriately manage the risks posed to the security of networks and services. Having regard to the state of the art, these measures must ensure a level of security appropriate to the risk presented. In particular, measures have to be taken to prevent and minimize the impact of security incidents on users and interconnected networks. The undertakings providing public communications networks must also take all appropriate steps to guarantee the integrity of their networks and thus ensure the continuity of the supply of services provided over those networks. This provision is highly relevant for ISPs because an ISP might filter botnet traffic and traffic between exploited computers and the command and control server (C&C server) and at some point simply cut off botnet clients.

Data protection law might be another legal basis to take and justify mitigation measures. Data protection law entails data security provisions as a means to protect personal data. One of the goals of data security is to ensure the availability of and access to personal data. DDoS attacks typically aim at making services inaccessible, e.g., there might be the situation where customers cannot access their data held in an online account. Furthermore, there are services that are accessed not only by customers but by employees too (e.g., ticketing systems). Internal services might also suffer from a DDoS attack on external services when internal services depend on external ones. If such services entail personal data that is not available or is inaccessible due to a DDoS attack, this might be a data protection concern too. Directive 95/46/EC (Data Protection Directive 95/46/EC) provides provisions in Art. 17 concerning the security of processing, stating that the controller must implement appropriate technical and organizational measures to protect personal data against accidental or unlawful destruction or accidental loss, alteration, unauthorized disclosure or access, in particular where the processing involves the transmission of data over a network, and against all other unlawful forms of processing. Having regard to the state of the art and the cost of their implementation, such measures must ensure a level of security appropriate to the risks represented by the processing and the nature of the data to be protected.

The GDPR regulates the security of personal data in Art. 32 according to which the controller and the processor must implement appropriate technical and organizational measures to ensure a level of security appropriate to the risk, thereby taking into account the state of the art, the costs of implementation, and the nature, scope, context, and purposes of processing as well as the risk of varying likelihood and severity for the rights and freedoms of natural persons. This explicitly includes the ability to restore the availability and access to personal data in a timely manner.

Comparing these security-relevant provisions from European network and information security, telecommunications and data protection law, it is apparent that the security measures comprise technical as well as organizational measures, that they all take the state of the art into account and that they have a risk-based approach in common.

In particular, the NIS Directive and the Framework Directive demand prevention and minimization of the impact of security incidents and focus on the continuity of the supply of services. Security measures laid down in data protection law protect the availability of and access to personal data. Both the continuity of the supply of services and the availability of and access to personal data may be endangered when a DoS attack on the network and information systems occurs, thus triggering the legal obligation to take active security measures. An effective measure to encounter a DoS attack is to block the IP addresses from which the requests amounting to an information overload originate. Identifying the "attacking" IP addresses and blocking them necessarily means to process the IP addresses. However, the IP addresses may qualify as personal data, raising the question of whether processing the IP address is lawful under data protection law (refer to case study 1 for more details on the qualification of IP addresses as personal data).

Even if the IP address qualifies as personal data, recital 49 GDPR declares that the processing of personal data to the extent strictly necessary and proportionate for the purposes of ensuring network and information security (i.e., the ability of a network or an information system to resist, at a given level of confidence, unlawful or malicious actions that compromise the availability, authenticity, integrity, and confidentiality of stored or transmitted personal data, and the security of the related services offered by, or accessible via, those networks and systems) constitutes a legitimate interest for providers of electronic communications networks and services and providers of security technologies and services. This explicitly includes stopping DoS attacks. Thus, ISPs as providers of electronic communications networks and services have a legitimate interest in processing "attacking" IP addresses under (future) data protection law.

It must also be asked how long it is allowed to block IP addresses. Recital 49 GDPR states that the processing of personal data—here the IP addresses—constitutes a legitimate interest to the extent strictly necessary and proportionate for the purposes of ensuring network and information security. Hence, when it is no longer necessary to process personal data in order to resist a DoS attack, there is no longer a legitimate interest in doing so. An entry containing the "attacking" IP addresses must be cleared when the network and information security can be ensured again. When a company's defense measure against a DDoS attack is to block the "attacking" IP addresses, the company must after a reasonable amount of time—probably a couple of hours—delist the blocked IP addresses to evaluate whether the attack is still carried out and poses a threat to the network and information security. It should also be taken into account that many IP addresses are dynamically assigned, which is why "old" entries of once-attacking IP addresses should be cleared on a regular basis.

Companies other than the entities listed in recital 49 GDPR cannot rely on recital 49. According to Art. 6 Sec. 1 (f) GDPR, the processing of data is lawful when the processing is necessary for the purposes of the legitimate interests pursued by the controller or by a third party, except where such interests are overridden by the interests or fundamental rights and freedoms of the data subject that require protection of personal data, in particular where the data subject is a child. Processing IP addresses to encounter a DDoS attack is necessary for the purposes of the legitimate interest to ensure data, network, and information security, and this interest is unlikely to be overridden by the interests or fundamental rights and freedoms of the data subject.

8.5.4 Legal Analysis—Self-Defense

Apart from laws protecting the security of networks, services, and data, the legal basis for mitigation measures can be identified in the legal mechanism of self-defense. In Austria, self-defense is enshrined in Sec. 3 para. 1 of the Austrian Criminal Code[20] and is equally applied in civil law where it is stipulated in Sec. 19 General Civil Code of Austria (Welser and Zöchling-Jud 2015, 382). In Germany, self-defense is enshrined in Sec. 32 para. 2 German Criminal Code[21] and in Sec. 227 para. 2 Civil Code of Germany.[22] Although the legal principle of self-defense

---

[20] For further details see Lewisch in Höpfel and Ratz (2016), § 3.

is a globally recognized principle of law, it varies greatly in detail depending on the individual jurisdiction.

In general, self-defense allows a person to defend himself or herself against a present or imminent threat of an unlawful attack on his or her or on other people's legal interests, be they life, health, physical integrity, freedom, or property.

DDoS attacks pose a threat to the legal interest property as they disturb the use of computer systems. DDoS attacks are illegal in at least the countries that are parties to the Budapest Convention on Cybercrime. The Budapest Convention requires the parties in Art. 5 (System interference) to establish as criminal offences under its domestic laws, when committed intentionally, the serious hindering without right of the functioning of a computer system by inputting, transmitting, damaging, deleting, deteriorating, altering, or suppressing computer data. System interference is also illegal under the Directive 2013/40/EU (Cybercrime Directive 2013/40/EU).

Countermeasures against cyber attacks such as DDoS can therefore be justified under self-defense. In order to be justified, though, it is essential that the attack is ongoing or imminently threatening and has the severity to be considered an illegal attack. Depending on the jurisdiction, self-defense may only justify interventions in the legally protected rights of the aggressor, not in the protected rights of third parties. These can, however, be justified or excused by emergency. Justification by emergency usually only applies to the intervention in clearly lower value legal goods in order to save a higher ranking legal entity.

8.5.5 Conclusion

In case of a cyber attack, various mitigation measures may be taken to react thereto. The question arises as to what happens if mitigation measures do not only affect the attacker. In the course of a DDoS attack, the botnet clients are usually owned not by the attacker but by third parties. As a mitigation measure an attacked company might block "attacking" IP addresses. Processing IP addresses therefore constitutes a legitimate reason under data protection law. Also, data protection law requires data security measures against DDoS attacks in particular to ensure the availability and accessibility of personal data. Providers of essential services and digital service providers under the NIS Directive must also take appropriate and proportionate technical and organizational measures to protect the security of their network and information systems and must prevent and minimize the impact of incidents affecting the security of the network and information systems with a view to ensuring the continuity of those services.

ISPs must take appropriate technical and organizational measures to appropriately manage the risks posed to security of networks and services according to

---

[21] For further details see Momsen and Savic in Heintschel-Heinegg (2016), § 32.
[22] For further details see Dennhardt in Bamberger and Roth (2016), § 227.

the Framework Directive. Measures have to be taken to prevent and minimize the impact of security incidents on users and interconnected networks. ISPs must also take all appropriate steps to guarantee the integrity of their networks and thus ensure the continuity of supply of services provided over those networks. ISPs that block IP addresses on behalf of attacked companies or introduce "rate limits" or filter botnet traffic and traffic between botnet clients and the C&C server are obliged to take such measures and act in accordance with the Framework Directive if the measures are appropriate to the risk posed. It must not be forgotten that using the networks of an ISP for the purpose of a DDoS attack constitutes a misuse of these networks and, thus, undermines the integrity thereof and might threaten the continuity of supply of services provided over those networks.

In conclusion, the network and information security legislation requires in particular providers of critical services and ISPs to take measures against cyber attacks that pose a threat to their networks and information systems as well as services provided using networks and information systems. Taking such measures will be justified under the network and information security legislation if they are appropriate to the risks posed. Apart therefrom, mitigation measures taken against cyber attacks such as DDoS attacks will be justified under self-defense. Consequently, damages as a result of these mitigation measures cannot be claimed.

8.6 Case Study 5: Legal Implications of the Involvement of Service Providers

8.6.1 Case Description

The final subchapter examines the legal implications of the involvement of IT service providers offering managed services with particular regard to incident reporting and communication. For example, in the course of providing services to customer A, a service provider becomes aware of IP addresses of botnet members within the domain of customer A (Figure 8.8). Is it lawful to share this information with customer B to mitigate risks of this customer? Who is responsible for reporting such information under the NIS Directive?

8.6.2 Introduction

It is common that a company's IT is run or maintained by an IT service provider. The service provider becomes aware of incidents in customer's IT infrastructure sooner due to specialized knowledge and gained experience. It is indubitable that the service provider must by contract mitigate risks and take action where necessary to protect the customer's IT. For that purpose, the service provider must assess risks

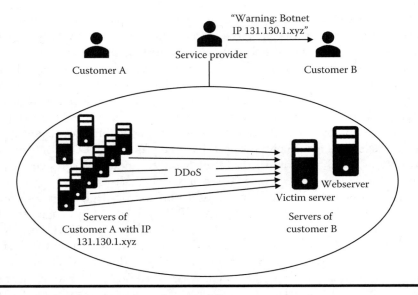

Figure 8.8 Involvement of service providers.

based on knowledge about vulnerabilities. However, the scope and the details of the service provider's duties are the object of negotiation and may differ by what is agreed on in a contract and particularly in the SLA. Still, it must be assumed that as soon as a service provider has knowledge of a severe vulnerability, it is obliged to mitigate the risk for its customer. Otherwise the service provider would not be taking actions to protect one of its customers despite better knowledge, which would most likely lead to the service provider's liability due to breach of contract.

The relevant question is what the service provider has to do or rather is allowed to do when the knowledge about a vulnerability comes from the domain of another customer. In this case, the service provider finds itself in the peculiar situation to potentially breach one of the contracts, regardless of whether it decides to take action or to refrain therefrom. For example, in the course of providing services to customer A, the service provider becomes aware of IP addresses of botnet members or spamming mail servers within the domain of customer A. Is it lawful to share this information with customer B to mitigate risks for customer B?

FURTHER INFORMATION: SPAMMING

Spam is the electronic version of "junk mail." The term spam refers to unsolicited, often unwanted, email messages. Spam does not necessarily contain viruses, and valid messages from legitimate sources could fall into this category (US-CERT, 2009). Different forms of spam and countermeasures can be differentiated. For a comparison of the European, German, and American legal situation, refer to Wendlandt (2004). Concerning the legal aspects for using spam and virus filters in Germany, refer to Eisentraut and Wirt (2005, p. 313). A legal analysis of backlisting and greylisting can be found in Banholzer et al. (2010). On the unlawful competition of backlisting in Germany, see the judgment of LG Lüneburg (2007).

Before sharing the information, the service provider should take any action necessary to eliminate customer A's vulnerability to avoid the conflict of interests in the first place. If that's not possible or feasible, the service provider must evaluate what information cannot be shared because of legal barriers (refer to Chapter 7 for more details on such legal barriers). In this case study, the information concerned comprises IP addresses of botnet members.

As elaborated above, IP addresses may qualify as personal data protected by data protection law (refer to case study 1 for more details). Thus, the service provider would need to make sure it is complying with data protection law when sharing the IP addresses.

Although it is not illegal to unknowingly be part of a botnet—in fact the company is a victim itself—being part of a botnet is harmful to the reputation of a company. Reporting thereof as an individual citizen would in most cases not have any legal consequences because there are no false accusations made (refer to case study 2 for more details). However, the service provider only became aware thereof in the course of providing services to the customer and, therefore, the information has not yet become public knowledge. When the service provider is not obliged to confidentiality by contract, it might, depending on a nation's contract law, be obliged to confidentiality as a consequence of an accessory contractual obligation. Another reason to keep such information confidential may lie in trade secret law.

8.6.3 Legal Analysis—Trade Secret Legislation

Vulnerabilities in the IT infrastructure may qualify as trade secrets. The national laws in EU Member States governing trade secrets[23] are about to be harmonized by the Directive 2016/943 (Trade Secret Directive 2016/943) that was adopted on June 8, 2016 (Kalbfus, 2016). In order for information to be considered a trade secret, the information must, according to Art. 2 Sec. 1,

1. be secret in the sense that it is not generally known among or readily accessible to persons within the circles that normally deal with the kind of information in question,

---

[23] For the Austrian legal situation with an excursion to the legal situation in the US, see Schramböck (2002); for Germany, see Wolff (1997).

2. have commercial value because it is secret, and
3. have been subject to reasonable steps under the circumstances, by the person lawfully in control of the information, to keep it secret.

The question of whether a vulnerability in the IT infrastructure qualifies as a trade secret largely depends on the nature of the vulnerability and various circumstances. Accordingly, the question can only be answered on a case-by-case basis. In general, however, it can be said that a vulnerability that only occurs in or is caused by the specific IT infrastructure of a company is likely to be unique and, thus, meets the secrecy requirement (requirement (a)). The same holds for a general vulnerability in standard software discovered by a company that affects not only the company in question (i.e., a zero-day exploit) as long as it is not generally known. In order to be considered a trade secret, the information must also have "commercial value because it is secret" (requirement (b)). So do vulnerabilities that are secret have commercial value? This question can be answered affirmatively. There is a legal market for vulnerabilities meaning that vulnerabilities are not only traded on the black market, but that there are legitimate legal ways to trade with vulnerabilities. For instance, vendors of software or hardware may pay rewards when customers report a vulnerability to them and not to others. Furthermore, there are rewards given to security researchers for discovering and submitting zero day whereby the amounts paid may depend on the popularity and security strength of the affected software/system, as well as the quality of the submitted exploit.[24] Moreover, recital 14 Trade Secret Directive clarifies that information should be considered to "have a commercial value, for example, where its unlawful acquisition, use or disclosure is likely to harm the interests of the person lawfully controlling it, in that it undermines that person's scientific and technical potential, business or financial interests, strategic positions or ability to compete." It can be argued that public knowledge of a vulnerability is most likely to undermine business or financial interests as well as strategic positions or the ability to compete. The last requirement (c) demands that the person in control of the information takes reasonable steps to keep it secret. It is to be expected that a company, as soon as it becomes aware of the vulnerability, will not only take action to diminish the vulnerability, but will also try to avoid the revelation of the vulnerability. In conclusion, a vulnerability in a company's IT infrastructure can qualify as a trade secret. Art. 4 stipulates that the use or disclosure of such a trade secret is amongst other things unlawful whenever carried out by a person who is in breach of a confidentiality agreement or any other duty not to disclose the trade secret. Hence, a service provider should only share information about a vulnerability with the customer's consent. Since no business would want to lose its trade secret, it

---

[24] Programs to reward security researchers for discovering vulnerabilities are run, e.g., by Google (https://bughunter.withgoogle.com/; accessed March 23, 2017), Microsoft (https://technet.microsoft.com/en-us/library/dn425036.aspx; accessed March 23, 2017) or Zerodium (https://www.zerodium.com/program.html; accessed March 23, 2017).

will avoid sharing any information that could be interpreted as revealing (parts of) the trade secret or not keeping it reasonably secure. As a result, the service provider and customer B would need to enter into a confidentiality agreement to keep the vulnerability a trade secret and to achieve the consent of customer A.

8.6.4 Legal Analysis—Notification Duty

The following paragraph deals with the responsibility for notifying under the NIS Directive.

The NIS Directive obliges the Member States to ensure that operators of essential services notify the competent authority or the CSIRT of incidents having a significant impact on the continuity of the essential services they provide. The same applies to digital service providers who will have to notify the competent authority or the CSIRT of any incident having a substantial impact on the provision of a service they offer within the EU. In practice, however, it's common that a company's IT is run or at least maintained by IT service providers. In comparison to the client, these service providers become aware of incidents in their client's IT infrastructure sooner. Moreover, the service providers have more knowledge and experience concerning incidents than a company that outsourced its IT. Thus, the question arises if it wouldn't be more efficient to let the service provider carry out notification duties. Hence, it must be asked who is responsible for notifying the competent authority or the CSIRT of incidents. Obviously, the answer must be sought in the laws requiring incident notifications. When it comes to network and information security, those laws are the Directive 2009/140/EC and the NIS Directive in particular. Reading the explicit legal text, Art. 13a Sec. 3 Directive 2009/140/EC addresses undertakings providing public communications networks or publicly available electronic communications services to notify the competent national regulatory authority. Under the NIS Directive, operators of essential services and digital service providers must notify the competent authority or the CSIRT of incidents. Furthermore, the NIS Directive states that where an operator of essential services relies on a third-party digital service provider for the provision of a service that is essential for the maintenance of critical societal and economic activities, any significant impact on the continuity of the essential services due to an incident affecting the digital service provider shall be notified by that operator (Art. 16 Sec. 5). The plain text suggests that the companies and not their service providers are obliged to report incidents. However, according to Art. 288 of the Treaty on the Functioning of the European Union (TFEU), a directive shall be binding, as to the result to be achieved, upon each Member State to which it is addressed but shall leave to the national authorities the choice of form and methods. The result that is to be achieved is to provide competent national authorities the information necessary to carry out their duties (especially to inform the national regulatory authorities in other Member States or the public) as well as to create awareness about severe incidents in authorities in general. This result is equivalently achieved when service providers notify incidents on behalf of their clients, meaning that the Directives don't inhibit notifications by service providers. Nevertheless, national laws implementing the directives must provide the opportunity to do so. As there is no Austrian national law implementing the NIS Directive yet,[25] it is not clear whether service providers will be able to notify incidents on behalf of their clients. Regarding the notification duty of digital service providers, it must be considered that Art. 16 Sec. 10 NIS Directive prohibits Member States to impose any further security or notification requirements on digital service providers. Moreover, the Commission may adopt implementing acts laying down the formats and procedures applicable to notification requirements (Art. 16 Sec. 9).

Assuming that the national laws implementing the NIS Directive do not prevent the transfer of the notification duty to service providers, it must be borne in mind that the ultimate responsibility to notify the competent authority or the CSIRT stays with the operators of essential services and the digital service providers. If the service provider fails the duty to notify, the penalties laid down pursuant Art. 22 will be against the operators of essential services and the digital service providers. If the company and the service provider agree by contract that the service provider notifies the competent authority or the CSIRT in case of incidents, the service provider is liable to indemnify the company. In any event, it is advisable and most likely imperative that the company and its service provider cooperate in incident situations and that they have proper and trained notification processes.

8.6.5 Conclusion

Generally, a service provider is obliged to mitigate the risks for its customers. However, when the knowledge about a vulnerability in the IT comes from the domain of another customer, a conflict of interest may arise. On the one hand, the service provider must mitigate the risks for customer B who might be exposed to the risk of a vulnerability in the domain of customer A, while on the other hand this must not result in inadequate reputational harm for customer A. The service provider might be obliged to confidentiality by contract. In the absence of a confidentiality agreement, a legal obligation to confidentiality or not to harm customer A in its reputation can arise as a consequence of an accessory contractual obligation that, in detail, depends on domestic contract law. Furthermore, vulnerabilities may qualify as trade secrets according to the Directive 2016/943 (Trade Secret Directive) according to which the disclosure of a trade secret is unlawful when disclosed in breach of a confidentiality agreement or any other duty not to disclose the trade secret. In conclusion, customer A must consent to the disclosure of the trade secret.

In regard to the question of whether service providers can notify security incidents to the competent authority or the CSIRT under the NIS Directive on behalf of their clients, it must be noted that the plain text of the NIS Directive suggests

---

[25] Time of writing: March 2017.

otherwise. However, EU Member States have certain leeway in the implementation of the NIS Directive. Thus, national laws implementing the NIS Directive might foresee the possibility to transfer the notification duty to service providers. Nevertheless, the responsibility to notify stays with the companies addressed by the NIS Directive.

List of Abbreviations

Art.	Article
C&C server	Command and control server
CERT	Computer Emergency Response Team
CERT/CC	CERT Coordination Center
CJEU	Court of Justice of the European Union
CSIRT	Computer Security Incident Response Team
CT	Cyber threat
CTI	Cyber threat intelligence
DNS	Domain Name System
ECJ	European Court of Justice
EEA	European Economic Area
EU	European Union
GDPR	General Data Protection Regulation
GRUR	Gewerblicher Rechtsschutz und Urheberrecht
MMR	MultiMedia und Recht
NJW	Neue Juristische Wochenschrift
para.	Paragraph
IoT	Internet of Things
IP	Internet Protocol
ISP	Internet service provider
IT	Information technology
SLA	Service-level agreement
TFEU	Treaty on the Functioning of the European Union
U.S.	United States

References

Article 29 Data Protection Working Party

Article 29 Data Protection Working Party (Art29WP). 2014. Opinion 06/2014 on the notion of legitimate interests of the data controller under Article 7 of Directive 95/46/EC, WP 217. http://ec.europa.eu/justice/data-protection/article-29/documentation/opinion-recommendation/files/2014/wp217_en.pdf (accessed March 11, 2017).

Books

Eisentraut, P. and A. Wirt. 2005. *Mit Open Source-Tools Spam & Viren bekämpfen*. Cologne, Germany: O'Reilly. https://www.oreilly.de/german/freebooks/spamvirger/pdf/313-318.pdf (accessed March 24, 2017), Beijing, Cambridge, Farnham, Köln, Paris, Sebastopol, Taipei, Tokyo.

Hilgendorf, E. and B. Valerius. 2012. *Computer-und Internetstrafrecht*, 2nd edition. Berlin and Heidelberg: Springer.

Knyrim, R. (ed.). 2016. *Datenschutz-Grundverordnung*. Vienna, Austria: Manz.

Paal, B. and D. Pauly. 2017. *Datenschutz-Grundverordnung*. Munich, Germany: Beck.

Reindl-Krauskopf, S. 2009. *Computerstrafrecht im Überblick*, 2nd edition. Vienna, Austria: Facultas.

Schramböck, M. 2002. *Der Schutz von Geschäfts-und Betriebsgeheimnissen mit Exkurs zur Rechtslage in den USA*. Vienna, Austria: Manz.

Welser, R. and B. Zöchling-Jud. 2015. *Bürgerliches Recht. Band II: Schuldrecht Allgemeiner Teil, Schuldrecht Besonderer Teil, Erbrecht,* 14th edition. Vienna, Austria: Manz.

Zankl, W. 2016. *E-Commerce-Gesetz*. Vienna, Austria: Verlag Österreich.

Commentaries

Bamberger, H. and H. Roth. 2016. *Beck'scher Online-Kommentar BGB*, 41st edition (status November 1, 2016). Munich, Germany: C.H. Beck.

Heintschel-Heinegg, B. 2016. *Beck'scher Online Kommentar StGB*, 33rd edition (status December 1, 2016). Munich, Germany: C.H. Beck.

Höpfel, F. and E. Ratz. 2016. *Wiener Kommentar zum StGB*, 2nd edition (status October 1, 2016, rdb.at). Munich, Germany: C.H. Beck.

Journals

Cormack, A. 2016. Incident response: Protecting individual rights under the general data protection regulation. *SCRIPTed*, vol. 13 no. 3, 258–282, doi:10.2966/scrip.130316.258 (accessed March 11, 2017).

Hall E., G. Howells and J. Watson. 2012. The Consumer Rights Directive—An Assessment of Its Contribution to the Development of European Consumer Contract Law. *European Review of Contract Law*, vol. 8 no. 2, 139–166.

Kalbfus, B. 2016. Die EU-Geschäftsgeheimnis-Richtlinie. Welcher Umsetzungsbedarf besteht in Deutschland? *GRUR* 2016, 1009.

Wendlandt, B. 2004. Europäische, deutsche und amerikanische Regelungen von E-Mail-Werbung—Überlegungen zum Nutzen des CAN-SPAM Act. *MMR* 2004/06, 365–369.

Wolff, H. 1997. Der verfassungsrechtliche Schutz der Betriebs-und Geschäftsgeheimnisse. *NJW* 1997, 98–101.

Reports/Studies/Websites/Miscellaneous

Banholzer, F., E.-M. Herring and H. Obex. 2010. Rechtliche Zulässigkeit von Blacklisting. Expert Opinion. Münster. https://www.dfn.de/fileadmin/3Beratung/Recht/Stellungnahmen/Final_Rechtliche_Zulaessigkeit_von_Blacklisting.pdf (accessed March 22, 2017).

CERT/CC. 2017. Vulnerability Disclosure Policy. http://www.cert.org/vulnerability-analysis/vul-disclosure.cfm? (accessed March 25, 2017).

McDowell, M. 2009. Understanding Denial-of-Service Attacks. Security Tip (ST04–015). U.S. Department of Homeland Security (DHS) US-CERT. https://www.us-cert.gov/ncas/tips/ST04-015 (accessed March 24, 2017).

Rouse, M. 2012. Definition Botnet (Zombie Army). TechTarget SearchSecurity. http://searchsecurity.techtarget.com/definition/botnet (accessed March 24, 2017).

US-CERT. 2009. Reducing Spam. Security Tip (ST04–007). U.S. Department of Homeland Security (DHS) US-CERT. https://www.us-cert.gov/ncas/tips/ST04-007 (accessed March 24, 2017).

US-CERT. 2016. Heightened DDoS threat posed by Mirai and other botnets. Alert (TA16–288A). U.S. Department of Homeland Security (DHS) US-CERT. https://www.us-cert.gov/ncas/alerts/TA16-288A (accessed March 24, 2017).

European Regulation

Council Decision of September 23, 2013 on the security rules for protecting EU classified information (2013/488/EU). OJ L 274, October 15, 2013, pp. 1–50.

Council Directive 2008/114/EC of December 8, 2008 on the identification and designation of European critical infrastructures and the assessment of the need to improve their protection. OJ L 345, December 23, 2008, pp. 75–82.

Council of Europe, European Treaty Series-No. 185, Budapest, November 23, 2001, Convention on Cybercrime/Budapest convention.

Council Framework Decision 2005/222/JHA of February 24, 2005 on attacks against information systems. OJ L 69, March 16, 2005, pp. 67–71.

Directive 95/46/EC of the European Parliament and of the Council of October 24, 1995 on the protection of individuals with regard to the processing of personal data and on the free movement of such data. OJ L 281, November 23, 1995, pp. 31–50.

Directive 2000/31/EC of the European Parliament and of the Council of June 8, 2000 on certain legal aspects of information society services, in particular electronic commerce, in the Internal Market (Directive on Electronic Commerce). OJ L 178, July 17, 2000, pp. 1–16.

Directive 2002/21/EC of the European Parliament and of the Council of March 7, 2002 on a common regulatory framework for electronic communications networks and services. OJ L 108, April 24, 2002, pp. 33–50.

Directive 2009/140/EC of the European Parliament and of the Council of 25 November 2009 amending Directives 2002/21/EC on a common regulatory framework for electronic communications networks and services, 2002/19/EC on access to, and interconnection of, electronic communications networks and associated facilities, and 2002/20/EC on the authorisation of electronic communications networks and services. OJ L 337, December 18, 2009, pp. 37–69.

Directive 2011/83/EU of the European Parliament and of the Council of October 25, 2011 on consumer rights, amending Council Directive 93/13/EEC and Directive 1999/44/EC of the European Parliament and of the Council and repealing Council Directive 85/577/EEC and Directive 97/7/EC of the European Parliament and of the Council. OJ L 304, November 22, 2011, pp. 64–88.

Directive 2013/40/EU of the European Parliament and of the Council of August 12, 2013 on attacks against information systems and replacing Council Framework Decision 2005/222/JHA. OJ L 218, August 14, 2013, pp. 8–14.

Directive (EU) 2015/2366 of the European Parliament and of the Council of November 25, 2015 on payment services in the internal market, amending Directives 2002/65/EC, 2009/110/EC and 2013/36/EU and Regulation (EU) No 1093/2010, and repealing Directive 2007/64/EC. OJ L 337, December 23, 2015, pp. 35–127.

Directive (EU) 2016/943 of the European Parliament and of the Council of June 8, 2016 on the protection of undisclosed know-how and business information (trade secrets) against their unlawful acquisition, use and disclosure. OJ L 157, June 15, 2016, pp. 1–18.

Directive (EU) 2016/1148 of the European Parliament and of the Council of July 6, 2016 concerning measures for a high common level of security of network and information systems across the Union. OJ L 194, July 19, 2016, pp. 1–30.

Regulation (EU) No 910/2014 of the European Parliament and of the Council of July 23, 2014 on electronic identification and trust services for electronic transactions in the internal market and repealing Directive 1999/93/EC. OJ L 257, August 28, 2014, pp. 73–114.

Regulation (EU) 2016/679 of the European Parliament and of the Council of April 27, 2016 on the protection of natural persons with regard to the processing of personal data and on the free movement of such data, and repealing Directive 95/46/EC (General Data Protection Regulation). OJ L 119, May 4, 2016, pp. 1–88.

National Regulation

Agreement between the Austrian Federal Government and NATO on the protection of information, Federal Law Gazette No. 18/1996.

(Austrian) Criminal Code (Strafgesetzbuch, abbreviated StGB), Federal Law Gazette No. 60/1974, as amended.

(Austrian) Federal Act Against Unfair Competition (Bundesgesetz gegen den unlauteren Wettbewerb, abbreviated UWG), Federal Law Gazette No. 448/1984, as amended.

(Austrian) Federal Law on the implementation of international obligations for the safe use of information (Information Security Act), Federal Law Gazette I No. 23/2002.

(Austrian) Federal Constitutional Law (Bundes-Verfassungsgesetz, abbreviated B-VG), in the version promulgated in 1930 (Federal Law Gazette No. 1/1930), last amended Federal Law Gazette I No. 106/2016.

Belgium Penal Code (Wetboek van Strafrecht) of 8 June 1867, as amended.

Civil Code of Germany (Bürgerliches Gesetzbuch, abbreviated BGB) of August 18, 1896 in the version promulgated on January 2, 2002, Federal Law Gazette I p. 42, 2909; 2003 I p. 738, as amended.

General Civil Code of Austria (Allgemeines Bürgerliches Gesetzbuch, abbreviated ABGB) of January 1, 1812, last amended Federal Law Gazette I No. 43/2016.

German Criminal Code (Strafgesetzbuch, abbreviated StGB), in the version promulgated on November 13, 1998, Federal Law Gazette I p. 3322, as amended.

Case Law

CJEU Judgement Case C-582/14, October 19, 2016 (Breyer), ECLI:EU:C:2016:779.

LG Lüneburg, September 27, 2007, 7 O 80/07: Wettbewerbswidrigkeit von IP-Blacklisting, *MMR* 2008, 61 (with remarks by Heidrich).

Chapter 9

Real-World Implementation of an Information Sharing Network: Lessons Learned from the Large-Scale European Research Project ECOSSIAN

Giuseppe Settanni and Timea Pahi

Austrian Institute of Technology

Contents

9.1 Introduction

In order to efficiently detect and counter modern targeted multistage cyber threats, organizations must cooperatively exchange security-relevant information with each other and the competent national authorities. By doing this, they can obtain broader knowledge on the current cyber threat landscape and subsequently derive new security insights regarding their infrastructures, hence be able to timely react if necessary.

National authorities responsible for the security of Network and Information Systems (NIS), as set forth by the European NIS directive (European Commission, 2016), are to be established to collect cyber incident reports issued by Critical Infrastructure (CI) providers. Such reports, describing critical security issues

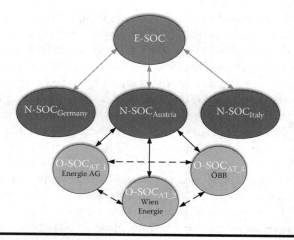

Figure 9.1   The ECOSSIAN ecosystem.

revealed in the CI networks (cf. Chapter 5), have to be analyzed and correlated by the responsible national NIS authority to establish national cyber-situational awareness (cf. Chapter 6) to eventually provide coordinated support and mitigation strategies to the affected organizations.

The ECOSSIAN[1] research project proposes a pan-European three-layered approach (Kaufmann et al., 2015), to protect CIs by detecting cyber incidents and in a timely manner generating and distributing early warnings to the potentially affected infrastructures. As depicted in Figure 9.1, the ECOSSIAN ecosystem foresees three types of Security Operation Centers: Organization SOC (O-SOC), National SOC (N-SOC), and European SOC (E-SOC).

At O-SOC-level organizations deploy multiple sensors and tools for intrusion and threat detection and report to N-SOCs about incidents that might have cross-organizational relevance. There are several different types of information O-SOCs share with their respective N-SOC. Security-relevant information (such as incidents, vulnerabilities, and observations) obtained by analyzing locally detected anomalies is manually reported to the N-SOC by O-SOC operators; structured data automatically generated by sensors at O-SOC level is first reviewed by O-SOC operators and then, if feasible, forwarded to the N-SOC. Additionally, O-SOCs, especially those operating in the same sector, may also share security data in a peer-to-peer fashion.

N-SOCs are deployed by European Member States joining the ECOSSIAN network; they are responsible for gaining cyber-situational awareness on the network of national critical infrastructures. Here cyber intelligence is acquired by analyzing

---

[1] ECOSSIAN—European Control System Security Incident Analysis Network—is a European collaborative research project started on June 1, 2014, and ended on May 31, 2017. This project has received funding from the European Union's Seventh Framework Programme (FP7) for research, technological development, and demonstration under grant agreement no. 607577.

information gathered from different data sources such as reporting O-SOCs, federated N-SOCs, and publicly available sources. Cyber incident information aggregation, correlation, classification, and analysis are the main functionalities provided at this level. Once the evaluation of analysis results is concluded, mitigation steps, advisories, or early warnings are sent back to the reporting and other involved O-SOCs.

At the highest level the E-SOC performs analysis of strategic information shared by the different N-SOCs and distributes advisories to targeted lower level SOCs. The E-SOC identifies supranational attack campaigns and provides a pan-European view on the security situation to the Member States and to the connected European bodies of relevance (e.g., Europol, ENISA, CERTs, etc.).

Based on the experience gained in the ECOSSIAN project, this chapter studies how the building blocks discussed in this book can be harmonized into a cross-national cybersecurity information sharing network. Moreover, this chapter analyzes the processes necessary to efficiently manage such a network and the technologies required to implement it.

Section 9.2 presents the technical requirements and the overall architecture designed for the ECOSSIAN ecosystem. The main technical components employed on each level of such a hierarchical cross-national incident analysis network are also outlined here. Considering the presented architecture, Section 9.3 introduces the CIC framework for cyber intelligence sharing, which defines roles and responsibilities of the actors involved in a national sharing network. The applicability of such a framework to the ECOSSIAN system is discussed in this section. Section 9.4 illustrates three different application scenarios, demonstrated in the ECOSSIAN project, highlighting the benefits of adopting the proposed approach in different domains. Finally, Section 9.5 discusses the lessons learned in the ECOSSIAN project and provides relevant recommendations for a large-scale rollout.

9.2 Overall Architecture and Technologies to Implement a National TI Framework

As discussed in the previous chapters, cyber threat intelligence comprises a vast number of aspects, both technical and procedural, that need to be carefully considered when designing a cross-national sharing and analysis network. In this and the following sections, the ECOSSIAN research project and its corresponding developed system prototype is taken as an example of a possible implementation of such a network.

The goal of the ECOSSIAN project was to create a platform to detect, analyze, and respond to security incidents and attacks on critical infrastructures, specifically in industrial control systems. The platform was designed to operate on three interconnected levels: organization, national, and EU-wide. This section describes the technical requirements the ECOSSIAN system had to fulfill in order to successfully achieve these goals, the derived system architecture, and the main components implemented at the different architectural layers.

9.2.1 System Requirements

The requirements examined in the following are grouped in two main categories: architectural requirements and functional requirements. Architecture requirements are established by looking at the system from inside and understanding how it should be built in order to successfully achieve functional requirements. These requirements define how the system should be supported and maintained and which resources should be available (Viktoriya Degeler et al., 2015).

Functional requirements are obtained by answering basic questions such as "What is the system supposed to do?" and "Which features should the system provide in order to successfully solve its tasks?" Functional requirements are the most user-centric, as they are directly derived from the expected usage of the final system.

Non-functional requirements were also defined for the ECOSSSIAN system. They specify the criteria that can be used to judge the operation of the system, rather than specific behavior. Non-functional requirements are not reported in this section for the sake of brevity.

ECOSSIAN NON-FUNCTIONAL REQUIREMENTS

Among the *non-functional requirements,* the following main aspects are addressed:

- System–user interaction, content presentation, and usability of the system
- System performance (capacity, availability, maintainability, monitoring, etc.)
- Security (access control, encryption, operation and communication security, privacy)
- Legal and regulatory requirements (with focus on data protection)

9.2.1.1 System and Architecture Requirements

The ECOSSIAN system needs to follow certain architectural requirements in order to archive its goal while offering architectural integrity, meaning that the system itself follows a clear paradigm and structure. Since the system is distributed, this is even more important, because the complexity increases exponentially with every new interface/component.

The ECOSSIAN system must consist of three layers: operator, national, and European. At each of the layers it is assumed that a SOC, following a CSIRT organization model (ENISA, 2006), is already present. The components of the ECOSSIAN system should communicate using open interfaces and data formats in order to achieve interoperability with existing tools. The ECOSSIAN system must offer a threat detection module, which allows the detection of cyber attacks based on sensor (security e.g., IDS) data, must have a data sharing component, which

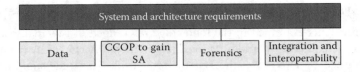

Figure 9.2 ECOSSIAN system and architecture requirements.

is responsible for reliable and secure data sharing based on the sharing requirements, and must have a Situational Awareness component, which allows decision makers to assess complex situations from a high-level perspective. Moreover, the ECOSSIAN system must have a collaboration component that allows all actors participating in the system to communicate in an efficient way.

The system must be distributed across the partners and also across the different nations collaborating together operating at different geographical locations.

As depicted in Figure 9.2, four main aspects are analyzed when deriving system and architecture requirements; each of them is discussed in more detailed in Sections 9.2.1.1.1 through 9.2.1.1.4.

9.2.1.1.1 Data Requirements

The data exchange format for sharing and the sharing mechanisms are essential parts of the ECOSSIAN system. Since the data sharing is one of the core functionalities, appropriate data formats must be selected to allow for efficient data sharing. At the O-SOC level, the data formats should include all information that can be gathered with the sensors as well as additional information originating from manual analysis and additional user activities. At the N-SOC level, the adopted data formats should be capable of holding the information necessary to instruct first responders in the corresponding country. In order to provide contextual information and ease root–cause analysis, it should be possible to include operational information about entire infrastructure sectors of one country explicitly also related to noncyber events. At this level, the data sharing component must ensure that all relevant information can be exchanged between the ECOSSIAN member organizations and external agencies. Based on the legal framework relevant for the N-SOC constituency, the SOC may indeed need to maintain a strong link with local or national law enforcement agencies in order to start a prosecution of potential attackers.

Given that the role of the E-SOC is more strategic and less technical than the N-SOC, it should be possible to share only aggregated and summarized information instead of raw technical data with the E-SOC. Nonstructured data formats should be foreseen for this communication.

The data formats adopted across all layers must support tagging of exchanged information with national, EU, and ECOSSIAN internal classifications (e.g., EU

Confidential). They should also allow privacy-related tagging of the information. It should optionally be possible to transfer anonymized or pseudonymized data instead of raw data. The data format should allow indicating the use of data that is protected in that way. As a pan-European system, it should be possible to state the applicable data protection legislation (e.g., EU + national German law). Data formats must support both human- and machine-readable data; additionally, they should be able to handle information about threats, attacks, TTPs, and malware-related information including common Indicators of Compromise (IoCs).

9.2.1.1.2 Using Common Cyber Operational Pictures to Gain Situational Awareness

The Common Cyber Operational Picture (CCOP) should provide enhanced situational awareness (SA). This component of the ECOSSIAN system is the main interface for the N-SOC and the E-SOC layer. The component must support the SOC staff at the corresponding layers to assess the current security and safety state of the monitored infrastructure. The SA module should allow the visualization of nontrivial relationships and situations that otherwise would result in an information overload for the operators. The CCOP should allow the operators to quickly assess the state of their monitored infrastructure.

The visualization component should provide different levels of visualization, depending on the ECOSSIAN layer at which it is employed. At the O-SOC layer, the focus should be on the individual organization's security status. At the N-SOC layer, the visualization should give an overview of the different sectors and their status. In case of attacks, critical dependencies between the sectors or big operators will also be pointed out, so that reactive actions can be taken. At the E-SOC layer, the visualization should mainly show the state of entire nations and sectors, with a simplified breakdown of sector per nation. For infrastructures that work cross-border or across significant parts of Europe, information should be displayed on a per-country basis, highlighting problems in one country that could have influence on the whole system.

9.2.1.1.3 Forensics

The ECOSSIAN system should support its operators when conducting threat/incident response activities like forensic investigations. At different layers of the ECOSSIAN system, the response capabilities will be very different. While at the O-SOC layer the support offered by the ECOSSIAN system will deal with classical incident response (data collection, forensics, containment), at higher levels of ECOSSIAN, the threat response module will support nation-states to deal with cyber crises and the coordination of responses against large-scale targeted attacks including physical effects on real infrastructures. At the N-SOC layer, the response capabilities will also include interfaces to first responders in order to deal with severe attacks that have physical effects.

9.2.1.1.4 Integration and Interoperability

The ECOSSIAN system should be able to integrate with existing solutions that may be in place already at all of the ECOSSIAN layers. Those interfaces can be designed for different purposes and have different complexities. The interoperability with those systems is important, since ECOSSIAN should allow data from different sources and systems to be integrated and allow reactions to be triggered with existing systems.

At the O-SOC layer, the ECOSSIAN system should be able to integrate with existing security products, such as SIEM (security information and event management) solutions, IDS (intrusion detection system) and log-management systems.

At the N-SOC layer, the ECOSSIAN system should integrate with existing situational awareness and early warning tools. Bidirectional interfaces should be present to exchange information with those systems. The system should moreover provide interfaces with national first responders. These interfaces should allow triggering warnings to the relevant entities.

At the E-SOC layer, the ECOSSIAN system should integrate with existing European Situational Awareness and early warning tools.

9.2.1.2 *Functional Requirements*

Functional requirements ultimately formulate what the system is supposed to do. In this section, the ECOSSIAN system is assumed to contain a set of interacting functional modules that react to or help the operator to react to disturbing, disabling, or destructive events in or toward CIs. Functional requirements describe the need for performing functions required for the world external to the ECOSSIAN ICT system. The problems the system has to solve or support and the end users represent this outside world. Main addressees are the system's operators, with whom the system communicates via the user interface(s).

The main aspects considered while deriving the functional requirements are summarized in Figure 9.3 and are further described in the following sections.

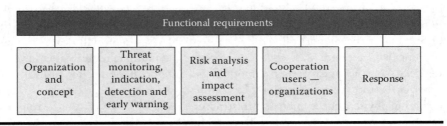

Figure 9.3   ECOSSIAN functional requirements.

9.2.1.2.1 Organizational and Concept Requirements

The overall requirement of the ECOSSIAN project is to design a functional command and control system for threat monitoring, detection, evaluation, mitigation, and incident management. The ECOSSIAN system should be based on a generic architecture of the three-level (or three-tier) approach representing and serving the levels of objects and processes, industrial control systems, and networks of certain CIs including their O-SOCs, N-SOCs, and a generic E-SOC. The system needs to provide functional support in all three tactical areas of command and control: detection, evaluation, and response.

9.2.1.2.2 Threat Monitoring, Indication, Detection, and Early Warning

Monitoring, detection, early warnings, and effective information provision and handling concerning cyber attacks to a CI component are key functions of the ECOSSIAN demonstrator. The communication among the three levels comprises quick and reliable status information from the O/N-level to the N/E-level as well as information and potentially briefing/instruction in the opposite direction. Monitoring the situation and detecting and indicating treats shall facilitate the extraction of trends (from historical data), as well as the prediction of future threats and impacts.

9.2.1.2.3 Risk Analysis and Impact Assessment

Risk analysis is performed within ECOSSIAN by an analytic tool operating with data collected during the daily operation and combines and interprets it in a systematic way. The analysis of risks not only refers to the frequencies and consequences of dedicated critical events but also includes the assessment of complete scenarios; such scenarios may consist of a sequence and distribution of events. Additionally, the risk analysis shall be based on and correlated with the most critical assets and business processes affected or expected to be affected.

Whereas such a risk-analysis function allows an assessment of monetary risks for the future (derived from many past events), incident management and impact assessment refer directly to a present incident and assess and calculate financial and other types of impacts of this incident under the present conditions.

9.2.1.2.4 Cooperation between Users/User Organizations

The ECOSSIAN system needs to provide functions that facilitate cooperation and coordination between different stakeholder organizations. This will comprise "horizontal" cooperation, i.e., between peer organizations like CI SOCs or between nations and "vertical" cooperation in the three-tier hierarchy of CIs, N-SOC(s) and E-SOC. Information exchange and coordination will be up, down, and lateral. One of the most important organizational instruments will be public–private partnership (PPP) frameworks (Center for Strategic and International Studies, 2013).

PPPs in CIP are essential, as it must be assumed that CIs can be vital targets of deliberate attacks or accidental disablers. Vulnerabilities in CIs plus cascading effects caused by interdependencies could cause serious CI breakdowns that create disasters of catastrophic dimension, both economically and politically.

Vertical and horizontal cooperation requires the common development and agreement on policies and rules to be followed for information and task sharing. These must be based on a common analysis and model on mutual interdependencies of related CIs, data conventions, and visualization in the CCOP adaptive to the hierarchical cooperation.

Cooperative functions need to be available for all phases of an incident response cycle (see Figure 9.4): monitoring, detection, alerting, assessment, response, and recovery.

Good coordination schemes need to use two-way or multiway sharing via trusted collaborative networks for cross-organizational and cross-national information sharing. It is necessary in ECOSSIAN to assume and establish a generic organizational policy that represents a compromise between different typical organizations from Member States. Shared information must be filtered and processed in a hierarchical model according to the needs at the different levels included. Rules for propagation in the hierarchical order need to be implemented.

Ultimately, it is expected that ECOSSIAN will contribute to developing pan-European strategies to include policies, procedures, and response teams' interactions and data sharing activities.

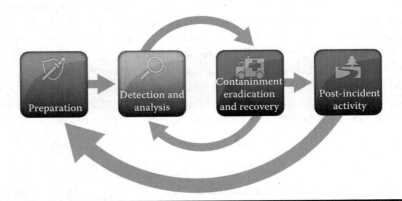

Figure 9.4   Incident response cycle defined by NIST (2012).

9.2.1.2.5 Response: Threat Mitigation, Planning, Incident Management, Decision Support, and Recovery

By incident response functionalities system users will be enabled to generally improve the response to an incident by mitigating its causes and origins and limiting or reducing imminent or forecast/future damages.

The response toolkit needs to start with identifying and assessing information and information sources that are critical for reaction. The response function then needs to assess in a process model for mitigation that delivers recommendations of response measures. This model will be different on the CI, national, or EU level. Criticality should account for both the threat event and its likely development, as well as the damages caused and the forecast of damage development. The response function will be provided by a decision support system that merges critical information with response options available, giving recommendations on actions to be taken. This needs to include an analysis of the inventory of possible response measures and mapping them against the threat and damage spectrum.

Besides decision support, the ECOSSIAN system will also include a Forensics Toolset. This forensic analysis and reporting tools need to operate at any of the O-SOC, N-SOC, or E-SOC levels and needs to trace events back to their origins and create timelines. It needs to correlate information from different sources relevant to forensic analysis and conclusions. In addition to forensic information logging and management, the system should give recommendations on forensic incident response.

Continuity planning should be enabled with the ultimate goal of contributing to pan-European strategies to include policies, procedures, and response teams' interactions and data sharing activities to ensure that a minimum level of services is maintained during a disruption to the ECOSSIAN platform. Minimum levels of continuity need to be defined and maintained at all levels. Continuity standards such as ISO 22301 (International Organization for Standardization, 2012) or BS 25999 (BSI-Global, 2006) should be applied. Governance of this continuity process needs to be provided via an organization of defined roles and responsibilities.

Technical mitigation measures at the CI level will be assumed in place in the CIs' O-SOCs. Here only requirements for the ECOSSIAN system above or aside existing proprietary CI mitigation tools and measures are addressed. From ECOSSIAN's point of view, an overall process model for mitigation at the EU level is required. This will be necessary or is at least strongly advised because CIs across Europe are under different management (public, private, mixed), most operate transnationally, and CIs may have different business models and business objectives. The main function of the mitigation module, therefore, should be to provide a balanced assessment of the criteria of SLAs (if in place) or equivalent levels of performance of the CI systems. The SLA should define constraints related to mitigation aspects, such as common reporting formats, incident reporting timing, and response latency.

The system is required to limit incident and consequence propagation by mapping CI interconnections and interdependencies and by identifying criticalities, which require coordination between dependent CIs and mitigation coordination from above the CI level.

The ultimate goal of this function is to provide input to a well-balanced CIP service and supply level throughout Europe in case of disruption or degradation of the infrastructures in question. Overarching contingency and continuity management should support this.

Moreover, ECOSSIAN needs to predict the actual aim of a distributed attack against multiple CIs. It needs to derive the actual aim of an attack based on known CI interdependencies. For that purpose, it must analyze the map of interdependencies between CIs in terms of the aim of a distributed attack, identify the most probable aim of the distributed attack, and distribute the aim throughout the system.

ECOSSIAN must warn partners that employ a vulnerable component. In case of an attack targeted at a specific component, ECOSSIAN warns all participants employing the same or similar component. This should trigger the search to identify all components that are vulnerable to the attack and attack trend detected.

After the attack and trend have been identified, appropriate countermeasures have to be initiated, implemented, and controlled, whether they have been started and are running properly. Success (and failure) needs to be identified and reported.

9.2.2 System Architecture

The ECOSSIAN architecture was defined using the modularization paradigm, where each type of function and each type of operation can be represented by a functional block. These functional blocks define how the system was designed; in order to implement the system architecture, the functional and the non-functional requirements presented in Section 9.2.1 need to be followed (Giuseppe Settanni et al., 2016).

The first part of this section presents the global architecture of the different SOC levels (O-SOC to E-SOC), the interconnections, and the hierarchical information flows. The basic architecture has been defined to be generic and valid for every SOC level. Each SOC level can, in turn, implement the different functional blocks for specific operations.

Due to the different domains addressed and the distributed nature of critical infrastructures, the ECOSSIAN system is distributed through a large number of geographical locations, in a highly heterogeneous way. Moreover, national information is aggregated by each country, further shared and aggregated at the European level. To achieve these objectives, a decentralized multilayer architecture with clear definition of the components' interfaces was designed.

9.2.2.1 Three Levels of Security Operation Centers

The ECOSSIAN approach relies on the implementation of a monitoring and detection system that enables an operator to obtain consistent information related to the status of the infrastructure (plant, distribution network, IT network, or the like). The ECOSSIAN approach relies on distributed network and system monitoring where legacy systems are integrated as well.

The approach adopted in ECOSSIAN extends the one applied by NOCs when dealing with distributed data aggregation; an O-SOC is here defined, where operators have the ability to get a real-time view on the cybersecurity state of the control network and the processes controlled. The raw data behind this information is stored and aggregated and can be used later to conduct forensic analysis of incidents.

However, securing each operator site in an isolated fashion is not enough. Because of existing interdependencies among CIs, complex threats to interconnected infrastructures would frequently remain undetected. It is also obvious that the implementation of one O-SOC is not sufficient to provide security on a national level. Thus, it is necessary to establish an O-SOC in each sector and each operator of critical services and share information between them. Therefore, the need for a trusted instance beyond each individual operator arises, to share sensitive information with each other and to establish nationwide cyber-situational awareness for the critical infrastructures deployed on the national territory. The ECOSSIAN approach addresses this issue introducing N-SOCs.

To address the interdependencies between the critical infrastructures of different Member States, ECOSSIAN proposes an E-SOC as a third tier in its early warning and incident response/management framework. Given that the capabilities provided by the E-SOC are similar to those the N-SOC support, the N-SOC architecture is designed to meet the E-SOC requirements.

From a technical perspective, a comprehensive interconnection of O-SOCs and N-SOCs into the E-SOC is feasible and would allow near-real-time situational awareness of the European cybersecurity state of critical infrastructures (see Figure 9.5).

FURTHER INFORMATION

However, as discussed in Chapters 7 and 8, numerous regulatory and legal issues need to be considered when establishing such interconnections across different Member States, complying with diverse legislation.

Due to the inherent distributed nature at the level of the N-SOC, and even more at the level of the E-SOC, the provision of a central physical installation of each SOC is not viable. In many cases, this argument applies to the level of the O-SOC, because the underlying infrastructure has a highly distributed nature (e.g., power transmission networks, oil and gas infrastructures, or transport and logistics).

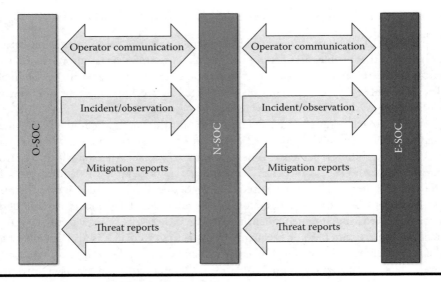

Figure 9.5   Cross-SOC information flow.

9.2.2.2 SOC Architecture

This section provides the overall concept for the three-level incident analysis network designed to allow horizontal information exchange at each of the individual SOC levels, as well as among the levels. On the one hand, the system needs to address all issues defined by the requirements specification (see previous section); on the other hand, the model has to be flexible enough, allowing individual and scalable implementations of all system aspects. This requires defining architectural elements and relations between these elements in an abstract manner and allowing subsequent customized implementation of each part depending on context and available resources. In order to reach that high level of abstraction, the concept of *functional blocks* (FBs) is introduced here.

Each FB is characterized by the typical functional behavior it exposes in a beacon context. If such functionality is too generic, diverse from its definition, or needs to be specialized in any way, subfunctions can be defined, which describe in detail the custom capabilities provided by the FB. Each function or subfunction is defined based on a single or set of requirements, guaranteeing a maximum set of system capabilities and supporting basic capabilities like inherent security capabilities.

In the diagram presented in Figure 9.6, an arrow indicates the direction of information flow between two FB. Blocks not connected by arrows are of general nature and are linked to all or several other FBs at the same SOC level.

The diagram in Figure 9.6 is applicable to each SOC level, meaning that from an abstract point of view all three levels can be modeled in a unique manner. Information exchange between different SOC levels occurs via interconnection

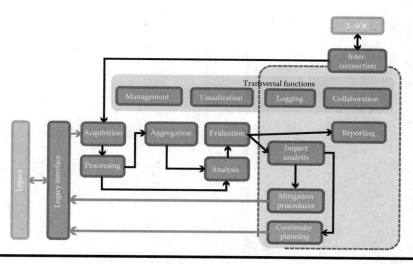

Figure 9.6 Functional block architecture applicable to SOC levels (ECOSSIAN Project Consortium, 2015).

blocks. Data accessible and sharable through the interconnection block is indicated by the dashed box.

Differentiation can be noticed when deriving concrete implementations (e.g., data acquired at different SOC levels will be of different nature, syntax, semantics, etc.). For example, raw data acquired at the O-SOC level is usually very detailed, closely related to the specific application or process implemented by the single CI. At the N-SOC or E-SOC level, the collected information is preprocessed and does not require further elaboration to be analyzed; interpretation of the collected information in terms of the impact on the national (or European) level can be directly performed; event-based procedures are used here for data acquisition.

ECOSSIAN FBs are technology independent and can be implemented within different software and hardware tools; they communicate with one another using different service paradigms (like polling, publish/subscribe, etc.) and are exposed by different interfaces and supported by diverse protocols.

Each tool, implemented at a given SOC level, can host an individual set of FB instances. If several FBs are implemented within a single host, local interfaces may exist not being accessible individually from outside the hosting tool.

9.2.2.3 Functional Blocks

This section lists the general characteristics provided by each individual FB, independent from the SOC level at which it is employed (Table 9.1). The main technologies adopted to instantiate these FBs at each SOC level are outlined in Section 9.4, where illustrative examples demonstrate how the FBs can be implemented in different application cases in different CI sectors.

Table 9.1 Description of Functional Blocks

Functional Block	General Description
Legacy interface	The FB "Legacy Interface" allows physical and logical access to an interface exposed by the system providing data to the ECOSSIAN system. "Legacy Interfaces" are of manifold nature. They may be unidirectional or bidirectional
Acquisition	The FB "Acquisition" is used to acquire data needed for analyzing the CI Systems status from different sources like networks, SCADA/ICS components, external sensors and other data sources dedicated to the "Legacy." At the N-SOC or E-SOC level, data may be acquired from other SOCs and from external sources such as OSINT. Data acquired is intended to be passed to the "Processing" component
Processing	The FB "Processing" receives data from the "Acquisition" FB. Data received by the "Processing" FB will be • Processed and transferred to the "Aggregation" FB • Processed and transferred to the "Analysis" FB or • Simply logged as raw data. Within the "Processing" FB, data is transformed into a format that can be treated by the ECOSSIAN system
Aggregation	The FB "Aggregation" collects data from different sources, such as • The "Processing" FB or • The "Logging" FB combines and possibly processes this data set according to specific rules and transfers it • To the "Analysis" FB or • To the "Logging" FB

(Continued)

Table 9.1 (*Continued*)   Description of Functional Blocks

Functional Block	General Description
Analysis	The main goal of the "Analysis" FB is to detect cyber threats that might affect the operation of SCADA, ICS, or interconnected information systems deployed in critical infrastructures in a timely manner. Depending on the SOC level, different types of data are used as input for the analysis. Whereas on O-SOC level data is analyzed for detecting threats within a dedicated control environment, N-SOC or E-SOC incidents detected at O-SOCs are analyzed to investigate more complex situations with the purpose of detecting threats affecting multiple CIs. Analysis may be performed with different levels of automation: • Automated analysis • Semiautomated analysis • Review by the human operator on duty • Review by the SOC expert team
Evaluation	The "Evaluation" FB consists of identifying abnormal situations, such as system degradations in terms of quality, performance, availability, or cyber attacks, with special focus on industrial automation and control systems and classifying information security incidents. The output of the "Evaluation" FB is sent to the "Impact Analysis" FB to assess direct and indirect adverse impacts on the operations
Logging	The "Logging" FB fulfils the task of • Storing data in a data storage over time and in relation to the data source (any other ECOSSIAN functional block). • Logging workflow. • Logging activities of operators. Information may be logged/stored in centralized or distributed databases. ECOSSIAN defines certain attributes (meta-data) attached to the data as required for fulfilling data analysis tasks. There are several services applicable for retrieving data from the storage

(Continued)

Table 9.1 (Continued) Description of Functional Blocks

Functional Block	General Description
Reporting	The "Reporting" FB provides the capability to improve alert information and enable a more accurate view of the vulnerabilities. It consists in • Early warning mechanisms. • Alert mechanisms and intelligent reporting to SOC operators. • Cybersecurity dashboards (ongoing incidents, level of threats, etc.) for executives. Reporting information, security vulnerabilities, events, and incidents must ensure, when required, anonymity
Impact analysis	The main task of the "Impact Analysis" FB is to identify the potential impact of an emerging threat. Impact analysis may be done in advance to be prepared in case a threat is detected, or "on-line" in case of an unforeseeable threat. Impact analysis is based on the characterization of a specific incident as well as of a CI-specific process and technical equipment knowledge. It is mainly performed by SOC expert teams
Mitigation procedure	The "Mitigation Procedures" FB receives data from the "Impact Analysis" FB in the case of attacks discovered by O-SOCs. Additionally, it can receive data from external SOCs through the "Inter-Connection" FB. There are two main functions for mitigation actions: The first function is for rapid mitigation actions based on incident information. This function lets the SOC expert team create preventive actions, based on standard operating procedures, as soon as possible, based on the received information. The second function stores information about incidents and derives new mitigation actions based on this stored information

(Continued)

Table 9.1 (*Continued*)   Description of Functional Blocks

Functional Block	General Description
Continuity planning	Continuity planning function implements an appropriate process around the ECOSSIAN framework and its associated O-SOC, N-SOC, and E-SOC stakeholders, applying an appropriate management system with human, process, and technology controls. This underpins the ability of ECOSSIAN operations to continue in the event of a significant disruption. This function has visibility of all components that comprise ECOSSIAN. This will include configurations, operating systems (OS), applications, and network devices
Visualization	The "Visualization" FB represents all means of interaction between the ECOSSIAN system and the operators at the respective SOC levels. Depending on the SOC level, different types of interfaces and presentation styles are used. Mobile visualization is dedicated to operators in the field at the O-SOC level. Here local operators work as a long arm of the O-SOC operator. A local operator is enabled to process ECOSSIAN data. This requires the visualization of local domain-specific data related to security incidents on the one hand and on the other hand the top-down notification from E-SOC and N-SOC levels
Interconnection	The "Interconnection" FB represents an interface supporting the information exchange between different SOCs of an ECOSSIAN system. As an elementary function, it provides the means for security (authentication, integrity check, or anonymization where applicable) and control depending on a security policy
Management	The "Management" FB has the tasks of monitoring and controlling the proper operation of the ECOSSIAN infrastructure at the respective SOC level
Collaboration	The "Collaboration" FB represents functionalities dedicated to inter-SOC collaboration, or with other related entities, information exchange for management, problem solving, training, or simply information exchange purposes

9.2.2.4 O-SOC Components

In this section the focus is drawn toward the components that, at the O-SOC level, implement the functional blocks previously introduced. A shown in Figure 9.7, several components are employed to provide acquisition and processing functions. Their main goal is to monitor and reveal in a timely manner any abnormal behavior occurring on different traits of the infrastructure, such as network traffic (by employing software tools such as BroLHG, BroIDS, and Nagios), the business process (with BPIDS), systems activities (using AECID), etc. Alarms generated at this stage are aggregated and analyzed by a centralized SIEM instance, which supports O-SOC human operators in the process of evaluating detected anomalies or potential threats. Further analysis capabilities are provided by advanced visualization components (like the hypervisor Cymerius) at the disposal of the O-SOC security managers, as well as on mobile devices used by on-site operators. When an incident occurs and is detected, the O-SOC team examines it and decides whether to report it to the N-SOC.

In this case an incident message in IODEF[2] (Incident Object Description Exchange Format) format is generated by the operator employing the hypervisor (Cymerius); it is opportunely encrypted (through the attribute-based encryption component) and exported, through a secure gateway (SGW) implementing the interconnection functionality. The message is received and decrypted by its counterpart at the N-SOC level.

9.2.2.5 N-SOC and E-SOC Components

Similar functionalities are provided at the national and European levels; for this reason, the main system components employed at these levels are identical; their configuration and their adoption are however tailored to the specific level. This section refers to the workflow governing the incident analysis and response processes in place at the N-SOC; the E-SOC implements similar procedures, on a higher abstraction level.

As depicted in Figure 9.8, the acquisition function at the N-SOC is implemented through a series of importing components, which in turn collect and aggregate data from a number of different sources including the O-SOCs running at the CIs deployed on the national territory, secret services, national CERTs, any other national relevant authorities, other affiliated N-SOCs, as well as Open Source Intelligence (OSINT) feeds.

Incident reports in IODEF format are received from the O-SOCs; STIX format is adopted for threat information (cf. Chapter 5), while generic open standards and formats are adopted for vulnerability reports (such as CVE[3]), security

---

[2] https://www.ietf.org/rfc/rfc5070.txt.
[3] https://cve.mitre.org/.

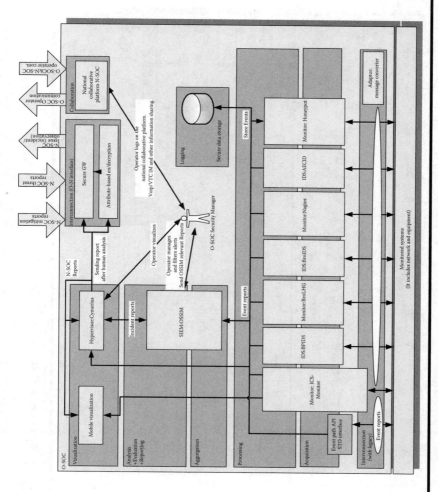

Figure 9.7 O-SOC architecture (Settanni, G. et al., 2016).

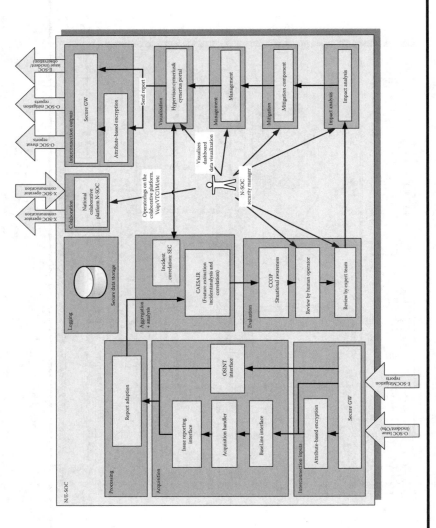

Figure 9.8   N/E-SOC architecture (Settanni, G. et al., 2016).

bulletins (such as Microsoft Security Bulletins[4] and US-CERT bulletins[5]) and any other security relevant intelligence collected here. The incident reports issued by the O-SOC are carefully analyzed and thoroughly examined by the N-SOC expert team. The security managers adopt advanced correlation software tools (e.g., CAESAIR[6]) to quickly identify implicit relations between the collected information, suitably evaluate connections through occurred events, and perform impact analysis. Once the security managers pinpoint the mitigation procedures that need to be put in place by the affected CIs to counter the reported incident, a detailed advisory is produced and forwarded to the corresponding O-SOCs, after being opportunely encrypted, through the SGW. If a threat is suspected to span across the national borders, or national security is at stake, N-SOC managers file a corresponding threat report and forward it to the E-SOC, where strategic decision-making occurs.

9.3 Roles, Responsibilities, and Processes within the National TI Framework

This section presents the organizational dimension of a national TI framework, drawn from the theoretical Cyber Intelligence Centre (CIC) framework (Pahi, 2016), focusing on the necessary roles and responsibilities for enhancing cyber-security in international, national, and organizational scope. This three-layered approach maps to the hierarchical architecture of the ECOSSIAN ecosystem presented in the previous sections. The framework assumes that all actors gain their own cyber-situational awareness (CSA) and create CCOPs (cf. Chapter 6). Given that CI providers and ICT companies are largely owned by private organizations, a strong PPP (cf. Chapter 7) plays a key role in this context. Various strategies and guidelines recommend the establishment of centralized cyber centers in the national and international scope. The centers have different names worldwide; they can be organized as SOCs (like in ECOSSIAN), CERTs, CSIRTs, or Cyber Defense Centers (CDCs).

This section refers to this concept with the term *CIC* in order to distinguish this framework from other approaches. These authorities have the required expertise and assets important to the state in the delivery of the goals usually set in their respective National Cybersecurity Strategies (NCSS). They provide incident response services to attack victims, share information regarding cybersecurity, and offer help or recommendations to improve computer and network security in the public and private sectors. These entities are very different in every state; the

---

[4] https://technet.microsoft.com/en-us/security/bulletins.aspx.
[5] https://www.us-cert.gov/ncas/bulletins.
[6] http://caesair.ait.ac.at.

theoretical framework described here presents one possible way without implying any obligations.

9.3.1 The CIC Framework

The framework describes the potential functionality of a CIC and gives guidance on cross-domain cooperation between private or public organizations and the CIC at the national level. The CIC and its frameworks need to be flexible and adaptable to allow governments to opportunely address the necessary steps to implement their NCSSs. The presented CIC Framework provides an approach to enhance cyber-situational awareness at the national level and to protect critical infrastructures. The following section offers guidance to nation-states in enhancing cyber resilience at the national level and in developing CICs.

The general goals, based on the wide range of existing NCSS, and on the evaluation of the European Union Agency for Network and Information Security (ENISA, 2014), are the following:

- Achieve cyber resilience
- Secure critical information infrastructures (CIIs)
- Tackle cybercrime
- Raise and maintain awareness
- Support economic and social development
- Develop industrial and technological resources for cybersecurity
- Develop national and international partnerships

In accordance with the objectives set in the NCSSs, the CIC Framework presents the following principal purposes:

- Providing a national framework for securing the cyberspace (CTO, 2014)
- Enhancing cyber resilience and preparedness
- Building PPP to promote the safety and security of CIs
- Building international partnerships to address cross-border cybercrime

The purpose of cyber-situational awareness is the support of strategic and political decision-making on the national level in order to strengthen the cybersecurity and resilience of infrastructures. Developing a picture of the national situation is a complex process. The main goal of cyber-situational awareness is to process and present all the relevant cyber incident information from the relevant public and private organizations, in order to gain a holistic view of the cyber situation and threat landscape. The purpose of data collecting is to process the relevant information in order to identify new trends at an early stage and prevent the potential escalation at the national level. The CIC Framework is designed for cooperation and efficient collaboration among all relevant public and private stakeholders and building on existing initiatives to avoid duplicating efforts and promote cybersecurity. This presented concept reconsiders security around five focal points:

- Contemporary multilevel data processing
- Proper communication channels
- Visualization-enhanced decision-making
- Early warning
- Holistic mitigation measures

The implemented design approach for the CIC Framework aims to be derived from a risk-based assessment that considers the assets and services that are essential to the state in the delivery of its national strategic goals. Risk-based means to assess risks by identifying threats, vulnerabilities, and consequences and then manage the risks through mitigations, controls and similar measures (CTO, 2015). Implementing this risk-based design approach helps to put the preventive and mitigating measures into practice.

9.3.2 Abstraction Level in the CIC Framework

The framework defines national priorities and assigns roles and responsibilities with the required resources. Stakeholders and partner organizations at different levels are the backbone of the relevant information exchange. The framework allows information to be shared among the public and private sectors in a structured manner, in order to provide a greater understanding of CSA derived from information about vulnerabilities, intrusions, incidents, mitigation, and recovery actions. The regular information exchange among the stakeholders in the international scope is required to gain cross-border CSA and to identify complex relationships and interdependencies. The nation-states are not isolated from each other anymore, especially not relating to critical resources and infrastructures. Also, international cooperation and regulations can minimize the risk for the participating Member States. The ENISA offers, for instance, recommendations on cybersecurity and supports the policy development and its implementation in the participating EU Member States. The nation-states have numerous mutual interactions with international stakeholders, such as the European Union, international law enforcement agencies and regulations, or the global security community. Possible information sources are the following in this scope: guidelines and recommendations of international organizations, internationally recognized standards and good practices, national cybersecurity reports from other nation-states, international reports of cross-border authorities (such as Europol, Interpol databases related to the cyber domain), etc.

FURTHER INFORMATION: THE CIC FRAMEWORK

The CIC Framework foresees three different spheres of interest: the international, the national, and the organizational scope.

The *international scope* covers the international security community.

The *national scope* forms the national nexus for cybersecurity issues with the leading role of the CIC.

The framework divides this center into two levels: *strategic* and *tactical*.

The CIC provides a centralized platform for cyber experts to collaborate with the relevant stakeholders in a trusted environment. The key employees of the CIC are the cyber threat analysts of the National Incident Response Team (NIRT). The narrowest scope is the *organizational scope,* divided into three different levels, namely, *executive, business,* and *implementation.*

The main objective of the three-layered CIC Framework is to gain nationwide CSA through Cyber Situational Pictures (CSPs) in order to support high-level decision-making relating to cyber incidents affecting the national security.

Every stakeholder has his own obligations and liabilities as integral part of the multilateral process of securing cyberspace. The CIC Framework focuses on the connection between the international security community and the National Security Council through international negotiations (see Figure 9.9). An example for the international negotiations is the EU NIS Directive (European Commission, 2016) relating to enhancing cybersecurity (cf. Chapter 7).

The framework divides the *national scope* into two levels, into strategic and tactical level. The relevant stakeholders within the national scope are the National Security Council (NSC) and the CIC. The NSC belongs to the strategic level; the CIC belongs to the tactical level of the national scope. The NSC is usually the main forum for coordinating national security issues and high-level decision-making on matters related to homeland security, including the protection of essential critical infrastructures using ICT. The NSC should be steered by experts from the most relevant domains, such as senior members and government authorities, sector-specific agencies, legislative authorities, law enforcement agencies, and the CI providers of the public and private sector related to cybersecurity. In order to gain a holistic picture of the cyber situation and the state of the CIs, the CIC develops CCOPs with different aspects and statistics for increasing the CSA and enhancing appropriate decision-making at the strategic level.

The Cyber Intelligence Centre (CIC) provides a centralized platform for cyber experts to collaborate with the relevant stakeholders in a trusted environment.

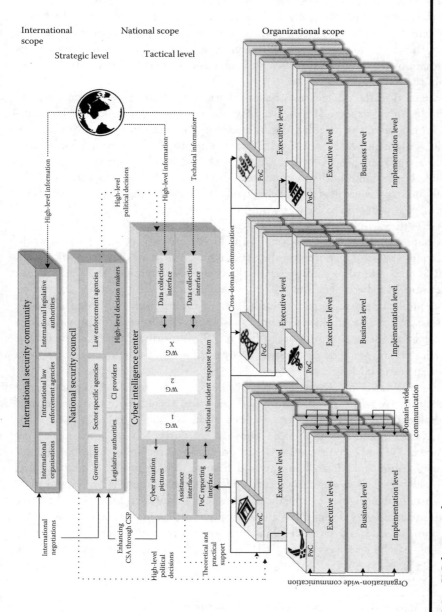

Figure 9.9 CIC framework.

The Centre is authorized to collect information, to undertake formal investigations regarding large-scale cyber attacks, to warn potential victim organizations and to manage incident response activities. Key employees of the CIC are the cyber threat analysts of the NIRT. The information management processes of the NIRT span across the data collection interfaces on two levels, namely, the tactical level with technical information and the strategic level with high-level information. This information needs to be correlated to enable proper cyber intelligence activities within the CIC.

The tactical data correlation processes use special and concrete data related to the technical aspects of cybersecurity, such as the details about vulnerabilities; for example, that the Bar Mitzvah security vulnerability takes advantage of the RC4 algorithm used in the TLS and SSL protocols.[7] The strategic information management processes use abstract and high-level information about the possible background and consequences of cyber attacks, such as the list of the widely used network devices at CI providers. Malware targeting a specific network device widely used by CIs would have a significant impact on the critical infrastructures, for instance SYNful Knock Malware for special Cisco devices (cf. Chapter 2). The threat analysts of the NIRT are divided into various working groups (WGs) depending on the cyber issue or incident they are working on. The CIC has a kind of interpreter role between the technical and the political dimension in cyberspace. The CIC provides theoretical support for all participating public or private organizations. In crisis situation, the NSC can authorize the CIC to provide additional practical support for targeted CI providers (see practical and theoretical support in Figure 9.9). In normal operation the CIC is not allowed to intervene in companies' operations, just to collect reports from the organizational scope.

The organizational scope contains the public and private CI providers in a country. The providers are divided into CI domains according to the categories of the national critical infrastructures, defined in the NCSS.

The CIC Framework applies the following categorization of CI providers: electric power, oil and gas distribution, transportation systems, information technology and communications, banking and finance, public health and healthcare, emergency services, water, agriculture and food, government facilities and military installation. Figure 9.9 illustrates just a few CI domains with several sample organizations. Every domain has a (single) point of contact (PoC) responsible for the domain-wide and cross-domain communication and information sharing. The PoC can be a sector-specific CERT, such as the Austrian Energy CERT[8] (cf. Chapter 5).

---

[7] NIST—National Vulnerability Database, Vulnerability Summary for CVE-2015-2808, https://web.nvd.nist.gov/view/vuln/detail?vulnId=CVE-2015-2808, Last accessed on July 22, 2016.

[8] https://cert.at/reports/report_2016_chap06/content.html. Last accessed on February 21, 2017.

EXAMPLE: TRUSTWORTHY REPORTING IN ECOSSIAN

The ECOSSIAN ecosystem employs specific components to enable trustworthy and efficient incident reporting from operational SOCs (which can also be grouped in a sectorial SOC) to the national PoC (i.e., the N-SOC) and response in the opposite direction. Advanced encryption techniques made available by the ABE module operating in the interconnection FB, anonymization methods, and secure communication channels established by the SGW allow the achievement of this goal.

The participating organizations report their incidents through the PoC reporting interface to the CIC in order to establish the nationwide CSA.

The organizational scope is not described in detail in this section, since every organization can have different structures. In the CIC framework the organizational scope is divided into three different stages: executive, business, and implementation. Handling cybersecurity incidents in the organizational scope has a considerably higher maturity level than in the national scope. Stakeholders of the executive level are able to understand the effects of the vulnerable elements in the infrastructure in the organization. They are in charge of strategic (investment) decisions and future implementations in the company.

The business level receives notifications about a critical incident that could not be solved by the technical team at the implementation level or that might have a larger impact. Their tasks cover threat analysis, event classification, and report generation about cyber incidents. The business level bridges the executive and the implementation levels. There can be any number of levels, but the business management directly above the implementation level is responsible for whether a current incident should be reported to the executive level or the incident is below a critical threshold. The *implementation level* is the lowest level in the organizational scope. The main goal at this level is technical data collection, asset management, infrastructure monitoring, and anomaly detection. They are responsible for enabling the uninterrupted operation of the key technical system and services within an organization. Decisions at this level relate to the day-to-day tasks of running business infrastructures. The level in the organizational scope has a strict hierarchy, but flexible communication channels between levels.

These scopes and their stakeholders are the basis for a working CIC Framework in cyberspace. The roles, responsibilities, and information channels regarding the national scope are discussed in the following section. These descriptions contain only recommendations and refer to the CIC Framework.

9.3.3 Roles and Responsibility in the National Scope

The government is responsible for protecting the nation's critical infrastructures against physical and cyber attacks. Information sharing is a key part of the government's mission to create cyber-situational awareness of nationwide malicious cyber activity. The absence of consolidated monitoring systems of national critical infrastructures' stability in near real-time jeopardizes national cybersecurity. The ECOSSIAN project aims, as discussed in the previous sections, to fill this gap. Gaining CSA includes a process for collecting, correlating, analyzing, and sharing cyber incident information across the private and governmental sector for protecting the national critical infrastructures. By collecting information from participating organizations, the related responsible agencies can build and enhance national cyber-situational awareness. Diverse legal spaces motivate the need for a formal partnership, for example in a form of a NCSC or NSC (cf. Chapter 7). In the CIC Framework the national scope comprises these entities. The scope is divided into two levels (strategic and tactical) and consists of (among others) governmental and private organizations, the intelligence community, and law enforcement.

In the following sections discuss the roles and responsibilities of the main national stakeholders on both strategic and tactical levels, as summarized in Table 9.2.

Table 9.2 Roles and Responsibilities in the National Scope

Level	Strategic	Tactical
Stakeholder	NSC	NIRT
Role	Provide a strategic platform for cooperation between the members of the relevant state actors	Provide a collaborative platform for authorized cyber experts to collaborate with each other in a trusted environment
Responsibilities	- Share and exchange information in international and national cooperation - Obtain a holistic view about the cyber situation - Prepare action plans for extensive cyber attacks - Adapt the legal framework and institutional dynamically to the threats - Trace criminals and prosecutions - Expand national expertise and national CSA of information security	- Create CCOPs for the decision makers - Early warning: warn possibly affected organizations - Enrich proprietary cyber threat intelligence data to see the context - Assist Organizations

9.3.3.1 National Scope at the Strategic Level

The primary stakeholder is the National Security Council at the strategic level. The *NSC* provides a strategic platform for cooperation between the members of the relevant state actors:

- *Government*, such as representatives of the Ministry of the Interior or Ministry of Defense
- *Law enforcement*, such as the Cyber Crime Department of the police
- *Legislative authorities*, for instance members of the NSC (or equivalent, depending on the political structures)
- *Sector-specific agencies*, such as the Cyber Competence Centers and sector-specific CERTs
- *CI providers*, for instance, the representatives of the essential companies in each domain

At the strategic level, an NSC is responsible for long-term decision-making. The mission of the NSC is to reduce the severity of cyber incidents that may significantly compromise the security and resilience of the national critical infrastructure and communication network. This mission defines the CSA framework's specific contribution to achieving the goal described above. To execute the mission effectively, the NSC will focus on the following objectives (U.S. Department of Justice, 2015).

9.3.3.1.1 Share and Exchange Information in International and National Cooperation

Given that cyber threats often occur in parallel, exploiting similar vulnerable circumstances, and spread simultaneously in different locations, nations could learn from each other and efficiently acquire cyber-situational awareness. Each nation may have different cultural, legal, and political backgrounds and therefore slightly different approaches to establish cyber-situational awareness. National capacity building should be considered as an investment, a commitment, and a valuable opportunity for fostering partnerships with international security councils. The NSC should also facilitate relationships among countries developing cybersecurity capacities and promote the sharing of best practices, lessons learned, and international technical exchanges. For instance, a yearly Cyber Security Awareness Report, such as the annual ENISA reports for telecommunication providers (ENISA, 2016), could provide awareness or solicit feedback from critical infrastructure owners, integrators, and operators concerning ongoing cyber events or activities with the potential to impact computing networks in critical infrastructures.

9.3.3.1.2 Obtain a Holistic View about the Cyber Situation

For the NSC to make correct strategic decisions, it must account for the current data interpretation from the tactical level. Decision makers should use the international internal reports and other international external sources to build proper cyber-situational awareness. The NSC should promote interoperable and reliable information and communication infrastructures that support national cooperation and strengthen cybersecurity.

9.3.3.1.3 Prepare Action Plans for Extensive Cyber Attacks

The NSC (and the executives in organizations) should have an incident-handling plan before large-scale or high-impact cyber attacks occur. During an extensive cyber attack, national stakeholders should focus on containing the intrusion, mitigating the damage, and collecting and preserving essential information that will help to assess the scope and the nature of the harm and the potential source of the cyber threat. The plan should provide specific, concrete procedures that in the event of an attack will:

- Address the responsibilities for different elements of a cyber incident response (e.g., NSC is responsible for strategic decision-making, PoC of the expert team for public communications, IT department on organization for information technology, IT employees for the implementation of security measures).
- Contact the list of critical personnel.
- Select backup critical personnel.
- Prioritize mission critical data, network, and services for effective protection.
- Preserve data related to the cyber attack for forensic analysis.
- Define criteria to ascertain who should be notified in case of an advanced cyber attack.
- Define notifying procedures.

All stakeholders should have access and familiarity with the plan, particularly members who play a role in strategic and tactical decisions during a national incident. The plan may also include regularly conducted exercises to ensure that the plan is proper and current.

9.3.3.1.4 Adapt the Legal Framework and Institution Dynamically to the Threats

Cyber incidents can raise several legal questions (for more information about legal issues, see Chapter 8). An organization faced with decisions about how to interact with government agents, its obligation to report the loss of customer information

(European Commission, 2016; Senate and House of Representatives of the United States of America, 2015), the types of protection technologies it can lawfully use, and its potential accountability for taking specific remedial measures will benefit from obtaining legal guidance from lawyers who are conversant with technology and knowledge about relevant laws. National stakeholders should attempt to establish a relationship with the federal law enforcement offices before an advanced cyber incident happens. Having a PoC and a good relationship with law enforcement will facilitate any subsequent interaction.

Cybersecurity on a national scale will require internationally agreed norms of state behavior, effective law enforcement, measures that build confidence and enhance transparency, appropriate deterrence, and the right to self-defend. Statutory provision should require private and public organizations to share cyber incident and risk data with the NIRT (which might be implemented by the national CERT) to accomplish a collective and collaborative information sharing and early warning framework.

9.3.3.1.5 Tracing Criminals and Prosecutions

In the cyber domain, the current state of practice regarding the technical ability to trace cyber attacks is primitive at best. Sophisticated attacks can be almost impossible to trace back to their routes. The anonymity leveraged by today's cyber attackers poses a heavy threat to the global information society, the prosperity of the information-based economy, and the advancement of global collaboration and cooperation (Lipson, 2002). Nation-states should identify and trace cyber criminals, ensure laws and practices deny criminals' safe havens, and cooperate with international crime investigation, e.g., Europol and Interpol, in a timely manner.

9.3.3.1.6 Expand National Expertise and National Cyber-Situational Awareness of Information Security

Almost a third of the world's population uses the Internet; there are more than four billion digital wireless devices in the world today (Obama, 2010). The NSC should build new initiatives to share information among government, key industries, critical infrastructure sectors, other stakeholders, and citizens.

Many of the activities that contribute to protecting national critical infrastructures from cyber attacks will be coordinated and developed collaboratively with strategic partners, such as the NIRT of the CIC.

9.3.3.1.7 Information Sources at the Strategic Level
Developing a picture of the national situation is a tedious process. The main goal of cyber-situational awareness is to process and present all the relevant technical data from the operational and technical levels in order to gain a holistic view about the cyber situation.

The NSC has both external and internal information sources. The primary internal information sources are the CCOP (for more information see Chapter 6) created by the WGs of the NIRT in the CIC.

9.3.3.2 National Scope at Tactical Level

In contrast to long-term strategic decisions, tactical decisions usually help to *implement the strategy* developed at higher levels. The tactical level, with the guiding role of the CIC and its *NIRT, provides a collaborative platform for authorized cyber experts to collaborate with each other in a trusted environment.* The NIRT is a high-level expert group that assesses cyber threats and risks, responds to a cyber incident so that the network can recover as fast as possible and avoid potential future incidents. The members of the NIRT include threat analysts and *PoC* for every CI domain (see the PoCs in Figure 9.9). They provide guidance in each domain and across all domains. Threat analysts of the NIRT are trained to identify anomalous activities and focus on detecting extensive attacks and advanced persistent threats (APTs) crossing several organizations or domains. At the tactical level, the NIRT is responsible for internal and external data collection, incident classification, early warning, and nationwide rapid cyber incident response.

The *threat analysts* and/or security analysts of the NIRT are responsible for analyzing and assessing existing vulnerabilities in the IT infrastructure (software, hardware, and networks), investigating available tools and countermeasures to fix identified failures and vulnerabilities, and suggesting solutions and best practices. A threat analyst also analyzes and assesses damage as a result of security incidents, examines available recovery tools and processes, and recommends solutions. Analysts check for compliance with security policies and procedures and may assist in the development, implementation, or management of certain cyber solutions (Albanese and Jajodia, 2014). They are divided into different working groups organized by cyber incidents or CI domains. The CIC and its NIRT have the following tasks and objectives.

9.3.3.2.1 Create CCOPs for the Decision Makers

The main objective of the NIRT is creating structured CCOPs (see description in Section 9.3.3.1) in order to enhance strategic decision-making in the NSC. Near real-time report and CCOP generation with increased quality, concerning the incident, vulnerabilities in the system, and further potential victims is essential in the CIC Framework. The CIC analyzes the received data from the organizations in near real time and promptly notifies involved organizations about identified IoCs. After detecting and identifying anomalies at the national level, the analysts are able to forecast upcoming threats and risks. The primary objective of the reporting is to discover ongoing threats by analyzing internal and OSINT for evidences of suspicious activities associated with a predefined set of targets to present an accurate CCOP and establish situational awareness for strategic decision-making.

9.3.3.2.2 Early Warning: Warn Possibly Affected Organizations

Early warning is a key component in minimizing the harmful effect of cyber attacks. The primary information source is the channel between the organizations and the CIC through the *PoC reporting interface* (see Figure 9.9). Based on the reports relating to cyber incidents, the CIC can create CCOPs and monitor the protection level of the critical infrastructures in the country. The CIC processes the reports from the organizations in order to identify common failures and trends within a sector and notifies the possibly affected organizations within the domain and potentially connected other domains. *Early warnings* and alerts provide timely notification to critical infrastructure owners and operators concerning threats to critical infrastructure networks.

9.3.3.2.3 Enrich Proprietary Cyber Threat Intelligence Data to See the Context

The CIC provides *near-real-time situational awareness of emerging cyber incidents* to support critical decision-making at the strategic level. This is done by analyzing numerous internal and external information sources daily. The data comprehension must combine recent information with already existing knowledge to produce a holistic picture of the CI situation as it evolves at the national level. This additional data input is the *OSINT* for completing the CCOP (see OSINT marked with the world icon in Figure 9.9). The open-source environment is turning more complex, and knowing where and how to look for information is critical to gain appropriate cyber-situational awareness. OSINT refers to the intelligence that can be gained from open or public sources and from which new information of interest can be derived (Polancich, 2015). Public sources are, for instance, newspapers or scientific studies websites, search engines, forums, IRC channels, blogs, social networks, places in the Deep Web, etc. Notice, while, e.g., ENISA does not require deep technical details for creating overview reports about the status of the implementation of national cybersecurity strategies, the CIC needs both high-level information to understand the context and technical information in order to describe the techniques of recent cyber attacks. Therefore, open source data is an integral part of the threat intelligence and the CCOP (Polancich, 2015).

9.3.3.2.4 Assistance for Organizations

The NIRT WGs of the CIC provide assistance for victim organizations in order to accelerate the recovery processes when the organization needs help. In this case, the NIRT could share open and trusted best practices, lessons learned, or white papers through the *assistance interface* (see Figure 9.9) with the affected organization. If needed, the NIRT provides additional assistance, such as creating tailored solutions or providing technical support locally. The victim organization should record all the steps taken to mitigate damage. This information is essential for recovering from damages, preventing similar attacks in the future, and crime investigation. Additionally, periodically the NIRT publishes best practices against the recent cyber threats and makes them available for reading and downloading for the participating organizations.

9.3.3.2.5 Information Sources for CSA at the Tactical Level

A wide range of information sources is processed by the CIC. The incident reports of the organizations serve as the primary internal information source. These reports cover the description of incident-related events, including dates and times, information about the affected networks and components within the organization, information relating to the nature and scope of damage inflicted by cyber attacks, and occasionally information about the possible effect on the national CIs or other potential victim organizations. A secondary information source is made up of reports from other NCSCs.

The main external information source is the OSINT with its huge amount of data covering—among other things—specialized portals, government resource guides, and official government sites, business, legal and economics portals, various search engines, blogs, forums and social network records about past and future attacks, patches, CVE data, breach databases, exploit databases, mailing lists, and subscriptions. Besides the open source information, data mining from the Dark and Deep Webs might also uncover valuable information.

9.3.4 Application of CIC Framework to the ECOSSIAN Ecosystem

The main aim of the CIC Framework is gaining accurate cyber-situational awareness, at different levels, by collecting and analyzing information from various sources. The framework provides a three-layered approach, and, as depicted in Figure 9.10, maps the ECOSSIAN hierarchical ecosystem.

The levels can be seamlessly matched as follows: the ECOSSIAN E-SOC correspond to the International Security Community within the international scope, the N-SOC concerns the CIC at the national scope, and the O-SOCs matches the CI domains in the organizational scope. While the ECOSSIAN research project focused mostly on designing the system architecture, developing all the required technical components, as well as defining the procedures to set up an European incident analysis network, the CIC Framework defines the necessary

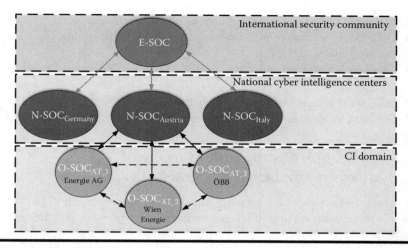

Figure 9.10   CIC-ECOSSIAN layers mapping.

roles and responsibilities of the involved actors, in order to protect CIs by detecting cyber incidents and in a timely manner generate and distribute early warnings to the potentially affected infrastructures. The CIC framework offers guidance to nation-states in enhancing cyber resilience at the national level and in developing their cyber capabilities in accordance with the European NIS Directive (European Commission, 2016).

9.4 Description of Application Cases for the EU FP7 Project ECOSSIAN

This section illustrates three different application cases in which the ECOSSIAN approach can be adopted to protect CIs, operating in different sectors, against common types of security threats and the cyber attacks targeting them. All the following scenarios have been implemented and demonstrated in the piloting phase of the ECOSSIAN project. The first two use cases have a national scope and show how the ECOSSIAN components employed at the O-SOC and N-SOC level can be leveraged to detect specific attacks and promptly react to them. The last case has a European scope; it involves several national SOCs, demonstrating how coordinated cross-country information sharing can be beneficial to reduce the impact of potentially disruptive threats and obtain European situational awareness.

The scenarios illustrated in this section assume a different connotation with respect to those described in Chapter 2. There a series of modern attack scenarios is analyzed; here we outline how the concepts and components developed within the ECOSSIAN project can be employed in realistic application cases to

- Efficiently detect realistic cyber attacks targeting different CIs.
- Collect and exchange relevant evidence among cooperating organizations and national SOCs.
- Thoroughly analyze and correlate the available TI to react to occurring incidents.
- Mitigate the impact of revealed incidents.
- Establish local, national, and European cyber-situational awareness.

9.4.1 Application Case 1: Early Warning of Attacks on Financial Infrastructures

In this application case, an external attacker gets access to the internal network of a financial institution by compromising an employee's PC. The attack is detected by the ECOSSIAN probes and, thanks to the support of the N-SOC, the institution's SOC operators are able to stop the intrusion. Moreover, the N-SOC establishes national situational awareness and warns similar critical infrastructures, providing them with the necessary information to cope with similar attacks in the future.

9.4.1.1 Context

This demonstration scenario shows how ECOSSIAN enables the early detection of a complex attack targeting the solvency department of a fictitious financial critical infrastructure named PIT. The solvency refers to an enterprise's financial health status, to the capacity to meet its long-term financial commitments. That is the reason the uncontrolled disclosure of the solvency of a company could have severe impacts, potentially leading to the complete disruption of its business. This scenario has been designed so that incidents and events match current threats that pose a real danger to today's financial institutions.

9.4.1.2 Scenario Description

The scenario evolves through three stages: attack, detection, and response. In the first stage, an external attacker gains access to PIT's internal network by compromising an employee's PC through a spear phishing attack. The attack is then detected by the ECOSSIAN probes, during the second stage, and hence, with the support of the N-SOC, the O-SOC operators stop the intrusion in the third stage.

The target of the attack demonstrated in this scenario is the internal network of a financial company, which is based on existing systems, technologies, and organizational structures typically employed in modern financial institutions (see Figure 9.11).

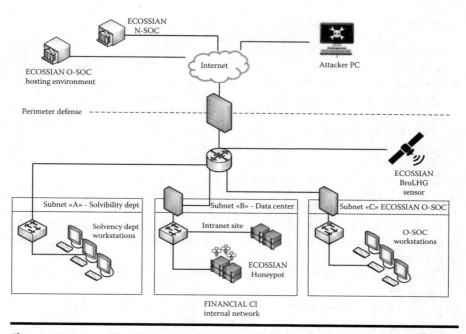

Figure 9.11 Application Case 1-demonstration setup (ECOSSIAN Project Consortium, 2017).

9.4.1.2.1 Stage 1: Attack

After retrieving, through social engineering, detailed information about a carefully identified PIT employee, the attacker crafts a malicious targeted HTML e-mail for the victim. The victim receives this spear phishing e-mail, and, by clicking on a button included in the e-mail, he downloads malicious software that infects his machine by exploiting a zero-day vulnerability. The attacker can now see and record everything happening on the compromised PC. The attacker is able to steal the credential of his victim, which allows him to penetrate the internal network of the company.

The attacker explores the corporate network trying to identify machines that host critical services. He also seeks and discovers vulnerabilities exploitable to gain higher privileges. As a result of the exploration, the attacker obtains knowledge about the exact corporate network topology, including the addresses of strategic and vulnerable machines. The attacker identifies a server class machine, scans it for known vulnerabilities, finds one and exploits it to gain administrative privileges; he therefore accesses the data stored on the server and exfiltrates sensitive information useful for further exploitation and fraud.

9.4.1.2.2 Stage 2: Detection

In the second stage, the attacker's activity raises alarms while further exploring the organization's infrastructure. The corporate network is monitored by ECOSSIAN sensors that detect isolated and uncorrelated *evidence* related to the running attack.

As shown in Figure 9.12, the first evidence is revealed by the threat detection sensor named *BroLHG*,[9] which detects unusual network traffic between the employee's compromised PC and the targeted server (see Chapter 3 for further details on network-based anomaly detection approaches). BroLHG triggers a warning-level alarm that is received by the O-SOC[10] (see arrow number 1 in Figure 9.12). As in any SOC infrastructure, a SIEM solution is deployed to centrally aggregate and correlate sensor events; in all the demonstrated scenarios *OSSIM*[11] is adopted as open source SIEM. ECOSSIAN does not intend to replace SIEM tools; it rather provides additional and complementary means to improve reliability in the detection, give a better level of understanding, and make the SOC team save time in the incident resolution process.

The alarms triggered by BroLHG are aggregated by OSSIM (arrow number 2 in Figure 9.12), which in turn forwards the evaluated alarms to Cymerius.[12] The O-SOC operator becomes aware of the situation by looking at the Cymerius' synoptic view: observing the incoming alarms the operator notices that they are caused by a corporate database server generating suspiciously large network traffic toward an employee's host machine. At the same time, the operator is notified, within Cymerius, about additional alarms triggered by another ECOSSIAN probe, the Honeypot[13] (arrow number 3), and aggregated by OSSIM (arrow

---

[9] The *BroLHG* sensor is one of the threat detection sensor prototypes developed in ECOSSIAN. It is based on Bro IDS (https://www.bro.org/) and provides network behavioral monitoring capabilities. It allows determining whether the detected monitored traffic is benign, by comparing it with previously observed network traffic patterns. If suspicious communications are detected, an alert message is sent to the SIEM.

[10] The O-SOC operators supervise the security issues of the company's IT infrastructure. Adopting the ECOSSIAN solutions, these operators have the ability to get a real-time view on the cybersecurity state of the controlled network and processes.

[11] *OSSIM*: https://www.alienvault.com/products/ossim (Last accessed on November 2016).

[12] *Cymerius* is a situation awareness solution used within a SOC. Cymerius allows O-SOC operators to be alerted when a new incident is reported; it proposes an incident view linked with a business impact evaluation; it provides situational overview and proposes courses of action. http://www.airbusds-optronics.com/web/guest/1299.html (Last accessed on November 2016).

[13] The Honeypot is another detection method developed in ECOSSIAN. It is able to detect APT attacks in discovery and capture phases. First, it discovers current machines available in the network segment and identifies for each the operating system and services provided (open ports). It then randomly generates virtual honeypots using this information in order to simulate the same services/operating systems. Finally, when the virtual honeypots are deployed, the honeypot hypervisor detects any communication attempts (Link layer and above) to those virtual honeypots and raises an alarm to the O-SOC.

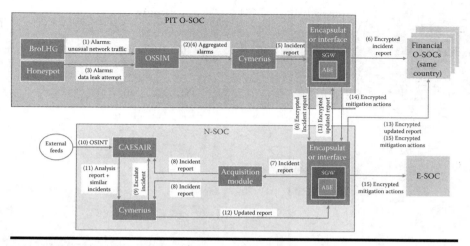

Figure 9.12   Application 1: detection and reaction flowchart.

number 4). The attacker is indeed additionally trying to leak further information he believes to be critical, from one of the deployed honeypots, which simulates a database server, and to which the attacker has previously obtained access. The ECOSSIAN *Honeypot* probe detects these attempts and warns the O-SOC operator with alert messages.

While still investigating the alarm triggered by the BroLHG sensor, the O-SOC operator receives a new series of alerts on the O-SOC console. In the Cymerius' incident view, an aggregation rule is automatically triggered as many alarms and updates of the situation are sent by the OSSIM instance. This reproduces a common situation that SOC operators face every day. In this particular case, the large number of alarms and the single source of scans strongly indicate that an attack is currently ongoing.

9.4.1.2.3 Stage 3: Incident Response

In the third stage, the O-SOC operator investigates the incident and validates the warnings received from the ECOSSIAN detection tools. Cymerius displays the aggregated incident messages to O-SOC security analysts who decide to investigate such an uncommon internal attack (see Figure 9.13).

A course of actions defined by PIT within its cybersecurity policy, and modeled into Cymerius, is proposed to the SOC operator. The SOC operator is then guided in the resolution process as well as in the process of sharing relevant information with the N-SOC. Once the analysis has been completed by the O-SOC team, a descriptive report is written and attached to one of the aggregated incidents.

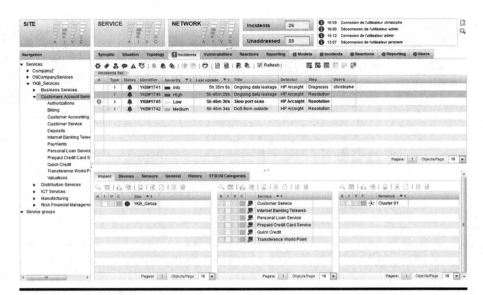

Figure 9.13 Cymerius dashboard presents to the O-SOC operator the list of detected incidents. ©Airbus.

The operator uploads the report through the *encapsulator interface*[14] and sends it to the N-SOC via the SGW[15] (arrow number 5 in Figure 9.12).

O-SOC operators select the list of SOCs to receive the incident reports they export, as well as the security level of the incident by setting its security domain (EU, IT, DE, etc.), and classification (PUBLIC, RESTRICTED, CONFIDENTIAL, SECRET, etc.). The O-SOC operator can also use the ABE module[16] (Bethencourt et al., 2007) to enforce the access control on the incident report and ensure that, in this case, only national CIs belonging to the financial sector may decrypt the received report (arrow number 6).

The incident report goes through the *acquisition module* (AM),[17] which acts as means of incident and threat reports collection (arrow number 7). The incident is then imported into the Cymerius instance deployed at the N-SOC (arrow number 8). The context here is different from the O-SOC; reports issued by multiple

---

[14] The *Encapsulator* provides the SOC operator with a graphical interface to customize the transmission of incident data through the *SGW* to selected recipients. Setting including anonymization, classification level, and encryption can be adjusted through this interface.

[15] The role of the *SGW* is to ensure that data flows appropriately between the various SOCs, upward and downward, preserving security and anonymity whenever required.

[16] The ABE module enables the encryption and decryption of a message based on a set of selected attributes while a message is sent through the *SGW*.

[17] The AM supports incident acquisition at N-SOC from O-SOC, trough SGW and other sources of relevant information (such as threat feeds), and incident querying by other components at N-SOC.

organizations on the national territory are collected by Cymerius at the N-SOC. The level of details included in the incident reports is lower than at the O-SOC level, to preserve companies' confidentiality; however, it is sufficient to assess the national security situation.

The N-SOC analysts identify the incident as a possible APT attack so they decide to look for similar attack patterns. In order to do so, they open the ECOSSIAN tool named *CAESAIR*,[18] directly available from the Cymerius interface (arrow number 9) and they look for threat intelligence related to the reported incident (arrow number 10). By correlating the incident information comprised in the report, with cyber intelligence acquired from several security-relevant data sources (e.g., security bulletins, vulnerability reports, security forums, etc.), CAESAIR discovers known APT attacks, which correspond to the analyzed incident, and outlines that they are classified as critical. Moreover it discovers that this type of attacks has been previously detected, in other CIs within the same country, as being carried out through e-mails from specific servers on a specific IP range, and command and control (CC) server is usually on one of three identified IP ranges. The N-SOC analyst using the information retrieved by CAESAIR can draft an analysis report and send it back to Cymerius (arrow number 11), stating that similar evidence has been found in other financial infrastructures operating within the national territory, usually related to an APT originating from malware often delivered through a spear phishing attack. The identified similar incident reports are attached to the analysis report and sent to Cymerius.

Cymerius displays the information to the N-SOC team, who decides to set the incident severity to high and send the updated report back to the originating O-SOC at PIT.

The N-SOC sends information on threat patterns of the potential APT attacks to the O-SOC through the SGW (arrow number 12). Similar to the O-SOC to N-SOC communications, the N-SOC operator selects the recipients (here PIT-SOC, and all the SOCs belonging to the financial sector) and the information's security level (EU, CONFIDENTIAL). The information classification is hence upgraded from RESTRICTED to CONFIDENTIAL as this report contains information that will cause damage to national security if publically available.

---

[18] CAESAIR is a Collaborative Analysis Engine for Situational Awareness and Incident Response developed to provide aggregation, analysis, and correlation functionalities within ECOSSIAN system. Using its correlation capability (Giuseppe Settanni, 2016b), CAESAIR provides analysts with the necessary support to handle reported incident information. It aggregates received incident reports and examines intelligence acquired from numerous OSINT feeds; it quickly identifies related threats and existing mitigation procedures; it allows the establishment of cyber-situational awareness by keeping track of security incidents and threats affecting the monitored critical infrastructures deployed on the national territory over time (Giuseppe Settanni, 2016a). For further information on the CAESAIR concept visit: http://caesair.ait.ac.at/. Last accessed on May 5, 2017.

Again, the operator configures and enables ABE to secure the advisory before sending it. The Cymerius instance running at PIT's O-SOC displays the information to the security team with updated severity and analysis reports as attached files (arrow number 13). The operator analyzes the information provided by the N-SOC, is able to adjust the internal incident management process, to eventually remove the malware from the infected machines, to restore the normal systems' operation, and therefore terminate the attack.

During the containment and eradication phase of the APT (cf. Chapter 2), the analysts collect other useful information that is attached to the original threat intelligence report. Finally, the O-SOC sends the N-SOC an update about the incident, containing additional information on threat relevant patterns and actions taken to stop the attack, thus enriching the available information on this specific threat (arrow number 14). This feedback information will then be shared by the N-SOC with other potentially affected CIs on the national territory, as well as with the E-SOC (arrow number 15); this step will be further illustrated in the last demonstration scenario described in Section 9.4.3.

9.4.2 Application Case 2: Detection of Attacks in a Gas Distribution Infrastructure

This application case shows how ECOSSIAN enables the detection of a cyber attack targeting a fictitious national gas provider infrastructure named Gas Network National (GNN); the attack is based on information falsification causing grid control operators to make incorrect decisions.

9.4.2.1 Context

As illustrated in Figure 9.14, gas is transmitted cross-country in high-pressure pipelines at approximately 70 bar. The pressure of the gas is reduced at various offtakes to supply gas to customers at pressures for which their equipment is rated. As most of the gas network is below ground, any active equipment installations will generally be located above ground—hence Above Ground Installation (AGI). There are two types of AGI:

1. Block valves that are remotely controlled and can be shut off if there is ever a break in the pipeline between two block valves
2. Pressure reduction stations at every offtake branch on the transmission

The instrumentation of each AGI is wired back to a remote terminal unit (RTU). SCADA servers in gas networks read/write to these RTUs. A grid control operation room is located in the main data center where operators monitor gas processes 24/7 on SCADA clients.

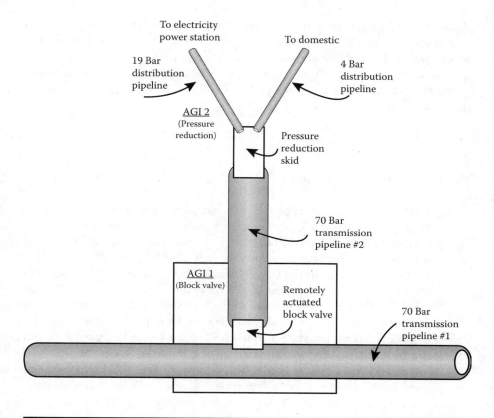

Figure 9.14   Gas distribution network.

9.4.2.2 Scenario Description

In this scenario, an external attacker compromises the gas provider network through a "man-in-the-middle" attack (Desmedt, 2011) on the telemetry readings. The aim of the attacker is to make the grid operator believe that there is a massive gas leak on the pipe. The grid operator would then close the block valves, thereby isolating the town and electricity power station from the gas network. The attack is detected by the ECOSSIAN probes and, consuming the support of the national SOC, the GNN O-SOC operators are able to stop the intrusion. The N-SOC also enables national situation awareness so that similar critical infrastructure providers receive the necessary information to effectively deal with similar attacks in the future.

This demonstration scenario is based on an accurate representation of how the SCADA network of GNN reads and writes telemetry data for its data center, grid control and AGIs around the country. It is based around information from AGI's being falsified causing grid control operators to make incorrect decisions and is a plausible representation of transmission gas networks. The demonstration setup is completely separated from the production environment. It consists of a SCADA server, two block valves and pressure reduction equipment.

The three major phases of the scenario are the attack, the detection of the attack by the ECOSSIAN probes, and the ECOSSIAN incident response at operational and national levels.

9.4.2.2.1 Stage 1: Attack

The attack consists of three steps:

1. *Network intrusion*: By applying the intrusion techniques presented in Chapter 2 (Section 2.3.3), the attacker penetrates the network and gathers information regarding the infrastructure, systems and operational routine of the gas provider. The attacker targets the leased MPLS (Multi-Protocol Label Switching) lines, used by the SCADA core to interact with the AGIs, through their service provider, such that he can get remote access into the AGIs' networks. The attacker then manages to get a remote persistent connection to AGI 1 and AGI 2 networks. He can then conduct an ARP spoofing attack (Whalen, 2011) against the RTU host and network switch, such that he can perform a man-in-the-middle attack on the communications between the RTU and SCADA Master. He can then tamper with the RTU readouts and inputs, but does not perform a detectable action so far. Within deeper analysis of the AGI 1 network, the attacker also identifies the PROFINET communication and tries to get access to this system.
2. *Suppression of the sensor readouts*: The attacker diverts the traffic coming from the pressure reduction equipment to the SCADA servers and suppresses some of the readouts of the sensors in order to create the false impression that some of the sensors are malfunctioning. This step of the attack is triggering an alarm on the O-SOC console. The attacker suppresses, at random points in time, and during an extended time period (might be hours, days, and weeks), the readout of the temperature from AGI 2, after gaining enough information.
3. *False telemetry readings*: The attacker starts to report a decrease in both the pressure and temperature readouts in the RTU from AGI 2, to make the grid operator believe that there is a leak on the pipe between AGI 1 and AGI 2. As a response, the grid operator instructs the block valve on AGI 1 to be shut with an unnecessary close valve request.

9.4.2.2.2 Phase 2: Detection

The SCADA network is monitored by ECOSSIAN sensors that detect isolated and uncorrelated evidence (i.e., observables among those listed in Chapter 3) related to the running attack, indicating network topology changes and business process anomalies. As a result of the ARP spoofing attack, there is a change on the network topology on the connection line to AGI 2, diverting or eventually suppressing the communication. This suppression is revealed by the *ICS-Monitor*,[19] which monitors and detects the communication interruption, and it is displayed on the *mobile visualization interface*[20] (see arrow number 1 in Figure 9.15); this addresses a potential threat to functional safety requirements of process automation plants. The alarm is then forwarded to the supervision console of the O-SOC Cymerius[21] (arrow number 2 in Figure 9.15).

BPIDS[22] detects that there is a correct sensor readout being sent by the RTU but that this temperature readout is not reaching the SCADA Master.

As in any SOC infrastructure, a SIEM is deployed to centrally aggregate and correlate sensor events. Also in this scenario, the SIEM tool used for aggregating

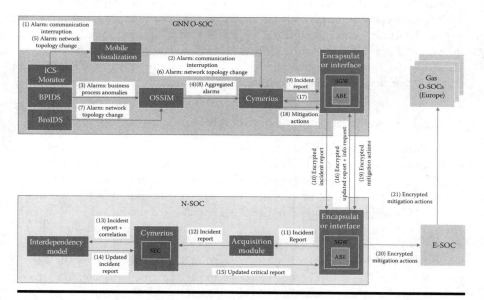

Figure 9.15   Application Case 2 detection and reaction flowchart.

---

[19] *ICS-Monitor* tool recognizes an unusually long drop in the SCADA-ICS communication.

[20] The *mobile visualization interface* allows O-SOC operators to visualize, on their mobile devices, possible attempts of tampering with the connection by monitoring the process values and observe periods of silence in the communication.

[21] See Section 9.4.1.2.2.

[22] The *BPIDS* detects that the sensors readouts at the SCADA server are incorrect, because the set of messages produced by the RTU and those received at the SCADA server do not match (i.e., the messages are being suppressed while in transit, since they are seen leaving the RTUs but never reach the SCADA server).

the alarms raised by the ECOSSIAN probes is OSSIM[23] (arrows number 3 and 7). Here, OSSIM forwards BPIDS and BroIDS alarms to Cymerius (arrows number 4 and 8). Cymerius also collects alarms directly forwarded from the ICS-Monitor sensor by the *mobile visualization* (arrows number 2 and 6).

BPIDS also detects that the original messages, being produced by the RTU, are not equal to those received on the SCADA master side; BPIDS detects that a block valve request is being issued by the SCADA server even though the temperature and pressure readouts from AGI 2 are not reaching the cut-off value.

As a result of the ARP spoofing attack, to perform the interception and change of process data, there is a change on the network topology on the connection line to AGI 2, the communication diverted or eventually suppressed; this change in topology is detected by the ICS-Monitor. The incident is displayed on the mobile visualization interface (arrow number 5). As only process values of valid connections are shown, the graph of the tampered process values shows no new values, while the packet frequency is constant, because of the parallel existence of the invalid parallel connections.

The BroIDS[24] sensor, analyzing the PROFINET[25] protocol, detects certain changes of the topology because of new IP requests for the second block valve, which have to be sent between attacker and HMI/motor by using the PROFINET *Discovery and Basic Configuration Protocol* (DCP).

9.4.2.2.3 Phase 3: Incident Response and Mitigation

In the third phase, the O-SOC operators investigate the incident and validate the warnings received from the ECOSSIAN system. Cymerius displays the report to O-SOC operators who decide to investigate such an uncommon internal anomaly. A course of action defined by cybersecurity experts from the O-SOC, and modeled into Cymerius, is proposed to the SOC operator (in the REACTION view). The SOC operator is guided then through the resolution process and through the sharing process of the information with the N-SOC. Once the analysis is completed by the O-SOC team, a report is written and attached to one of the aggregated incidents. The report is then uploaded to the *encapsulator*[26] interface (arrow number 9), which exports it to the N-SOC through the SGW[27] (arrow number 10). On this interface the operators select the country's N-SOC as recipient, the security level of the incident, by selecting its security domain (EU), and classification (RESTRICTED). By doing this they enforce that the reported incident will be received only by the N-SOC, and if necessary the E-SOC, and that it will not be

---

[23] See Section 9.4.1.2.2.
[24] The *BroIDS* sensor detects PROFINET packets for changing the IP address of a valve. It sends a detection message to the O-SOC to inform the operators about the IP address change. The unexpected IP address change alerts the operator about a possible intrusion.
[25] http://us.profinet.com/technology/profinet/ (Last accessed on December 2016).
[26] See Section 9.4.1.2.3.
[27] See Section 9.4.1.2.3.

available to other O-SOCs in the country. Operators also use the ABE[28] module to enforce the access control on the incident report and ensure that only European energy-related organizations are able to decrypt this information.

The incident report reaches the *AM*[29] (arrow number 11) at the country's N-SOC, which redirects it to the N-SOC Cymerius (arrow number 12). The N-SOC operator receives therefore a message on the console and starts investigating the incident using analysis and correlation tools such as *Cymerius Portal* and the *simple event correlator*[30] *(SEC)* (arrow number 12).

While performing the impact analysis, the N-SOC team finds out that the attack is relevant for all European gas providers, because of potential cascading effects that the exploited vulnerability would cause if it became known on a broader scale. The *interdependency model*[31] shows indeed which parts of other CIs are affected by the current attack (i.e., insufficient gas provisioning). This information is additionally sent to Cymerius and integrated in the incident report for a comprehensive evaluation of the criticality of the incident (arrow number 14). The N-SOC analyst does not find any similar attack that previously occurred, but evaluates that the incident is critical. So, he decides to set the incident severity to high and to ask for more information from the GNN O-SOC (arrow number 15). He sends the updated report back to the O-SOC through the *SGW* and the *ABE* (arrow number 16), and Cymerius'O-SOC instance displays the information to the respective on-site security engineer with the severity updated and analysis reports as attached files (arrow number 17). The O-SOC operator updates the incident report with complementary information on how the incident was detected, analyzed, and addressed (arrow number 18). The enriched incident report (see Table 9.3) is sent by the O-SOC operator to the N-SOC (arrow number 19), as explained before, and is also forwarded by the N-SOC to the E-SOC (arrow number 20) and to other CIs (arrow number 21).

9.4.3 Application in a Pan-European Network of Interconnected Infrastructures

This application case shows how ECOSSIAN enables the detection of a cyber attack targeting a fictitious national transportation infrastructure named National Railway and Road Administration (NRRA) operating in a given European country

---

28 See Section 9.4.1.2.3.

29 See Section 9.4.1.2.3.

30 The simple event correlator (SEC) is a module integrated into Cymerius, which aims at identifying relations between incident reports by looking at their characteristics, i.e., incident report time, size, source, etc.

31 *Interdependency Model* presents all CIs and their location in Europe within this scenario. After the attack, the model highlights all affected CIs and shows a list of immediately affected CIs and their availability.

Table 9.3 Fields of an Incident Report

Report Components	Report's Field	Description
Information about the sender	Title	Descriptive title
	Sender	Sender of the incident report
	Sector	Critical infrastructures may belong to several sectors
Time information	Reporting time	Time of reporting the incident (timestamp)
	Time of occurrence	Time when the incident happened/fault occurred (timestamp)
	Duration	Duration of the incident (make sense if the incident can be considered as closed)
Notification category	Support requested[a]	In case the providers of the CI need external support
	Confidentiality level	In case the report is confidential, possible categories: strictly confidential/only for the branch/not confidential
	Priority[a]	Set the priority of the incident report: 0 = only status information 1 = low 2 = middle 3 = high
	Personal data[a]	Whether the report includes personal data.

(Continued)

Table 9.3 (Continued) Fields of an Incident Report

Report Components	Report's Field	Description
Information about the attack	Target[b]	Is the attack targeting a specific organization?
	System level	Is attack targeting hardware level, OS, databases, network components, or the application level?
	Description	Description of the vulnerability entered as free text
	CVE-Link[a]	Possible CVE-Link to the exploited vulnerability
	Affected components	Description of the affected components entered as free text
	Estimated impact	Description of the possible impact, such as endangered services, external subcontractor, estimated damage, etc.
	Potential additional targets[b]	Possible targets (organizations) potentially hit by similar incidents resulting from the adoption of the same attack vector
	Stage of completion[a]	Estimated stage of completion related to the resolution of the incident
Magnitude of impact	Technical[a]	Estimated technical impact
	Business	Estimated business impact
	Temporal	Estimated temporal limits

(Continued)

Table 9.3 (*Continued*)   Fields of an Incident Report

Report Components	Report's Field	Description
Additional information	Free text	Description of other details, such as measures planned or already taken, results of analysis, etc.
	Attachments	Graphs, user manuals, network topology, etc.
	Response[a]	Is the first incident report, or just additional reporting, related to an older incident?

Note: Incident reports include different information depending on the stage of the incident response phase and on the SOC level they are generated at. This table lists the fields comprised in incident reports exchanged among O-SOCs, N-SOCs, and the E-SOC.

[a] Specified only in reports sent by O-SOCs to their respective N-SOC.
[b] Included only in reports sent by N-SOCs to the E-SOC.

X; this application case does not focus much on the detection stage, which was largely demonstrated in the two previous application cases; it rather outlines the incident response and mitigation procedures put in place by ECOSSIAN, at operational, national, and European levels.

9.4.3.1 Context

NRRA has deployed a SCADA system for two purposes: the operation of several railway systems (i.e., level crossing, tunnel and station management, object detection on railways, etc.), and the operation of the electric grid (power lines and substation) that powers the train traction. The SCADA system allows supervision and control of these railway systems in real-time and in a centralized manner. Each has a three-level architecture: acquisition, automation, and application.

At the acquisition level, the remote terminal unit (RTU) is responsible for the direct interface with the infrastructure and executes local automation functions. The information acquired by the RTU is sent toward the automation level to the programmable logic controller (PLC), which executes broader and more distributed automation functions. At the application level, the central servers execute the SCADA functions taking into account all the information gathered by the PLC. The central system has two UNIX servers to guarantee the redundancy of the databases and SCADA applications, as shown in Figure 9.16.

9.4.3.2 Scenario Description

In this scenario, the attacker intends to target the NRRA railway system in a way to generally disrupt railway traffic. In order to achieve his goals, the attacker plans to gain access to the production railway network, gather technical and operational information of potentially vulnerable systems, and then use that knowledge to launch an attack with the purpose of generating a service disruption in the normal operation of the national railway.

The attack is detected by the ECOSSIAN probes and, thanks to the support of the national SOC, the SOC operators will be able to stop the intrusion.

The N-SOC of country X will also enable national situational awareness so that similar critical infrastructure will have the necessary information to face and counteract such attacks. Considering the event of interest for the E-SOC, this N-SOC shares the incident information with the E-SOC.

With the received information, the E-SOC specialists determine the impact on other European critical infrastructures. In the meantime, the E-SOC correlates the incident and reveals that a similar event has occurred in a critical infrastructure (fictitiously named *RailY* and belonging to the transportation sector) deployed in a different Member State (we refer to it as country Y).

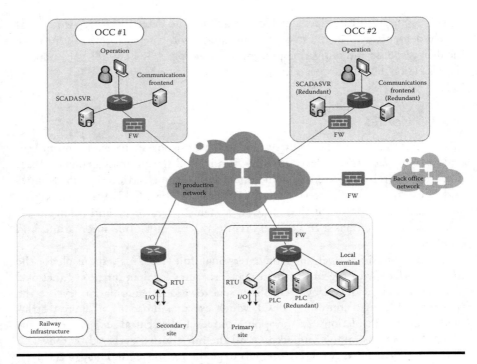

Figure 9.16   Railway SCADA architecture.[1]

---

[1] This diagram was presented during the ECOSSIAN final demonstration. The event was organized by the ECOSSIAN consortium and hosted by Airbus Defence and Space in Èlancourt (France) on April 26, 2017. External stakeholders including scholars, critical infrastructures operators, military, regulator, and law enforcement agencies, attended the event.

The entire incident response workflow across the three ECOSSIAN SOC levels is depicted in Figure 9.18 and is described in detail in Sections 9.4.3.2.1 through 9.4.3.2.5.

9.4.3.2.1 Attack

The attack consists of three phases as depicted in Figure 9.17. In the first phase, the attacker intrudes on the corporate network through exploiting a maintenance VPN (social engineering) and applying a discovery process (network scanning); the attacker gathers information in order to find exploitable vulnerabilities on key network equipment and systems. In the second phase, after gaining access to the operation infrastructure, the attacker takes control of the PLC from the catenary system powering the actual trains, as well as of some network equipment. The attacker proceeds, in the third phase, by forcing off the power supply to the catenary system

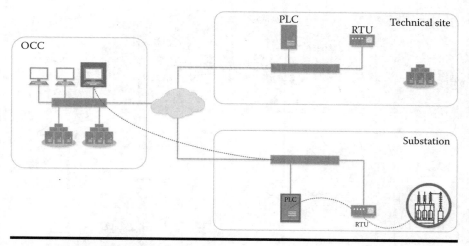

Figure 9.17   Attack scenario.[1]

---

[1] This diagram was presented during the ECOSSIAN final demonstration. The event was organized by the ECOSSIAN consortium and hosted by Airbus Defence and Space in Èlancourt (France) on April 26, 2017. External stakeholders including scholars, critical infrastructure operators, military, regulator, and law enforcement agencies attended the event.

at that particular track segment, while simultaneously using a specially contrived filter applied on the relevant switch/router interfaces, in order to prevent related sensor information from reaching the SCADA master at the OCC and tentatively prolong the response time to the problem.

9.4.3.2.2 Detection

The detection is achieved by utilizing one of the ECOSSIAN probes (BPIDS[32]), which monitors the flow of commands to open and close the energy circuits and detects that the SCADA commands do not follow the specified process, namely, that the command executed at the PLC level did not originate from the OCC. This generates an alert that an inconsistent command was triggered at the PLC level; the alert is then forwarded as incident report to the O-SOC hypervisor (Cymerius[33]) for further investigation (arrows 1 and 2 in Figure 9.18).

9.4.3.2.3 Incident Response and Mitigation at the O-SOC Level

In this phase, the O-SOC operator starts to investigate the incident and validates the warnings received from the ECOSSIAN probes. Based on all the correlated events

---

[32] See Section 9.4.2.2.2.
[33] See Section 9.4.1.2.2.

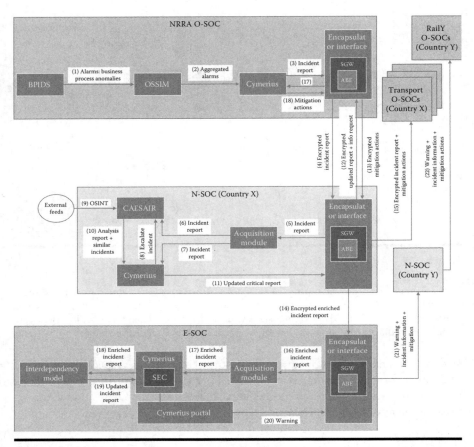

Figure 9.18 European application case: incident response flowchart.

displayed by Cymerius, the O-SOC analysts identify the malicious user's VPN connection and the potentially breached workstations. Following the predefined reaction plan, the O-SOC incident response team shuts down the suspicious VPN and disables the user account. The O-SOC team notifies the network and SCADA teams in the field, supplying them with relevant details on the potentially affected systems and equipment. The field teams initiate an emergency plan to secure the affected devices and change the compromised credentials, either remotely where applicable or locally where necessary. Once the analysis has been completed by the O-SOC team, the severity is set to medium in every incident related to the attack, and the analysis report is written and attached to the incident message. This incident is considered of interest for other critical infrastructures and is therefore shared with country X's N-SOC. This happens following the secure information exchange procedure illustrated in the previous application cases, based on the adoption of a SGW[34] and the application of ABE[35]; see arrows 3 and 4 in Figure 9.18.

9.4.3.2.4 Incident Response and Mitigation at the N-SOC Level (Country X)

In this phase the N-SOC team receives the incident reported by the O-SOC, and it starts its investigation, which leads to forensic analysis and subsequently provides awareness at the national level. As described in the first application case (se Section 9.4.1.2.3) the incident report is collected and processed at the N-SOC level by using the ECOSSIAN incident response tool-chain comprising the AM, Cymerius, and CAESAIR (arrows 5, 6, and 7 in Figure 9.18).

By leveraging CAESAIR's correlation capabilities, the N-SOC team recognizes that similar incidents occurred previously and were reported by other critical infrastructures in country X. The acquisition of this information makes the N-SOC team increase the severity level of the incident; an updated incident report including this additional insight is sent back to the NRRA O-SOC (arrow 12).

At the NRRA O-SOC, the operators use the received information to stop the attack; moreover, during the containment and eradication of the attack, the analysts collect other useful information that is attached to enrich the original report. Finally, the O-SOC sends an update to the N-SOC about the incident containing detection and mitigation feedback that can help to detect and mitigate similar attacks in the future (arrow 13). The tools used for the exchange of incident information and the respective feedback are the Encapsulator, SGW, and ABE.

The feedback information, including the enriched incident report, received by the N-SOC is then shared by the N-SOC with the E-SOC (arrow 14). Nonconfidential information on the incident and its mitigation recommendations are also shared with other critical infrastructures in the transport sector on the national territory of country X (arrow 15).

9.4.3.2.5 Incident Response and Mitigation at the E-SOC Level

The information flow between N-SOC and E-SOC follows the same procedure and is based on the adoption of the same tools, illustrated before for the communication between O-SOC and N-SOC. Once the incident report reaches the Cymerius instance running at the E-SOC, the analysis team can observe the impact of such an incident on all federated European CIs. To do so, the E-SOC team makes use

---

[34] See Section 9.4.1.2.3.
[35] See Section 9.4.1.2.3.

of the ECOSSIAN interdependency model[36] (arrow 18). During this impact analysis the E-SOC team finds out that the incident reported by NRRA has an impact on other critical infrastructures operating in other European countries. The interdependency model shows the list of such CIs on a map and stores the calculated impact in a summary, which is additionally attached to the received incident report (arrow 19).

The overall security situation is monitored and visualized through Cymerius Portal.[37] At the same time the incident is processed by the *SEC* correlator,[38] which detects whether any similar situation was already reported from other transport-related CIs in Europe. The correlator identifies that this is the case in country Y. Cymerius Portal shows indeed that the organization RailY, in country Y, reported very similar issues only a few hours before; the E-SOC team examines the available information related to the incidents reported by RailY, and decides to notify the respective N-SOC with a warning message (arrow 20) indicating a possible cross-national attack. The nonsensitive available information collected during the response of the incident affecting NRRA in country X are anonymized and securely shared (through the SGW) with the country Y's N-SOC (arrow 21).

Warnings received from the E-SOC are processed by the N-SOC following a dedicated procedure that involves the assessment of the information obtained, the evaluation of the relevance to their constituencies, and if necessary the notification of the interested critical infrastructures on their territory. Hence, in this case, the N-SOC informs the RailY O-SOC (arrow 22) about the warning received from the E-SOC and recommends it adopt the suggested countermeasures to mitigate the security incident.

9.5 Lessons Learned and Recommendations for a Large-Scale Rollout

This section provides a summary of the main findings derived throughout the design, implementation, integration, and demonstration of the ECOSSIAN ecosystem. Based on the lessons learned in the execution of the ECOSSIAN research project, the chapter concludes with recommendations for a large-scale rollout of the system.

---

[36] The interdependency model presents all CIs and their location in Europe. After an attack the model highlights all the potentially affected CIs and shows a list of immediately impacted CIs and their availability.

[37] Cymerius Portal displays a situation overview and a map of Europe with the monitored CIs including their security status and some summary of the cyber situation: incident, risk, mitigation actions. Correlated situations are shown in a specific view in the portal. The situation evolution can also be seen on a set of dashboards with graphs, and pie charts.

[38] See Section 9.4.2.2.3.

9.5.1 Lessons Learned in the ECOSSIAN Project

The key aspect introduced by the ECOSSIAN approach is the *secure exchange of incident-related information* amongst end users, including operators of critical infrastructures, national, and E-SOCs.

At the organizational level, innovative solutions have been proposed aiming at the detection of highly sophisticated cybersecurity attacks. The integration of such solutions delivers an extensive suite of tools and methods at disposal of the SOC, including systems for the detection of behavioral characteristics, extended protocol analysis tools, machine learning approaches, and dynamic low interaction honeypot systems. This enables the operator of critical infrastructures to improve the *detection of incident in real-time, not only focusing on traditional IT systems but also paying special attention to operational technology (OT) systems as well.*

Due to the *open architecture* of the ECOSSIAN framework, organizations can adopt the most suitable operating model for their O-SOC. The O-SOC can indeed be deployed in-house allowing different organizational models or can be contracted as a service from specialized managed security service providers, sector specific security operations centers, or the N-SOC.

In the original design of the ECOSSIAN architecture, the O-SOCs operating at critical infrastructures of a Member State are linked to an N-SOC. However, dedicated *sectorial security operations centers* can optionally be foreseen, as an intermediate layer, to interface groups of similar O-SOCs to the respective N-SOC; this can reduce the workload of the N-SOC and improve the effectiveness of decision-making and incident response capabilities. From the O-SOC perspective this would allow the operators of critical infrastructures to receive tailored early warnings about ongoing attacks that can potentially target their business, as well as insights in terms of interdependencies with other sectors and critical infrastructures.

The reception of warnings, advisories, IoCs, and mitigation procedures distributed by the N-SOCs allows organizations to effectively implement *preventive security measures and thus to enhance the resilience of the affiliated critical infrastructure.*

By applying the advanced *data fusion* techniques, *information analysis* and *correlation* approaches, and near-real-time *situational awareness* capabilities, the N-SOCs are indeed featured by an improved efficiency in decision-making and a higher effectiveness in incident response.

By casting *early warnings* to potentially affected O-SOCs, and by deriving interdependencies between different CIs, N-SOCs can also improve their abilities in disaster prevention, disaster mitigation, preparedness, response, and recovery. Additionally, this feature enables the N-SOC to detect large-scale attacks at the national level by incident correlation and aggregation.

The implementation of the E-SOC brings further benefits on a cross-national level; enhanced disaster management, through prevention, mitigation, response and recovery of incidents, supports the establishment of the European cyber-situational awareness.

Considering the aforementioned aspects, which outline the benefits provided by the ECOSSIAN framework, other considerations can be derived, mostly on a nontechnical level.

In particular, it is crucial in such a framework to ensure *trustworthiness, anonymity,* and *legal compliance* for information sharing among all stakeholders and end users, conforming to the national and European regulations on data protection, such as the General Data Protection Regulation (GDPR) (Regulation (EU) 2016/679) and the NIS Directive (cf. Chapter 7).

Another key lesson, learned from the numerous discussions held with end users and external stakeholders, concerns the involvement of *humans in the incident-handling* process. Decisions related to the content of messages to be shared, the selection of the recipients of such messages, and the timing of information exchange are very critical and shall not be automatized.

Finally, it is important to mention that the whole paradigm of information sharing and early warning distribution, upon which the ECOSSIAN concept is conceived, holds as long as the entity involved has a clear and *evident advantage in sharing relevant information*, while the *confidentiality of sensitive data is guaranteed*. The benefits of being part of such a collaborative platform have been largely discussed and demonstrated in previous chapters.

9.5.2 *Recommendations for a Large-Scale Rollout*

Implementing and maintaining an operational information sharing network requires the consideration of multiple aspects: technical, organizational, procedural, legal, ethical, societal, and political. Section 9.2 addresses the architectural and technological features, derived from the ECOSSIAN project, such a network could provide; Section 9.3 discusses organizational and procedural facets, as proposed in the CIC framework, which would complement the technical features in a possible real-world implementation of such a sharing network. Finally, Section 9.4 demonstrates a series of different national and cross-national application cases, where the presented approach is contextualized in diverse attack scenarios, and the benefits of the sharing network are outlined.

In this section the main recommendations covering all aforementioned aspects, obtained within the project, collected from relevant stakeholders and derived from the demonstrations, are provided for a possible large-scale rollout of the proposed sharing network.

The designed ECOSSIAN architecture can be seen as a template architecture that can be instantiated and customized in terms of components and technologies adopted. The selection of a subset of tools could be the natural development of this framework in order to obtain a tailored solution to a specific case and domain.

Furthermore, given the provisions set forth by the NIS directive (cf. Chapter 7), it will soon become necessary for the European Member States to define which governmental body or organization will operate the so-called *National Security*

Authority. The same question applies at the European level: it is currently not defined yet which organization will be responsible for operating this entity. In any case, the ECOSSIAN architecture would be flexible enough to be seen as a possible technical layer to be adopted and suitably customized when implementing this directive on both national and European levels.

Additionally to the three-tiered architecture, *sectorial SOCs* could be foreseen as intermediary entities between the CIs and the (public) N-SOC, which could act as "buffer level," and decide which security events to forward to the national entity.

When considering critical infrastructure protection, vulnerabilities and threats have been largely identified, while the consequences to business, politics, and societies of related security incidents are still not fully understood, resulting in a lack of preparedness and response measures. High investments, cutting-edge technologies, and a system of advanced functionalities, which are the basic characteristics of the ECOSSIAN system, are prerequisites but not sufficient for success. *The system must be tested and its behavior assessed, proven, and measured in a real environment.*

ECOSSIAN must be seen as a highly complex security measure, a system of technology, procedures, and organizations that will operate in various CI sectors, across sectors, with national governments, and in an international environment with a dedicated role of the EU.

Prior to its rollout, the *evaluation of the ECOSSIAN system* is therefore fundamental. This assessment can be broken down into four "pillars" of evaluation, reflecting the four main challenges a system such as ECOSSIAN has to address the following:

1. The system shall *reduce risks* in CI environments: this is an important requirement, and the benefits of ECOSSIAN are measured by criteria that allow it to quantify or at least estimate the fulfillment of these requirements.
2. The system shall follow basic system characteristics for implementation and operation: Such a system is expected to be *flexible to different kinds of CI threats and national rules*, adaptable to future challenges, easy to understand, learned, and operated, and it must be interoperable with existing systems.
3. The system shall generate positive and *avoid negative implications in politics and legal settings*, be acceptable to society and create no ethical problems.
4. *Costs* for introduction and operation of the system and cost *savings* when operated shall be *favorable*.

ECOSSIAN, when implemented on national and international scale, will have major effects in all four categories. Due to its *societal importance*, special attention needs to be paid to *ECOSSIAN's expected legal, ethical, and social foundations.* The whole project was accompanied by in-depth analyses of legal frameworks, ethical principles concerning privacy and data protection, and the need and models for cooperation between governments and the private sector.

An important point of focus, which can also be found in the considerations addressed in Chapter 7, is on *data protection legislation*. In this regard, with the adoption of the GDPR, applicable from 2018, an important development occurred during the project run-time. Even though data protection legislation is often considered a showstopper for information sharing, the sharing of information is allowed under certain circumstances.

However, data protection legislation provides certain requirements and principles that need to be adhered to when *processing personal data*. The ECOSSIAN approach provides a broad solution that can be integrated in very different situations and with different legacy systems. Therefore the system is not adjusted to a specific type of data, but instead different parts were built that provide flexibility in the possible integration to allow for a data protection compliant system. For an assessment of whether captured data comprises personal data and to enable data minimization within the system, a central function comes to the *human operator* at each level. This decision is a part that cannot easily be automated but can be supported by way of a Data Protection Impact Assessment. Furthermore, a legal analysis was made regarding information sharing, especially obligations for breach notifications and the obligations provided by the NIS Directive. The ECOSSIAN system provides solutions that are beneficial for integrating the requirements of the NIS Directive, especially regarding *standardized information sharing solutions and incident notification*. The proposed ECOSSIAN system goes, with the possible integration of an E-SOC, even further than the current legal system provides and is therefore also a showcase of technical possibilities for a potential future information sharing system with a central European component, which at the moment is not possible for subsidiarity concerns.

Main focuses of the *ethical considerations* in the project were *privacy and data protection* and potential risks arising from the sensors and information sharing structure. Regarding data protection, this was deeply assessed in the legal reports for compliance with data protection legislation, and regarding the project itself in the reports of the data protection coordinator. For assessing potential privacy and other possible infringements of fundamental rights by the ECOSSIAN system, a specific assessment tool was developed, considering amongst other factors specifically a potential ethical and societal impact of the ECOSSIAN system.

Economic impacts of security measures, such as the introduction of the ECOSSIAN system, are mainly estimations that hold for certain security scenarios. Nevertheless, CI enterprises would surely gain appreciation of such a system if some information on *cost–benefit and ROSI (return-on-security investment)* could be generated. ECOSSIAN would also require an unprecedented *legal, contractual, and procedural framework for cooperation between the private/entrepreneurial and the PPP*. This would particularly comprise models of and rules for sharing of information, sharing of responsibilities and cost, sharing of tasks and resources, and agreement on mutual incentives.

The CIC framework illustrated in Section 9.3 outlines opportunities and constraints, providing some guideline and role models on how such a PPP framework could look like and which prerequisites and procedures should be established in order to make it a success story for all: for the CI industry, for national governments and for the EU.

Several additional factors of relevance need to be regarded when implementing such a sophisticated information sharing system. Most of these criteria on expected societal reactions, ethical risks, or political preferences cannot usually be expressed in physical or monetary units, often not even in logical ones. These "qualitative" criteria have been identified and grouped into the following categories:

1. *Ethical criteria* address social values, trust of citizens in such a system, risk of privacy violations, integrity of decision makers, etc.
2. *Political criteria* allow the assessment under political preferences, possible political conflicts, or international political reputation and agreements.
3. *Societal criteria* address the security impact of the ECOSSIAN system perceived by society, welcoming, or rejection of new and possibly intrusive technologies and possible health impact.

Summarizing, the factors influencing the sociopolitical impact of the ECOSSIAN system are as follows:

■ The potential of impacting on societal values and individual rights
■ Its broad acceptance by societal groups and politicians
■ The need of substantially new ways of cooperation among CI sectors and among CI providers/operators, governmental bodies, and the EU
■ Its compliance with national laws and regulations and with the EU CIP strategic endeavors; it may even need new or modified rules of law
■ Its economic and societal implications that imply a number of uncertainties

List of Abbreviations

ABE	Attribute-based encryption
AECID	Automatic event correlation of incident detection
CAESAIR	Collaborative Analysis Engine for Situational Awareness and Incident Response
CDC	Cyber Defense Centers
CERT	Computer emergency response team
CI	Critical infrastructure
CIC	Cyber Intelligence Center
CCOP	Common Cyber Operational Picture
COTS	Commercial off-the-shelf
CSIRT	Computer security incident response team

DoS	Denial of service
ECOSSIAN	European Control System Security Incident Analysis Network
E-SOC	European SOC
FB	Functional block
HTML	Hypertext Markup Language
HTTP	Hypertext Transfer Protocol
HTTPS	Hypertext Transfer Protocol Secure
ICS	Industrial control system
ICT	Information and communication technology
ID	Identifier
IDS	Intrusion detection system
IODEF	Incident Object Description Exchange Format
IP	Internet Protocol
ISO	International Organization for Standardization
IT	Information technology
MPLS	Multi-Protocol Label Switching
NOC	Network operations center
N-SOC	National SOC
OT	Operational technology
O-SOC	Organization SOC
OSSIEM	Open-source SIEM
PLC	Programmable logic controller
SCADA	Supervisory control and data acquisition
SDS	Secure data storage
SEC	Simple event correlator
SIEM	Security information and event management
SOC	Security operations center
STIX	Structured Threat Information eXpression
TAXII	Trusted Automated eXchange of Indicator Information
TLS	Transport Layer Security
VPN	Virtual private network
X-SOC	O-SOC or N-SOC or E-SOC

References

Albanese, M. and Jajodia, S. (2014). Formation of awareness, In: *Cyber Defense and Situational Awareness*, (pp. 47-62). A. Kott, R. Erbacher, and C. Wang, eds, Springer: Heidelberg.

Bethencourt, J., Sahai, A., and Waters, B. (2007). Ciphertext-policy attribute-based encryption. In: *SP'07 Proceedings of the 2007 IEEE Symposium on Security and Privacy*, 2007, pp. 321–334.

BSI-Global (2006). BS 25999—Business continuity management. http://www.bsi-global.com/. Last accessed on February 21, 2017.

Center for Strategic and International Studies (2013). Public private partnerships for critical infrastructure protection. http://csis.org/files/publication/130819_PPP.pdf, part4. Last accessed on February 21, 2017.

CTO (2014). Commonwealth approach for developing National Cybersecurity Strategies. https://www.sbs.ox.ac.uk/cybersecurity-capacity/system/files/Commonwealth%20 Approach%20for%20National%20Cybersecurity%20Strategies.pdf. Last accessed on April 16, 2016.

CTO (2015). Commonwealth approach for developing National Cybersecurity Strategies. https://www.sbs.ox.ac.uk/cybersecurity-capacity/system/files/Commonwealth%20 Approach%20for%20National%20Cybersecurity%20Strategies.pdf. Last accessed on April 16, 2016.

Degeler, V. et al. (2015). ECOSSIAN Deliverable D1.2: Requirements report. http://ecossian.eu/downloads/D1.2-Requirements-PU-M09.pdf. Last accessed on May 05, 2017.

Desmedt, Y. (2011). Man-in-the-middle attack. In *Encyclopedia of Cryptography and Security*, pp. 759–759. Springer: Heidelberg.

ECOSSIAN Project Consortium (2015). Newsletter November 2015-Issue 3. http://ecossian.eu/downloads/ECOSSIAN-Newsletter-Issue3-November2015.pdf. Last accessed on May 5, 2017.

ECOSSIAN Project Consortium (2017). Newsletter March 2017-Issue 6. http://ecossian.eu/downloads/ECOSSIAN-Newsletter-Issue6-March2017.pdf. Last accessed on May 5, 2017.

ENISA (2006). A step-by-step approach on how to set up a CSIRT. https://www.enisa.europa.eu/publications/csirt-setting-up-guide. Last accessed on February 21, 2017.

ENISA (2014). An evaluation framework for National Cyber Security Strategies. https://www.enisa.europa.eu/publications/an-evaluation-framework-for-cyber-security-strategies-1. Last accessed on March 19, 2016

ENISA (2016). Incident reporting for Telcos 2015. October 2016. https://www.enisa.europa.eu/publications/annual-incident-reports-2015. Last accessed on February 21, 2017.

European Commission (2016). European Directive on security of network and information systems. https://ec.europa.eu/digital-single-market/en/network-and-information-security-nis-directive. Last accessed on February 21, 2017.

International Organization for Standardization (2012). ISO 22301:2012. Societal Security—Business Continuity Management Systems—Requirements. https://www.iso.org/obp/ui/#iso:std:iso:22301:ed-1:v2:en. Last accessed on February 21, 2017.

Kaufmann, H., Hutter, R., Skopik, F., Mantere, M. (2015). A structural design for a pan-European early warning system for critical infrastructures. *Elektrotechnik und Informationstechnik*, Volume 132, Issue 2, pp. 117–121.

Lipson, H.F. (2002) Tracking and tracing cyber-attacks: Technical challenges and global policy issues. (No. CMU/SEI-2002-SR-009). Software Engineering Inst., Carnegie-Mellon University, Pittsburgh, PA.

NIST (2012). *Computer Security Incident Handling Guide.* Recommendations of the National Institute of Standards and Technology. http://nvlpubs.nist.gov/nistpubs/SpecialPublications/NIST.SP.800-61r2.pdf. Last accessed on February 21, 2017.

Obama, B. (2010). *National Security Strategy of the United States.* DIANE Publishing: Darby, PA.

Pahi, T. (2016). Cyber Intelligence Centre framework, Bachelor Thesis, University of Applied Sciences St Poelten, Austria. https://www.fhstp.ac.at/de/studium-weiterbildung/informatik-security/it-security/bachelorarbeiten/cyber-intelligence-centre-framework.

Polancich, J. (2015). OSINT alone does not equal threat intelligence. http://www.securityweek. com/osint-alone-does-not-equal-threat-intelligence. Last accessed on July 17, 2015.

Senate and House of Representatives of the United States of America (2015). Cybersecurity Information Sharing Act. https://www.congress.gov/bill/114th-congress/senate-bill/754/text. Last accessed on February 22, 2017.

Settanni, G. et al. (2016). A collaborative cyber incident management system for European interconnected critical infrastructures. *Journal of Information Security and Applications*, Volume 34, Part 2, June 2017, pp. 166-182.

Settanni, G. et al. (2016a). A collaborative analysis system for cross-organization cyber incident handling. *Proceedings of the 2nd International Conference on Information Systems Security and Privacy, IEEE*, pp. 105–116.

Settanni, G. et al. (2016b). Correlating cyber incident information to establish situational awareness in critical infrastructures. *14th Annual Conference on Privacy, Security and Trust (PST)*, 2016. IEEE, Auckland, New Zealand.

U.S. Department of Justice (2015). Best practices for victim response and reporting of cyber incidents, Version 1. https://www.justice.gov/sites/default/files/criminal-ccips/legacy/2015/04/30/04272015reporting-cyber-incidents-final.pdf. Last Accessed on June 22, 2016.

Whalen, S. (2001). An introduction to ARP spoofing. Node99, April 2001. http://www.leetupload.com/database/Misc/Papers/arp_spoofing_slides.pdf.

Index

A

Actions of intent, 35
AD (anomaly-based detection), 109
Address Resolution Protocol, *see* ARP
Advance persistent threats, *see* APTs
Adwind, 3
AGI (Above Ground Installation), 398
Anomaly detection, 107–108, *see also* AD; IDS
Application-specific observables, 84
APTs (advance persistent threats), 28
    advanced victims, 29
    characteristics, 29
    history, 28
    threat actors, 29
Arbitrary organization network diagram, 71–72
ARP (Address Resolution Protocol), 94
Asset adaption, 80–81
Asset components, 263
Asset disposal, 81
Asset groups, 263
Asset identification, 79–80
Asset information, 79
Asset lifecycle, 77–78
Asset operation, 80
Asset type, 263
Attacker campaigns, 189

B

Big Data, 26
Binary patterns, 98
BIPT (Belgisch Instituut voor Postdiensten en Telecommunicatie), 287
BlackEnergy 3 malware, 42
BSI IT-Krisenreaktionszentrum, 243
BSI IT-Lage und Analysezentrum, 243
Business network, 71

C

C2 (command and control), 34
Capturing network data and process, 2–3
CCOP (cyber common operating pictures)
    contextual information, 259
        best practices, 265
        critical infrastructure provider list, 262–263
        current political environment, 264
        dependencies, 264
        domain, 264
        incident reports, 264
        industry knowledge, 264
        international law, 265
        lessons learned, 265
        national law, 265
        organizational assets, 263
        public incident documentation, 264–265
        technical reports, 264–265
    core information, 259, 260–262
    decision makers, 388–389
    ECOSSIAN research project, 361
    sources, 265–266
        accessibility, 266
        information modeling, 267–268
        ownership, 268–269
CERTs (Computer Emergence Response Teams), 132
CIC (cyber intelligence center) framework
    business level, 383
    design approach, 379
    goals, 378
    implementation level, 383
    national scope, 380
    nation-states, 379
    organizational scope, 382, 383